MW01672480

CASES AND MATERIALS

CORPORATE FINANCE

2010 SUPPLEMENT to SIXTH EDITION

by
WILLIAM W. BRATTON
Professor of Law, University of Pennsylvania Law School

FOUNDATION PRESS
EAGAN, MINNESOTA
2010

1 New York Plaza, 34th Floor
New York, NY 10004
Phone Toll Free 1–877–888–1330
Fax 646–424–5201
foundation–press.com

Printed in the United States of America

ISBN 978–1–59941–959–6

Mat #40951263

ANALYTICAL TABLE OF CONTENTS

2010 Supplement Page No.		Sixth Edition Page No.
	PART I. Valuing the Firm and Its Securities	
	Section B. Elements of Fundamental Value	
	5. Risk Reduction through Hedging	
	(1) Counterparty Relationships	
1	Note: Swaps	184
	(2) Hedging and Corporate Law Rights and Duties	
4	CSX Corporation v. The Children's Investment Fund Management (UK) LLP	196
	(3) Systemic Risk and Transparency	
	(c) The Financial Crisis of 2008	
23	Ben S. Bernanke, Four Questions about the Financial Crisis	204
33	Ben S. Bernanke, Financial Reform to Address Systemic Risk	204
44	Department of the Treasury, Financial Regulatory Reform, A New Foundation--Large Interconnected Financial Firms	204
52	The Turner Review: A Regulatory Response to the Global Banking Crisis	204
	PART II. Debt Financing	
	Section B. Basic Terms and Concepts	
	1. Introduction	
64	In re Merrill Lynch Auction Rate Securities Litigation	248
74	Note: ARS Enforcement Proceedings	248
	3. The Bondholder and the Going Concern	
	(A) The Promise to Pay	
74	Note: Refunding Cases	267
	(B) Promises that Protect the Promise to Pay	
	(2) Judicial Interpretation of Covenants	
79	Affiliated Computer Services, Inc. v. Wilmington Trust Company	279
	Section C. Security and Seniority	
	4. Asset Securitization	
	(A) Overview	
86	Note: Securitization and the Financial Crisis of 2008	294
	(C) Transaction Structure	

2010 SUPPLEMENT

to

CORPORATE FINANCE

CASES AND MATERIALS

SIXTH EDITION

PART I. VALUING THE FIRM AND ITS SECURITIES

Section B. Elements of Fundamental Value

5. RISK REDUCTION THROUGH HEDGING

(E) REGULATION OF DERIVATIVES

(1) Counterparty Relationships

Insert at Casebook 184 as the second item in "Note: Swaps":

3. *The Terms of Equity Swaps*

In **CSX Corporation v. The Children's Investment Fund Management (UK) LLP.**, 526 F. Supp. 2d 511 (S.D.N.Y. 2008), the court offered a useful description of the terms of equity swaps:

"The term 'derivative,' as the term is used in today's financial world, refers to a financial instrument that derives its value from the price of an underlying instrument or index. Among the different types of derivatives are swaps, instruments whereby two counterparties agree to 'exchange cash flows on two financial instruments over a specific period of time.' These are (1) a 'reference obligation' or 'underlying asset' such as a security, a bank loan, or an index, and (2) a benchmark loan, generally with an interest rate set relative to a commonly used reference rate (the 'reference rate') such as the London Inter-Bank Offered Rate ('LIBOR'). A TRS is a particular form of swap.

"The typical-or 'plain vanilla'-TRS is represented by Figure 1.

Figure 1

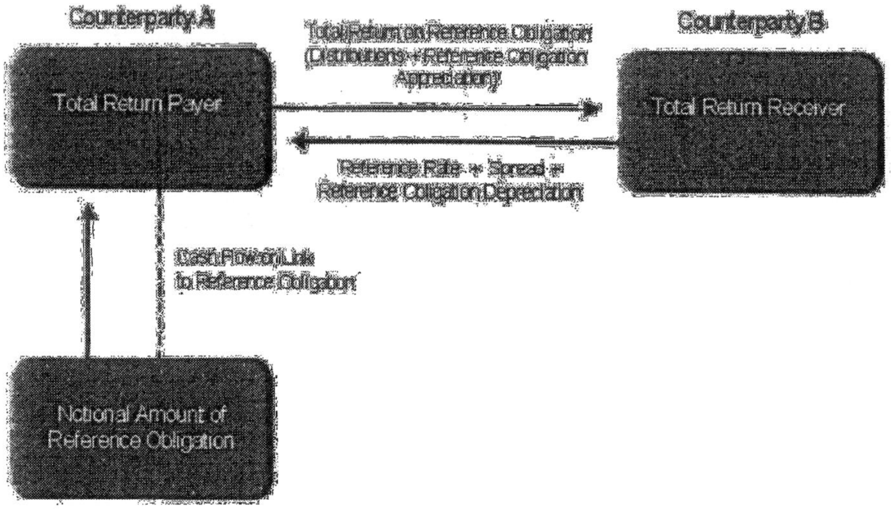

Counterparty A-the 'short' party-agrees to pay Counterparty B-the 'long' party-cash flows based on the performance of a defined underlying asset in exchange for payments by the long party based on the interest that accrues at a negotiated rate on an agreed principal amount (the 'notional amount'). More specifically, Counterparty B, which may be referred to as the 'total return receiver' or 'guarantor,' is entitled to receive from Counterparty A the sum of (1) any cash distributions, such as interest or dividends, that it would have received had it held the referenced asset, and (2) either (i) an amount equal to the market appreciation in the value of the referenced asset over the term of the swap (if the TRS is cash-settled) or, what is economically the same thing, (ii) the referenced asset in exchange for its value on the last refixing date prior to the winding up of the transaction (if the TRS is settled in kind). Counterparty A, referred to as the 'total return payer' or 'beneficiary,' is entitled to receive from Counterparty B(1) an amount equal to the interest at the negotiated rate that would have been payable had it actually loaned Counterparty A the notional amount, and (2) any decrease in the market value of the referenced asset.

"For example, in a cash-settled TRS with reference to 100,000 shares of the stock of General Motors, the short party agrees to pay to the long party an amount equal to the sum of (1) any dividends and cash flow, and (2) any increase in the market value that the long party would have realized had it owned 100,000 shares of General Motors. The long party in turn agrees to pay to the short party the sum of (1) the amount equal to interest that would have been payable had it borrowed the notional amount from the short party, and (2) any depreciation in the market value that it would have suffered had it owned 100,000 shares of General Motors.

"In practical economic terms, a TRS referenced to stock places the long party in substantially the same economic position that it would occupy if it owned the referenced stock or security. There are two notable exceptions. First, since it does not have record ownership of the referenced shares, it does not have the right to vote them. Second, the long party looks to the short party, rather than to the issuer of the referenced security for distributions and the marketplace for any appreciation in value.

"The short party of course is in a different situation. It is entitled to have the long party place it in the same economic position it would have occupied had it advanced the long party an amount equal to the market value of the referenced security. But there are at least two salient distinctions, from the short party's perspective, between a TRS and a loan. First, the short party does not actually advance the notional amount to the long party. Second, it is subject to the risk that the referenced asset will appreciate during the term of the TRS. As will appear, the institutions that make a business of serving as short parties in TRSs deal with this exposure by hedging, a fact pivotal to one of CSX's claims here.

* * *

"The goals of those who enter into TRSs vary.

* * *

"As a generic matter, a short party may be motivated to enter into a TRS simply to obtain the cash flow generated by the long party's payment of the negotiated rate on the notional amount over the term of the swap. But the *quid pro quo* for that cash flow is the exposure to the risk of market appreciation in the referenced security.

"As a matter of theory and on occasion in practice, a short party may accept that exposure either because it thinks the risk of appreciation is small-in other words, it is making its own investment decision with respect to the referenced security-or because it has a more or less offsetting long exposure that it wishes to hedge. But that is not what we are dealing with in this case.

"The defendants' counterparties in this case are major financial service institutions that are in the business, among others, of offering TRSs as a product or service and seeking an economic return via the pseudo-interest, if it may be so called, that they receive on the notional amount and from other incidental revenue sources. They are not, in this aspect of their endeavors, in the business of speculating on the market fluctuation of the shares referenced by the TRSs into which they enter as short parties. Accordingly, they typically hedge their short exposures by purchasing the referenced securities in amounts identical to those referenced in their swap agreements.

"Institutions that hedge short TRS exposure by purchasing the referenced shares typically have no economic interest in the securities. They are, however, beneficial owners and thus have the right to vote the referenced shares.

* * *

"A long party to a TRS referencing equity in a public company gains economic exposure to the equity. In other words, it is exposed to essentially the same potential benefits and detriments as would be the case if it held the referenced security, and it gains that exposure without the need for the capital to fund or maintain such a purchase directly. This may permit such investors to operate with greater leverage or a lower cost than might be the case if they bought the security directly."

4. *Enron and the Equity Swaps that Weren't.*

———

(2) Hedging and Corporate Law Rights and Duties

Insert at Casebook 196 after "Note: Empty Voting":

CSX Corporation v. The Children's Investment Fund Management (UK) LLP

United States District Court, Southern District of New York, 2008
526 F. Supp. 2d 511

KAPLAN, J.

Some people deliberately go close to the line dividing legal from illegal if they see a sufficient opportunity for profit in doing so. A few cross that line and, if caught, seek to justify their actions on the basis of formalistic arguments even when it is apparent that they have defeated the purpose of the law.

This is such a case. The defendants--two hedge funds that seek extraordinary gain, sometimes through "shareholder activism"--amassed a large economic position in CSX Corporation ("CSX"), one of the nation's largest railroads. They did so for the purpose of causing CSX to behave in a manner that they hoped would lead to a rise in the value of their holdings. And there is nothing wrong with that. But they did so in close coordination with each other and without making the public disclosure required of 5 percent shareholders and groups by the Williams Act, a statute that was enacted to ensure that other shareholders are informed of such accumulations and arrangements. They now have launched a proxy fight that, if successful, would result in their having substantial influence and perhaps practical working control of CSX.

Defendants seek to defend their secret accumulation of interests in CSX by invoking what they assert is the letter of the law. Much of their position in CSX was in the form of total return equity swaps ("TRSs"), a type of derivative that gave defendants substantially all of the indicia of stock ownership save the formal legal right to vote the shares. In consequence, they argue, they did not beneficially own the shares referenced by the swaps and thus were not obliged to disclose sooner or more fully than they did. In a like vein, they contend that they did not reach a formal agreement to act together, and therefore did not become a "group" required to disclose its collaborative activities, until December 2007 despite the fact that they began acting in concert with respect to CSX far earlier. But these contentions are not sufficient to justify defendants' actions.

The question whether the holder of a cash-settled equity TRS beneficially owns the referenced stock held by the short counterparty appears to be one of first impression. There are persuasive arguments for concluding, on the facts of this case, that the answer is "yes"--that defendants beneficially owned at least some and quite possibly all of the referenced CSX shares held by their counterparties. But it ultimately is unnecessary to reach such a conclusion to decide this case.

Rule 13d-3(b) under the Exchange Act provides in substance that one who creates an arrangement that prevents the vesting of beneficial ownership as part of a plan or scheme to avoid the disclosure that would have been required if the actor bought the stock outright is deemed to be a beneficial owner of those shares. That is exactly what the defendants did here in amassing their swap positions. In consequence, defendants are deemed to be the beneficial owners of the referenced shares.

As for the question whether defendants made prompt disclosure after they formed a "group" within the meaning of Section 13(d) of the Exchange Act, the evidence, as in virtually all such cases, is circumstantial. But it quite persuasively demonstrates that they formed a group many months before they filed the necessary disclosure statement. Their protestations to the contrary rest in no small measure on the premise that they avoided forming a group by starting conversations by stating that they were not forming a group and by avoiding entry into a written agreement. But the Exchange Act is concerned with substance, not incantations and formalities.

This is not to say that CSX is entitled to all of the relief that it seeks. The Williams Act was intended not only to prevent secret accumulation and undisclosed group activities with respect to the stock of public companies, but to do so without "tipping the balance of regulation either in favor of management or in favor of the person making the takeover bid." It must be applied, especially in private litigation, with due regard for the principle that the purpose of private equitable relief is "to deter, not to punish." Moreover, the Court's ability to formulate a remedy is sharply constrained by precedent. Accordingly, while the Court will enjoin defendants from further Section 13(d) violations, it may not preclude defendants from voting their CSX shares and declines to grant any of the other drastic relief that CSX seeks. Any penalties for defendants' violations must come by way of appropriate action by the Securities and Exchange Commission ("SEC") or the Department of Justice.

Background

I. Parties

[Plaintiff CSX Corporation ("CSX") is incorporated in Virginia and headquartered in Jacksonville, Florida. Its shares are traded on the New York Stock Exchange, and it operates one of the nation's largest rail systems through its wholly owned subsidiary, CSX Transportation, Inc. Defendants The Children's Investment Fund Management (UK) LLP ("TCIF UK") and The Children's Investment Fund Management (Cayman) LTD. ("TCIF Cayman") are, respectively, an English limited liability partnership and a Cayman Islands company. Defendant The Children's Investment Master Fund ("TCI Fund") also is a company organized under the laws of the Cayman Islands and is managed by both TCIF UK and TCIF Cayman. These entities are run by defendant Christopher Hohn, who is managing partner and a controlling person of TCIF UK and the sole owner and a controlling person of TCIF Cayman. Defendant Snehal Amin is a partner of TCIF UK. These five defendants are referred to collectively as TCI. Defendants 3G Fund L.P. ("3G Fund") and 3G Capital

Partners L.P. ("3G LP") are Cayman Islands limited partnerships. Defendant 3G Capital Partners Ltd. ("3G Ltd.") is a Cayman Islands company and the general partner of 3G LP, which in turn is the general partner of 3G Fund. They are run by defendant Alexandre Behring, also known as Alexandre Behring Costa, who is the managing partner of 3G Ltd. These four defendants are referred to collectively as 3G.]

II. Proceedings

TCI and 3G currently are engaged in a proxy fight in which they seek, *inter alia,* to elect their nominees to five of the twelve seats on the CSX board of directors and to amend its by-laws to permit holders of 15 percent of CSX shares to call a special meeting of shareholders at any time for any purpose permissible under Virginia law.

CSX brought this action against TCI and 3G on March 17, 2008. The complaint alleges, among other things, that defendants failed timely to file a Schedule 13D after forming a group to act with reference to the shares of CSX and that both the Schedule 13D and the proxy statement they eventually filed were false and misleading. It seeks, among other things, an order requiring corrective disclosure, voiding proxies defendants have obtained, and precluding defendants from voting their CSX shares. * * *

III. Total Return Swaps

[For the Court's presentation of the terms of equity swaps, see Note: Swaps, supra this Supplement.]

The swap agreements at issue in this case are cash-settled TRSs entered into by TCI with each of eight counterparties, most significantly Deutsche Bank AG ("Deutsche Bank") and Citigroup Global Markets Limited ("Citigroup"), and by 3G with Morgan Stanley.

* * *

Institutions that hedge short TRS exposure by purchasing the referenced shares typically have no economic interest in the securities. They are, however, beneficial owners and thus have the right to vote the referenced shares.

Institutional voting practices appear to vary. As noted below, some take the position that they will not vote shares held to hedge TRS risk. Some may be influenced, at least in some cases, to vote as a counterparty desires. Some say they vote as they determine in their sole discretion. Of course, one may suppose that banks seeking to attract swap business well understand that activist investors will consider them to be more attractive counterparties if they vote in favor of the positions their clients advocate. In any case, however, the accumulation of substantial hedge positions significantly alters the corporate electorate. It does so by (1) eliminating the shares constituting the hedge positions from the universe of available votes, (2) subjecting the voting of the shares to the control or influence of a long party that does not own the shares, or (3) leaving the vote to be determined by an institution that has no economic interest in the fortunes of the issuer, holds nothing more than a formal interest, but is aware that future swap business from a particular client may depend upon voting in the "right" way.

* * *

A long party to a TRS referencing equity in a public company gains economic exposure to the equity. In other words, it is exposed to essentially the same potential benefits and detriments as would be the case if it held the referenced security, and it gains that exposure without the need for the capital to fund or maintain such a purchase directly. This may permit such investors to operate with greater leverage or a lower cost than might be the case if they bought the security directly. But those are by no means the only reasons motivating long parties to engage in TRSs. There can be tax advantages. Most importantly for purposes of this case, if the long party to a cash-settled TRS is not the beneficial owner of the referenced shares-a question hotly contested here-one interested in amassing a large economic exposure to the equity of a registered company may do so without making the public disclosure that is required when a person or group acquires 5 percent or more of the outstanding shares.

The avoidance of public disclosure can confer significant advantages on the long party. By concealing its activities, it may avoid other investors bidding up the referenced stock in anticipation of a tender offer or other corporate control contest and thus maximize the long party's profit potential. Second, it permits a long party who is interested in persuading an issuer to alter its policies, but desirous of avoiding an all-out battle for control, to select the time of its emergence to the issuer as a powerful player to a moment of its choosing, which may be when its exposure is substantially greater than 5 percent. In other words, it permits a long party to ambush an issuer with a holding far greater than 5 percent.

One other point bears mention here. TRSs, like all or most derivatives, are privately negotiated contracts traded over the counter. Their terms may be varied during their lives as long as the counterparties agree. In consequence, a TRS that in its inception contemplates cash settlement may be settled in kind-i.e., by delivery of the referenced shares to the long party-as long as the parties consent.

This confers another potential advantage on a long party that contemplates a tender offer, proxy fight, or other corporate control contest. By entering into cash-settled TRSs, such an investor may concentrate large quantities of an issuer's stock in the hands of its short counterparties and, when it judges the time to be right, unwind those swaps by acquiring the referenced shares from those counterparties in swiftly consummated private transactions. Moreover, even if such TRSs were settled in cash, the disposition by the short counterparties of the referenced shares held to hedge their swap exposures would afford a ready supply of shares to the market at times and in circumstances effectively chosen and known principally by the long party. The long party therefore likely would have a real advantage in converting its exposure from swaps to physical shares even if it does not unwind the swaps in kind.

IV. The Events of Mid-2006 Until Late 2007

[TCI, determined to profit by forcing change at CSX, acquired a long interest in up to 14.1 percent of CSX common entirely through TRSs. TCI disclosed its interest to CSX, noting that it could switch to outright ownership at any time; meetings were held. TCI also consulted investment bankers and CSX about the possibility of a leveraged buyout of CSX. CSX, in turn, announced plans to repurchase 2 million shares. TCI then filed a premerger notification under the Hart-Scott-Rodino Act, stating an intention to buy (directly) up to $500 million in CSX shares. TCI also approached other hedge funds, encouraging them to take positions in CSX and support its initiative.

[TCI, getting no cooperation from CSX management, began to prepare for a proxy fight, and so began to transfer its holdings from TRSs to stock held outright. It also continued to pitch its plan to investment institutions, toward the end of getting them to take supportive stock positions.]

From the inception of its TRS acquisitions * * * TCI carefully distributed its swaps among eight counterparties so as to prevent any one of them from acquiring greater than 5 percent of CSX's shares and thus having to disclose its swap agreements with TCI. On October 30, 2007, however, TCI began unwinding its TRSs with Credit Suisse, Goldman Sachs, J.P. Morgan, Merrill Lynch, Morgan Stanley, and UBS and replacing them with TRSs with Deutsche Bank and Citigroup. Ultimately, it shifted exposure equal to approximately 9 percent of CSX from other counterparties into Deutsche Bank and Citigroup.

[3G began looking at CSX as a potential target in 2005 and began taking large positions in its stock in 2007. As events developed, TCI and 3G communicated with each other and eventually agreed to conduct a proxy contest jointly and agreed on board nominees. On December 19, 2007, TCI, 3G, and their board nominees (the "Group") filed a Schedule 13D with the SEC. The Group filed its preliminary proxy statement on March 10, 2008. It proposed Hohn and Behring, and three outside nominees for election to the board and advocated its proposal to permit investors holding at least 15 percent of CSX stock to call a special meeting for any purpose permissible under Virginia law. The materials noted that the Group collectively held 35.1 million shares, representing approximately 8.7 percent of those outstanding, and that the value of its investment in CSX exceeded $1.65 billion. It disclosed its members' swap arrangements and the aggregate percentage of CSX shares to which they provided economic exposure. It disclosed also that Deutsche Bank beneficially owned 36.7 million shares of CSX, or 9.1 percent of the common stock.

[CSX contends, *inter alia*, that TCI violated Section 13(d) of the Exchange Act by failing to disclose its beneficial ownership of shares of CSX common stock referenced in their TRSs.]

Discussion

I. Section 13(d)

The Williams Act, which enacted what now is Section 13(d) of the Exchange Act, was passed to address the increasing frequency with which hostile takeovers were being used to effect changes in corporate control. Section 13(d) in particular was adopted "to alert the marketplace to every large, rapid aggregation or accumulation of securities, regardless of technique employed, which might represent a potential shift in corporate control."

[Section 13(d) requires holders of more than 5 percent of a registered class of stock to file a statement within 10 days of acquisition.[1] The present dispute concerns whether TCI's investments in cash-settled TRSs referencing CSX shares conferred beneficial ownership of those shares upon TCI. The term beneficial ownership is defined in Rule 13d-3:

> (a) For the purposes of sections 13(d) and 13(g) of the Act a beneficial owner of a security includes any person who, directly or indirectly, through any contract, arrangement, understanding, relationship, or otherwise has or shares:(1) Voting power which includes the power to vote, or to direct the voting of, such security; and/or, (2) Investment power which includes the power to dispose, or to direct the disposition of, such security.
>
> (b) Any person who, directly or indirectly, creates or uses a trust, proxy, power of attorney, pooling arrangement or any other contract, arrangement, or device with the purpose of [*sic*] effect of divesting such person of beneficial ownership of a security or preventing the vesting of

---

1

[Ed note:]The core of the statute for present purposes is Section 13(d)(1), which provides in relevant part that

> "Any person who, after acquiring directly or indirectly the beneficial ownership of any equity security of a class which is registered pursuant to section 78*l* of this title, ... is directly or indirectly the beneficial owner of more than 5 per centum of such class shall, within ten days after such acquisition, send to the issuer of the security at its principal executive office, by registered or certified mail, send to each exchange where the security is traded, and file[ ] with the Commission, a statement containing such of the following information, and such additional information, as the Commission may by rules and regulations, prescribe as necessary or appropriate in the public interest or for the protection of investors-
>
> "(A) the background, and identity, ... and the nature of such beneficial ownership by, such person and all other persons by whom or on whose behalf the purchases have been or are to be effected;
>
> "(C) if the purpose of the purchases or prospective purchases is to acquire control of the business of the issuer of the securities, any plans or proposals which such persons may have to liquidate such issuer, to sell its assets to or merge it with any other persons, or to make any other major change in its business or corporate structure;
>
> "(D) the number of shares of such security which are beneficially owned, and the number of shares concerning which there is a right to acquire, directly or indirectly, by (i) such person, and (ii) by each associate of such person, giving the background, identity, residence, and citizenship of each such associate...."

> such beneficial ownership as part of a plan or scheme to evade the reporting requirements of section 13(d) or (g) of the Act shall be deemed for purposes of such sections to be the beneficial owner of such security.]

The SEC intended Rule 13d-3(a) to provide a "broad definition" of beneficial ownership so as to ensure disclosure "from all those persons who have the ability to change or influence control." This indeed is apparent from the very words of the Rule. By stating that a beneficial owner "includes" rather than "means" any person who comes within the criteria that follow, it made plain that the language that follows does not exhaust the circumstances in which one might come within the term. The phrases "directly or indirectly" and "any contract, arrangement, understanding, relationship, or otherwise" reinforce that point and demonstrate the focus on substance rather than on form or on the legally enforceable rights of the putative beneficial owner. It therefore is not surprising that the SEC, at the very adoption of Rule 13d-3, stated that the determination of beneficial ownership under Rule 13d-3(a) requires

> [a]n analysis of all relevant facts and circumstances in a particular situation ... in order to identify each person possessing the requisite voting power or investment power. For example, for purposes of the rule, the mere possession of the legal right to vote securities under applicable state or other law ... may not be determinative of who is a beneficial owner of such securities inasmuch as another person or persons may have the power whether legal, economic, or otherwise, to direct such voting.

Nor does Rule 13d-3(a) exhaust the Commission's efforts to cast a very broad net to capture all situations in which the marketplace should be alerted to circumstances that might result in a change in corporate control. Rule 13d-3(b) was adopted so that Rule 13d-3(a) "cannot be circumvented by an arrangement to divest a person of beneficial ownership or to prevent the vesting of beneficial ownership as part of a plan or scheme to evade the reporting requirements of [S]ection 13(d)."

With these considerations in mind, the Court turns to CSX's contentions. It first considers whether TCI had beneficial ownership, within the meaning of Rule 13d-3(a), of the shares of CSX stock referenced by its swap agreements and held by its counterparties by considering the facts and circumstances surrounding those contracts. It then turns to the question of whether TCI, assuming it were not a beneficial owner of the hedge shares under Rule 13d-3(a), nevertheless would be deemed a beneficial owner under Rule 13d-3(b) because it used the TRSs as part of a plan or scheme to evade the disclosure requirements of Section 13(d) by avoiding the vesting of beneficial ownership in TCI.

1. Rule 13d-3(a)

The contracts embodying TCI's swaps did not give TCI any legal rights with respect to the voting or disposition of the CSX shares referenced therein. Nor did they require that its short counterparties acquire CSX shares to hedge their positions. But the beneficial ownership

> inquiry focuses on any relationship that, as a factual matter, confers on a person a *significant ability to affect* how voting power or investment power will be exercised, because it is primarily designed to ensure timely disclosure of market-sensitive data about changes in the identity of those who are able, as a practicable matter, to influence the use of that power. [SEC v. Drexel Burnham Lambert Inc., 837 F.Supp. 587, 607 (S.D.N.Y.1993), aff'd sub nom .SEC v. Posner, 16 F.3d 520 (2d Cir.1994), cert. denied,513 U.S. 1077 (1995)]

It therefore is important to consider whether TCI's TRSs contemplated that its counterparties would hedge their positions with CSX shares and, if so, whether TCI had "a significant ability to affect how voting power or investment power will be exercised."

a. Investment Power

TCI acknowledges, as it must, that its swaps contemplated the possibility that the counterparties might--indeed would--hedge by acquiring physical shares. It emphasizes, however, that they were under no contractual obligation to do so and, indeed, had other means of hedging their short positions. Moreover, TCI asserts that it had no influence over how its counterparties disposed of physical shares used to hedge a swap, if any, at the time of termination. TCI therefore maintains that it had no investment power over any shares used to hedge its swaps.

TCI correctly describes the legal instruments constituting the swaps. They do not require the counterparties to hedge their positions by purchasing CSX stock and do not in terms address the question of how the counterparties will dispose of their hedges at the conclusion of the swaps. But the evidence is overwhelming that these counterparties in fact hedged the short positions created by the TRSs with TCI by purchasing shares of CSX common stock. * * * [T]hey did so on virtually a share-for-share basis and in each case on the day or the day following the commencement of each swap.

This is precisely what TCI contemplated and, indeed, intended. None of these counterparties is in the business, so far as running its swap desk is concerned, of taking on the stupendous risks entailed in holding unhedged short (or long) positions in significant percentages of the shares of listed companies. As a practical matter, the Court finds that their positions could not be hedged through the use of other derivatives. Thus, it was inevitable that they would hedge the TCI swaps by purchasing CSX shares.

TCI knew that the banks would behave in this manner and therefore sought at the outset to spread its TRS agreements across a number of counterparties so as to avoid pushing any counterparty, individually, across the 5 percent threshold that would have triggered an obligation on the counterparty's part to disclose its position under Regulation 13D. This would have been a cause for concern only if TCI understood that its counterparties, although not legally obligated to do so, in fact would hedge by purchasing CSX shares equal or substantially equal to the shares referenced by the TCI swaps.

Moreover, TCI understood that there were advantages to TCI of its short counterparties hedging with physical shares. The fact that these are nominally cash-settled TRSs does not necessarily mean that they all will be settled for cash. TCI and its counterparties have the ability to agree to unwind the swaps in kind, i.e., by delivery of the shares to TCI at the conclusion of each transaction, as indeed commonly occurs. That simple fact means that the hedge positions of the counterparties hang like the sword of Damocles over the neck of CSX. Once the Hart-Scott-Rodino waiting period expired, nothing more was required to move the legal ownership of the hedge shares from the banks to TCI than the stroke of a pen or the transmission of an email. This greatly enhances TCI's leverage over CSX, even if it never settles any of the TRSs for cash, as indeed has been the case to date. And TCI so views the realities as evidenced by [its] statement to CSX that TCI's swap position could be converted to shares at any time as well as [its] assertion * * * that TCI "owned" a quantity of shares that clearly included the shares held by its counterparties.

The corollary to the bank's behavior at the front end of these transactions, viz. purchasing physical shares to hedge risk, is that the banks would sell those shares at the conclusion of the swaps (assuming cash settlement) so as to avoid the risk that holding the physical shares would entail once the downside protection of the swap was removed. And that is exactly what happened here. With very minor exceptions, whenever TCI terminated a swap, the counterparty sold the same number of physical shares that were referenced in the unwound swap and it did so on the same day that the swap was terminated. * * *

To be sure, there is no evidence that TCI explicitly directed the banks to purchase the hedge shares upon entering into the swaps or to sell them upon termination. Nor did it direct the banks to dispose of their hedge shares by any particular means. But that arguably is not dispositive.

On this record, it is quite clear that TCI significantly influenced the banks to purchase the CSX shares that constituted their hedges because the banks, as a practical matter and as TCI both knew and desired, were compelled to do so. It significantly influenced the banks to sell the hedge shares when the swaps were unwound for the same reasons.

b. Voting Power

There is no evidence that TCI and any of its counterparties had explicit agreements that the banks would vote their hedge shares in a certain way. Moreover, the policies and practices of the counterparties with respect to voting hedge shares vary. But these are not the only pertinent considerations.

(1) Deutsche Bank

Between October and November 2007, TCI moved swaps referencing 28.4 million and 18.0 million shares into Deutsche Bank and Citigroup, respectively, while leaving swaps referencing 1,000 shares with each of its remaining six counterparties. [TCI claimed that it did so in order to reduce counterparty default risk and conceded that it expected "beneficial" results respecting any share voting. The Court expressed skepticism respecting the credit risk argument, but noted that TCI's interests respecting CSX were directly aligned with those of Austin Friars, a hedge fund within Deutsche Bank that held a proprietary position in CSX common stock. In addition, there was speculation from CSX that Deutsche Bank recalled, for voting purposes, loaned shares prior to the CSX record date for its 2008 annual meeting.]

In the last analysis, the question whether there was an agreement--explicit or implicit--between Deutsche Bank and TCI with respect to the voting of the shares is a close one. In view of the grounds on which the Court ultimately disposes of this case, however, it is unnecessary to make a finding on the point.

(2) All of the Counterparties

* * * [T]he SEC has made plain that a party has voting power over a share under Rule 13d-3(a)(1) if that party has the "ability to control *or influence*

the voting ... of the securities." So the question of influence must be considered with respect to all of the banks.

As an initial matter, TCI, which knew that the banks would hedge the swaps by purchasing physical shares, could and at least to some extent did select counterparties by taking their business to institutions it thought would be most likely to vote with TCI in a proxy contest. D.F. King's "Preliminary Vote Outlook" presentation concerning the proxy contest indicates that certain types of investors adhere to particular voting patterns in contested elections and are influenced by the recommendations made by institutional proxy advisory firms such as RiskMetrics (formerly ISS). Although D.F. King was clear that it could not guarantee the manner in which a particular investor would vote, patterns of behavior made it possible for TCI to predict the likelihood of that vote and place its swap transactions accordingly.

Further, some of the banks' policies gave TCI the power to prevent a share from being voted. Credit Suisse, for example, appears to follow a policy of not voting its hedge shares if it is solicited by its counterparty in a contested situation. In such instances, then, TCI could ensure that that bank's hedge shares would not be voted against it by the simple expedient of soliciting its counterparty. Thus, by entering into a TRS with Credit Suisse, TCI was in a position to ensure that Credit Suisse would purchase shares that otherwise might have been voted against TCI in a proxy fight and then to ensure that those shares would not be so voted. While this would not be as favorable a result as dictating a vote in its favor, it would be better than leaving the votes of those shares to chance.

Finally, the fact that TCI thought it could influence Citigroup at least suggests that its relationship with Citigroup permitted it to do so. Nevertheless, the proof on this point is not sufficient to find that TCI in fact had that ability.

c. Synthesis

In the last analysis, there are substantial reasons for concluding that TCI is the beneficial owner of the CSX shares held as hedges by its short counterparties. The definition of "beneficial ownership" in Rule 13d-3(a) is very broad, as is appropriate to its object of ensuring disclosure "from all ... persons who have the ability [even] to ... influence control." It does not confine itself to "the mere possession of the legal right to vote [or direct the acquisition or disposition of] securities," but looks instead to all of the facts and circumstances to identify situations in which one has even the ability to influence voting, purchase, or sale decisions of its counterparties by "legal, economic, or other[ ]" means.

On this record, TCI manifestly had the economic ability to cause its short counterparties to buy and sell the CSX shares. The very nature of the TRS transactions, as a practical matter, required the counterparties to hedge their short exposures. And while there theoretically are means of hedging that do not require the purchase of physical shares, in the situation before the Court it is perfectly clear that the purchase of physical shares was the only practical alternative. Indeed, TCI effectively has admitted as much. It did so by spreading its swap transactions among eight counterparties to avoid any one hitting the 5 percent disclosure threshold and thus triggering its own reporting obligation-a concern that was relevant only because TCI knew that the counterparties were hedging by buying shares. And it did so in closing argument, where its counsel said that the banks' purchases of CSX shares were "the natural consequence" of the swap transactions. Thus, TCI patently had the power to cause the counterparties to buy CSX. At the very least, it had the power to influence them to do so. And once the counterparties bought the shares, TCI had the practical ability to cause them to sell simply by unwinding the swap transactions. Certainly the banks had no intention of allowing their swap desks to hold the unhedged long positions that would have resulted from the unwinding of the swaps.

The voting situation is a bit murkier, but there nevertheless is reason to believe that TCI was in a position to influence the counterparties, especially Deutsche Bank, with respect to the exercise of their voting rights.

TCI nevertheless argues strenuously against a finding that it has beneficial ownership of the shares, focusing heavily on the fact that it had no legal right to direct its short counterparties to buy or sell shares or to vote them in any particular way, indeed at all. Some *amici,* more cautiously, urge that any finding of beneficial ownership be rooted in unique facts of this case to avoid upsetting what they say is the settled expectation of the marketplace that equity swaps, *in and of themselves,* do not confer beneficial ownership of the referenced shares. They contend that a broader ruling could have extensive implications and that the subject therefore is dealt with more appropriately by administrative agency rule making than case-by-case adjudication. And the SEC Division of Corporation Finance argues--perhaps inconsistently with some of the Commission's past statements about the breadth of the definition of beneficial ownership--that there is no beneficial ownership where the short counterparties buy, sell, or vote their hedge shares as a result of their own economic incentives and not pursuant to legal obligations owed to their long counterparties, although it does not comment on the facts of this case. The Division, moreover, suggests that a contrary ruling would be novel and upset settled expectations of the market.

The focus on TCI's legal rights under its swap contracts, while those rights certainly are relevant, exalts form over substance. The securities markets operate in the real world, not in a law school contracts classroom. Any determination of beneficial ownership that failed to take account of the practical realities of that world would be open to the gravest abuse. Indeed, this Court is not alone in recognizing that abuses would be facilitated by a regime that did not require disclosure of the sort that would be required if "beneficial ownership" were construed as advocated by CSX.

Moreover, the Court is inclined to the view that the Cassandra-like predictions of dire consequences of holding that TCI has beneficial ownership under Rule 13d-3(a) have been exaggerated. For one thing, there is no reason to believe that there are many situations in which the 5 percent reporting threshold under Section 13(d) would be triggered by such a ruling. The overwhelming majority of swap transactions would proceed as before without any additional Regulation 13D or G reporting requirements. The issue here, moreover, is novel and hardly settled. And markets can well adapt regardless of how it ultimately is resolved. Indeed, the United Kingdom reportedly now requires disclosure of economic stakes greater than 1 percent in companies involved in takeovers and is considering requiring disclosure at the 3 percent level in other companies, levels lower than would be required to trigger Section 13(d), assuming that the TRSs here fall within Rule 13d-3(a). Yet there is no reason to believe that the sky has fallen, or is likely to fall, in London.

Nor do potentially broad implications or any supposed advantage of administrative rule making over adjudication permit a court to decline to decide an issue that must be decided in order to resolve a case before it. But it is equally true that courts should decide no more than is essential to resolve their cases.

In this case, it is not essential to decide the beneficial ownership question under Rule 13d-3(a). As is discussed immediately below, TCI used the TRSs with the purpose and effect of preventing the vesting of beneficial ownership of the referenced shares in TCI as part of a plan or scheme to evade the reporting requirements of Section 13(d). Under Rule 13d-3(b), TCI, if it is not a beneficial owner under rule 13d-3(a), therefore is deemed--on the facts of this case--to beneficially own those shares. The Court therefore does not rule on the legal question whether TCI is a beneficial owner under Section 13d-3(a).

2. Rule 13d-3(b)

In construing any statute or rule, the Court is governed by well-established principles. It first must examine "the language of the provision at issue," which governs " 'unless that meaning would lead to absurd results.'" In addition, the provision "should be construed so that effect is given to all its provisions, so that no part will be inoperative or superfluous, void or insignificant, and so that one section will not destroy another unless the provision is the result of obvious mistake or error."

We begin with the language. Rule 13d-3(b) provides:

> "Any person who, directly or indirectly, [1] creates or uses a trust, proxy, power of attorney, pooling arrangement or any other contract, arrangement, or device [2] with the purpose of [*sic*] effect of divesting such person of beneficial ownership of a security or preventing the vesting of such beneficial ownership [3] as part of a plan or scheme to evade the reporting requirements of section 13(d) or (g) of the Act shall be deemed for purposes of such sections to be the beneficial owner of such security."

Thus, the Rule by its plain terms is triggered when three elements are satisfied:

• the use of a contract, arrangement, or device

• with the purpose or effect of divesting such person of beneficial ownership of a security or preventing the vesting of such beneficial ownership

• as part of a plan or scheme to evade the reporting requirements of Section 13(d) or (g).It is undisputed that TCI's cash-settled TRSs are contracts. The first element therefore concededly is satisfied.

The evidence that TCI created and used the TRSs, at least in major part, for the purpose of preventing the vesting of beneficial ownership of CSX shares in TCI and as part of a plan or scheme to evade the reporting requirements of Section 13(d) is overwhelming. Joe O'Flynn, the chief financial officer of TCI Fund told its board, albeit not in the specific context of CSX, that one of the reasons for using swaps is "the ability to purchase without disclosure to the market or the company." TCI emails discussed the need to make certain that its counterparties stayed below 5 percent physical share ownership, this in order to avoiding triggering a disclosure obligation on the part of a counterparty. TCI admitted that one of its motivations in avoiding disclosure was to avoid paying a higher price for the shares of CSX, which would have been the product of front-running that it expected would occur if its interest in CSX were disclosed to the market generally. Indeed, TCI acquired only approximately 4.5 percent in physical CSX shares to remain safely below the 5 percent reporting requirement until it was ready to disclose its position.

To be sure, there is evidence that TCI argues points in the opposite direction. It did disclose to CSX the fact that it had exposure to its stock well before it made a Schedule 13D filing. But that does not carry the day. Telling an issuer that an investor has exposure to its stock is quite a different matter than timely disclosing to the marketplace generally the details of the investor's position, its plans and intentions, its contracts and arrangements with respect to the issuer's securities, and its financing and then keeping that information up to date as Regulation 13D requires. For one thing, the market in general does not necessarily know even what the issuer knows. And the issuer is left to guess as to many of the important matters that compliance with Regulation 13D requires. Here, TCI's limited disclosure to CSX and its concealment of broader, more timely, and more accurate information from the marketplace served its objectives. It exerted pressure on CSX, a pressure that was enhanced by the lack of complete information. And it kept the marketplace entirely and, after CSX filed its Form 10-Q, largely in the dark, thus serving TCI's interest in permitting it to build its position without running up the price of the stock. In all the circumstances, the Court finds that each of the elements of Rule 13d-3(b) is satisfied here.

This outcome is supported by the views of the SEC's Division of Corporation Finance as the Court understands them. While the Division did not comment upon or attempt to analyze the facts of this case in light of governing legal standards, its *amicus* letter appears to take two positions. First, it states the view that "the long party's underlying motive for entering into the swap transaction generally is not a basis for determining whether there is 'a plan or scheme to evade." ' It goes on to say that it believes "that the mental state contemplated by the words 'plan or scheme to evade' is generally the intent to enter into an arrangement that creates a false appearance." It states that "a person who entered into a swap would be a beneficial owner under Rule 13d-3(b) if it were determined that the person did so with the intent to create the false appearance of non-ownership of a security ." But it adds that it "cannot rule out the possibility that, in some unusual circumstances, a plan or scheme to evade the beneficial ownership provisions of Rule 13d-3 might exist where the evidence does not indicate a false appearance or sham transaction." Having said that, however, the letter concludes that "as a general matter, a person that does nothing more than enter into an equity swap should not be found to have engaged in an evasion of the reporting requirements."

As an initial matter, no one suggests that TCI did "nothing more than enter into an equity swap."At a minimum, it entered into the TRSs rather than buying stock for the purpose, perhaps among others, of avoiding the disclosure requirements of Section 13(d) by preventing the vesting of beneficial ownership in TCI.

Passing on to its other point, the Division's assertion that "a person who entered into a swap would be a beneficial owner under Rule 13d-3(b) if it were determined that the person did so with the intent to create the false appearance of non-ownership of a security" suffers from some degree of ambiguity. On the one hand, the statement may be intended merely to illustrate a specific intent that would satisfy the test, without intending to exhaust the possibilities. On the other, it may intend to convey the thought that an intent to create a false appearance of non-ownership is indispensable to a Rule 13d-3(b) finding. Two considerations persuade the Court that the former is the case.

First, the Division declined to "rule out the possibility that ... a plan or scheme to evade ... might exist [without] a false appearance or sham transaction."It follows that it cannot be saying that, in its view, a false appearance of non-ownership is a necessary condition for application of Rule 13d-3(b).

Second, reading Rule 13d-3(b) as requiring an intent to create a false appearance of non-ownership would violate a fundamental principle of statutory construction. An appearance of non-ownership cannot be false unless one in fact is at least a beneficial owner. That beneficial ownership would satisfy Rule 13d-3(a), thus making Rule 13d-3(b) superfluous. In consequence, Rule 13d-3 as a whole is inconsistent with any view that a false appearance of non-ownership is a prerequisite to application of Rule 13d-3(b).

This leaves us with the Division's more likely position, viz. that Rule 13d-3(b) is satisfied only where the actor intends to create some false appearance, albeit not necessarily a false appearance of non-ownership. But false appearance of what?

The goal of Section 13(d) "is to alert the marketplace to every large, rapid aggregation or accumulation of securities ... which might represent a potential shift in corporate control." In consequence, the natural reading is that the Division refers to a false appearance that no such accumulation is taking place. Put another way, Rule 13d-3(b) applies where one enters into a transaction with the intent to create the false appearance that there is no large accumulation of securities that might have a potential for shifting corporate control by evading the disclosure requirements of Section 13(d) or (g) through preventing the vesting of beneficial ownership in the actor.

If that is what the Division means, then its proposed standard is more than satisfied in this case. TCI intentionally entered into the TRSs, with the purpose and intent of preventing the vesting of beneficial ownership in TCI, as part of a plan or scheme to evade the reporting requirements of Section 13(d) and thus concealed precisely what Section 13(d) was intended to force into the open. And if this is not what the Division means, the Division's argument would be unpersuasive. After all, there is not one word in Section 13(d) or in Rule 13d-3 that supports a requirement of an intent to create a false appearance of non-ownership if that term requires anything more than concealment of the sort of secret market accumulations that went on here.

Undaunted, TCI argues that it did not trigger Rule 13d-3(b). It relies in part on a letter from Professor Bernard Black to the SEC in which the professor argued that "it must be permissible for an investor to acquire equity swaps, rather than shares, in part--or indeed entirely--*because* share ownership is disclosable under § 13(d) while equity swaps are not." He bases this argument on the premise that "the underlying [i.e., evasive] activity must involve holding a position which is 'beneficial ownership' under the *statute* (Exchange Act § 13(d) or (g)), but would otherwise fall outside the *rule*-outside the SEC's effort to define the concept of beneficial ownership elsewhere in Rule 13d-3." With respect, the Court finds the argument unpersuasive.

As an initial matter, the SEC, in the Court's view, has the power to treat as beneficial ownership a situation that would not fall within the statutory meaning of that term. Section 23(a) of the Exchange Act grants the Commission the "power to make such rules and regulations as may be necessary or appropriate to implement the provisions of this chapter for which [it is] responsible...." The validity of a rule or regulation promulgated under such a grant of authority will be sustained so long as it is "reasonably related to the purposes of the enabling legislation."

The purpose of Section 13(d) is to alert shareholders of "every large, rapid aggregation or accumulation of securities, regardless of technique employed, which might represent a potential shift in corporate control." Rule 13d-3(b) was promulgated to further this purpose by preventing circumvention of Rule 13d-3 with arrangements designed to avoid disclosure obligations by preventing the vesting of beneficial ownership as defined elsewhere--in other words, where there is accumulation of securities by any means with a potential shift of corporate control, but no beneficial ownership. As Rule 13d-3(b) therefore is reasonably related to the purpose of the statute, it is a perfectly appropriate exercise of the Commission's authority even where it reaches arrangements that otherwise would not amount to beneficial ownership.

Second, while it may be debated whether the term "beneficial ownership" as used in the Williams Act is broader than or coextensive with the same language as used in Rule 13d-3(a), one thing is quite clear. If Rule 13d-3(b) reaches only situations that involve beneficial ownership, then it reaches only situations that are reached by Rule 13d-3(a). Professor Black's view thus would render Rule 13d-3(b) superfluous.

In sum, the Court finds that TCI created and used the TRSs with the purpose and effect of preventing the vesting of beneficial ownership in TCI as part of a plan or scheme to evade the reporting requirements of Section 13(d). Under the plain language of Rule 13d-3(b), it thus is deemed to be a beneficial owner of the shares held by its counterparties to hedge their short exposures created by the TRSs.

———

(3) Systemic Risk and Transparency

(c) the Financial Crisis of 2008

Chairman Ben S. Bernanke, Speech at the Morehouse College, Atlanta, Georgia

April 14, 2009

Four Questions about the Financial Crisis

* * *

My remarks today will focus on the ongoing turmoil in financial markets and its consequence, the global economic recession. The financial crisis, the worst since the Great Depression, has severely affected the cost and availability of credit to both households and businesses. Credit is the lifeblood of market economies, and the damage to our economy resulting from the constraints on the flow of credit has already been extensive. With recent job losses exceeding half a million per month, this year's college graduates are facing the toughest labor market in 25 years. In the communities in which you and I grew up, many families are trying to cope with lost employment and depleted savings or are facing foreclosure on their homes. Firms have shut factories and cancelled construction projects. States and municipalities are scrambling to find the funding to provide critical services. And although we naturally tend to be most aware of conditions in the United States, we should not overlook the impact that the crisis is having virtually everywhere in the world, particularly on many citizens of countries that struggle economically even when the global economy is doing well.

In the midst of all of these concerns, many Americans have recently celebrated Easter or Passover. As you may know, a highlight of the traditional Passover meal occurs when the youngest child asks four questions, the answers to which tell the history of the Jews when they were slaves in Egypt and during their exodus to the Promised Land. In the spirit of the holiday, today I will pose and answer four important questions about the financial crisis. Of course, my answers will have to be brief, but we will have more time for additional questions at the conclusion of my prepared remarks.

How Did We Get Here?

The first question I would like to address is: How did we get here? What caused our financial and economic system to break down to the extent it has? Not surprisingly, the answer to this question is complex, and experts disagree on how much weight to give various explanations. In my view, however, to tell the story fully--and, in particular, to understand its international scope--we need to consider how global patterns of saving and investment have evolved over the past decade or more, and how those changes affected credit markets in the United States and some other countries.

At the most basic level, the role of banks and other financial institutions is to take the savings generated by households and businesses and put them to use by making loans and investments. For example, financial institutions use the funds they receive from savers to provide loans that help families buy homes or allow businesses to finance inventories and payrolls. Financial markets, such as the stock and bond markets, perform a similar function, as when a firm raises funds for a new factory by selling a bond directly to investors. When the financial system is working as it should, it allocates funds both prudently (that is, with proper attention to risk) and efficiently (to the most productive uses).

Importantly, in our global financial system, saving need not be generated in the country in which it is put to work but can come from foreign as well as domestic sources. In the past 10 to 15 years, the United States and some other industrial countries have been the recipients of a great deal of foreign saving. Much of this foreign saving came from fast-growing emerging market countries in Asia and other places where consumption has lagged behind rising incomes, as well as from oil-exporting nations that could not profitably invest all their revenue at home and thus looked abroad for investment opportunities. Indeed, the net inflow of foreign saving to the United States, which was about 1-1/2 percent of our national output in 1995, reached about 6 percent of national output in 2006, an amount equal to about $825 billion in today's dollars.

Saving inflows from abroad can be beneficial if the country that receives those inflows invests them well. Unfortunately, that was not always the case in the United States and some other countries. Financial institutions reacted to the surplus of available funds by competing aggressively for borrowers, and, in the years leading up to the crisis, credit to both households and businesses became relatively cheap and easy to obtain. One important consequence was a housing boom in the United States, a boom that was fueled in large part by a rapid expansion of mortgage lending. Unfortunately, much of this lending was poorly done, involving, for example, little or no down payment by the borrower or insufficient consideration by the lender of the borrower's ability to make the monthly payments. Lenders may have become careless because they, like many people at the time, expected that house prices would continue to rise--thereby allowing borrowers to build up equity in their homes--and that credit would remain easily available, so that borrowers would be able to refinance if necessary. Regulators did not do enough to prevent poor lending, in part because many of the worst loans were made by firms subject to little or no federal regulation.

Mortgage markets were not the only ones caught up in the credit boom. The large flows of global saving into the United States drove down the returns available on many traditional long-term investments, such as Treasury bonds, leading investors to search for alternatives. To satisfy the enormous demand for investments both perceived as safe and promising higher returns, the financial industry designed securities that combined many individual loans in complex, hard-to-understand ways. These new securities later proved to involve substantial risks--risks that neither the investors nor the firms that designed the securities adequately understood at the outset.

The credit boom began to unravel in early 2007 when problems surfaced with subprime mortgages--mortgages offered to less-creditworthy borrowers--and house prices in parts of the country began to fall. Mortgage delinquencies and defaults rose, and the downturn in house prices intensified, trends that continue today. Investors, stunned by losses on assets they had believed to be safe, began to pull back from a wide range of credit markets, and financial institutions--reeling from severe losses on mortgages and other loans--cut back their lending. The crisis deepened last September, when the failure or near-failure of several major financial firms caused many financial and credit markets to freeze up. Stock prices fell sharply as investors lost confidence in the financial sector and became gloomy about economic prospects. Declining stock values, a teetering financial system, and difficulties in obtaining credit triggered a remarkably rapid and deep contraction in global economic activity and employment, a contraction that has persisted through the first months of 2009. Both the ongoing financial crisis and economic contraction have posed major challenges to economic policymakers.

What Is the Fed Doing to Address the Situation?

Those challenges bring me to my second question: What has the Federal Reserve been doing to address the economic and financial crisis?

The Fed's mandate from the Congress is to promote maximum sustainable employment and stable prices. In addition, the Fed is expected to contribute to financial stability by acting to contain financial disruptions and prevent their spread outside of the financial sector. Thus, we have been serving as a first responder to the crisis.

The Fed's basic policy tool for influencing economic activity and inflation is its ability to control very short-term interest rates--specifically, the federal funds rate, which is the rate that banks pay each other for overnight loans. Lower interest rates can be used to stimulate private-sector borrowing and spending at times like the present when the economy is suffering from a lack of demand. In September 2007, shortly after the turbulence in financial markets began and signs of economic weakness started to appear, the Federal Open Market Committee (FOMC), the body that determines the Federal Reserve's monetary policy, began to aggressively reduce the federal funds rate. By the spring of 2008, we had cut that interest rate from 5-1/4 percent to 2 percent, a highly proactive policy that helped to cushion the economy from some of the effects of the financial turmoil. But, as I mentioned a moment ago, the intensification of the financial crisis in the fall of 2008 led to a further significant deterioration in the economic outlook. The FOMC responded with additional interest rate cuts, and since December, our policy interest rate has been essentially zero. In addition, the FOMC has made clear that it expects economic conditions to warrant holding the federal funds rate low for an extended period.

However, given the ongoing problems in credit markets, conventional monetary policy alone is not adequate to provide all the support that the economy needs. The Fed has therefore taken a number of steps to help the economy by unclogging the flow of credit to households and businesses. In doing so, we have demonstrated that the Fed's toolkit remains potent, even though the federal funds rate is close to zero and thus cannot be reduced further.

We have taken a wide range of actions to help restore the flow of credit, of which I will only mention a few of the most important. One set of actions involves making short-term loans to banks and other financial institutions. Banks and other financial intermediaries normally make longer-term commitments--such as residential mortgages and business loans--yet rely on funding that may be relatively short-term, such as customer deposits that can be withdrawn at any time. To have the confidence to commit to longer-term loans and investments, banks must be sure that they will have ample access to funding when necessary. To give this assurance to banks, the Federal Reserve has made clear that it will provide short-term credit to sound financial institutions as needed. Indeed, serving as a lender of last resort to financial institutions is a method that central banks have used for centuries to try to calm financial crises.

To underscore our commitment to providing short-term funding to banks when they need it, we have lowered the interest rate we charge for short-term loans and extended the term of the loans to up to three months. We have also begun to auction funds to financial institutions, thereby allowing the interest rate paid to depend on the level of demand. Importantly, this lending is extremely safe from the point of view of both the Fed and the taxpayer. Not only is our lending short-term and restricted to healthy institutions, but we require that the borrowers pledge, as security, collateral whose value exceeds the amount we are lending. The Fed's lending to financial institutions has helped to ease conditions in a number of key financial markets, reduced important benchmark interest rates (such as the London interbank offered rate, or Libor, to which payments on some mortgages and other types of loans are tied), and increased the willingness of banks to make credit available.

A second strategy the Fed has employed is to use targeted lending to help free up critical credit markets outside of the banking system. A good example of targeted lending is our efforts in the commercial paper market. Commercial paper is a form of short-term debt issued by a variety of businesses to finance their operations; paychecks and payments to suppliers can depend on it. Among the largest investors in commercial paper are money market mutual funds. At the peak of the crisis last fall, many people who had invested in money market mutual funds lost confidence in those funds and withdrew their money; this loss of funding forced money market mutual funds to reduce their own investments, which in turn caused serious problems in the commercial paper market. Through a series of lending programs, and in coordination with steps taken by the Treasury, the Federal Reserve helped restore confidence in both money market mutual funds and the commercial paper market. Over time, withdrawals from money market mutual funds have been replaced by modest net inflows, and borrowers in the commercial paper market have seen significant improvements in the cost and availability of funding.

More recently, the Federal Reserve has also initiated a lending program, with the cooperation of the Treasury, designed to free up the flow of credit to households and small businesses. Among the forms of credit on which the program is currently focused are auto loans, credit card loans, student loans, and loans guaranteed by the Small Business Administration. We are currently reviewing other types of credit for possible inclusion in this program. In all cases, we will be taking the appropriate measures to minimize the risk of loss to the Federal Reserve.

Restoring stability to the market for housing and home mortgages has been a particular area of concern. To address this problem, the Fed has employed a third type of policy tool--namely, buying securities in the open market. The FOMC has approved purchases of well over $1 trillion this year of mortgage-related securities guaranteed by the government-sponsored mortgage companies, Fannie Mae and Freddie Mac. Buying mortgage-related securities helps to drive down the interest rates that consumers pay on mortgages, and, indeed, the rate on a traditional 30-year fixed-rate mortgage has recently fallen to less than 5 percent, the lowest level since the 1940s. Certainly, the housing market remains depressed, but lower interest rates and house prices are making houses more affordable. For example, two years ago, when mortgage rates were higher than 6percent, payments on a mortgage covering 80 percent of the cost of a $215,000 home would have been more than $1,000 per month; today, the price of that same house may have fallen to $170,000, and, at today's mortgage interest rates, the monthly payment would be about $700. Lower mortgage rates are also helping some homeowners refinance their mortgages to reduce their monthly payments.

The Federal Reserve will continue to take the necessary steps to unclog the credit markets and strengthen the economy. We will also continue to work closely with other agencies, such as the Treasury and the Federal Deposit Insurance Corporation (FDIC), each of which has also taken a variety of actions to help stabilize financial markets, as well as with other central banks around the world.

Does the Fed's Aggressive Response Risk Inflation Down the Road?

The multifaceted policy response that I've described has been aggressive. I am confident that such a proactive policy response is well justified by the serious ongoing problems in financial markets and the economy. However, some have raised the third question I will address: Could the Fed's aggressive actions to stabilize the economy today lead to an inflation problem down the road?

I mentioned earlier that the Fed's mandate from the Congress is to foster price stability as well as maximum sustainable employment. The FOMC treats its obligation to ensure price stability extremely seriously. Price stability supports healthy economic growth, for example, by making it easier for households and businesses to plan for the future. In practice, price stability does not require that inflation be literally zero; indeed, although inflation can certainly be too high, it can also be too low. Experience suggests that inflation rates that are close to zero or even negative (corresponding to deflation, or falling prices) can at times be associated with poor economic performance. Cases in point include the United States in the 1930s and the more recent experience of Japan. In their latest quarterly projections of the economy, most members of the FOMC indicated that they would like to see an annual inflation rate of about 2 percent in the longer term. Right now, because of the weakness in economic conditions here and around the world, inflation has been running less than that, and our best forecast is that inflation will remain quite low for some time. Thus, the Fed's proactive policy approach is not at all inconsistent with the goal of price stability in the medium term.

Although inflation seems set to be low for a while, the time will come when the economy has begun to strengthen, financial markets are healing, and the demand for goods and services, which is currently very weak, begins to increase again. At that point, the liquidity that the Fed has put into the system could begin to pose an inflationary threat unless the FOMC acts to remove some of that liquidity and raise the federal funds rate. We have a number of effective tools that will allow us to drain excess liquidity and begin to raise rates at the appropriate time; that said, unwinding or scaling down some of our special lending programs will almost certainly have to be part of our strategy for reducing policy stimulus once the recovery is under way.

We are thinking carefully about these issues; indeed, they have occupied a significant portion of recent FOMC meetings. I can assure you that monetary policy makers are fully committed to acting as needed to withdraw on a timely basis the extraordinary support now being provided to the economy, and we are confident in our ability to do so. To be sure, decisions about when and how quickly to proceed will require a careful balancing of the risk of withdrawing support before the recovery is firmly established versus the risk of allowing inflation to rise above its preferred level in the medium term. However, this delicate balancing of risks is a challenge that central banks face in the early stages of every economic recovery. I believe that we are well equipped to make those judgments appropriately. In addition, when the time comes, our ability to clearly communicate our policy goals and our assessment of the outlook will be crucial to minimizing public uncertainty about our policy decisions.

Why Did the Fed and the Treasury Act to Prevent the Bankruptcy of Some Major Financial Firms?

The final question is as difficult as it is important: Why did the Fed and the Treasury act to prevent the bankruptcy of some major financial firms, such as the investment bank Bear Stearns and the insurance company American International Group, or AIG? We must answer that question not only because the decisions have been controversial, but also because it bears on the steps we need to take as a country if we are to avert a repetition of the crisis.

As a general rule, my strong preference is that any firm that cannot meet its obligations should bear the consequences of the marketplace. But recent circumstances have been truly extraordinary. Consider the situation on September 16 of last year, when the insurance conglomerate AIG faced pressures that threatened to force it imminently into bankruptcy. At that time, the strains in the global financial system were unprecedented and extreme, and the confidence of financial market participants in the system was rapidly eroding. The investment bank Lehman Brothers had filed for bankruptcy the day before, and the mortgage giants Fannie Mae and Freddie Mac, after suffering losses that threatened their solvency, had effectively been taken over by the government just two weeks earlier. As waves of panic and fear washed over the markets, the Fed and the Treasury became very concerned about the stability of a number of other major financial firms.

Large, complex financial institutions tend to be highly interconnected with other firms and markets, and AIG was more interconnected than most. For example, AIG had insured many billions of dollars of loans and securities held by banks around the world, and its failure would have rendered those insurance contracts worthless, imposing large losses on the global banking system. In addition, banks had extended more than $50 billion in credit to the company, much of which would have been lost. Many other serious consequences would have followed from a default by AIG: Insurance policyholders would have faced considerable uncertainty about the status of their policies; state and local governments, which had lent more than $10 billion to AIG, would have suffered losses; workers whose 401(k) plans had purchased $40 billion of insurance from AIG against the risk of loss would have seen that insurance disappear; and holders of AIG's substantial quantities of commercial paper would have also borne serious losses.

But much more important, the disorderly failure of AIG would have put at risk not only the company's own customers and creditors but the entire global financial system. Historical experience shows that, once begun, a financial panic can spread rapidly and unpredictably; indeed, the failure of Lehman Brothers a day earlier, which the Fed and the Treasury unsuccessfully tried to prevent, resulted in the freezing up of a wide range of credit markets, with extremely serious consequences for the world economy. The financial and economic risks posed by a collapse of AIG would have been at least as great as those created by the demise of Lehman. In the case of AIG, financial market participants were keenly aware that many major financial institutions around the world were insured by or had lent funds to the company. The company's failure would thus likely have led to a further sharp decline in confidence in the global banking system and possibly to the collapse of other major financial institutions. At best, the consequences of AIG's failure would have been a significant intensification of an already severe financial crisis and a further worsening of economic conditions. Conceivably, its failure could have triggered a 1930s-style global financial and economic meltdown, with catastrophic implications for production, incomes, and jobs.

The Federal Reserve and the Treasury agreed that in the environment then prevailing, AIG's failure would have posed unacceptable risks for the global financial system and for our economy. Accordingly, the Federal Reserve, with the full support of the Treasury, made a loan to AIG to prevent its failure. The loan imposed tough terms; in addition, senior management was replaced, and shareholders lost almost all of their investments. However, because the firm avoided a declaration of bankruptcy, creditors of AIG were protected.

In my view, preventing the failure of AIG was the best of the very bad options available, but it nevertheless involved major costs, including financial risks to the taxpayer. The American people also quite correctly see as unfair that AIG was saved from bankruptcy because of the dangers to the system that its failure would have posed, even as many other companies, including nonfinancial and smaller financial firms, have not received the same treatment. Allowing AIG to at least partly avoid the discipline of the marketplace also sets a bad precedent.

For these reasons, it is essential that we make changes to the financial rules of the game to prevent a similar episode from occurring in the future. First, we must ensure that all types of financial institutions, especially large and interconnected ones like AIG, receive strong and effective government oversight. AIG's regulatory oversight was limited, which allowed it to take dangerous risks largely out of sight of federal regulators.

Second, the AIG experience demonstrates that federal regulators urgently need a new set of procedures for dealing with a complex, systemically important financial institution on the brink of failure. Such rules already exists for banks: If a bank approaches insolvency, the FDIC is empowered to intervene as needed to protect depositors, sell the bank's assets, and take any necessary steps to prevent broader consequences to the financial system. However, for an insurance conglomerate like AIG, or for a large financial holding company that owns many subsidiary companies, these rules do not apply. Among other things, a good system for resolving nonbank financial institutions would allow federal regulators to unwind a failing company in ways that minimize disruptions in financial markets. An effective regime would also provide the authorities greater latitude to negotiate with creditors and to modify contracts entered into by the company, including contracts that set bonuses and other compensation for management. More generally, we need significant reforms to financial regulation and financial practices that will reduce the risk of future financial crises like the one we are currently experiencing. The Federal Reserve strongly supports such reform efforts.

Conclusion

The current crisis has been one of the most difficult financial and economic episodes in modern history. Recently we have seen tentative signs that the sharp decline in economic activity may be slowing, for example, in data on home sales, homebuilding, and consumer spending, including sales of new motor vehicles. A leveling out of economic activity is the first step toward recovery. To be sure, we will not have a sustainable recovery without a stabilization of our financial system and credit markets. We are making progress on that front as well, and the Federal Reserve is committed to working to restore financial stability as a necessary step toward full economic recovery.

I am fundamentally optimistic about our economy. Among its many intrinsic strengths are universities and colleges like Morehouse, which help talented students gain not only a command of a body of knowledge but also the capacity to think creatively and independently. Institutions like this one train the professionals, entrepreneurs, and leaders who will shape our economy in the future. Today's economic conditions are difficult, but the foundations of our economy are strong, and we face no problems that cannot be overcome with insight, patience, and persistence. The Federal Reserve will certainly do its part to help restore prosperity and opportunity to our economy.

Chairman Ben S. Bernanke, Speech at the Council on Foreign Relations, Washington, D.C.,

March 10, 2009

Financial Reform to Address Systemic Risk

The world is suffering through the worst financial crisis since the 1930s, a crisis that has precipitated a sharp downturn in the global economy. Its fundamental causes remain in dispute. In my view, however, it is impossible to understand this crisis without reference to the global imbalances in trade and capital flows that began in the latter half of the 1990s. In the simplest terms, these imbalances reflected a chronic lack of saving relative to investment in the United States and some other industrial countries, combined with an extraordinary increase in saving relative to investment in many emerging market nations. The increase in excess saving in the emerging world resulted in turn from factors such as rapid economic growth in high-saving East Asian economies accompanied, outside of China, by reduced investment rates; large buildups in foreign exchange reserves in a number of emerging markets; and substantial increases in revenues received by exporters of oil and other commodities. Like water seeking its level, saving flowed from where it was abundant to where it was deficient, with the result that the United States and some other advanced countries experienced large capital inflows for more than a decade, even as real long-term interest rates remained low.

The global imbalances were the joint responsibility of the United States and our trading partners, and although the topic was a perennial one at international conferences, we collectively did not do enough to reduce those imbalances. However, the responsibility to use the resulting capital inflows effectively fell primarily on the receiving countries, particularly the United States. The details of the story are complex, but, broadly speaking, the risk-management systems of the private sector and government oversight of the financial sector in the United States and some other industrial countries failed to ensure that the inrush of capital was prudently invested, a failure that has led to a powerful reversal in investor sentiment and a seizing up of credit markets. In certain respects, our experience parallels that of some emerging-market countries in the 1990s, whose financial sectors and regulatory regimes likewise proved inadequate for efficiently investing large inflows of saving from abroad. When those failures became evident, investors lost confidence and crises ensued. A clear and highly consequential difference, however, is that the crises of the 1990s were regional, whereas the current crisis has become global.[1]

In the near term, governments around the world must continue to take forceful and, when appropriate, coordinated actions to restore financial market functioning and the flow of credit. I have spoken on a number of occasions about the steps that the U.S. government, and particularly the Federal Reserve, is taking along these lines.[2] Until we stabilize the financial system, a sustainable economic recovery will remain out of reach. In particular, the continued viability of systemically important financial institutions is vital to this effort. In that regard, the Federal Reserve, other federal regulators, and the Treasury Department have stated that they will take any necessary and appropriate steps to ensure that our banking institutions have the capital and liquidity necessary to function well in even a severe economic downturn. Moreover, we have reiterated the U.S. government's determination to ensure that systemically important financial institutions continue to be able to meet their commitments.

At the same time that we are addressing such immediate challenges, it is not too soon for policymakers to begin thinking about the reforms to the

---

1

Another important difference is that, unlike in the Asian crisis, investors have not fled U.S. markets. They have, however, fled from many private credit markets.

2

See, for example, Ben S. Bernanke (2009), "Federal Reserve Policies to Ease Credit and Their Implications for the Fed's Balance Sheet," speech delivered at the National Press Club Luncheon, National Press Club, Washington, D.C., February 18.

financial architecture, broadly conceived, that could help prevent a similar crisis from developing in the future. We must have a strategy that regulates the financial system as a whole, in a holistic way, not just its individual components. In particular, strong and effective regulation and supervision of banking institutions, although necessary for reducing systemic risk, are not sufficient by themselves to achieve this aim.

Today, I would like to talk about four key elements of such a strategy. First, we must address the problem of financial institutions that are deemed too big--or perhaps too interconnected--to fail. Second, we must strengthen what I will call the financial infrastructure--the systems, rules, and conventions that govern trading, payment, clearing, and settlement in financial markets--to ensure that it will perform well under stress. Third, we should review regulatory policies and accounting rules to ensure that they do not induce excessive procyclicality--that is, do not overly magnify the ups and downs in the financial system and the economy. Finally, we should consider whether the creation of an authority specifically charged with monitoring and addressing systemic risks would help protect the system from financial crises like the one we are currently experiencing. My discussion today will focus on the principles that should guide regulatory reform, leaving aside important questions concerning how the current regulatory structure might be reworked to reduce balkanization and overlap and increase effectiveness. I also will not say much about the international dimensions of the issue but will take as self-evident that, in light of the global nature of financial institutions and markets, the reform of financial regulation and supervision should be coordinated internationally to the greatest extent possible.

Too Big to Fail

In a crisis, the authorities have strong incentives to prevent the failure of a large, highly interconnected financial firm, because of the risks such a failure would pose to the financial system and the broader economy. However, the belief of market participants that a particular firm is considered too big to fail has many undesirable effects. For instance, it reduces market discipline and encourages excessive risk-taking by the firm. It also provides an artificial incentive for firms to grow, in order to be perceived as too big to fail. And it creates an unlevel playing field with smaller firms, which may not be regarded as having implicit government support. Moreover, government rescues of too-big-to-fail firms can be costly to taxpayers, as we have seen recently. Indeed, in the present crisis, the too-big-to-fail issue has emerged as an enormous problem.

In the midst of this crisis, given the highly fragile state of financial markets and the global economy, government assistance to avoid the failures of major financial institutions has been necessary to avoid a further serious destabilization of the financial system, and our commitment to avoiding such a failure remains firm. Looking to the future, however, it is imperative that policymakers address this issue by better supervising systemically critical firms to prevent excessive risk-taking and by strengthening the resilience of the financial system to minimize the consequences when a large firm must be unwound.

Achieving more effective supervision of large and complex financial firms will require a number of actions. First, supervisors need to move vigorously--as we are already doing--to address the weaknesses at major financial institutions in capital adequacy, liquidity management, and risk management that have been revealed by the crisis. In particular, policymakers must insist that the large financial firms that they supervise be capable of monitoring and managing their risks in a timely manner and on an enterprise-wide basis. In that regard, the Federal Reserve has been looking carefully at risk-management practices at systemically important institutions to identify best practices, assess firms' performance, and require improvement where deficiencies are identified.[3] Any firm whose failure would pose a systemic risk must receive especially close supervisory oversight of its risk-taking, risk management, and financial condition, and be held to high capital and liquidity standards.[4] In light of the global reach and diversified operations of many large financial firms, international supervisors of banks, securities firms, and other financial institutions must collaborate and cooperate on these efforts.

Second, we must ensure a robust framework--both in law and practice--for consolidated supervision of all systemically important financial firms organized as holding companies. The consolidated supervisors must have clear authority to monitor and address safety and soundness concerns in all parts of the organization, not just the holding company. Broad-based application of the

---

3

The Federal Reserve has issued enhanced guidance on consolidated supervision of bank and financial holding companies. See Board of Governors of the Federal Reserve System (2008), "Federal Reserve Issues Guidance for Consolidated Supervision of Bank Holding Companies and Combined U.S. Operations of Foreign Banking Organizations," press release, October 16.

4

Such an approach would also help offset the incentives for financial firms to become too big to fail.

principle of consolidated supervision would also serve to eliminate gaps in oversight that would otherwise allow risk-taking to migrate from more-regulated to less-regulated sectors.

Third, looking beyond the current crisis, the United States also needs improved tools to allow the orderly resolution of a systemically important nonbank financial firm, including a mechanism to cover the costs of the resolution. In most cases, federal bankruptcy laws provide an appropriate framework for the resolution of nonbank financial institutions. However, this framework does not sufficiently protect the public's strong interest in ensuring the orderly resolution of nondepository financial institutions when a failure would pose substantial systemic risks. Improved resolution procedures for these firms would help reduce the too-big-to-fail problem by narrowing the range of circumstances that might be expected to prompt government intervention to keep the firm operating.

Developing appropriate resolution procedures for potentially systemic financial firms, including bank holding companies, is a complex and challenging task. Models do exist, though, including the process currently in place under the Federal Deposit Insurance Act (FDIA) for dealing with failing insured depository institutions and the framework established for Fannie Mae and Freddie Mac under the Housing and Economic Recovery Act of 2008. Both models allow a government agency to take control of a failing institution's operations and management, act as conservator or receiver for the institution, and establish a "bridge" institution to facilitate an orderly sale or liquidation of the firm. The authority to "bridge" a failing institution through a receivership to a new entity reduces the potential for market disruption while limiting moral hazard and mitigating any adverse impact of government intervention on market discipline.

The new resolution regime would need to be carefully crafted. For example, clear guidelines must define which firms could be subject to the alternative regime and the process for invoking that regime, analogous perhaps to the procedures for invoking the so-called systemic risk exception under the FDIA. In addition, given the global operations of many large and complex financial firms and the complex regulatory structures under which they operate, any new regime must be structured to work as seamlessly as possible with other domestic or foreign insolvency regimes that might apply to one or more parts of the consolidated organization.

Strengthening the Financial Infrastructure

The first element of my proposed reform agenda covers systemically important institutions considered individually. The second element focuses on interactions among firms as mediated by what I have called the financial infrastructure, or the financial plumbing if you will: the institutions that support trading, payments, clearing, and settlement. Here the aim should be not only to help make the financial system as a whole better able to withstand future shocks, but also to mitigate moral hazard and the problem of too big to fail by reducing the range of circumstances in which systemic stability concerns might prompt government intervention. I'll give several examples.

Since September 2005, the Federal Reserve Bank of New York has been leading a major joint initiative by the public and private sectors to improve arrangements for clearing and settling credit default swaps (CDS) and other over-the-counter (OTC) derivatives. As a result, the accuracy and timeliness of trade information has improved significantly. However, the infrastructure for managing these derivatives is still not as efficient or transparent as that for more mature instruments. The Federal Reserve Bank of New York, in conjunction with other domestic and foreign supervisors, will continue to work toward establishing increasingly stringent targets and performance standards for market participants. To help alleviate counterparty credit concerns, regulators are also encouraging the development of well-regulated and prudently managed central clearing counterparties for OTC trades.[5] Just last week, we approved the application for membership in the Federal Reserve System of ICE Trust, a trust company that proposes to operate as a central counterparty and clearinghouse for CDS transactions.

The Federal Reserve and other authorities also are focusing on enhancing the resilience of the triparty repurchase agreement (repo) market, in which the primary dealers and other major banks and broker-dealers obtain very large amounts of secured financing from money market mutual funds and other short-

---

5

International standards for central counterparties have been developed, and national authorities should work to ensure that all covered entities adhere to these standards. See Committee on Payment and Settlement Systems and Technical Committee of the International Organization of Securities Commissions, Bank for International Settlements (2004), "Recommendations for Central Counterparties," November. The benefits and costs of a central counterparty are discussed in "Assessing the Potential for Instability in Financial Markets," a speech delivered by Randall S. Kroszner (2008) at the Risk Minds Conference, International Center for Business Information, Geneva, Switzerland, December 8.

term, risk-averse sources of funding.[6] For some time, market participants have been working to develop a contingency plan for handling a loss of confidence in either of the two clearing banks that facilitate the settlement of triparty repos. Recent experience demonstrates the need for additional measures to enhance the resilience of these markets, particularly as large borrowers have experienced acute stress. The Federal Reserve's Primary Dealer Credit Facility, launched in the wake of the Bear Stearns collapse and expanded in the aftermath of the Lehman Brothers bankruptcy, has stabilized this critical market, and market confidence has been maintained. However, this program was adopted under our emergency powers to address unusual and exigent circumstances. Therefore, more-permanent reforms are needed. For example, it may be worthwhile considering the costs and benefits of a central clearing system for this market, given the magnitude of exposures generated and the vital importance of the market to both dealers and investors.

More broadly, both the operational performance of key payment and settlement systems and their ability to manage counterparty and market risks in both normal and stressed environments are critical to the stability of the broader financial system. Currently, the Federal Reserve relies on a patchwork of authorities, largely derived from our role as a banking supervisor, as well as on moral suasion to help ensure that critical payment and settlement systems have the necessary procedures and controls in place to manage their risks. By contrast, many major central banks around the world have an explicit statutory basis for their oversight of these systems. Given how important robust payment and settlement systems are to financial stability, a good case can be made for granting the Federal Reserve explicit oversight authority for systemically important payment and settlement systems.

Another issue that warrants attention is the potential fragility of the money market mutual fund sector. Last fall, as a result of losses on Lehman Brothers commercial paper, a prominent money market mutual fund "broke the buck"--that is, was unable to maintain a net asset value of $1 per share. Over subsequent days, fearful investors withdrew more than $250 billion from prime money market mutual funds. The magnitude of these withdrawals decreased only after the Treasury announced a guarantee program for money market mutual fund investors and the Federal Reserve established a new lending program to

---

6

Primary dealers are broker-dealers that trade in U.S. government securities with the Federal Reserve Bank of New York. The New York Fed's Open Market Desk engages in trades on behalf of the Federal Reserve System to implement monetary policy.

support liquidity in the asset-backed commercial paper market.

In light of the importance of money market mutual funds--and, in particular, the crucial role they play in the commercial paper market, a key source of funding for many businesses--policymakers should consider how to increase the resiliency of those funds that are susceptible to runs. One approach would be to impose tighter restrictions on the instruments in which money market mutual funds can invest, potentially requiring shorter maturities and increased liquidity. A second approach would be to develop a limited system of insurance for money market mutual funds that seek to maintain a stable net asset value. For either of these approaches or others, it would be important to consider the implications not only for the money market mutual fund industry itself, but also for the distribution of liquidity and risk in the financial system as a whole.

Procyclicality in the Regulatory System

It seems obvious that regulatory and supervisory policies should not themselves put unjustified pressure on financial institutions or inappropriately inhibit lending during economic downturns. However, there is some evidence that capital standards, accounting rules, and other regulations have made the financial sector excessively procyclical--that is, they lead financial institutions to ease credit in booms and tighten credit in downturns more than is justified by changes in the creditworthiness of borrowers, thereby intensifying cyclical changes.

For example, capital regulations require that banks' capital ratios meet or exceed fixed minimum standards for the bank to be considered safe and sound by regulators.[7] Because banks typically find raising capital to be difficult in economic downturns or periods of financial stress, their best means of boosting their regulatory capital ratios during difficult periods may be to reduce new lending, perhaps more so than is justified by the credit environment. We should review capital regulations to ensure that they are appropriately forward-looking, and that capital is allowed to serve its intended role as a buffer--one built up during good times and drawn down during bad times in a manner consistent with

---

7

In addition to ensuring that banking organizations comply with minimum regulatory capital requirements, supervisors also must ensure that organizations have the ability to assess their overall capital needs and hold capital commensurate with their individual risk profiles.

safety and soundness.[8] In the area of prudential supervision, we should also ensure that bank examiners appropriately balance the need for caution and the benefits of maintaining profitable lending relationships when evaluating bank loan policies.

The ongoing move by those who set accounting standards toward requirements for improved disclosure and greater transparency is a positive development that deserves full support. However, determining appropriate valuation methods for illiquid or idiosyncratic assets can be very difficult, to put it mildly. Similarly, there is considerable uncertainty regarding the appropriate levels of loan loss reserves over the cycle. As a result, further review of accounting standards governing valuation and loss provisioning would be useful, and might result in modifications to the accounting rules that reduce their procyclical effects without compromising the goals of disclosure and transparency. Indeed, work is underway on these issues through the Financial Stability Forum, and the results of that work may prove useful for U.S. policymakers.[9]

Another potential source of procyclicality is the system for funding deposit insurance. In recognition of this fact--as well as the weak economic outlook and the current strains on banks and the financial system--the Federal Deposit Insurance Corporation recently announced plans to extend from five years to seven years the period over which it would restore the deposit insurance fund to its minimum required level. This plan, if implemented, should help reduce the costs imposed on banks at a time when capital and lending are already under pressure. Policymakers should consider additional steps to reduce the possible procyclical effects of deposit insurance costs while still ensuring that riskier banks pay higher premiums than safer banks. One possibility would be to raise the level to which the designated reserve ratio may grow in benign economic environments, so that a larger buffer is available to be drawn down when economic conditions worsen and insurance losses are high.

Systemic Risk Authority

8

Internationally, the Financial Stability Forum and the Basel Committee have already begun such a review.

9

Financial Stability Forum (2008), "Report of the Financial Stability Forum on Enhancing Market and Institutional Resilience: Follow-Up on Implementation.

The policy actions I've discussed would inhibit the buildup of risks within the financial system and improve the resilience of the financial system to adverse shocks. Financial stability, however, could be further enhanced by a more explicitly macroprudential approach to financial regulation and supervision in the United States. Macroprudential policies focus on risks to the financial system as a whole. Such risks may be crosscutting, affecting a number of firms and markets, or they may be concentrated in a few key areas. A macroprudential approach would complement and build on the current regulatory and supervisory structure, in which the primary focus is the safety and soundness of individual institutions and markets.

How could macroprudential policies be better integrated into the regulatory and supervisory system? One way would be for the Congress to direct and empower a governmental authority to monitor, assess, and, if necessary, address potential systemic risks within the financial system. The elements of such an authority's mission could include, for example, (1) monitoring large or rapidly increasing exposures--such as to subprime mortgages--across firms and markets, rather than only at the level of individual firms or sectors; (2) assessing the potential for deficiencies in evolving risk-management practices, broad-based increases in financial leverage, or changes in financial markets or products to increase systemic risks; (3) analyzing possible spillovers between financial firms or between firms and markets, such as the mutual exposures of highly interconnected firms; and (4) identifying possible regulatory gaps, including gaps in the protection of consumers and investors, that pose risks for the system as a whole. Two areas of natural focus for a systemic risk authority would be the stability of systemically critical financial institutions and the systemically relevant aspects of the financial infrastructure that I discussed earlier.

Introducing a macroprudential approach to regulation would present a number of significant challenges. Most fundamentally, implementing a comprehensive systemic risk program would demand a great deal of the supervisory authority in terms of market and institutional knowledge, analytical sophistication, capacity to process large amounts of disparate information, and supervisory expertise.

Other challenges include defining the range of powers that a systemic risk authority would need to fulfill its mission and then integrating that authority into the currently decentralized system of financial regulation in the United States. On the one hand, it seems clear that any new systemic risk authority should rely on the information, assessments, and supervisory and regulatory programs of existing financial supervisors and regulators whenever possible.

This approach would reduce the cost to both the private sector and the public sector and allow the systemic risk authority to leverage the expertise and knowledge of other supervisors. On the other hand, because the goal of any systemic risk authority would be to have a broader view of the financial system, simply relying on existing structures likely would be insufficient.

For example, a systemic risk authority would need broad authority to obtain information--through data collection and reports, or when necessary, examinations--from banks and key financial market participants, as well as from nonbank financial institutions that currently may not be subject to regular supervisory reporting requirements. A systemic risk authority likely would also need an appropriately calibrated ability to take measures to address identified systemic risks--in coordination with other supervisors, when possible, or independently, if necessary. The role of a systemic risk authority in setting standards for capital, liquidity, and risk-management practices for the financial sector also would need to be explored, given that these standards have both microprudential and macroprudential implications.

In general, much discussion will be needed regarding what can reasonably be expected from a macroprudential regime and how expectations, accountability, and authorities can best be aligned. Important decisions must be made about how the systemic risk regulation function should be structured and located within the government. Several existing agencies have data and expertise relevant to this task, so there are a variety of organizational options. In any structure, however, to ensure accountability, the scope of authorities and responsibilities must be clearly specified.

Some commentators have proposed that the Federal Reserve take on the role of systemic risk authority; others have expressed concern that adding this responsibility would overburden the central bank. The extent to which this new responsibility might be a good match for the Federal Reserve depends a great deal on precisely how the Congress defines the role and responsibilities of the authority, as well as on how the necessary resources and expertise complement those employed by the Federal Reserve in the pursuit of its long-established core missions.

It seems to me that we should keep our minds open on these questions. We have been discussing them a good deal within the Federal Reserve System, and their importance warrants careful consideration by legislators and other policymakers. As a practical matter, however, effectively identifying and addressing systemic risks would seem to require the involvement of the Federal

Reserve in some capacity, even if not in the lead role. As the central bank of the United States, the Federal Reserve has long figured prominently in the government's responses to financial crises. Indeed, the Federal Reserve was established by the Congress in 1913 largely as a means of addressing the problem of recurring financial panics. The Federal Reserve plays such a key role in part because it serves as liquidity provider of last resort, a power that has proved critical in financial crises throughout history. In addition, the Federal Reserve has broad expertise derived from its wide range of activities, including its role as umbrella supervisor for bank and financial holding companies and its active monitoring of capital markets in support of its monetary policy and financial stability objectives.

Conclusion

In the wake of the ongoing financial crisis, governments have moved quickly to establish a wide range of programs to support financial market functioning and foster credit flows to businesses and households. However, these necessary short-term steps must be accompanied by new policies to limit the incidence and impact of systemic risk. In my remarks today, I have emphasized the need to address the problems posed by firms that are perceived to be too big to fail, the importance of efforts to strengthen the financial infrastructure, the desirability of reducing the procyclical effects of capital regulation and accounting rules, and the potential benefits of taking a more macroprudential approach to the supervision and regulation of financial firms. Some of the policies I propose can be developed and implemented under the existing authority of financial regulators. Indeed, we are in the process of doing just that. In other cases, congressional action will be necessary to create the requisite authority and responsibility.

Financial crises will continue to occur, as they have around the world for literally hundreds of years. Even with the sorts of actions I have outlined here today, it is unrealistic to hope that financial crises can be entirely eliminated, especially while maintaining a dynamic and innovative financial system. Nonetheless, these steps should help make crises less frequent and less virulent, and so contribute to a better functioning national and global economy.

Department of the Treasury, Financial Regulatory Reform, A New Foundation: Rebuilding Financial Supervision and

Regulation

June, 2009.
pages 21-28.

I. PROMOTE ROBUST SUPERVISION AND REGULATION OF FINANCIAL FIRMS

* **

B. Implement Heightened Consolidated Supervision and Regulation of All Large, Interconnected Financial Firms

1. *Any financial firm whose combination of size, leverage, and interconnectedness could pose a threat to financial stability if it failed (Tier 1 FHC) should be subject to robust consolidated supervision and regulation, regardless of whether the firm owns an insured depository institution.*

The sudden failures of large U.S.-based investment banks and of American International Group (AIG) were among the most destabilizing events of the financial crisis. These companies were large, highly leveraged, and had significant financial connections to the other major players in our financial system, yet they were ineffectively supervised and regulated. As a consequence, they did not have sufficient capital or liquidity buffers to withstand the deterioration in financial conditions that occurred during 2008. Although most of these firms owned federally insured depository institutions, they chose to own depository institutions that are not considered "banks" under the Bank Holding Company (BHC) Act. This allowed them to avoid the more rigorous oversight regime applicable to BHCs.

We propose a new, more robust supervisory regime for any firm whose combination of size, leverage, and interconnectedness could pose a threat to financial stability if it failed. Such firms, which we identify as Tier 1 Financial Holding Companies (Tier 1 FHCs), should be subject to robust consolidated supervision and regulation, regardless of whether they are currently supervised as BHCs.

2. *The Federal Reserve Board should have the authority and accountability for consolidated supervision and regulation of Tier 1 FHCs.*

We propose that authority for supervision and regulation of Tier 1 FHCs be vested in the Federal Reserve Board, which is by statute the consolidated supervisor and regulator of all bank holding companies today. As a result of changes in corporate structure during the current crisis, the Federal Reserve already supervises and regulates all major U.S. commercial and investment banks on a firm-wide basis. The Federal Reserve has by far the most experience and resources to handle consolidated supervision and regulation of Tier 1 FHCs.

The Council should play an important role in recommending the identification of firms that will be subject to regulation as Tier 1 FHCs. The Federal Reserve should also be required to consult with the Council in setting material prudential standards for Tier 1 FHCs.

The ultimate responsibility for prudential standard-setting and supervision for Tier 1 FHCs must rest with a single regulator. The public has a right to expect that a clearly identifiable entity, not a committee of multiple agencies, will be answerable for setting standards that will protect the financial system and the public from risks posed by the potential failure of Tier 1 FHCs. Moreover, a committee that included regulators of specific types of financial institutions such as commercial banks or broker-dealers (functional regulators) may be less focused on systemic needs and more focused on the needs of the financial firms they regulate. For example, to promote financial stability, the supervisor of a Tier 1 FHC may hold that firm's subsidiaries to stricter prudential standards than would be required by the functional regulator, whose focus is only on keeping that particular subsidiary safe.

Diffusing responsibility among several regulators would weaken incentives for effective regulation in other ways. For example, it would weaken both the incentive for and the ability of the relevant agencies to act in a timely fashion – creating the risk that clearly ineffective standards remain in place for long periods.

The Federal Reserve should fundamentally adjust its current framework for supervising all BHCs in order to carry out its new responsibilities effectively with respect to Tier 1 FHCs. For example, the focus of BHC regulation would need to expand beyond the safety and soundness of the bank subsidiary to include the activities of the firm as a whole and the risks the firm might pose to the financial system. The Federal Reserve would also need to develop new supervisory approaches for activities that to date have not been significant activities for most BHCs.

3. *Our legislation will propose criteria that the Federal Reserve must consider in identifying Tier 1 FHCs.*

We recommend that legislation specify factors that the Federal Reserve must consider when determining whether an individual financial firm poses a threat to financial stability. Those factors should include:

- the impact the firm's failure would have on the financial system and the economy;
- the firm's combination of size, leverage (including off-balance sheet exposures),
- and degree of reliance on short-term funding; and
- the firm's criticality as a source of credit for households, businesses, and state and local governments and as a source of liquidity for the financial system.

We propose that the Federal Reserve establish rules, in consultation with Treasury, to guide the identification of Tier 1 FHCs. The Federal Reserve, however, should be allowed to consider other relevant factors and exercise discretion in applying the specified factors to individual financial firms. Treasury would have no role in determining the application of these rules to individual financial firms. This discretion would allow the regulatory system to adapt to inevitable innovations in financial activity and in the organizational structure of financial firms. In addition, without this discretion, large, highly leveraged, and interconnected firms that should be subject to consolidated supervision and regulation as Tier 1 FHCs might be able to escape the regime. For instance, if the Federal Reserve were to treat as a Tier 1 FHC only those firms with balance-sheet assets above a certain amount, firms would have incentives to conduct activities through off-balance sheet transactions and in off-balance sheet vehicles. Flexibility is essential to minimizing the risk that an "AIG-like" firm could grow outside the regulated system.

In identifying Tier 1 FHCs, the Federal Reserve should analyze the systemic importance of a firm under stressed economic conditions. This analysis should consider the impact the firm's failure would have on other large financial institutions, on payment, clearing and settlement systems, and on the availability of credit in the economy. In the case of a firm that has one or more subsidiaries subject to prudential regulation by other federal regulators, the Federal Reserve should be required to consult with those regulators before requiring the firm to be regulated as a Tier 1 FHC. The Federal Reserve should regularly review the classification of firms as Tier 1 FHCs. The Council should have the authority to receive information from its members and to recommend to the Federal Reserve that a firm be designated as a Tier 1 FHC, as described above.

To enable the Federal Reserve to identify financial firms other than BHCs that require supervision and regulation as Tier 1 FHCs, we recommend that the Federal Reserve should have the authority to collect periodic and other reports from all U.S. financial firms that meet certain minimum size thresholds. The Federal Reserve's authority to require reports from a financial firm would be limited to reports that contain information reasonably necessary to determine whether the firm is a Tier 1 FHC. In the case of firms that are subject to federal regulation, the Federal Reserve should have access to relevant reports submitted to other regulators, and its authority to require reports should be limited to information that cannot be obtained from reports to other regulators.The Federal Reserve also should have the ability to examine any U.S. financial firm that meets certain minimum size thresholds if the Federal Reserve is unable to determine whether the firm's financial activities pose a threat to financial stability based on regulatory reports, discussions with management, and publicly available information. The scope of the Federal Reserve's examination authority over a financial firm would be strictly limited to examinations reasonably necessary to enable the Federal Reserve to determine whether the firm is a Tier 1 FHC.

4. ***The prudential standards for Tier 1 FHCs – including capital, liquidity and risk management standards – should be stricter and more conservative than those applicable to other financial firms to account for the greater risks that their potential failure would impose on the financial system.***

Tier 1 FHCs should be subject to heightened supervision and regulation because of the greater risks their potential failure would pose to the financial system. At the same time, given the important role of Tier 1 FHCs in the financial system and the economy, setting their prudential standards too high could constrain long-term financial and economic growth. Therefore, the Federal Reserve, in consultation with the Council, should set prudential standards for Tier 1 FHCs to maximize financial stability at the lowest cost to long-term financial and economic growth.

Tier 1 FHCs should, at a minimum, be required to meet the qualification requirements for FHC status (as revised in this proposal and discussed in more detail below).

Capital Requirements. Capital requirements for Tier 1 FHCs should reflect the large negative externalities associated with the financial distress, rapid deleveraging, or disorderly failure of each firm and should, therefore, be strict enough to be effective under extremely stressful economic and financial conditions. Tier 1 FHCs should be required to have enough high-quality capital during good economic times to keep them above prudential minimum capital requirements during stressed economic times. In addition to regulatory capital ratios, the Federal Reserve should evaluate a Tier 1 FHC's capital strength using supervisory assessments, including assessments of capital adequacy under severe stress scenarios and assessments of the firm's capital planning practices, and market-based indicators of the firm's credit quality.

Prompt Corrective Action. Tier 1 FHCs should be subject to a prompt corrective action regime that would require the firm or its supervisor to take corrective actions as the firm's regulatory capital levels decline, similar to the existing prompt corrective action regime for insured depository institutions established under the Federal Deposit Insurance Corporation Improvement Act (FDICIA).

Liquidity Standards. The Federal Reserve should impose rigorous liquidity risk requirements on Tier 1 FHCs that recognize the potential negative impact that the financial distress, rapid deleveraging, or disorderly failure of each firm would have on the financial system. The Federal Reserve should put in place a robust process for continuously monitoring the liquidity risk profiles of these institutions and their liquidity risk management processes.

Federal Reserve supervision should promote the full integration of liquidity risk management of Tier 1 FHCs into the overall risk management of the institution. The Federal Reserve should also establish explicit internal liquidity risk exposure limits and risk management policies. Tier 1 FHCs should have sound processes for monitoring and controlling the full range of their liquidity risks. They should regularly conduct stress tests across a variety of liquidity stress scenarios, including short-term and protracted scenarios and institution-specific and market-wide scenarios. The stress tests should incorporate both on- and off-balance sheet exposures, including non-contractual off balance sheet obligations.

Overall Risk Management. Supervisory expectations regarding Tier 1 FHCs' risk management practices must be in proportion to the risk, complexity, and scope of their operations. These firms should be able to identify firm-wide risk concentrations (credit, business lines, liquidity, and other) and establish appropriate limits and controls around these concentrations. In order to credibly measure and monitor risk concentrations, Tier 1 FHCs must be able to identify aggregate exposures quickly on a firm-wide basis.

Market Discipline and Disclosure. To support market evaluation of a Tier 1 FHC's risk profile, capital adequacy, and risk management capabilities, such firms should be required to make enhanced public disclosures.

Restrictions on Nonfinancial Activities. Tier 1 FHCs that do not control insured depository institutions should be subject to the full range of prudential regulations and supervisory guidance applicable to BHCs. In addition, the long-standing wall between banking and commerce – which has served our economy well – should be extended to apply to this new class of financial firm. Accordingly, each Tier 1 FHC also should be required to comply with the nonfinancial activity restrictions of the BHC Act, regardless of whether it controls an insured depository institution. We propose that a Tier 1 FHC that has not been previously subject to the BHC Act should be given five years to conform to the existing activity restrictions imposed on FHCs by the BHC Act.

Rapid Resolution Plans. The Federal Reserve also should require each Tier 1 FHC to prepare and continuously update a credible plan for the rapid resolution of the firm in the event of severe financial distress. Such a requirement would create incentives for the firm to better monitor and simplify its organizational structure and would better prepare the government, as well as the firm's investors, creditors, and counterparties, in the event that the firm collapsed. The Federal Reserve should review the adequacy of each firm's plan regularly.

> **5. *Consolidated supervision of a Tier 1 FHC should extend to the parent company and to all of its subsidiaries – regulated and unregulated, U.S. and foreign. Functionally regulated and depository institution subsidiaries of a Tier 1 FHC should continue to be supervised and regulated primarily by their functional or bank regulator, as the case may be. The constraints that the Gramm-Leach-Bliley Act (GLB Act) introduced on the Federal Reserve's ability to require reports from, examine, or impose higher prudential requirements or more stringent activity restrictions on the functionally regulated or depository institution subsidiaries of FHCs should be removed.***

The financial crisis has demonstrated the crucial importance of having a consolidated supervisor and regulator for all Tier 1 FHCs with a deep understanding of the operations of each firm. The crisis has made clear that threats to a consolidated financial firm and threats to financial stability can emerge from any business line and any subsidiary. It is not reasonable to hold the functional regulator of a single subsidiary responsible for identifying or managing risks that cut across many different subsidiaries and business lines.

The GLB Act impedes the Federal Reserve's ability, as a consolidated supervisor, to obtain information from or impose prudential restrictions on subsidiaries of a BHC that already have a primary supervisor, including banks and other insured depository institutions; SEC-registered broker-dealers, investment advisers and investment companies; entities regulated by the CFTC; and insurance companies subject to supervision by state insurance supervisors. By relying solely on other supervisors for information and for ensuring that the activities of the regulated subsidiary do not cause excessive risk to the financial system, these restrictions also make it difficult to take a truly firm-wide perspective on a BHC and to execute its responsibility to protect the system as a whole.

To promote accountability in supervision and regulation, the Federal Reserve should have authority to require reports from and conduct examinations of a Tier 1 FHC and all its subsidiaries, including those that have a primary supervisor. To the extent possible, information should be gathered from reports required or exams conducted by other supervisors. The Federal Reserve should also have the authority to impose and enforce more stringent prudential requirements on the regulated subsidiary of a Tier 1 FHC to address systemic risk concerns, but only after consulting with that subsidiary's primary federal or state supervisor and Treasury.

6. *Consolidated supervision of a Tier 1 FHC should be macroprudential in focus. That is, it should consider risk to the system as a whole.*

Prudential supervision has historically focused on the safety and soundness of individual financial firms, or, in the case of BHCs, on the risks that an organization's nondepository subsidiaries pose to its depository institution subsidiaries. The financial crisis has demonstrated that a narrow supervisory focus on the safety and soundness of individual financial firms can result in a failure to detect and thwart emerging threats to financial stability that cut across many institutions or have other systemic implications. Going forward, the consolidated supervisor of Tier 1 FHCs should continue to employ enhanced forms of its normal supervisory tools, but should supplement those tools with rigorous assessments of the potential impact of the activities and risk exposures of these companies on each other, on critical markets, and on the broader financial system. The Federal Reserve should continuously analyze the connections among the major financial firms and the dependence of the major financial markets on such firms, in order to track potential impact on the broader financial system. To conduct this analysis, the Federal Reserve should require each Tier 1 FHC to regularly report the nature and extent to which other major financial firms are exposed to it. In addition, the Federal Reserve should constantly monitor the build-up of concentrations of risk across all Tier 1 FHCs that may collectively threaten financial stability – even though no single firm, viewed in isolation, may appear at risk.

UK Financial Services Authority, The Turner Review: A Regulatory Response to the Global Banking Crisis

March 2009.
pages 39-49.

1.4 Fundamental theoretical issues

The analysis of the causes of the financial crisis implies the need for major changes in our approach to capital, liquidity, accounting, and institutional coverage * * *. But the crisis also raises important questions about the intellectual assumptions on which previous regulatory approaches have largely been built.

At the core of these assumptions has been the theory of efficient and rational markets. Five propositions with implications for regulatory approach have followed:

(i) Market prices are good indicators of rationally evaluated economic value.

(ii) The development of securitised credit, since based on the creation of new and more liquid markets, has improved both allocative efficiency and financial stability.

(iii) The risk characteristics of financial markets can be inferred from mathematical analysis, delivering robust quantitative measures of trading risk.

(iv) Market discipline can be used as an effective tool in constraining harmful risk taking.

(v) Financial innovation can be assumed to be beneficial since market competition would winnow out any innovations which did not deliver value added.

Each of these assumptions is now subject to extensive challenge on both theoretical and empirical grounds, with potential implications for the appropriate design of regulation and for the role of regulatory authorities.

1.4 (i) Efficient markets can be irrational

The predominant assumption behind financial market regulation – in the US, the UK and increasingly across the world – has been that financial markets are capable of being both efficient and rational and that a key goal of financial market regulation is to remove the impediments which might produce inefficient and illiquid markets. A large body of theoretical and empirical work has been devoted to proving that share prices in well regulated liquid markets, follow 'random walks', and that it is therefore impossible to make money on the basis of the knowledge of past patterns of price movement, with prices instead changing as new information becomes available and is assessed by a wide range of independently acting market participants. And the assumption has been that these independently acting market participants are in general rational in their assessments and that the overall level of prices as a result has a strong tendency towards a rational equilibrium.

These assumptions have always been subject to some challenge. Many market participants accept on the basis of pragmatic observation that significant temporary bubbles in market prices are possible. And scepticism about the rationality of markets and the benefits of liquidity has a long intellectual lineage. Keynes's General Theory contains a famous attack on the idea that equity prices are driven by the rational assessment of the available information. Hyman Minsky argued in 1986 that financial markets and systems are inherently susceptible to speculative booms which, if long lasting, will inevitably end in crisis. Charles Kindelberger's *Manias, panics and markets* illustrated how the tendency towards occasional speculative excess spanned different markets, countries and centuries. But the predominant tendency of financial markets theory of the last 20 to 30 years has been to assert that:

(i) efficient and liquid financial markets deliver major allocative efficiency benefits by making possible a full range of contracts, thus

enabling providers and users of funds more effectively to meet their preferences for risk, return and liquidity;
(ii) markets are sufficiently rational as to justify a strong presumption in favor of market deregulation; and
(iii) that even if markets are theoretically capable of irrational behaviour, policymakers will never be able to judge when and how far they are irrational with sufficient confidence to justify market intervention.

In the face of the worst financial crisis for a century, however, the assumptions of efficient market theory have been subject to increasingly effective criticism, drawing on both theoretical and empirical arguments. These criticisms include that:

• **Market efficiency does not imply market rationality**. There is nothing in empirical tests of market efficiency narrowly defined (i.e. tests of the non-existence of chartist patterns) which illustrates market rationality. The fact that prices move as random walks and cannot be predicted from prior movements in no way denies the possibility of self-reinforcing herd effects and of prices overshooting rational equilibrium levels.

• **Individual rationality does not ensure collective rationality**. There are good theoretical and mathematically modellable reasons for believing that, even if individuals are rationally self interested, their actions can, if determined in conditions of imperfect information and/or determined by particular relationships between end investors and their asset manager agents, result in market price movements characterised by self-reinforcing momentum.

• **Individual behaviour is not entirely rational**. There are moreover insights from behavioural economics, cognitive psychology and neuroscience, which reveal that people often do not make decisions in the rational front of brain way assumed in neoclassical economics, but make decisions which are rooted in the instinctive part of the brain, and which at the collective level are bound to produce herd effects and thus irrational momentum swings.

• **Allocative efficiency benefits have limits**. Beyond a certain degree of liquidity and market completion, the additional allocative efficiency benefits of further liquidity and market completion may be relatively slight, and therefore easily outweighed by additional instability risks which increasing liquidity or complexity might itself create. It is for instance arguable that the allocative efficiency benefits of the creation of markets for many complex structured credit securities (e.g. CDO-squareds) would have been at most trivial even if they had not played a role in creating financial instability.

• **Empirical evidence illustrates large scale herd effects and market overshoots.** Economists such as Robert Shiller have argued persuasively that empirical evidence proves that financial market prices can diverge substantially and for long periods of time from estimated economic values, with the calculated divergences at times so large that policymakers can reasonably conclude that market prices have become irrational.

Given this theory and evidence, a reasonable judgement is that policymakers have to recognise that all liquid traded markets are capable of acting irrationally, and can be susceptible to self reinforcing herd and momentum effects. This does not imply that liquid and efficient markets have no benefits nor that the only problems of financial instability arise within liquid financial markets: It is quite possible, for instance, that efficient and liquid markets provide useful and accurate price signals as to the *relative* attractiveness of different equities or credits even if the overall level of prices is subject to irrational overshoots. • And it is certainly the case that markets other than liquid financial markets can also be subject to irrational overshoots. Robert Shiller's work illustrates that irrational exuberance is possible in housing markets as well as in equity markets. And markets for on-balance sheet credit, provided via non-traded bank loans, have often displayed herd effects in the past, leading to underpricing of credit.

But the acceptance that financial markets are inherently susceptible to irrational momentum effects does imply that regulatory approaches should be based on striking a balance between the benefits of market completion and market liquidity and the potential disadvantages which may arise from inherent instabilities in liquid markets.

The optimal balance may moreover be different when considering securitised credit markets compared with other markets (such as those for equities and commodities). * * *

1.4(ii) Securitisation and financial instability: inherent or fixable with better regulation?

* * * [The] system of securitised credit intermediation was originally proposed as a mechanism for taking risk off the balance sheets of banks, placing it with a diversified set of end investors, and thus reducing banking system risks.

Subsequently the system grew massively in both scale and complexity. But even once it had done so the predominant intellectual assumption was that the new system had reduced financial instability risks. The IMF's *Global Financial Stability Report* of April, 2006 stated that 'the dispersion of credit risk by banks to a broader and more diverse set of investors, rather than warehousing such risk on their balance sheets, has helped make the banking and overall financial system more resilient'. It noted that this dispersion would help to 'mitigate and absorb shocks to the financial system' with the result that 'improved resilience may be seen in fewer bank failures and more consistent credit provision'.

This analysis has been proved wrong. Rather than improving financial system resilience, the development of securitised credit has ended up producing the worst financial crisis for a century. The crucial issue is whether increased instability is inherent to a securitised model of credit intermediation or the result of the particular form of securitised credit which developed over the last 15 years and the manner in which these developments were regulated.

There are some theoretical reasons for believing that a securitised credit model may be inherently more vulnerable to financial instability shocks that a model of on-balance sheet credit intermediation.

• In a securitised system credits become marketable instruments, tradeable in liquid markets. And * * * all liquid markets are inherently susceptible to periodic swings in sentiment which produce significant divergence from rational equilibrium prices. Internet equity prices in 2000 were driven irrationally high by rational exuberance and subsequently fell. Bond yields were driven irrationally low and prices irrationally high by self reinforcing exuberance between 2002 and early 2007; when confidence disappeared yields subsequently soared, and prices collapsed.

• But while the former boom and bust in equity prices had surprisingly small consequences for the real economy the latter upswing and reversal is having an enormous one. That contrast may be inherent. The world economy may have greater ability to absorb without dire consequences severe cases of irrational exuberance and then depression in equity prices, than in the prices of a broad range of credit instruments, held to a significant extent on the trading books of banks, shadow banks or near banks.

• This is because of the characteristics of banks, their central role in the economy, and the specific risks they face. Banks are highly leveraged: they perform maturity transformation which exposes them to liquidity risks: and they are involved in a process of continual rollover of new credit supply to the real economy without which economies will contract. So irrational swings in prices of credit securities held by banks, and thus in their capital resources, are likely to be far more economically significant than irrational swings in the prices of equity investments held by end investors.

• It is therefore possible that the growth of the securitised credit intermediation model has increased systemic risk in ways which are not just the result of poor execution – bad remuneration policies, inadequate risk management or disclosure, failures in the credit rating process – but inherent.

But it is also important not to overstate this case and to recognise the potential for better regulation to ensure a more robust model of securitised credit intermediation.

• Some of the arguments originally advanced in favour of securitised credit are sound: taking regionally or concentrated credit risk off bank balance sheets and distributing it to diversified investors can be beneficial.

• Many forms of credit, for instance residential mortgages, are best assessed via quantitative scoring techniques, rather than by individual bank officer judgement, and can therefore be turned into securities, the risk of which can be well captured in credit ratings. Credit ratings indeed * * * worked reasonably well as indicators of relative probability of default until the development of overly complex structured credit instruments.

• Many of the problems of the securitised credit model as it emerged over the last 15 years were the direct result of poor regulation: e.g. the emergence of off-balance sheet shadow banking activities and inadequately low capital requirements against trading books.

• And while we are now facing a crisis of the securitised credit model, history has provided many examples of credit crises involving almost entirely on-balance sheet banking – the US savings and loans debacle of the 1980s, the Japanese and Swedish banking crises of the 1990s, the US banking crisis of 1929-33. Some of these cases (e.g. the Japanese banking crisis) illustrate the point * * * that irrational exuberance can operate in the market for traditional on balance sheet loans and in the property market, as well as in liquid financial instrument markets. And some of the factors which played a role in those crises e.g. the regionally specific concentration of bank exposures in US banks in the 1930s, could have been partially offset by appropriate application of an originate and distribute model of securitised credit.

A reasonable judgement therefore is that future system for credit intermediation will and should involve a combination of traditional on-balance sheet mechanisms and securitisation. The challenge is to design regulatory responses which will produce a safer version of the securitized credit model – less complex, more transparent to end investors, with less packaging and trading of securitised credit through multiple balance sheets, more true distribution to end investors and more real risk diversification.

This conclusion has implications for the debate about whether regulation should seek a clear distinction between traditional on balance sheet banks and investment banking style trading activities (sometimes labeled 'utility banking' and 'casino banking'). * * *

1.4 (iii) Misplaced reliance on sophisticated maths: fixable deficiencies or inherent limitations?

* * * [The] development of a greatly expanded financial sector and the rapid growth and increased complexity of the securitised model of credit intermediation was accompanied and, it was believed, made safe by the development of increasingly sophisticated mathematical techniques for the measurement and management of position taking risks. The techniques entailed numerous variants to cope with the different mathematics of, for instance different categories of option. And their application required significant computing power to capture, for instance, relationships between different market prices, the complex nature of structured credit instruments, and the effects of diversification across partially but not wholly correlated markets. But the underlying methodological assumption was straightforward: the idea that analysis of past price movement patterns could deliver statistically robust inferences relating to the probability of price movements in future. The financial crisis has revealed, however, severe problems with these techniques. They suggest at very least the need for significant changes in the way that [Value at Risk (VAR)]-based methodologies have been applied: some, however, pose more fundamental questions about our ability in principle to infer future risk from past observed patterns.

Four categories of problem can be distinguished:

• **Short observation periods** . * * * Measures of VAR were often estimated using relatively short periods of observation e.g. 12 months. As a result they introduced significant procyclicality, with periods of low observed risk driving down measures of future prospective risk, and thus influencing capital commitment decisions which were for a time self-fulfilling. At very least much longer time periods of observations need to be used.

• **Non-normal distributions** However, even if much longer time periods (e.g. ten years) had been used, it is likely that estimates would have failed to identify the scale of risks being taken. Price movements during the crisis have often been of a size whose probability was calculated by models (even using longer term inputs) to be almost infinitesimally small. This suggests that the models systematically underestimated the chances of small probability high impact events. Models frequently assume that the full distribution of possible events, from which the observed price movements are assumed to be a random sample, is normal in shape. But there is no clearly robust justification for this assumption and it is possible that financial market movements are inherently characterized by fat-tail distributions. This implies that any use of VAR models needs to be buttressed by the application of stress test techniques which consider the impact of extreme movements beyond those which the model suggests are at all probable. Deciding just how stressed the stress test should be, is however inherently difficult, and not clearly susceptible to any mathematical determination.

• **Systemic versus idiosyncratic risk** . One explanation of fat-tail distributions may lie in the importance of systemic versus idiosyncratic risk i.e. the presence of 'network externalities'. The models used implicitly assume that the actions of the individual firm, reacting to market price movements, are both sufficiently small in scale as not themselves to affect the market equilibriums, and independent of the actions of other firms. But this is a deeply misleading assumption if it is possible that developments in markets will induce similar and simultaneous behaviour by numerous players. If this is the case, which it certainly was in the financial crisis, VAR measures of risk may not only fail adequately to warn of rising risk, but may convey the message that risk is low and falling at the precise time when systemic risk is high and rising. According to VAR measures, risk was low in spring 2007: in fact the system was fraught with huge systemic risk. This suggests that stress tests may need (i) to be defined as much by regulators in the light of macro-prudential concerns, as by firms in the light of idiosyncratic concerns; and (ii) to consider the impact of second order effects i.e. the impact on one bank of another bank's likely reaction to the common systemic stress.

• **Non-independence of future events; distinguishing risk and uncertainty**. More fundamentally, however, it is important to realize that the assumption that past distribution patterns carry robust inferences for the probability of future patterns is methodologically insecure. It involves applying to the world of social and economic relationships a technique drawn from the world of physics, in which a random sample of a definitively existing universe of possible events is used to determine the probability characteristics which govern future random samples. But it is unclear whether this analogy is valid when applied to economic and social relationships, or whether instead, we need to recognise that we are dealing not with mathematically modellable risk, but with inherent 'Knightian' uncertainty.21 This would further reinforce the need for a macro-prudential approach to regulation. But it would also suggest that no system of regulation could ever guard against all risks/uncertainties, and that there may be extreme circumstances in which the backup of risk socialization (e.g. of the sort of government intervention now being put in place) is the optimal and the only defence against system failure.

1.4 (iv) The failure of market discipline

The challenge to efficient market theory has consequences for the extent to which we can rely on market discipline rather than regulatory action to constrain risks. In the past, an important school of thought has argued that market discipline can play a key role in incentivising banks to constrain capital and liquidity risks. The Basel II capital adequacy framework includes the assumption that improved disclosure under 'Pillar 3' will play a significant role alongside regulation, in incentivising appropriate behaviour. Proposals have also been put forward in the past to require banks to issue subordinated debt, in the belief that a transparent market price for bank credit will in itself improve discipline, either directly through its influence on management behaviour, or indirectly by providing information which might trigger intervention by bank regulators. The development of the CDS market has also been assumed by some commentators to create an increased discipline, since it provides a clear external measure of risk. And many r responses to the crisis have focused heavily on the need for increased disclosure and transparency as a key response, and – in some cases – the single most important response. But a strong case can be made that the events of the last five years have illustrated the inadequacy of market discipline: indeed, they suggest that in some ways market prices and market pressures may have played positively harmful roles.

• Bank CDS prices before the crash of 2007 did not provide forewarning of the scale of problems ahead. They were moderately successful in indicating the *relative* riskiness of different institutions – e.g. suggesting that Northern

Rock was more risky than other banks. But their overall sector wide level suggested that risks were at historically low not historically high levels.

• Bank share prices similarly failed to indicate that risks were increasing, but rather delivered strong market price reinforcement to management's convictions that their aggressive growth strategies were value creative.

• And while * * * capital adequacy regulations are sometimes criticised as procyclical, it is clear that market pressures from investors and analysts were far more so. Far from banks being pressured to build up capital buffers in the good times before 2007, ahead of potential future problems, the pressure of the market was for them to return capital in order to reduce capital ratios from what were perceived as inefficiently high levels.

• Finally, while it is clear in retrospect that some major corporate actions, in particular the RBS bid for ABN AMRO, were risky mistakes, and while several institutional shareholders expressed significant concerns that the time, they were not able or willing to force a change of strategy.

A reasonable conclusion is that market discipline expressed via market prices cannot be expected to play a major role in constraining bank risk taking, and that the primary constraint needs to come from regulation and supervision. There may, however, be potential to achieve more effective institutional shareholder influence over corporate strategies * * *.

1.4 (v) Financial innovation and value added

* * * [One] one of the striking features of the last 15 years has been a dramatic increase across the world in the relative size of wholesale financial services within the real economy. [Financial] system balance sheets had increased far more rapidly than lending and deposit taking to and from the non-financial sectors of the economy. This increase in balance sheets was moreover matched by similar trends in measures of value added and profit. Financial sector 'value added' as a % of GDP increased significantly. * * * Banking sector profits grew as a % of total profits. And the market capitalisation of financial companies, and in particular banks, grew as a % of GDP and as a % of total market capitalisation.

This growth appears to be at variance with one of the arguments made in favour of securitisation, that it would be a more cost efficient system, delivering the service of credit intermediation to the real economy at a lower total cost. An important theoretical issue is therefore why wholesale financial services have grown so significantly.

A reasonable assessment is while that while there are some inherent reasons why financial services tend to grow in importance as income per capita rises, the increase over the last ten to 15 years has also been driven by unnecessary and undesirable factors which raise questions about the value of some financial innovation and about appropriate regulatory responses.

There are some fundamental and benign factors which tend to increase the relative importance of financial services (both retail and wholesale) as incomes grow. The wealthier people become, the more life cycle consumption smoothing occurs, and the more diverse they become in their preferences for consumption at different points in their life. As a result there is a simultaneous increase in demand for both savings and borrowing products. And the more globalised the world economy becomes, the more complex are the functions which global banks have to perform in intermediating credits and other flows and in themselves managing and helping corporates to manage the risks that arise from global operations, and from fluctuating exchange rates, interest rates and commodity prices. In general income per capita and financial sector value added as a % of GDP are somewhat correlated, across at least a range of income per capita levels, for inherent and benign reasons.

But it also seems likely that the importance of financial services as a % of GDP has been swollen by two other factors, one illusory and the other harmful:

- The illusory affect can arise from mark-to-market profits in a rising market. The bank and near-bank system in total holds a net long position in those assets which are marked to market. As a result, if irrational exuberance pushes the price of assets to irrationally high levels, mark to market accounting will swell declared profit in an unsustainable way. A significant element of trading book profits recorded in the years running up to the crisis proved in retrospect illusory. These illusory profits were however used as the basis for bonus decisions, and created incentives for traders and management to take further risk. This carries implications for remuneration policies * * *
- The possible harmful effect is rent extraction. For it seems likely that some and perhaps much of the structuring and trading activity involved in the complex version of securitised credit, was not required to deliver credit intermediation efficiently. Instead, it achieved an economic rent extraction made possible by the opacity of margins, the asymmetry of information and knowledge

between end users of financial services and producers, and the structure of principal/agent relationships between investors and companies and between companies and individual employees. Wholesale financial services, and in particular that element devoted to securitised credit intermediation and the trading of securitised credit instruments, grew to a size unjustified by the value of its service to the real economy.

If this is true, it could carry implications for appropriate regulatory approaches. An underlying assumption of financial regulation in the US, the UK and across the world, has been that financial innovation is by definition beneficial, since market discipline will winnow out any unnecessary or value destructive innovations. As a result, regulators have not considered it their role to judge the value of different financial products, and they have in general avoided direct product regulation, certainly in wholesale markets with sophisticated investors. * * *

PART II. DEBT FINANCING

SECTION B. BASIC TERMS AND CONCEPTS

1. INTRODUCTION

Insert at Casebook page 248, after the first full paragraph:

In re Merrill Lynch Auction Rate Securities Litigation

United States District Court, Southern District of New York, 2010
--- F.Supp.2d ----, 2010 WL 1257597

LORETTA A. PRESKA, Chief Judge.

Plaintiffs Colin Wilson, Ronald Levy, and Michael Bonde, purchasers of auction rate securities ("ARS"), bring this purported class action against Merrill Lynch & Co., Inc. ("Merrill Lynch & Co."), a financial firm that offers wide-ranging financial services and products through its subsidiaries, and Merrill Lynch, Pierce, Fenner & Smith, Inc. ("Merrill Lynch"), a securities broker-dealer and a wholly-owned subsidiary of Merrill Lynch & Co. Plaintiffs bring their claim under Section 10(b) of the Securities Exchange Act of 1934 ("Exchange Act"), and Rules 10b-5 (a) and 10b-5(c) thereunder. * * * Defendants now move to dismiss the Plaintiffs' complaint for failure to state a claim. For the reasons discussed below, the Defendants' motion is GRANTED.

I. Background

* * *

The Lead Plaintiffs purport to represent all persons or entities who purchased ARS for which Merrill Lynch served as sole auction dealer, lead auction dealer, co-lead auction dealer, or joint lead auction dealer between March 25, 2003, and February 13, 2008 (the "Class Period"). A summary of the factual allegations of the Complaint follows.

A. Auction Rate Securities

Auction rate securities were equity or debt instruments that were traded through periodic Dutch auctions held every seven, twenty-eight, thirty-five, or forty-nine days. The securities were issued by closed-end preferred funds, states, state agencies, municipalities, student loan originators and lenders, and other corporations and entities. While the market for ARS was initially populated by sophisticated institutional investors in the 1980s, issuers and underwriters subsequently attracted unsophisticated investors by lowering the minimum investment to $25,000. By February 2008, the market for ARS had grown to over $330 billion.

Investors participated in the periodic auctions by submitting orders to buy, sell, or hold ARS at particular interest rates. An auction succeeded if the number of purchase orders at a particular interest rate equaled or exceeded the number of sell orders at that same rate. The clearing rate was then set as the lowest interest or dividend rate at which all sale orders could be fulfilled. This clearing rate applied until the next auction.

An auction failed if the number of sell orders exceeded the number of buy orders. In the event of a failed auction the interest rate on a security was reset to a predetermined rate, referred to as the maximum rate. If the maximum rate was sufficiently high it would attract new buyers or prompt the issuer to refinance; if the maximum rate was sufficiently low, on the other hand, it would not attract new buyers and the holder would be left with an illiquid security.

Plaintiff Colin Wilson purchased ARS from E*Trade on July 17, 2007. Plaintiff Ronald Levy, as Trustee of the Levy Family Trust, purchased ARS from Wells Fargo Investments, LLC ("Wells Fargo") on March 16, 2006. Plaintiff Michael Bonde purchased ARS from Wells Fargo on December 24, 2007.

B. Defendants' Conduct

Plaintiffs allege that Merrill Lynch engaged in a scheme to manipulate the ARS market "to create the appearance of a functioning auction market in which auction rate securities traded in accordance with actual supply and demand." Merrill Lynch participated in the ARS market as an underwriter, an auction dealer, and a bidder for its own account. As an underwriter, Merrill Lynch allegedly issued ARS with maximum rates that were insufficient to attract liquidity in the event of a failed auction. As an auction dealer, Merrill Lynch accepted orders from investors and managed the auctions. Investors could also place orders through other brokerages, which would then submit orders to Merrill Lynch.

The central component of the alleged scheme was Merrill Lynch's intervention to prevent auction failures in every auction for which it served as sole or lead auction dealer. From January 3, 2006, to May 27, 2008, for example, Merrill Lynch prevented more than 5,800 auctions from failing by placing bids for its own account. This intervention occurred pursuant to tacit agreements with ARS issuers that Merrill Lynch would suppress auction failures.

By placing support bids with its own capital, Merrill Lynch masked the lack of investor demand for ARS and led investors to "believe their investments could be readily liquidated through arm's-length sales at periodic auctions." In reality, the market for ARS was not dictated by the natural interplay of supply and demand but was upheld only because of Merrill Lynch's constant interventions.

Merrill Lynch's support bidding also allowed it to set the clearing rate at each auction. Merrill Lynch was able to bid for its own account after all other buy and sell bids were submitted, allowing the Merrill Lynch ARS Trading Desk to bid at specific rates and in specific amounts that guaranteed that auctions would clear at those rates. These interest rates were set high enough to encourage continued investment by customers but low enough to satisfy issuers. After placing support bids and acquiring ARS for its own account, Merrill Lynch would reduce excess inventory by selling ARS between auction periods; by setting the clearing rate higher, Merrill Lynch could "clear more product" before the next auction period.

Merrill Lynch allegedly furthered its manipulative scheme by misstating and omitting facts about its ARS practices and procedures and by pressuring Merrill Lynch sales representatives to sell ARS to investors. Merrill Lynch described ARS to investors as "highly liquid, safe investments similar to money market funds" and classified ARS as "Other Cash" on clients' account statements. Despite the purported existence of a protective wall designed to restrict the flow of material non-public information between various Merrill Lynch groups, the ARS Trading Desk shared information about Merrill Lynch's ARS inventory with the Research Department. Individuals at the ARS Trading Desk pushed the Research Department to issue favorable research reports, caused an unfavorable research report to be retracted and amended, and used research analysts to tout the benefits of ARS to Merrill Lynch's financial advisors. Finally, Merrill Lynch pressured its financial advisors to sell ARS to customers through national sales conference calls, emails, and by paying advisors greater commissions than they could have earned selling other financial products.

C. The 2006 SEC Order and Merrill Lynch's Website Disclosure

The Securities and Exchange Commission ("SEC") began to investigate the auction practices of Merrill Lynch and other auction dealers in 2004. The SEC s inquiry was reported in the *Associated Press, The Wall Street Journal, Dow Jones Newswires, The Los Angeles Times, and The Bond Buyer.* The investigation culminated on May 31, 2006, when the SEC filed an Order Instituting Administrative and Cease-and-Desist Proceedings, Making Findings, and Imposing Remedial Sanctions and a Cease-and-Desist Order Pursuant to Section 8A of the Securities Act of 1933 and Section 15(b) of the Securities Exchange Act of 1934 ("2006 SEC Order").

The 2006 SEC Order noted that, among other conduct, certain auction dealers had "submitted bids to ensure that all of the securities would be purchased to avoid failed auctions and thereby, in certain instances, affected the clearing rate." Such conduct was improper because it was not accompanied by adequate disclosure; the Order specified that it did "not prohibit broker-dealers from bidding for their proprietary accounts when properly disclosed."

The Order included several remedial provisions. Merrill Lynch agreed to pay a civil monetary penalty of $1,500,000. The Order also required Merrill Lynch to provide its customers who held ARS, issuers of ARS, and customers who were first-time purchasers of ARS with a written description of Merrill Lynch's material auction practices and procedures. The SEC stated that Merrill Lynch could satisfy these requirements by sending customers the written material description itself or by including a written notification with the trade confirmation directing the purchaser to a specific page on Merrill Lynch's website containing the written description. The Order required Merrill Lynch to "at all times make a description of its then-current material auction practices and procedures available to (1) all customers and broker-dealers who are participating through [Merrill Lynch] in an [ARS auction] on the portion of its website that is accessible to such customers and broker-dealers and is related to such action and (2) the general public on another portion of its website accessible to the general public."

Merrill Lynch subsequently placed a document on its website titled "Description of Merrill Lynch's Auction Rate Securities Practices and Procedures." The document noted that "because of the multiple roles that Merrill Lynch play[ed] in the [ARS] market, Merrill Lynch's interests in participating in that market [could] differ from [other investors]." These roles included "providing services to issuers of [ARS], acting as an agent for investors ... and purchasing and selling as principal for Merrill Lynch's own account."

The document also contained a section titled "Risk Factors and Special Considerations." Under a subheading titled "Bidding by Merrill Lynch," the document stated that "Merrill Lynch [was] permitted, but not obligated, to submit orders in auctions for its own account either as a bidder or a seller, or both, and routinely d[id] so in its sole discretion." (*Id.*) Merrill Lynch disclosed that if it

> submit[ted] an order for its own account, it would likely have an advantage over other bidders because Merrill Lynch would have knowledge of some or all of the other orders ... and, thus, could determine the rate and size of its order so as to ensure that its order [was] likely to be accepted in the auction and that the auction [was] likely to clear at a particular rate.

Where Merrill Lynch was the sole auction dealer, it "could discern the clearing rate before the orders [were] submitted to the auction agent and set the clearing rate with its order."

The document disclosed certain facts surrounding the possibility of a failed auction. It noted that "Merrill Lynch may routinely place one or more bids in an auction for its own account to acquire auction rate securities ... to prevent an auction failure." (*Id.*) The document also noted that "[b]ids by Merrill Lynch or by those it may encourage to place bids [were] likely to affect the clearing rate." (*Id.*) "Because of these practices," the document stated,

> the fact that an auction clear d[id] successfully d[id] not mean that an investment in the securities involve[d] no significant liquidity or credit risk. Merrill Lynch [was] not obligated to continue to place such bids or encourage other bidders to do so in any particular auction to prevent an auction from failing.

Investors were not to "assume that Merrill Lynch [would] do so or that auction failures [would] not occur."

Finally, under a section titled "Holder's Ability to Resell Auction Rate Securities May Be Limited," the document noted that

> Merrill Lynch may submit a bid in an auction to keep it from failing, but it is not obligated to do so. There may not always be enough bidders to prevent an auction from failing in the absence of Merrill Lynch bidding in the auction for its own account or encouraging others to bid. Therefore, auction failures are possible, especially if the issuer's credit were to deteriorate, if a market disruption were to occur or if, for any reason, Merrill Lynch were unable or unwilling to bid.

D. The Prospectuses

The prospectuses for the securities at issue also revealed the broker-dealer's ability to intervene in auctions. The prospectus for Blackrock MuniHoldings Fund Inc., Series C, purchased by Lead Plaintiffs Colin Wilson and Ronald Levy, provided that:

> A broker-dealer may bid in an auction in order to prevent what would otherwise be (i) a failed auction, (ii) an "all-hold" auction, or (iii) an applicable dividend rate that the broker-dealer believes, in its sole discretion, does not reflect the market for the [ARS] at the time of the auction.

The prospectus further stated that as "a result of bidding by broker-dealers in an auction for their own account, the dividend rate that would apply at the auction may be higher or lower than the rate that would have prevailed had the broker-dealer not bid" and that "[n]either broker-dealers nor the Fund are [sic] obligated to purchase shares of [ARS] in an auction or otherwise."

The prospectus for Nuveen Premium Income Municipal Fund, Series M, purchased by Lead Plaintiff Michael Bonde, stated that "A Broker-Dealer may also submit Orders to the Auction Agent for its own account as an Existing Holder or Potential Holder." The prospectus also noted that a broker-dealer that submitted bids for its own account "might have an advantage over other Bidders because it would have knowledge of all Orders submitted by it in that Auction."

E. The Collapse of the ARS Market

The credit market deteriorated in the summer of 2007. In August and September 2007, Merrill Lynch and several other major broker-dealers allowed a number of auctions for collateralized residential mortgage-backed ARS to fail. Merrill Lynch continued to monitor the ARS landscape throughout the rest of 2007 to determine if other broker-dealers were continuing to support their auctions. On February 12, 2008, after learning that two other major broker-dealers had allowed auctions to fail, Merrill Lynch executives decided to stop supporting auctions. Beginning on February 13, Merrill Lynch and all other major auction dealers stopped supporting auctions. Since the collapse of the market, the Plaintiffs have been unable to sell at par the ARS they purchased during the Class Period.

* * *

III. Discussion

A. The Plaintiffs Have Not Stated a Claim for Market Manipulation under Section 10(b)

The Plaintiffs allege that Merrill Lynch manipulated the ARS market in violation of the securities laws. * * "Market manipulation requires a plaintiff to allege (1) manipulative acts; (2) damage (3) caused by reliance on an assumption of an efficient market free of manipulation; (4) scienter; (5) in connection with the purchase or sale of securities; (6) furthered by the defendant's use of the mails or any facility of a national securities exchange."

* * *

2. The Plaintiffs Have Failed to Allege Manipulative Conduct

Defendants argue that the Plaintiffs have failed sufficiently to allege that Merrill Lynch engaged in manipulative conduct. "Manipulation is virtually a term of art when used in connection with securities markets. The term refers generally to practices, such as wash sales, matched orders, or rigged prices, that are intended to mislead investors by artificially affecting market activity." *Santa Fe Indus., Inc. v. Green,* 430 U.S. 462, 476, 97 S.Ct. 1292, 51 L.Ed.2d 480 (1977) (internal quotations and citations omitted). Section 10(b)'s "broad language, on its face, extends to manipulation of all kinds, whether by making false statements or otherwise."

A plaintiff alleging market manipulation typically must show "that an alleged manipulator engaged in market activity aimed at deceiving investors as to how other market participants have valued a security." *ATSI,* 493 F.3d at 100. Such activity misleads investors into thinking "that prices at which they purchase and sell securities are determined by the natural interplay of supply and demand, not rigged by manipulators." *Id.* (quoting *Gurary v. Winehouse,* 190 F.3d 37, 45 (2d Cir.1999)). In other words, "while misrepresentations affect investor beliefs by directly injecting false information into the marketplace, market manipulation affects beliefs indirectly by creating circumstantial evidence that positive information has entered the market." *Catton v. Defense Tech. Sys., Inc.,* No. 05 Civ. 6954(SAS), 2006 WL 27470, at *6 (S.D.N.Y. Jan.3, 2006).

* * *

The Plaintiffs in the instant case have not sufficiently alleged that Merrill Lynch sent a false pricing signal to the market. The fact that Merrill Lynch could prevent failed auctions through the placement of support bids was disclosed in numerous publicly available documents. The 2006 SEC Order, for example, highlighted that auction dealers had placed support bids to prevent failed auctions and specifically noted that the Order did not prohibit such conduct as long as it was properly disclosed. The Order, moreover, indicated that Merrill Lynch was required to place a written description of its material auction practices and procedures on a specific page of its website accessible to the general public.

Merrill Lynch's website disclosed "that Defendants could engage in the very conduct of which Plaintiff[s] complain[ ], the advantages that Defendants would have if they did engage in such conduct, the ability of such conduct to affect clearing rates and the possibility that the auctions would fail if Defendants did not intervene in them." *In re Citigroup Auction Rate Sec. Litig.*, ---F.Supp.2d ----, No. 08 Civ. 3095(LTS)(FM), 2009 WL 2914370, at *7 (S.D.N.Y. Sept. 11, 2009) (dismissing similar claims against Citigroup based on the disclosure of Citigroup's material ARS practices and procedures on its website). These disclosures negate the Plaintiffs' claims that Merrill Lynch misled the market into believing that the price of the securities and the clearing rates set by the auctions were dictated by the natural interplay of supply and demand. * * *

The Plaintiffs' argument that the disclosures were insufficient is unavailing. The Plaintiffs characterize Merrill Lynch's acknowledgment that it "routinely" submitted support bids as inaccurate because Merrill Lynch "systematically" submitted support bids. (Pls. Mem. of Law 19.) This semantic distinction is not persuasive, particularly in light of the Plaintiffs' own use in the Complaint of the word "routinely" to describe Merrill Lynch's conduct. (*See* Compl. ¶ 44 ("Merrill used its own capital to routinely place 'support bids.' "); *id.* at 13 ("Merrill Routinely Intervened In Auctions to Set The Rates Of Interest Paid On ML ARS.").)

Another court in this district recently came to the same conclusion in a similar case. In *Teva Pharmaceutical Industries v. Deutsche Bank AG, et al.*, 09-cv-6205 (AKH), the plaintiff alleged that Deutsche Bank manipulated the ARS market by, *inter alia,* placing support bids in every auction for which it served as a broker-dealer. Deutsche Bank had disclosed in the private placement memorandum for the ARS that it might buy for its own account. The court held that the plaintiff's allegations did not amount to market manipulation because the disclosure informed investors that Deutsche Bank might or might not intervene, "which meant it might or might not affect the demand and supply for the instruments that were being auctioned." Accordingly, the court dismissed the claims with prejudice.

Contrary to the Plaintiffs' assertions in the instant case, Merrill Lynch also disclosed that the lack of auction failures was not indicative of the health of the ARS market. * * * Indeed, disclosing that Merrill Lynch might routinely intervene to prevent failed auctions necessarily implied that there might not be sufficient demand to support the auctions and to create liquidity.

* * *

3. Plaintiffs Have Failed Sufficiently to Plead Reliance

A plaintiff alleging market manipulation must plead "reliance on an assumption of an efficient market free of manipulation." *ATSI,* 493 F.3d at 101. * * *

* * *

The fraud on the market theory is based on the premise that "the market price of shares traded on well-developed markets reflects all publicly available information, and, hence, any material misrepresentations." *Basic Inc. v. Levinson,* 485 U.S. 224, 246, 108 S.Ct. 978, 99 L.Ed.2d 194 (1988). When a plaintiff alleges that "materially misleading statements have been disseminated into an impersonal, well-developed market for securities, the reliance of individual plaintiffs on the integrity of the market price may be presumed." *Id.* at 247.

* * *

Even if the Plaintiffs have sufficiently alleged the efficiency of the ARS market, however, they still cannot benefit from the fraud on the market presumption of reliance. An efficient market incorporates "all publicly available information." *ATSI,* 493 F.3d at 101 n. 4 (quoting *Basic,* 485 U.S. at 246). Under this theory the ARS market would have incorporated the 2006 SEC Order, Merrill Lynch's website disclosure, and the prospectuses for the ARS at issue. * * *

Combined, these materials preclude the Plaintiffs from establishing a presumption of reliance on the efficiency of the ARS market. * * * Here, Merrill Lynch's participation in the ARS market was revealed to the public with the degree of credibility and intensity necessary to counterbalance any misinterpretations resulting from the alleged manipulation.

* * *

The prospectuses, 2006 SEC Order, and Merrill Lynch's ARS website demonstrate that "[t]he 'total mix' of available information included the very information plaintiffs claim was concealed." *White,* 2004 WL 1698628, at *13. These sources were widely available, easily accessible, and disclosed in detail Merrill Lynch's ability to place support bids, the reasons it might place support bids, the advantages it might have if it placed support bids, and the consequences of an auction failure. In addition to this information's wide availability, investors would have had every reason to trust the sources: an investigation and settlement by the SEC, Merrill Lynch itself, and the SEC-filed prospectuses for the ARS. Given the detail and credibility with which the sources discussed auction-dealer participation in ARS auctions, no reasonable investor could have been misled by Merrill Lynch's alleged failure to disclose its involvement in the ARS market. * * *

* * *

Without a presumption of reliance, the Plaintiffs must establish that they directly, and reasonably, relied on an assumption of the efficiency of the ARS market. "An investor may not justifiably rely on a misrepresentation if, through minimal diligence, the investor should have discovered the truth." *Starr ex rel. Estate of Sampson v. Georgeson S'holder, Inc.,* 412 F.3d 103, 109 (2d Cir.2005) (quoting *Brown v. E.F. Hutton Group, Inc.,* 991 F.2d 1020, 1032 (2d Cir.1993)). "Under this standard, § 10(b) liability will not be imposed when an investor's conduct rises to the level of recklessness." *Brown,* 991 F.2d at 1032.

* * *

* * * Merrill Lynch's participation in the ARS market was disclosed in several sources that were widely available and easily accessible to the Plaintiffs. The Plaintiffs do not allege the existence of a longstanding business relationship or a fiduciary relationship with Merrill Lynch. The Plaintiffs also do not allege that Merrill Lynch or any other entity initiated their purchases of ARS. Rather, the Plaintiffs took the opportunity to purchase ARS on their own initiative without availing themselves of the opportunity to detect the alleged fraud. The disclosures discussed above highlighted that broker-dealers such as Merrill Lynch could submit bids for their own accounts to prevent failed auctions and

to determine clearing rates. "[A]bsent specific allegations of the basis for Plaintiff[s'] incorrect assumptions about the ARS market and the reasonableness of the alleged reliance in the face of such disclosure, Plaintiff[s'] market manipulation claim must be dismissed." *Citigroup,* 2009 WL 2914370, at *8.

NOTE: ARS ENFORCEMENT PROCEEDINGS

The ARS meltdown presents a case in which private antifraud litigation such as that against Merrill Lynch played a distinctly secondary role in protecting investors. When ARS market imploded each of the SEC, FINRA, and multitudinous state securities commissioners initiated enforcement actions grounded in fraud allegations. The principal actors in the market–Citibank, Merrill, Wachovia, Goldman Sachs, etc.-- all settled during 2008 and 2009. The settlements followed a pattern. Individual investors with accounts under a threshhold size (say, $10 million), small businesses, and charities, had their holdings of ARSs paid down at par immediately. The settling bank also promised to use "best efforts" to liquidate the holdings of its institutional customers over a longer timetable.

3. The Bondholder and the Going Concern

(A) THE PROMISE TO PAY

Insert in "Note: Refunding Cases," at the end of the incomplete paragraph at the top of Casebook page 267:

3. *Payments for Consent.*

In re Loral Space and Communications Inc., 2008 WL 4293781 (Del.Ch.), concerned an issue of notes issued in connection with the effectuation of a chapter 11 reorganization. The notes, issued by Loral's subsidiary, Loral Skynet, were redeemable for 110 percent of face value but only in the event that two-thirds of the noteholders registered no objection. Skynet redeemed the notes, and two-thirds of the noteholders did not object. The noteholder plaintiffs claimed a breach of the good faith duty on the ground that 45 percent of the notes were held MHR Financing, which held a large block of stock of Skynet's parent and had traded away its right to object in the course of negotiating a sweetheart financing deal with the parent, a deal that entailed a transfer of effective control to MHR.

The court held that there was no breach:

"* * * The noteholders contend that their rights were violated because MHR received consideration for its decision not to object, in the form of the favorable terms of the MHR Financing, that were not offered to other noteholders.

"I reject that argument. The terms of the notes contain no restriction on payments for consents. Unlike most note issuances, here, one holder, MHR, owned a large position and was singularly able to deliver a non-objection that would enable early redemption. During the negotiations over the indenture governing the notes, the creditors' committee tried to get a provision inserted prohibiting any payments in connection with consents. That provision was rejected, as was a contrary provision, and the eventual indenture was silent on the question. But noteholders were clearly told that MHR had a sufficient number of notes to unilaterally consent to early redemption.

"The implied covenant in a bond indenture is not a license for judges to invent market terms that should act as a default rule simply because plaintiffs or the judge think that would be a good thing. Bond indentures are carefully negotiated instruments filled with many restrictions. Therefore, courts should be chary in assuming that there are gaps to be filled, particularly when parties actually considered the question and the agreement ultimately reached incorporated no restriction on the rights of the issuer to bargain with a large holder for its consent. And that is particularly the case when it is clear that many indentures expressly prohibit such payments, that such an express restriction was sought, and did not make it into the indenture. What the noteholders got here is precisely the fruits of the bargain they struck, which was a full 110% of principal value plus accrued interest, in a situation when fewer than two-thirds of the noteholders did not object. Indeed, what happened was highly foreseeable, as the other noteholders should have foreseen that MHR, which was Loral's largest stockholder, might have reasons to not object to early redemption in connection with a strategic transaction good for Loral's equity holders that would not be identical with respect to noteholders who did not have a similar equity stake. No reasonable expectancy was upset here; the other noteholders got the compensation provided by the notes themselves.

* * *

"* ** The Noteholder Plaintiffs contend * * * that 'the implied covenant of good faith and fair dealing prohibits unequal payments for consent to noteholders during a redemption in the absence of an expression provision' allowing such payments. They do not ground that assertion in any particular provision of the Notes or any decision of a New York court so holding, but rather in the supposedly 'bedrock principle of the bond markets' that unequal payments to bondholders are not allowed. The Noteholder Plaintiffs bolster their argument that selective payments for consent are not allowed by stating that such payments 'simply do not occur in the debt market'

* * *

"In contrast, Loral has seized upon the 'Payments for Consent' restrictive covenant that was included in the original publicly filed draft of the Indenture but ultimately removed from the final Indenture. * * * The drafting history is of importance for two independent reasons.

"For starters, it demonstrates that this is not a case where the negotiators failed to address a possibility and the court must fill the void by trying to figure out what to do in an unforeseen circumstance that has now come to pass. * * *

"The other reason the bargaining history is relevant is that it demonstrates that there is no universally accepted default rule prohibiting payments for consent. The negotiators for the Noteholders no doubt recognized that and sought out an express protection, precisely because MHR's large stake gave it sufficient power to unilaterally consent to an early redemption and its equity interest in Loral gave it potential reasons to consent that other Noteholders might not share.

"This inference is justified by the record evidence regarding the presence of express covenants prohibiting payments for consents in many indentures. Loral introduced into the record a compendium of the indentures that were publicly filed in the five months before the Skynet Notes were issued that shows that approximately 10% of those indentures contained Payments for Consent restrictive covenants. As Loral argues, the existence of such Payments for Consents restrictive covenants in a material percentage of these indentures undermines the Noteholder Plaintiffs' assertion that there is a bedrock principle in the bond market that selective payments for consent are not allowed. Why would these sophisticated parties contract to include such a restrictive covenant if it is such an indisputable proposition that it is implied in all bond indentures? The Noteholder Plaintiffs counter that the Payments for Consent restrictive covenants are included as 'belts and suspenders language' That doesn't make sense. The indenture is the primary source of rights for Noteholders.

"Candidly, the record suggests that selective payments for consent are rarely made. But, it also suggests that it is extremely rare for one noteholder to own so much of an issue of notes that it has a control position over a consent vote. in a situation like this one, where it has been previously disclosed that a single noteholder whose interests might differ from other noteholders has control over a consent and there exists in common usage a covenant that prevents selective payments for consent, it would be unprincipled for a court to speculate, based solely on the self-serving testimony of the plaintiffs about their understanding of the market's view of a default rule proscribing such action, that the fruits of the bargain were such that the controlling noteholder could not extract a selective payment for consent. Implying the covenant requested by the [Noteholder Plaintiffs] would also be 'troublesome' in view of the fact that the Indentures 'could easily have been drafted to incorporate expressly the terms the [Noteholder Plaintiffs] now urge this court to imply.'

"Given that indentures are highly negotiated contracts forged by sophisticated parties and that such parties clearly know how to craft Payments for Consent restrictive covenants, it would be exceedingly odd for me to craft a common law rule of New York law prohibiting noteholders from receiving payments for consent. Such a rule would be akin to adopting a prohibition on the receipt of an equity control premium by a controlling stockholder of a corporation. The common law of corporations of New York has never embraced such a ban. That is the case even though stockholders have far less specific contractual rights than noteholders and a less practical ability to negotiate for themselves. Admittedly, equitable limitations, in the form of fiduciary duties, place some restraints on the circumstances in which a controller can receive an equity control premium, but the default rule remains that such a premium can be extracted. * * *

* * *

"Finally, the Noteholder Plaintiffs have also attempted to sway me by pointing to judicial decisions suggesting that it would be a breach of the implied covenant of good faith and fair dealing for an issuer to pay some noteholders more in order to get their consent. But those decisions involve dictum and nothing more. In this regard, it is important to note that the Noteholder Plaintiffs find no support in the terms of the Skynet Indenture for their argument that the Indenture impliedly prohibits unequal payments for consent are not allowed.

"That makes this case distinguishable from the only case the Noteholder Plaintiffs claim *holds* that all bondholders must be treated equally. That unreported federal decision applying New York law, *Whitebox Convertible Arbitrage Partners, L.P. v. World Airways, Inc.*, 2006 WL 358270 (N.D.Ga.2006), involved a corporation that wanted to redeem all of a series of convertible debentures (the '2004 Convertibles') but did not have the cash to do so. The corporation originally extended a public exchange offer to all holders that would have exchanged a portion of the 2004 Convertibles for convertible debentures with more favorable terms (the '2009 Convertibles') and redeemed the remaining portion for cash so long as 95% of the 2004 Convertibles were tendered into the exchange offer. But while the public exchange offer was outstanding, the corporation consummated a private exchange offer with a select group of 2004 Convertible holders. That select group was allowed to convert into the 2009 Convertibles. After the private exchange offer took place, the remaining 2004 Convertible holders were forced to redeem their 2004 Convertibles for cash. The plaintiffs sued alleging a non-pro-rata partial redemption in violation of an express covenant that the Convertibles selected for an oversubscribed partial redemption would be selected 'pro rata or by such other method as the Trustee shall deem fair and appropriate.' The court found that the private exchange offer and subsequent redemption were 'two partial redemptions' that treated the holders differently in violation of the express covenant on partial redemptions. It then held that the provision of 'a special incentive to certain bondholders in an effort to obtain their approval of a bond exchange while not making the same offer to other bondholders' was the type of 'manipulation that [the express covenant on partial redemptions] and the principles of good faith and fair dealing are designed to avoid.' The good faith and fair dealing comment is clearly dictum in light of an express covenant on point and not backed up by any reasoning. In fact, what is most notable about the *Whitebox* case is that the instrument at issue included in its language an equal treatment covenant that directly required pro-rata treatment in a partial redemption, the particular type of transaction at issue. In other words, the only case the Noteholder Plaintiffs cite for the equal treatment of all bondholders principle actually demonstrates that bondholders do not rely on the mercy of the court's enforcement of a default rule embracing such an implied principle but rather expressly demand such a covenant at the bargaining table. That is wise behavior given the absence of any decision of the New York State courts embracing any default rule of that kind."

(B) PROMISES THAT PROTECT THE PROMISE TO PAY

(2) Judicial Interpretation of Covenants

Insert after Sharon Steel *at Casebook page 279:*

Affiliated Computer Services, Inc. v. Wilmington Trust Company

United States Court of Appeals, Fifth Circuit, 2009
– F. 3d. –

Before JONES, Chief Judge, WIENER and STEWART, Circuit Judges.

CARL E. STEWART, Circuit Judge:

Affiliated Computer Services, Inc. ("ACS") brought a declaratory judgment action against The Bank of New York Trust Company ("Bank of New York"), later substituted by Wilmington Trust Company ("Wilmington Trust"), seeking a determination that ACS was not in breach of an indenture agreement ("Indenture") entered into between ACS and the Bank of New York. Wilmington Trust filed a counterclaim for a declaratory judgment that ACS breached the Indenture by failing timely to file a Form 10-K with the Securities and Exchange Commission ("SEC"), that ACS breached its covenant of good faith and fair dealing, and that ACS violated § 314(a) of the Trust Indenture Act of 1939 ("TIA"). The * * * district court granted ACS's [summary judgment] motion. * * * [W]e affirm.

I. FACTUAL AND PROCEDURAL BACKGROUND

The relevant facts are undisputed in this case. On June 6, 2005, ACS entered into the Indenture and supplemental indentures pursuant to which ACS issued two sets of notes, one at 5.20% and another at 4.70%. The notes issued at 5.20%, which are due on June 1, 2015, are the only notes relevant to this appeal. ACS timely made semi-annual interest payments on the notes.

The notes were publicly traded throughout the relevant time period, and thus, ACS was required to file reports with the SEC pursuant to Sections 13 and 15(d) of the Securities Exchange Act of 1934 * * *. ACS's Form 10-K for 2006 was due to be filed with the SEC on September 13, 2006. On September 14, 2006, ACS filed a Notification of Late Filing explaining that it was unable timely to file its 10-K because of an ongoing internal investigation into its historical stock option practices. ACS eventually filed its 10-K with the SEC on January 23, 2007, and two days later, it delivered a copy of the 10-K to Wilmington Trust.

The Indenture contains the following "Event of Default", among others: "[ACS] fails to comply with any of its other covenants or agreements in, or provisions of, the Securities of that series or this Indenture...." Indenture § 6.01(3). In the Event of Default, the trustee may accelerate the notes by written notice and declare the principal and interest due and payable immediately. Indenture § 6.02. On September 22, 2006, Cede & Co., acting on behalf of beneficial owners, delivered a Notice of Default to ACS and the [indenture] trustee at the time. On September 29, 2006, the [indenture trustee] delivered a similar Notice of Default to ACS, and on October 5, 2006, other holders of notes forwarded default notices to ACS. The notices asserted that ACS defaulted on the Indenture by failing timely to file the Form 10-K. Cede & Co. delivered a Demand to Accelerate Notes on September 29, 2006, and the [indenture trustee] submitted a similar demand on October 6, 2006. Both demands declared the principal and interest due and payable immediately. ACS did not honor either acceleration notice.

ACS responded to the notice of default by filing a declaratory judgment action * * * seeking a determination that it was not in default under the Indenture. * * * Wilmington Trust filed a counterclaim against ACS, bringing claims for breach of contract based on §§ 4.03 and 6.02 of the Indenture, breach of the covenant of good faith and fair dealing, and for violation of § 314(a) of the TIA.

> Section 4.03 of the Indenture provides in pertinent part as follows:
> [ACS] shall file with the Trustee, within 15 days after it files the same with the SEC, copies of the annual reports and the information, documents and other reports (or copies of those portions of any of the foregoing as the SEC may by rules and regulations prescribe) that [ACS] is required to file with the SEC pursuant to Section 13 or 15(d) of the Exchange Act. [ACS] shall also comply with the provisions of TIA 314(a).

Indenture § 4.03(a). Section 314(a) of the TIA similarly requires an issuer of bonds to

> file with the indenture trustee copies of the annual reports and of the information, documents, and other reports (or copies of such portions of any of the foregoing as the Commission may by rules and regulations prescribe) which such obligor is required to file with the Commission....

* * * The district court addressed the following issue: whether the Indenture requires ACS to timely file with the trustee the reports that it files with the SEC, even if the SEC filings are themselves untimely. The court agreed with ACS's interpretation that the provisions merely require ACS timely to file with the trustee the reports that ACS has filed with the SEC. * * *

II. STANDARD OF REVIEW

* * * The Indenture's choice-of-law provision specifies that it is to be governed and construed by New York law, while interpretation of the TIA is a matter of federal law. * * *

III. DISCUSSION

* * *

A. Section 314(a) of the TIA

Section 314(a) of the TIA requires an issuer of bonds to file with the trustee copies of the annual reports which it is "required to file" with the SEC. See 15 U.S.C. § 77nnn(a). The Indenture also requires compliance with § 314(a), and ACS does not dispute that it was required to comply with the provision of the section. The dispute turns on the interpretation of § 314(a), which is a matter of first impression for this court. Wilmington Trust contends that § 314(a) requires ACS to provide copies of the reports it is required to file with the SEC regardless of whether ACS actually filed the reports. ACS argues that § 314(a) requires that it only file with the trustee the reports that it has in fact filed with the SEC. The district court held that § 314 obligates ACS to file with Wilmington Trust "copies of the reports and documents that ACS files with the SEC, but § 314(a) does not require that ACS file anything with the SEC."

After the district court entered its judgment, the Eighth Circuit addressed this same issue in *UnitedHealth Group Inc. v. Wilmington Trust Co.,* 548 F.3d 1124 (8th Cir.2008). In *UnitedHealth,* the court held that "TIA § 314(a) requires only that debt issuers forward to their trustees copies of such reports as are actually filed with the SEC." *Id.* at 1131.The court explained that "the TIA's reference to §§ 13 and 15(d) of the Exchange Act merely identifies *which* reports must eventually be forwarded to the trustee. It does not independently impose any particular timetable for filing nor does it incorporate the SEC's regulatory deadlines." *Id.* at 1130.

Wilmington Trust argues that SEC Rule 19a-1 and circumstances surrounding it demonstrate that the SEC has interpreted the TIA to require timely filing of SEC reports. In 2002, the SEC issued the 34 Act Order permitting companies normally audited by Arthur Andersen LLP, an accounting firm, to file unaudited financials with their annual and quarterly reports with the SEC. * * * The SEC concurrently promulgated Rule 19a-1, titled "Compliance with Section 314(a)(1) of the Trust Indenture Act for certain eligible indenture obligors,"which states that

> [a]n "eligible indenture obligor" that files with the indenture trustee those Exchange Act reports filed with the Commission in accordance with the Release referred to in paragraph (b)(2) of this section has met its duty under Section 314(a)(1) of the Act * * * to "file with the indenture all reports required to be filed with the Commission pursuant to Section 13 or Section 15(d) of the Securities Exchange Act of 1934."

* * * The Release referred to in paragraph (b)(2) of the section is the 34 Act Order. * * * The 34 Act Order allowed certain exemptions to companies audited by Arthur Andersen LLP, provided those companies met certain conditions.

Wilmington Trust suggests that if the TIA imposed no time for filing SEC reports, there was no need to adopt Rule 19a-1 because issuers simply could have waited until they were able to obtain an audit, however long that may have taken, without violating Section 314(a)(1), and the only possible reason for the accommodation was that bond issuers unable to complete a timely audit due to Arthur Andersen's circumstances would have been late on the filings required of them by the TIA. Wilmington Trust also contends that the rule and circumstances surrounding it demonstrate that the SEC has recognized that the TIA requires timely filing of SEC reports. ACS suggests a different purpose for Rule 19a-1, stating that it simply recognizes that a report without audited financials is not the type of report required by the Exchange Act, but if a filer takes advantage of the 34 Act Order exemption and forwards to the trustee reports filed under the 34 Act Order, the filer has complied with § 314(a)(1).

* * * The circumstances surrounding Rule 19a-1 thus indicate that the rule was clarifying that companies potentially affected by the indictment of Arthur Andersen LLP may file unaudited financials as opposed to audited financials. The TIA does not impose any independent obligation timely to file reports with the SEC, and Wilmington Trust's import of Rule 19a-1 to conclude otherwise ignores the limited purpose of Rule 19a-1.

Wilmington Trust also seeks to rely on *Bank of New York v. BearingPoint, Inc.*, 824 N.Y.S.2d 752 (N.Y.Sup.Ct.2006) (unpublished table decision), arguing that this court should afford it "the weight due the only New York decision on point." Construction of § 314(a) is a matter of federal law, and we do not find *BearingPoint* to be persuasive. We agree with the reasoning of the Eighth Circuit and hold that § 314(a) of the TIA does not impose an independent obligation timely to file reports with the SEC. Rather, § 314(a) requires ACS to provide copies of reports that are actually filed with the SEC.

B. The Indenture

i. Indenture § 4.03

Wilmington Trust's other arguments center on the Indenture. Under New York law, "[t]he words and phrases used by the parties must, as in all cases involving contract interpretation, be given their plain meaning." *Brooke Group Ltd. v. JCH Syndicate 488,* 87 N.Y.2d 530, 534, 640 N.Y.S.2d 479, 663 N.E.2d 635 (N.Y.1996) (citing *Levine v. Shell Oil Co.,* 28 N.Y.2d 205, 211, 321 N.Y.S.2d 81, 269 N.E.2d 799 (N.Y.1971)).“[C]ourts may not fashion a new contract under the guise of contract construction; rather, they are required to discern the intent of the parties, to the extent that the parties evidenced what they intended by what they wrote." Slatt v. Slatt, 64 N.Y.2d 966, 967, 488 N.Y.S.2d 645, 477 N.E.2d 1099 (N.Y.1985) (internal quotation marks and citations omitted).

At least one New York state court has construed an indenture provision similar to the provision at issue in this case. In *BearingPoint,* the court considered the following provision:

> [T]he Company shall file with the Trustee, within fifteen days after it files such annual and quarterly reports, information, and documents and other reports with the SEC, copies of its annual report and of the information, documents and other reports (or copies of such portions of any of the foregoing the SEC may by rules and regulations prescribe) which the Company is required to file with the SEC pursuant to Section 13 or 15(d) of the Exchange Act. The Company shall comply with the other provisions of TIA Section 314(a).

BearingPoint, 2006 WL 2670143, at *2. The court rejected BearingPoint's argument that it did not breach the indenture by failing to provide the trustee with timely SEC filings. The court stated that the provision "unambiguously obligates BearingPoint to make the required SEC filings and to provide copies of them to the Trustee," and BearingPoint's "tortured parsing" of the provision vitiated the clear purpose of the indenture to provide information to investors so they could protect their investments. In making that determination, the court focused on the following phrases in the indenture provision: "[T]he Company shall file with the Trustee ... copies of its annual reports and of the information, documents, and other reports ... which the Company is required to file with the SEC pursuant to Section 13 or 15(d) of the Exchange Act." *Id.* (emphasis and omissions in original).

The Eighth Circuit, however, rejected *BearingPoint*'s parsing of the indenture provision.

> The [*BearingPoint*] court's analysis focused on the mandatory language of the indenture but did not distinguish between two distinct duties: one to file reports with the SEC in the first instance and another to forward copies of the reports to the trustee. More importantly, the court did not consider any timing issues and simply eliminated the phrase "within 15 days after it files such ... reports ... with the SEC," replacing it with a set of ellipses.

UnitedHealth, 548 F.3d at 1129-30 (omissions in original). The court in *UnitedHealth* did not set out the full text of the pertinent indenture provision in that case, but it stated its essence as follows: "the Company shall cause copies of ... financial reports ... which the Company is then required to file with the Commission pursuant to Section 13 or 15(d) of the Exchange Act to be filed with the Trustee ... within fifteen days of filing with the Commission." *Id.* at 1128 (omissions in original). The Eighth Circuit, in a matter of first impression, held that the plain meaning of the indenture provision imposed no independent obligation timely to file SEC reports. The court emphasized that "the plain language of [the indenture provision] makes clear that any duty actually to file the reports is imposed pursuant to Section 13 or 15(d) and *not* pursuant to the indenture itself. *Id.* At 1128-29 (internal quotation marks omitted). The court further explained the "then required to file" language:

> [T]he phrase "then required to file" is part of a longer clause introduced by the relative pronoun "which." The antecedent of "which" is clearly and unambiguously the word "reports." Thus, as a simple matter of syntax, the phrase "then required to file" modifies the word "reports" and indicates *which* reports are subject to § 504(i)'s terms. Just as clearly and just as unambiguously, the phrase "within fifteen days of filing with the Commission" modifies "shall cause ... to be filed" and indicates *when* § 504(i)'s commands must be fulfilled.

Id. at 1128 (omission in original).

We find *UnitedHealth's* reasoning persuasive. In this case, § 4.03 of the Indenture provides in part that "[ACS] shall file with the Trustee, within 15 days after it files the same with the SEC, copies of the annual reports ... that [ACS] is required to file with the SEC pursuant to Section 13 or 15(d) of the Exchange Act."The unambiguous language of § 4.03 does not impose an independent obligation actually timely to file reports with the SEC. Rather, the phrase "that [ACS] is required to file" indicates those reports copies of which ACS is required to file with the Trustee. "[W]ithin 15 days after it files the same with the SEC" designates the time in which to file the reports with the Trustee. At best, the provision anticipates that ACS "is required to file" reports with the SEC pursuant to Section 13 or 15(d), but the provision neither incorporates the SEC's timing requirements nor imposes a deadline by which ACS must actually file the reports. We therefore hold that § 4.03 of the Indenture does not impose an obligation timely to file reports with the SEC.

ii. Alleged Condition Precedent

Wilmington Trust also contends that ACS cannot take advantage of its failure to fulfill its statutory obligation timely to file reports with the SEC to argue that it has not breached its obligation to provide the Trustee with the required reports. ACS argues that in the absence of a deadline in § 4.03 for filing with the SEC, ACS did not fail to perform under the Indenture. We find no condition precedent timely to file reports with the SEC. We have already held that neither the Indenture nor § 314 of the TIA requires ACS timely to file reports with the SEC. Wilmington Trust may not rely on ACS's failure to comply with statutory obligations not made part of the parties' contract to argue that ACS breached its contractual obligation. *See Camp Kennybrook Inc. v. Kuller,* 214 A.D.2d 264, 632 N.Y.S.2d 874, 875 (N.Y.App.Div.1995) ("While plaintiff assumed a duty of care and supervision over Max, ..., such duty is imposed of law independent of and extraneous to the contract.... Accordingly, plaintiff had no contractual or quasi-contractual duty to care for and supervise Max.") (citations omitted); *see generally Nuzzi Family Ltd. Liability Co. v. Nature Conservancy, Inc.,* 304 A.D.2d 631, 758 N.Y.S.2d 364, 365 (N.Y.App.Div.2003) (rejecting time of the essence argument and stating that "[c]ontrary to the plaintiff's contention, the contract did not contain a condition precedent that its validity or the plaintiff's performance under the contract required its assignment to the DEC by a date certain") (citations omitted)

IV. CONCLUSION

Because we hold that neither § 314 of the TIA nor the Indenture requires ACS timely to file reports with the SEC, we need not address the parties' arguments regarding the acceleration of the notes. For the foregoing reasons, we affirm the district court's judgment.

Section C. Security and Seniority

4. Asset Securitization

(A) Overview

Insert after "Note: Risk and Return" at Casebook page 294:

NOTE: SECURITIZATION AND THE FINANCIAL CRISIS OF 2008

Securitizations figure prominently among the high risk transactions that brought about the financial crisis that commenced in 2008.

The negative shock that triggered the crisis originated in the subprime mortgage market. Securitization in turn figured prominently in that market's unprecedented growth – subprime loans accounted for 3 percent of the US mortgage market in 2002 and grew to 15 percent in 2006. During the subprime lending binge more than $600 billion crossed the table to borrowers previously deemed unqualified by institutional lenders. The stepped up lending triggered stepped up demand for real estate. An unprecedented price bubble resulted. Rising house prices in turn fueled willingness to lend, as actors in the credit markets assumed that increases in the value of the real estate securing the loans would make up for weakness in the borrowers' ability to pay. If a borrower who took an adjustable mortgage with a teaser interest rate could not assimilate an upward rate adjustment, the lender assumed that the borrower could refinance the loan because the property would have increased in value; if the borrower got stuck due to job loss or illness, the value of the foreclosed property would make the lender whole at all events.

Unfortunately, real estate values stopped rising in 2006. Subprime default rates promptly rose dramatically. But the end of 2007, 20.43 percent of subprime adjustable rate mortgages were in default, compared to 1.67 percent of conventional prime mortgages.

Securitization facilitated the rise in subprime lending. Banks and savings and loans found a ready market for securitized packages of subprime mortgages. They took the consideration received for the mortgage packages and promptly reloaned it in the subprime market, repeating the process over and over. Lending standards deteriorated. If a loan is not expected to be retained in the lending bank's portfolio, and also is expected to be readily saleable in a secondary market whatever the identity of the borrower, why expend resources on screening potential borrowers? Indeed, why narrow the range of one's opportunities by hewing to traditional credit standards? Thus did competitive pressures cause many banks lower their standards. The federal home mortgage packagers, Fannie Mae and Freddie Mac, were in this group.

Even as credit standards were dropping, the securitization process expanded the amount of credit available by expanding the universe of potential lenders. Subprime was only one sector contributing to a multi-trillion dollar output of securitized paper distributed throughout the financial system. Investment banks and hedge funds used borrowed money to buy the paper. So did the same banks that originated the mortgages, purchasing the paper through off-balance sheet "structured investment vehicles," and in so doing avoiding application of equity capital requirements.

The quantum of credit extended was unprecedented in US economic history. The figure below tracks total US credit market debt over gross domestic product from 1920 through 2006. It shows that during the decade that began in 2000, the national debt/equity ratio reached new and highly risky heights, outstripping the relative level of indebtedness reached during the Great Depression. Note an important difference between that debt spike and the one experienced more recently. The national debt/equity ratio peaked during the 1930s because GNP dropped. The ratio increased after 2000 during an economic expansion that in turn was fueled by expanding credit.

Total Credit Market Debt/U.S. GDP

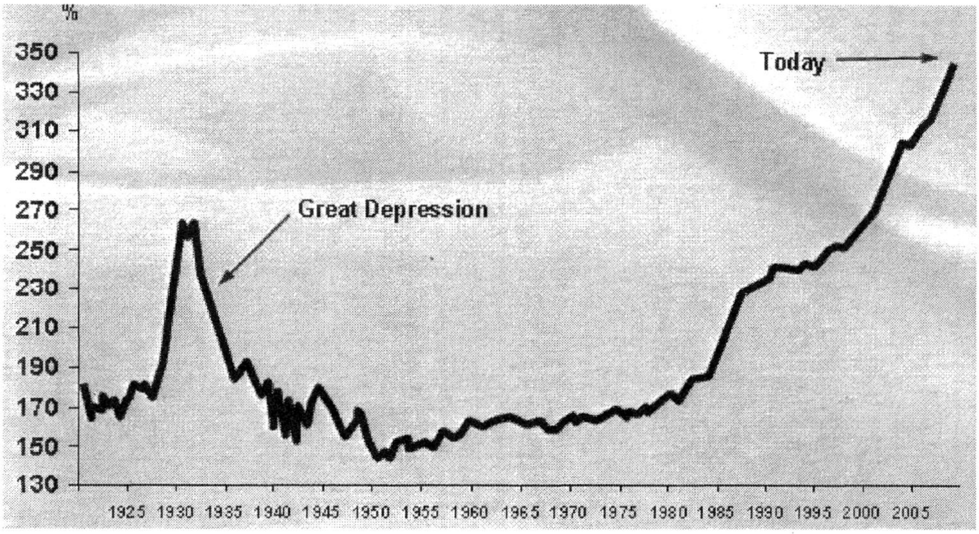

Summing up, securitization facilitated credit expansion in three ways. First, it expanded the capacity of primary lenders by enabling them to remove loans from their portfolios. Second, it opened the doors of US mortgage lending to new players – the hedge funds, bond funds, and other entities, many from offshore, that purchased securitized loans. Third, it precipitated a decline in lending standards.

But why did the third result follow from the first and second? This is where the "alchemy" of securitization figures in. The pooling of mortgages, when accompanied by the division of the securitized notes into tranches, has a portfolio effect. The higher tranches, which are protected from default by the lower ranked tranches, qualified for investment grade credit ratings, enhancing the attractiveness of securitized paper in the markets.

Mortgaged Backed Securities

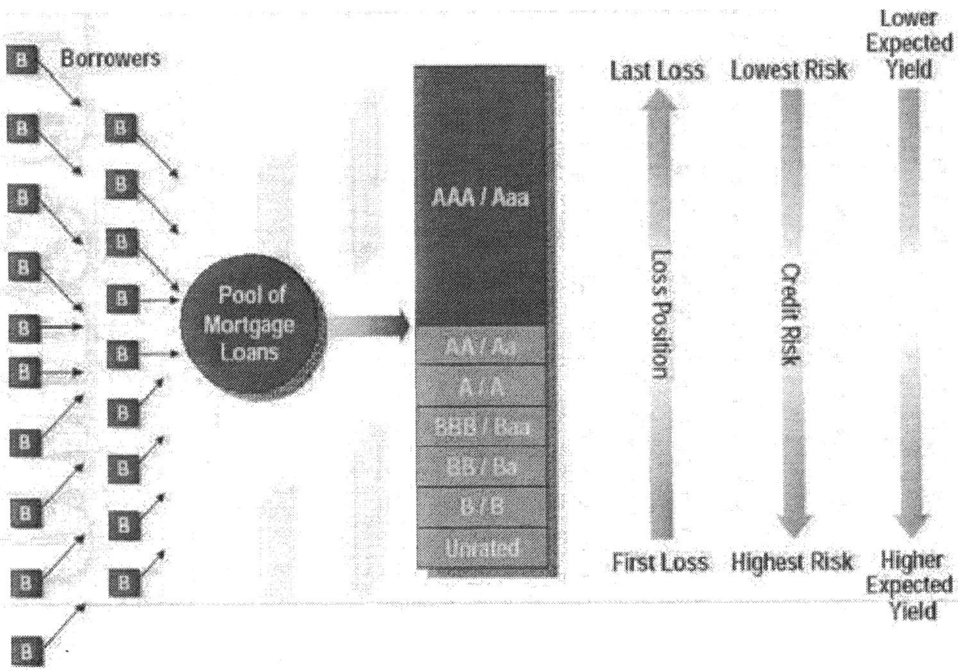

The figure above depicts how this works. Note that credit enhancement provided by mortgage insurers could be employed to expand the investment grade set. Investors loved investment grade securitized paper because it offered a higher yield than did comparable debt investments. For once, high return and low risk seemed to be walking hand in hand. But the overall picture was more than a little counter-intuitive. Loans to the worst credits in the economy were yielding AAA debt securities at a time when fewer than 20 US corporations were deemed to warrant a AAA rating.

Unfortunately, Wall Street's securitization alchemists had still further miracles of credit enhancement to perform. They collected pools of below investment grade mortgaged-backed securities and re-securitized them into secondary pools called "Collaterized Debt Obligations." The top tranches of these pools were elevated to investment grade status, as depicted in the figure below.

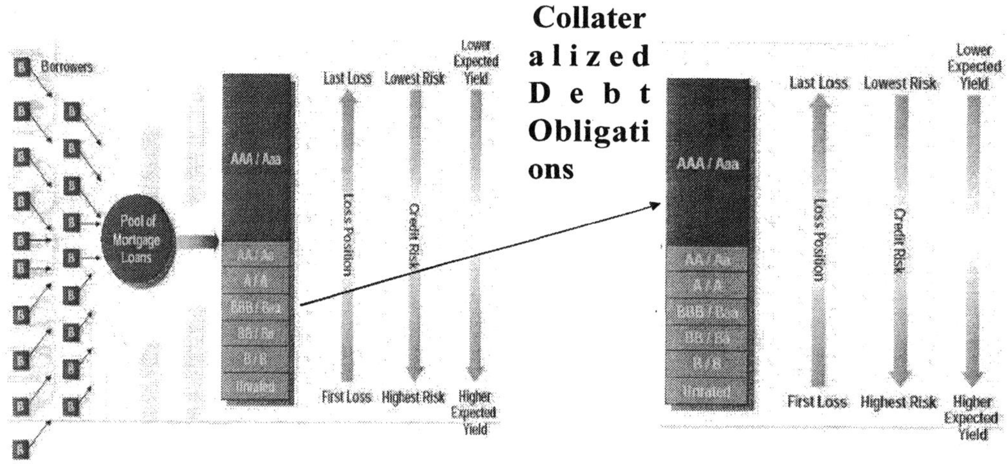

Needless to say, some very fancy mathematics must have producing investment grade CDO tranches built on pools of below investment grade paper backed in turn by risky mortgages. The basic insight is accessible enough, however.

Assume that there are two bonds, each of which will either pay $1 on maturity or default. There is a 10 percent risk of default on each bond. We can get a portfolio effect by placing both bonds in an SPE and dividing the payment stream into two tranches as follows: If both bonds default, neither tranche gets anything; if one bond defaults, the bottom tranche gets $0 and the top tranche gets $1; if neither defaults, both tranches get $1.

So far our slicing and dicing has directed the risk of loss to the bottom tranche. But how exactly does a high credit rating emerge for the top tranche? Make a further assumption: the 10 percent risk of default on the two bonds is *completely uncorrelated.* Given that, the risk of default on the top tranche declines to 1 percent while the risk of default on the bottom tranche is 19 percent. The result is intuitive. We have combined two bonds each of which carries a 10 percent risk of default. That creates a pooled 20 percent risk of default. The tranching reassigns the risk among the interest holders in the pool – five percent of the pooled risk (or one percent out of the total of 20 percent) goes to the top and 95 percent of the risk (or 19 percent of the total of 20 percent) goes to the bottom.

We are not yet at AAA for the top tranche, however. So let us add a third bond to the pool. This bond also has a 10 percent risk of default, risk that remains completely uncorrelated with the risk attached to the first two. Now we create three tranches. The top tranche only defaults if all three bonds default; the middle tranche defaults if two bonds default; the bottom tranche defaults if one bond defaults; if all three bonds pay, all three tranches get paid. With this arrangement, the top tier risk is 0.1 percent; the mid tier risk is 2.8 percent; and the bottom tier risk is 27.1 percent.

At this point we have roughed out the assumptions that yielded AAA ratings for the top tranches of mortgage-backed securitizations. Note that the tranches are directly supported by the pooled mortgages.

Having gotten that far, we are ready to create a collaterized debt obligation. Go back to the two bond pool. Assume that there are two such pools, each with bottom tranches of each holding out a 19 percent default risk. We take the notes in the two bottom tranches and resecuritize them into a new pool with two tranches. The top tier loses only if at least one bond defaults in each of the two underlying pools. Still assuming that defaults are completely uncorrelated, the default risk carried by the top tier is 3.6 percent. Voila!

All of the above follows from the assumption that default risk across the mortgages is completely uncorrelated. Now let us change this critical assumption respecting default correlation. Assume that the default risk on the bonds in the pools is 100% correlated. That is, all of the bonds will either default simultaneously or all will survive and pay 100 cents on the dollar. On this scenario, there is no risk enhancement for the top tranches – everybody gets paid or no one gets paid. The risk of default is 10 percent across the board, the tranching makes no difference, and a junk mortgage is a junk mortgage.

Clearly, the credit appeal of subprime securitization lay in the assumption that defaults would be uncorrelated. How could that have been projected? By hypothesis, systemic risk was thought to be negligible. And such would have been the case if real estate prices had continued to rise and the economy had stayed out of recession while the mortgages in the pools remained outstanding. Given that, default on any particular pooled mortgage could have resulted only from random, relatively uncorrelated events like catastrophic illness or accident on the part of a particular mortgagor.

But such has not been the case. The collapse in housing prices triggered widespread defaults. The defaults in turn caused credit to tighten, which in turn triggered recession. The recession triggered further real estate price declines and additional defaults due to job losses. Systemic risk proved salient after all and defaults have been highly correlated.

The market for new securitizations has dried up. Whither this mode of financing? Significantly, the Treasury and the Federal Reserve look to jump start the securitization market as one means to the end of economic recovery. This is the job of the Term Asset-Backed Securities Loan Facility or TALF. This supports the consumer and business credit markets by providing the financing to private investors to invest in securitized auto, student loan, small business, credit card and other consumer and business credit. As of this writing, the volume of TALF securitizations has not been impressive.

(C) TRANSACTION STRUCTURE

Insert after the first full paragraph on Casebook page 299:

Concord Real Estate CDO 2006-1, LTD. v. Bank of America N.A.

Court of Chancery of Delaware, 2010
--- A.2d ----, 2010 WL 2011616 (Del.Ch.)

LASTER, Vice Chancellor.

The plaintiffs are single-purpose entities that issued notes as part of a collateralized debt obligation known as Concord Real Estate CDO 2006-1 (the "Concord CDO"). The notes were issued subject to the Indenture Agreement for Concord Real Estate CDO 2006-1 dated December 21, 2006 (the "Indenture" or "IA"). The Indenture refers to plaintiff Concord Real Estate CDO 2006-1, Ltd.

as the Issuer and plaintiff Concord Real Estate CDO 2006-1, LLC as the Co-Issuer. Defendant Bank of America N.A. has been sued in its capacity as the Trustee under the Indenture * * *. The Trustee also serves as Paying Agent, Calculation Agent, Transfer Agent, Custodial Securities Intermediary, Backup Advancing Agent, and Notes Registrar, all of which are roles defined by the Indenture.

* * *

I. FACTUAL BACKGROUND

A. Concord Real Estate CDO 2006-1

In March 2006, Winthrop Realty Trust and Newkirk Realty Trust, Inc. formed Concord Debt Holdings LLC ("Concord Sponsor") to act as a sponsor of collateralized debt obligations and other structured financial products. In December 2006, Concord Sponsor put together the Concord CDO.

To assemble the Concord CDO, Concord Sponsor formed the Issuer and the Co-Issuer. The Issuer and Co-Issuer then issued notes with a face value of approximately $413,850,000 (the "Notes"), divided into tranches designated from Class A through Class H. Each Note will mature at par in December 2046 unless earlier redeemed or repaid. During the life of the Notes, each earns interest at a fixed spread over a published reference rate. The Issuer and Co-Issuer also issued $51,150,000 of preferred shares (the "Preferred Shares").

[The Notes and Preferred Shares, other than the Class G and H Notes and Preferred Shares, were issued subject to the Indenture in the Rule 144A private placement market. The G, H, and Preferred were not offered and are held by Concord Debt Funding Trust ("Concord Trust"), an affiliate of Concord Sponsor. The proceeds of the issuance of the Notes were invested in portfolio of assets, defined in the Indenture as "Collateral Interests," consisting of mortgage loans, mezzanine loans, real estate bank loans, collateralized mortgage-backed securities, other CDO securities, REIT debt, and other real estate related interests. Cash flow from the Collateral Interests is used to make payments on the Notes. The Indenture also allows specified amounts of cash flow to be reinvested in the Concord CDO and used to acquire other Collateral Interests.]

The different classes of Notes enjoy different priorities in the cash flows generated by the Collateral Interests, and they pay different rates of interest to compensate for their relative risk. So-called "super senior Notes"--the higher tranches--have first priority in payments of interest and principal but pay a lower rate of interest. So called "mezzanine Notes" are subordinate to the senior notes but pay a higher rate of interest. The equity tranche of Preferred Shares has the lowest priority of payment and receives any remaining cash flows. The sequential payout of available cash as it flows down the tiers of securities is commonly referred to as the "waterfall."

Section 11.1 of the Indenture sets forth a detailed waterfall for distribution of proceeds to the various holders of the Issuer and Co-Issuer's securities.

B. The Coverage Tests

The distribution of funds under the waterfall changes depending on the outcome of two coverage tests: the Par Value Test and the Interest Coverage Test. The Par Value Test resembles a leverage ratio, and the Interest Coverage Test resembles a debt service coverage ratio. For purposes of this dispute, only the Par Value Test is relevant.

Par value testing is performed at the Class A/B/C level, Class D level, Class E level, Class F level, and Class G level. The Par Value Test works the same way at each level, except that each level has its own compliance threshold.

For example, the Class F Par Value Test is defined as "[t]he test that is met as of any Measurement Date on which any Class F Notes remain Outstanding if the Class F Par Value Ratio on such Measurement Date is equal to or greater than 118.0%." The Par Value Ratio thresholds for the Class A/B/C, Class D, Class E, and Class G tests are, respectively, 135%, 126%, 122%, and 113%. The Class F Par Value Ratio is defined as follows:

> As of any Measurement Date, the number (expressed as a percentage) calculated by dividing (a) the Net Outstanding Portfolio Balance on such Measurement Date by (b) the sum of the Aggregate Outstanding Amount of the Class A Notes, the Class B Notes, the Class C Notes, the Class D Notes, the Class E Notes and the Class F Notes and the amount of any unreimbursed Interest Advances and any Class F Deferred Interest.

The Par Value Ratio for the Class A/B/C, Class D, Class E, and Class G tests are defined similarly, except that "Aggregate Outstanding Amount" is defined only with reference to the level of the security being tested and those classes senior to it.

The Par Value Ratio is thus a fraction with two inputs: the Net Outstanding Portfolio Balance, which serves as the numerator, and the

Aggregate Outstanding Amount, which serves as the denominator. The numerator is basically the value of the assets securing the Notes, and the denominator is the aggregate principal balance on the Notes through the class being tested. The resulting percentage quantifies the leverage of the Concord CDO through the tested class. If the percentage is equal to or greater than the compliance threshold, then the CDO passes the test. If not, the CDO fails the test.

If a Par Value Test is not met as of a given Measurement Date, then funds that otherwise would be used to pay interest on the class of Notes at the level where the test failed and on any junior securities are instead used to redeem the most senior class of Notes then outstanding. Redemptions continue until either the relevant Par Value Test is met or until the senior Notes are fully redeemed. Redeeming the senior Notes should result eventually in the Par Value Test being met, because redeeming Notes decreases the denominator in the test. Assuming that the numerator remains constant, decreasing the denominator increases the resulting percentage. Assuming the value of the Collateral Interests is stable, reducing the Aggregate Outstanding Amount by redeeming senior Notes should bring the Concord CDO back into compliance.

C. Concord Sponsor Anticipates A Par Value Test Failure.

In December 2009, Concord Sponsor became concerned that the Concord CDO might fail one or more levels of the Par Value Test because of a decline in the market value of the Collateral Interests. Through Concord Trust, Concord Sponsor approached the Trustee about canceling certain Notes. The Trustee took the position that Notes could not be canceled voluntarily under the terms of the Indenture.

[Nonetheless, Concord Trust formally renounced all of its rights, title, and interest in various Class C,D,E,F, and G Notes (the “Subject Notes”) with a principal amount aggregating $66.325 million, surrendering the Notes to the Issuer free of charge. The Issuer than delivered the Subject Notes for cancellation to the Trustee in its capacity as Notes Registrar and directed that the Notes be canceled. The Trustee declined to do so.]

The fate of the Subject Notes determines the outcome of the Par Value Tests at the Class E, F, and G levels for the Measurement Date that occurred on February 19, 2010. If the Subject Notes were "Outstanding," then the Par Value Ratios fell below their respective thresholds, as shown by the following table:

Testing Class	Aggregate Outstanding Amount Net	Outstanding Portfolio Balance	Par Value Ratio	Threshold	P/F
Class ABC	$292,950,000.00	$428,817,407.20	146.38%	135%	Pass
Class D	$330,150,000.00	$428,817,407.20	129.89%	126%	Pass
Class E	$352,237,000.00	$428,817,407.20	121.74%	122%	Fail
Class F	$376,650,000.00	$428,817,407.20	113.85%	118%	Fail
Class G	$395,250,000.00	$428,817,407.20	108.49%	113%	Fail

If the Subject Notes were no longer "Outstanding," then each Par Value Test was met, as shown by the following table:

Testing Class	Aggregate Outstanding Amount	Net Outstanding Portfolio Balance	Par Value Ratio	Threshold	P/F
Class ABC	$282,025,000.00	$428,817,407.20	152.05%	135%	Pass
Class D	$308,025,000.00	$428,817,407.20	139.22%	126%	Pass
Class E	$325,112,000.00	$428,817,407.20	131.90%	122%	Pass
Class F	$347,525,000.00	$428,817,407.20	123.39%	118%	Pass
Class G	$347,525,000.00	$428,817,407.20	123.39%	113%	Pass

When a Par Value Tests fails, then funds must be diverted to redeem the senior Notes. The following chart compares the allocation of cash flows if the Subject Notes were not canceled with the allocation of cash flows if the Subject Notes were canceled:

Security	Payments (Without Cancellation)	Payments (With Cancellation)
A-1	$88,942.17	$88,942.17
	$922,135.82 in redemptions	
A-2	$11,424.49	$11,424.49
B	$25,651.89	$25,651.89
C	$12,264.10	$5,860.98
D	$31,412.85	$21,955.22
E	$27,209.67	$21,050.01
F	0	$38,226.32
G	0	0
H	0	0
Preferred	0	$548,110.93

Thus, if the Subject Notes remain outstanding, then the Class A-1 Noteholders are entitled to have $922,135.82 of the principal amount of their Notes redeemed. If the Subject Notes are canceled, then no redemption payment is due, the Class F Notes receive $38,226.32 in interest, and the Preferred Shares receive $548,110.93 in distributions. In addition, if the Subject Notes are canceled, then the Issuer and Co-Issuer can reinvest an additional $406,710.55 of proceeds in the Concord CDO.

II. LEGAL ANALYSIS

[The Indenture is governed by New York law. Under New York law: (1) the construction and interpretation of an unambiguous written contract is an issue of law within the province of the court; (2) words of a contract are enforced in accordance with their plain meaning; (3) individual words and provisions should not be read in isolation, but rather in light of the plain purpose and object of the agreement; and (4) a contract should be read as a whole.]

Courts strive to give indenture provisions a consistent and uniform meaning because "[u]niformity in interpretation is important to the efficiency of capital markets." *Sharon Steel Corp. v. Chase Manhattan Bank, N.A.*, 691 F.2d 1039, 1048 (2d Cir.1982) (Winter, J.). "Whereas participants in the capital market[s] can adjust their affairs according to a uniform interpretation, ... the creation of enduring uncertainties as to the meaning of boilerplate provisions would decrease the value of all debenture issues and greatly impair the efficient working of capital markets." *Id.; accord Kaiser Aluminum Corp. v. Matheson,* 681 A.2d 392, 398-99 (Del.1996)* * * .

Courts enhance stability and uniformity of interpretation by looking to the multi-decade efforts of leading practitioners to develop model indenture provisions. [The Court then described Model Debenture Indenture and the *Commentaries on Indentures* (hereinafter, the "Commentaries") and the Model and Revised Model Simplified Indentures.]

A. The Common Law Rule That Governs Absent A Controlling Provision In The Indenture

The Indenture does not explicitly address the surrender of Notes for no consideration with an instruction that they be canceled. No provision expressly allows it. No provision expressly prohibits it. Unable to cite a provision directly on point, the parties have joined issue over two boilerplate provisions that speak indirectly to cancellation in general. I therefore first determine the common law rule that will apply to the surrender of the Subject Notes absent a governing contractual provision. I look to the common law because this body of jurisprudence provides a backdrop of standard default rules that supplement negotiated agreements and fill gaps when a contract is incomplete, whether by inadvertence or design. Parties can contract around virtually all common law rules. In a lengthy and sophisticated agreement like the Indenture, the terms of the agreement and not the common law will control many issues. But unless contradicted or altered by the parties' agreement, the common law rules form an implied part of every contract.

For over a century, New York courts have held that the delivery of a promissory note to the obligor with the intent to cancel the note discharges the obligation and cancels the debt. * * * I refer to this rule as the "Delivery Rule." [The Delivery Rule comports with black-letter authority and is codified in New York for negotiable instruments in UCC section 3-605. Moreover, the Rule reflects basic notions of property rights, which assume that a holder of property can alienate it as he or she sees fit.]

I conclude that absent a contrary provision in the Indenture, Concord Trust had the right to surrender the Subject Notes to the Issuer and Co-Issuer with the intent and for the purpose of discharging the contractual obligations the Subject Notes represented, and that this act operated as a release and discharge of the Subject Notes. Absent a contrary provision in the Indenture, the Subject Notes were discharged [on] the date on which Concord Trust surrendered them to the Issuer and Co-Issuer.

B. The Specific Provisions Of The Indenture

As noted, the Indenture does not specifically contract around the Delivery Rule. Implicitly recognizing the absence of any provision directly on point, the parties have joined issue over two boilerplate provisions that address cancellation generally: (i) Section 2.9, entitled "Cancellation," and (ii) the definition of "Outstanding," which drives the calculation of the Aggregate Outstanding Amount for purposes of the denominator in the Par Value Test. Neither provision alters the Delivery Rule.

Because the essence of their dispute is whether the Subject Notes should have been canceled, the parties have focused primarily on Section 2.9. This provision states:

> All Notes surrendered for payment, registration of transfer, exchange or redemption, or deemed lost or stolen, shall, if surrendered to any Person

> other than the Trustee, be delivered to the Trustee, and shall be promptly canceled by the Trustee and may not be reissued or resold. No Notes shall be authenticated in lieu of or in exchange for any Notes canceled as provided in this Section 2.9, except as expressly permitted by this Indenture. All canceled Notes held by the Trustee shall be destroyed or held by the Trustee in accordance with its standard retention policy unless the Issuer and the Co-Issuer shall direct by an Issuer Order that they be returned to them.

Citing the familiar maxim of *inclusio unius est exclusio alterius,* the Trustee argues that Section 2.9 identifies the exclusive instances in which Notes can be canceled and that only the Trustee can cancel Notes.

Although I agree with the Trustee that Section 2.9 identifies situations in which the Trustee must cancel Notes, I disagree that Section 2.9 eliminates the Delivery Rule. The venerable principle that the Trustee cites can be a helpful interpretive aid, but "[t]his maxim is not a rule of law" and is "not always dispositive."

[The court noted that the language of Section 2.9 does not attempt to define the term "cancellation." and is not framed as an exclusive provision.]

My interpretation of the plain language of Section 2.9 finds support in the Commentaries, the Model Simplified Indenture, and the Revised Model Simplified Indentures. The language of Section 2.9 has direct antecedents in the model provisions found in these documents. The model provision from the Commentaries states:

> All Debentures and coupons surrendered for payment, conversion or redemption shall, if surrendered to the Company or any agent of the Company, be delivered to the Trustee and, if not already cancelled, shall be promptly cancelled by it. *The Company may at any time deliver to the Trustee for cancellation any Debentures previously authenticated and delivered hereunder, together with all unpaid coupons appertaining thereto, which the Company may have acquired in any manner whatsoever, and all Debentures so delivered shall be promptly cancelled by the Trustee.* No Debentures shall be authenticated in lieu of or in exchange for any Debentures cancelled as provided in this Section, except as expressly permitted by this Indenture. All cancelled Debentures and coupons held by the Trustee shall be disposed of as directed by a Company Order.

Commentaries at 191-92 (emphasis added).

The model provision in the Commentaries thus expressly states that "[t]he Company may at any time deliver to the Trustee for cancellation any Debentures ... which the Company may have acquired in any manner whatsoever, and all Debentures so delivered shall be promptly cancelled by the Trustee." *Id.* at 191. The Commentaries explain that this language "specifically authorizes the Company to deliver to the Trustee for cancellation, debentures acquired by the Company." *Id.* at 192. The analysis continues:

> Typically, these would be treasury debentures acquired by purchase on the market that the Company desires to render no longer outstanding. *One might think that the Company's right to effect such cancellation would be implicit,* but instances are known where the propriety of such cancellation, in the absence of an express provision, was questioned.

Id. (emphasis added). The Commentaries thus view the explicit language addressing cancellation as confirming a right the issuer ordinarily would have. Although the Commentaries do not cite authorities, this appears to refer to the Delivery Rule.

Subsequent efforts at model provisions have continued this approach. * * *

Unlike the model provisions, Section 2.9 does not contain the language about an issuer's right to tender securities for cancellation. Because the history of the model provision shows that language was intended to confirm the common law right, the omission of the language from Section 2.9 does not alter the Delivery Rule.

The parties next focus on the definition of "Outstanding." The Indenture defines the term as follows:

> "Outstanding": With respect to the Notes, as of any date of determination, all of the Notes or any Class of Notes, as the case may be, theretofore authenticated and delivered under this Indenture except:
> (i) *Notes theretofore canceled by the Notes Registrar or delivered to the Notes Registrar for cancellation;*
> * * *

The parties debate subpart (i) of the definition, which refers to the cancellation of Notes by the Notes Registrar rather than the Trustee and argue over whether it conflicts with Section 2.9.

I conclude that subpart (i) of the definition of Outstanding and its reference to the Notes Registrar are consistent with the Delivery Rule. Section 2.5 of the Indenture makes clear that the Notes Registrar performs one of the administrative functions typically performed by a transfer agent: maintaining records identifying the owners of the Notes. Section 2.5(a) provides:

> The Issuer and Co-Issuer shall cause to be kept a register (the "Notes Register") in which, subject to such reasonable regulations as they may prescribe, the Issuer and the Co-Issuer shall provide for the registration of Notes and the registration of transfers of Notes. The Trustee is hereby initially appointed "Notes Registrar" for the purpose of registering Notes and transfers of such Notes with respect to the Notes Register and holding the Notes Register. Upon any resignation or removal of the Notes Registrar, the Issuer and the Co-Issuer shall promptly appoint a successor or, in the absence of such appointment, assume the duties of Notes Registrar.

Id. § 2.5(a) (emphasis added). Under Section 2.8, the Issuer, Co-Issuer, Trustee, and any of their agents "may treat as the owner of a Note the Person in whose name such Note is registered on the Notes Register...." *Id.* § 2.8. The Trustee currently serves as Notes Registrar.

The Notes Registrar thus takes care of the back-office function of maintaining the Notes Register. When Notes are canceled, the Notes Registrar records that fact on the Notes Register. *Id.* § 2.5(a). Because the Notes Registrar keeps the Notes Register, the term Outstanding is logically defined to exclude "Notes theretofore canceled by the Notes Registrar or delivered to the Notes Registrar for cancellation." *Id.* § 1.1 at 58. This definition recognizes that the Notes Registrar maintains the official ownership records of the Issuer and Co-Issuer, *viz.* the Notes Register, and thus it is the Notes Registrar's records that are used to determine what Notes are Outstanding.

I do not construe the definition of Outstanding as giving substantive authority to the Notes Registrar to determine whether or not to cancel Notes. The Indenture assigns ultimate responsibility for the Notes Register to the Issuer and Co-Issuer. *Id.* § 2.5(a) ("The Issuer and Co-Issuer shall cause to be kept a register...."). Unless they use an administrative agent like the Notes Registrar, the Issuer and Co-Issuer must keep track of the Notes themselves. * * *

Given this agency relationship, authority over the recording of ownership, including cancellation, rests with the Issuer and Co-Issuer. * * *

Except in situations when Section 2.9 assigns the Trustee a role in the cancellation process, the Trustee has no authority over cancellation. When the Trustee acts as Notes Registrar, it performs that function as agent of the Issuer and Co-Issuer. Notably, if the Issuer and Co-Issuer remove and replace the

Trustee as Notes Registrar, then the Trustee no longer bears any responsibility for maintaining the Notes Register or for verifying the ownership of Notes. Section 2.5(a) recognizes this fact. It provides that in such a case, the Trustee has the right to inspect the Notes Register and to rely on a certificate executed by an officer of the Notes Registrar as to the ownership of Notes. IA § 2.5(a).

I conclude that under the Indenture, the Issuer and Co-Issuer are responsible for maintaining the Notes Register. The Issuer and Co-Issuer therefore can instruct the Notes Registrar regarding the recordation of securities, including the cancellation of Notes. Except in situations where Section 2.9 of the Indenture empowers the Trustee to cancel Notes, the Issuer and Co-Issuer retain the authority to cancel Notes and to instruct the Notes Registrar to effect cancellation.

* * *

C. The Delivery Rule Is Consistent With The Reasonable Contractual Expectations Of The Senior Noteholders.

The Trustee argues that permitting the Subject Notes to be canceled would defeat the reasonable contractual expectations of the senior Noteholders by depriving them of the redemption payments they would receive if the Coverage Test failed. Under the Indenture, the Noteholders bargained for the return of their principal plus interest at the agreed-upon rate. Each Noteholder has a reasonable contractual expectation of receiving timely and periodic payments of principal and interest through the maturity of the Notes in December 2046.

In addition to this core entitlement, the Noteholders bargained for protections for their investment, including the right to redemption payments if a Coverage Test fails. The redemption payments are conditioned on the failure of a Coverage Test. The Noteholders did not bargain for a contractual right to hold the pool of Collateral Interests constant such that a Coverage Test must fail. The Noteholders also did not bargain for a covenant that would limit the ability of the Issuer or Co-Issuer to take actions designed to ensure that the Coverage Tests are met. The Indenture does not contain any covenant prohibiting the Issuer or Co-Issuer from taking actions that might affect the Coverage Tests.

"Issuers of corporate debt do not breach their contractual obligations by structuring transactions to avoid triggering a mandatory redemption provision in favor of Noteholders." *Law Debenture Trust,* 2007 WL 2248150, at *7 (applying New York law). The Noteholders purchased securities that carry protections in the form of a mandatory redemption provision triggered by the failure of a Coverage Test. As long as the Coverage Tests are met on each respective Measurement Date and timely payments of principal and interest are made, then the Noteholders' contractual expectations are being met. Provided that they do not run afoul of any other provision of the Indenture, the Issuer and Co-Issuer do not breach their contractual obligations by taking actions to remain in compliance with the Coverage Tests and avoid the mandatory redemption obligation. Permitting the cancellation of the Subject Notes in accordance with the Delivery Rule is thus consistent with and does not defeat the contractual expectations of the senior Noteholders.

* * *

Insert at the end of Section D at Casebook page 304:

(E) SPEs AS LEGAL ENTITIES

In re Parmalat Securities Litigation

United States District Court, Southern District of New York, 2010.
--- F.Supp.2d ----, 2010 WL 545964.

LEWIS A. KAPLAN, District Judge.

This case had its genesis in the desire of Parmalat, which collapsed in 2003, to raise money by selling a minority of the stock of its Brazilian subsidiary, Parmalat Administracao ("Parmalat Brazil"), at a time when that stock could not be sold in equity markets. Bank of America (together with its affiliates, "BoA") conceived of and Parmalat engaged in a pair of matched transactions that were intended to provide off-balance sheet debt financing to bridge the gap until the Parmalat Brazil stock could be sold on attractive terms.

In concept, the transactions were no different from many other structured finance deals. BoA arranged for the creation of two special purpose entities ("SPEs")-in this case, both Cayman Islands companies-that would exist only on paper and only for the purpose of completing the transaction. The SPEs would (a) borrow $300 million from institutional investors, and (b) buy the Parmalat Brazil stock from Parmalat Brazil for $300 million. The debt eventually was to have been repaid with the proceeds of the sale by the SPEs of the Parmalat Brazil stock.

This deal had at least two attractions to Parmalat beyond the fact that it raised $300 million. First, assuming that it was structured to conform to the relevant accounting rules-and no one suggests that it was not-the debt incurred by the SPEs would not appear on Parmalat's consolidated balance sheet. Second, by "selling" this minority interest to the SPEs for $300 million, the transaction implied a high value for Parmalat Brazil as a whole and thus for the majority stake in Parmalat Brazil that Parmalat continued to own.

But why would institutional investors pay $300 million for notes of the SPEs in circumstances in which the only source of money to pay the notes when due would have been the hoped-for proceeds of a minority interest in Parmalat Brazil that could not have been sold for such a price at the inception of the deal? The short answer is that they would not. So BoA, in order to make the deal salable, recommended and Parmalat provided two additional sources of funds to pay the debt in the event the Parmalat Brazil stock could not be sold at a price sufficient to satisfy the notes. The first was a "put" option to give the SPEs the right to sell their Parmalat Brazil stock to Parmalat Capital Finance Limited ("PCFL") for $300 million if that stock could not otherwise be sold for a sufficient sum. The second was a guarantee by Parmalat of PCFL's obligation to perform if the put option were exercised. Thus, the ability of the institutional investors to be repaid depended upon any one of three conditions being satisfied: (1) the successful sale of the SPEs' Parmalat Brazil stock for at least $300 million, (2) the performance by PCFL of its obligations under the put, or (3) Parmalat's performance of its guarantee.

In the end, none of these conditions was satisfied. The structure failed. The institutional investors-chief among them BoA, which had bought $165 million of the notes-were left holding the bag.

In hindsight, the reasons for this debacle are plain. Even when the deal closed, the likelihood that the Parmalat Brazil stock was worth or, in any reasonable time frame, likely to be worth $300 million was uncertain at best. The only apparently solid sources of funds to repay the debt issued by the SPEs were the PCFL put and the Parmalat guarantee. But Parmalat and its entire organization, including PCFL, collapsed in December 2003 upon the discovery of a massive fraud. This resulted in defaults on the PCFL put and on the Parmalat guarantee, not to mention a blizzard of lawsuits of which this is one. This case, however, is particularly interesting because the plaintiffs are the SPEs created by BoA, who claim that they were defrauded and otherwise wronged by the entity that created them and that held a majority of the debt they issued.

Like any other fraud plaintiffs, the SPEs argue that they would not have bought the overvalued Parmalat Brazil stock in the first place if they had known the truth regarding Parmalat Brazil and BoA's internal assessments of the deal. One focus of this case therefore must be on what BoA knew, when it knew it, what if any material information it failed to disclose, and the other facts pertinent to claims of fraud and breach of trust. But the fact that the plaintiffs are the SPEs creates a second focus.

SPEs formed to engage in structured finance transactions like this one have no past, no future, and no employees. They are creatures of the financial services companies that cause their creation. They are phantoms, endowed by law with legal personality but having no real existence. The questions whether these SPEs could have been deceived or whether they would have acted differently if only one or another piece of information had been fully and fairly disclosed therefore arise in a context rather different from that of the usual fraud or breach of fiduciary duty case.

In the last analysis, I conclude that BoA did not commit fraud because it lacked culpable intent. In the particular circumstances of this case, however, BoA owed the SPEs fiduciary duties and breached them by failing to disclose all material facts. But the SPEs were not injured because they never considered the business merits of this deal in the first place and would have gone forward regardless of any other or additional disclosures by BoA.

This conclusion would be almost inconceivable if the controversy had arisen between substantial and responsible companies. But it should not be surprising here. The SPE "directors" who nominally approved the deal were hired by BoA for a fee. They never met or discussed the transaction. They made no serious business judgment as to the desirability of the deal from the SPEs' standpoint-after all, had the deal worked, the SPEs neither would have benefitted nor been harmed. The directors consented to the transaction essentially on the basis that it was sponsored by Parmalat, then thought to be a reputable company, and BoA. In short, they were engaged to vote "yes." This they did. This they would have done even if the allegedly concealed information had been disclosed to them. Hence, there is no causal relationship between BoA's breach of fiduciary duty and any injury suffered by the SPEs.

I. Facts

Plaintiffs Food Holdings Limited ("FHL") and Dairy Holdings Limited ("DHL") (collectively, the "Companies") are two Cayman Islands SPEs that entered into the matched transactions at issue in this case. Defendants are Bank of America Corp., Bank of America, N.A., and Banc of America Securities, LLC (collectively, "BoA").

BoA created and used the Companies as vehicles for an investment in Parmalat's Brazilian operations.

Structured finance transactions typically involve an "originator" that transfers one or more assets to an SPE for the purpose of raising capital. The SPE is a separate corporate entity that raises funds from investors, uses the money to acquire specific assets from the originator, and later-if all goes well-repays the borrowed money with proceeds derived from the acquired assets. The SPE typically is liquidated once the transaction is completed.

As noted, structured transactions can be attractive means of raising capital because, perhaps among other things, the SPE's financial statements are not consolidated with those of the originator. Hence, the debt incurred by the SPE does not appear on the originator's consolidated balance sheet. In addition, such transactions are "bankruptcy remote" in that the bankruptcy of the sponsor usually would not affect the assets.

SPEs usually are located in and formed under the laws of tax neutral jurisdictions. The Caymans are a particularly attractive venue for SPEs because SPEs are not taxed there when they buy or sell assets. In addition, there are no foreign exchange controls or regulatory requirements applicable to Cayman Islands SPEs that lend, borrow, or issue debt securities.

[Parmalat was founded in 1961 as a small, family-run dairy distributor in Parma, Italy. It expanded rapidly in the 1990s by acquiring other food and dairy companies, including companies in Brazil. By 2003, Parmalat had operations in over thirty countries and was the leading milk distributor in Italy, Canada, and Brazil. It had tens of thousands of employees and reported more than $7 billion in revenues worldwide.

[Parmalat sought to raise hundreds of millions of dollars for its Brazilian subsidiary, Parmalat Brazil. In 1997, it contacted BoA to work on a deal that would achieve its objective. BoA agreed to structure a transaction allowing an SPE to sell debt to investors and then use the proceeds to purchase equity in Parmalat Brazil. An equity investor--BoA, a "pool of investors" led by BoA, or an SPE--would purchase a minority of the shares of Parmalat Brazil for $300 million. The investor was to be repaid with the proceeds of an anticipated initial public offering ("IPO") of the Parmalat Brazil shares. Repayment would be assured through a "put option ... in case the agreed price of the stocks to be placed is not consistent with the then prevailing market conditions."

[Luca Sala, an officer at BoA's Milan branch, served also as BoA's Parmalat relationship manager from 1997 through June 2003, and was instrumental in formulating the transaction for BoA. He was assisted by Luis Moncada , a senior credit officer at the Milan branch.

[Their proposals underwent multiple iterations before the transaction went through, however. Successive internal credit approval memoranda ("CAMs") and Standard Credit Memoranda ("SCMs") were sent to BoA superiors and rejected in 1988.

[There were a number of problems. First, Deloitte & Touche Corporate Finance in Sao Paolo ("Deloitte") performed a valuation of Parmalat Brazil. Deloitte issued a report that concluded that the equity value of Parmalat Brazil as a whole was between $1.36 billion and $1.57 billion, which implied a value of no more than $247 to $285 million for an 18.18 percent interest, the amount ultimately purchased. Second, the credit on the put option was to be Parmalat S.p.A., Parmalat Brazil's parent, the assets of which were essentially the same as those of Parmalat Brazil. Third, prospects for a successful Brazilian IPO were not promising..

[NationsBank took over BoA in September 1998. One month later, its investment banking arm, NationsBanc Montgomery Securities ("NMS"), valued Parmalat Brazil at between $9 million and roughly $2 billion according to various methodologies and assumptions.

[In January 1999, Moncada and Sala submitted a revised SCM, which yet again proposed the creation of an SPE to take on $300 million in debt and use the debt proceeds to purchase $300 million of Parmalat Brazil equity. As before, the debt ultimately was to be repaid with the proceeds of an anticipated public offering of the Parmalat Brazil shares. This time, however, repayment was to be assured by giving the SPE the right to put the Parmalat Brazil shares to a Parmalat Luxembourg subsidiary or to convert the SPE's investment into shares of Parmalat's Italian parent company. The performance by Parmalat Luxembourg under the put was to be fully guaranteed by Parmalat S.p.A. In addition, the proposal tweaked the framework of the debt tranches as follows:

(1) $150 million was to be underwritten by BoA and "sold down to zero in the U.S. private placement market," (2) $50 million was to be placed in the U.S. private placement market by NMS on a "best effort basis," and (3) $100 million was to come from an American investor. The SCM described the sale of debt in the U.S. private placement market as the "primary source of repayment" and the IPO of Parmalat Brazil shares as the "secondary source." BoA stood to receive a 1.5 percent fee "as well as most of the expected equity upside" for arranging the transaction.

[Unknown to BoA, Sala would be quoting a higher fee of 2.75 percent to Parmalat. Sala planned to pocket the difference himself. He would carry out the plan in full, siphoning the $3.75 million differential through a Swiss bank.

[This deal also was rejected within BoA. Despite that fact, work went ahead on the transaction, apparently in anticipation that it ultimately would be approved.

[BoA's counsel, Mayer Brown, already had retained Maples & Calder, a Cayman Islands law firm that had an extensive relationship with BoA and had worked on other BoA transactions, and its related entity, QSPV Limited ("Maples Finance"), to work on the proposed Parmalat transaction and to incorporate a Cayman Islands SPE. Among the tasks that Maples was to perform was to supply directors for the SPE. A Maples & Calder marketing brochure stated that the SPE directors it supplied typically approved structured transactions upon the receipt of the "fee[s] for undertaking the transaction[s]," the board's determination of the "overall integrity of the transaction documents," and a conclusion that "there is ultimately little risk to the SP[E]."

[In April, 1999, still long before BoA had approved any transaction, Bank of America Securities, LLC, and Bank of America, N.A., entered into an indemnification agreement with Parmalat S.p.A. in which they expressly acknowledged BoA's engagement ... to advise and assist FHL and DHL, the as-yet unformed SPEs, with respect to an as-yet unapproved $300 million private placement. Furthermore, in June 1999, BoA prepared and Parmalat chief financial officer Tonna approved a Parmalat private placement memorandum ("PPM") for use in selling the debt contemplated by the proposed transaction. The PPM included Parmalat's consolidated financial statements but contained also a disclaimer that stated that BoA "make[s] no representation or warranty, express or implied, and assume[s] no responsibility for the accuracy or completeness of the information contained herein and furnished herewith regarding Parmalat."

[On October 21, 1999, Maples & Calder sent BoA a letter quoting its fee for the deal. The letter stated that the necessary due diligence regarding investors and sources of funds would be the responsibility of Parmalat or BoA as opposed to the SPEs.

[Thereafter, Moncada finally got the deal approved. The revised structure added a credit default swap ("CDS") provision further to protect BoA. The deal closed inclusive of the swap.

[Neither FHL nor DHL had any management, staff, offices, or operations. Each had four directors-Hugh Thompson, Martin Couch, Phillip Hinds, and Anthony Baker-all supplied by Maples Finance for a fee. Each director served simultaneously on the boards of between three hundred and eight hundred other SPEs created and administered by Maples Finance.

[Each of the FHL and DHL boards approved the transactions. Although the FHL board "minutes" state that the board's formal approval came at a "meeting" at which "all the Directors were present in person or by proxy," no meeting in fact took place. The directors never met to discuss or deliberate and never asked any questions of BoA. Although Anthony Baker, the Companies' "lead director," did review the transaction documents, he approved the transaction based primarily on the reputations of Parmalat and BoA. He testified that the SPEs were not equipped to perform due diligence, which he understood to be the sole responsibility of BoA. Indeed, three of the four directors paid no material attention to the transactions at all and that none of the four evaluated the transactions from a business or economic perspective. Baker alone-simply read the contracts and other documents. Nor did Maples do anything more in terms of exercising business judgment. It did, however, issue an opinion letter to the FHL board on December 17, 1999-two days after the FHL board approved the deal-recommending its approval of the transaction based on its assessment of the transaction documents.

[From the perspective of the SPEs, these transactions were a $300 million equity purchase in Parmalat Brazil. Given the overall structure of the deals, however, BoA ultimately had come to view them internally as loans by the noteholders secured by (1) a pledge of Parmalat Brazil stock of uncertain value and liquidity, (2) the PCFL put, and (3) Parmalat's guarantee. In other words, the bank internally thought of these transactions in substance as loans made on the credit of Parmalat.

[Under the transaction documents, FHL and DHL and Parmalat Brazil entered into subscription agreements pursuant to which the Companies purchased Parmalat Brazil shares. Attached to those agreements was Parmalat Brazil's business plan, which contained Parmalat Brazil's 1998 annual financial statements and updated 1999 earnings projections. A comparison between the business plan earnings projections, on one hand, and even the downside projections upon which the Deloitte and NMS valuations rested, at least in part, shows that the outlook for Parmalat Brazil at the time of the closings was significantly worse than it had been when Deloitte and NMS had valued the company. The updated 1999 earnings projections in the business plan would have made clear to a knowledgeable business person aware of the Deloitte and NMS valuations that the minority interest in Parmalat Brazil the Companies bought probably was worth dramatically less than $300 million at the dates of the closings. BoA, however, never disclosed the Deloitte and NMS valuations to the Companies.

[The Companies also entered into support and inducement agreements with Parmalat S.p.A. and PCFL. These represented that the PPM "fairly describes, in all material respects, the general nature of the business and principal properties of Parmalat Italy and its Subsidiaries and does not contain any untrue statement of fact or omit to state any material of fact...." The Companies argue that BoA is chargeable with the Parmalat representations and that it thereby defrauded them because BoA knew that Parmalat's financial statements were materially false.

[Finally, BoA entered into management agreements, drafted by Mayer Brown, with the Companies. Pursuant to those agreements, each of the Companies appointed BoA "Manager," which "shall be fully invested with and responsible for the general management and conduct of the business of the [SPE] and shall advise the Board on all matters of policy." The Companies likewise "invest [ed] the Manager with all rights and powers" necessary to manage the SPEs' "day to day business affairs." In addition, BoA undertook to "keep the Board fully informed as to the discharge of the Manager's duties hereunder."

[In 2003, it became clear that Parmalat had perpetrated one of the largest financial frauds in history. From 1990 through 2003, it offered and sold more than $1 billion in debt securities in the United States based on fraudulent financial statements that concealed rising debts and shrinking assets and on materially false representations by its senior management. A subsequent investigation revealed that Parmalat in fact had operated at a loss during that period. In December 2003, Parmalat entered extraordinary administration in Italy upon the revelation of its fraud. Parmalat Brazil went into bankruptcy in Brazil, and PCFL was placed into liquidation. The Companies' Parmalat Brazil shares could not be sold. PCFL defaulted on the put, Parmalat S.p.A. defaulted on the guarantee, and the Companies defaulted on the notes. The noteholders filed "winding up" petitions in a Cayman Islands court, and the Companies too were placed into liquidation.]

II. Discussion

The Companies' fraud and breach of fiduciary duty claims share a common factual basis. They assert that BoA misstated or failed to disclose facts material to the SPEs' decisions to approve the transaction. * * *

* * *

A. The Fraud Claim

* * *

The Companies assert [that actors] at BoA, particularly those in the hierarchy that passed on the various deal proposals, knew or were recklessly indifferent to the fraudulent nature of Parmalat's financial statements and the vastly overstated picture of its financial soundness that Parmalat portrayed. The testimony of BoA's credit officers, including those who approved and promoted the transactions, however, reveals that BoA was unaware of Parmalat's fraud and that the Parmalat financial information contained in the PPM was inaccurate. In fact, BoA bought $165 million of the Companies' debt based on its faith in Parmalat's guarantee, whereas its fee for the deal was only $4.5 million. It would not have done so, even in the extraordinary atmosphere that brought about the financial crisis that befell the world in the fall of 2008, if it had had any real inkling that Parmalat was a financial house of cards. In short, there is no persuasive evidence that BoA knew of or recklessly disregarded Parmalat's disastrous financial situation. This aspect of the fraud claim lacks merit.

The Companies claim also that BoA fraudulently failed to disclose the Deloitte and NMS valuations and the earnings projections they contained which, they assert, were material to their decision to approve the transaction.

* * *

There is no persuasive evidence that BoA ever made the analysis that underlies this claim, i.e., a comparison of the projections disclosed in the business plan with those contained in the earlier Deloitte and NMS work coupled with an evaluation of the effect that the much poorer December 1999 EBIT figures would have had on the earlier valuations had those figures been known to Deloitte and NMS. The fact is that BoA ultimately viewed these transactions internally as loans on the strength of a pledge of Parmalat Brazil stock of uncertain value, the PCFL put, and Parmalat's guarantee. At the time it approved the transaction, BoA's credit group believed that the put and guarantee were reliable and compensated for the potential uncertainty of an IPO of Parmalat Brazil shares.

B. The Breach of Fiduciary Duty Claim

The alleged misstatements and omissions that ground plaintiffs' fraud claim are the basis of its claim of breach of fiduciary duty. Under New York law, a claim for breach of a fiduciary duty requires a showing of (1) the existence of a fiduciary relationship, (2) the intentional or negligent breach of that duty, and (3) damages suffered because of that breach. The Companies therefore need not prove *scienter* to recover on this theory, and the claim must be proven only by a preponderance of the evidence.

[The court concluded that despite the structure of negotiated contract, that BoA owed the Companies fiduciary duties, including a duties of perfect candor, full disclosure, and good faith. The court further found that BoA had breached the duty in failing to disclose details respecting its sequence of internal rejections of (and reservations respecting) the transaction and the Deloitte and NSM valuations.]

A plaintiff seeking damages for breach of fiduciary duty must demonstrate that the defendant's conduct proximately caused its injury. Where, as here, a plaintiff seeks compensatory damages for injuries allegedly sustained as a result a defendant's misstatements or omissions, it therefore must establish a causal link between the wrongful conduct and any damages sustained. The Court therefore passes to the question whether BoA's breach of its fiduciary duty proximately caused any loss to the Companies.

To be sure, disclosure to the directors of BoA's internal credit memoranda and the Deloitte and NMS materials would have been unusual for transactions like these. The Companies, moreover, emphasize Baker's testimony that the value of the Parmalat Brazil stock was material to the directors and that they would not have approved the transaction if they had known the stock was not worth $300 million. They likewise assert that it would have been illogical for the directors to have approved the purchase of stock worth a fraction of the purchase price. But Baker's claim is subject to substantial doubt in and of itself, and other evidence points in the opposite direction.

* * *

There is * * * ample evidence that the Companies' directors would have approved the transaction notwithstanding any disclosure of the internal credit memoranda and the Deloitte and NMS materials. Three of the four SPE directors testified that they did not engage in any substantive analysis of the transaction, read the transaction documents, or ask any questions of BoA. The board conducted no due diligence, and Baker, the only SPE director who reviewed even the transaction documents, testified that he approved the transaction based primarily on the reputation of the parties involved and saw "no reason" to carry out a detailed business analysis. He did not even review the financial statements or the PPM. * * * [None] of the directors of either company made any business judgment about the wisdom or attractiveness of the transactions. It was, quite simply, not the job they were hired to do. Nor is this surprising. As an expert on Caymans practice in these situations, Andrew Galloway, testified, it was the custom and practice of Caymans directors to assume the trustworthiness of the promoter and approve such transactions on the basis of its reputation.

In addition, the Companies' directors had a strong financial incentive not to disrupt or refuse approval for the transactions that BoA had assembled. The directors were employees of Maples Finance, a company controlled by Maples & Calder, which had a "preexisting" and "extensive relationship with BoA." As would have been expected of individuals who, as a result of their relationships with Maples Finance, served simultaneously as directors of several hundred companies, their common interest was to generate additional business for Maples and appointments as directors of SPEs for themselves in exchange for fees paid to Maples Finance, their employer. They therefore had a powerful motive to further Maples Finance's business relationship with BoA, of which the Food and Dairy Holdings transactions were only a small part.

In all of the circumstances, disclosure of the materials BoA withheld would not likely have altered the directors' decision to approve the deal. I therefore am not convinced that BoA's breach of fiduciary duty was a proximate cause of the Companies' alleged injury. While BoA most assuredly did not conduct itself in an appropriate manner, it is not liable for damages for its breach of duty.

(F) FINANCIAL COLLAPSE AND PROPOSED REFORM

In re Citigroup Inc. Shareholder Derivative Litigation

Delaware Court of Chancery, 2009
964 A.2d 106

CHANDLER, Chancellor.

* * *

I. BACKGROUND

A. The Parties

Citigroup is a global financial services company whose businesses provide a broad range of financial services to consumers and businesses. * * *

Defendants in this action are current and former directors and officers of Citigroup.* * * Plaintiffs allege that a majority of the director defendants were members of the Audit and Risk Management Committee ("ARM Committee") in 2007 and were considered audit committee financial experts as defined by the Securities and Exchange Commission.

Plaintiffs * * * are all owners of shares of Citigroup stock.

B. Citigroup's Exposure to the Subprime Crisis

Plaintiffs allege that since as early as 2006, defendants have caused and allowed Citigroup to engage in subprime lending that ultimately left the Company exposed to massive losses by late 2007. Beginning in late 2005, house prices, which many believe were artificially inflated by speculation and easily available credit, began to plateau, and then deflate. Adjustable rate mortgages issued earlier in the decade began to reset, leaving many homeowners with significantly increased monthly payments. Defaults and foreclosures increased, and assets backed by income from residential mortgages began to decrease in value. By February 2007, subprime mortgage lenders began filing for bankruptcy and subprime mortgages packaged into securities began experiencing increasing levels of delinquency. In mid-2007, rating agencies downgraded bonds backed by subprime mortgages.

Much of Citigroup's exposure to the subprime lending market arose from its involvement with collateralized debt obligations ("CDOs")-repackaged pools of lower rated securities that Citigroup created by acquiring asset-backed securities, including residential mortgage backed securities ("RMBSs"), and then selling rights to the cash flows from the securities in classes, or tranches, with different levels of risk and return. Included with at least some of the CDOs created by Citigroup was a "liquidity put"-an option that allowed the purchasers of the CDOs to sell them back to Citigroup at original value.

According to plaintiffs, Citigroup's alleged $55 billion subprime exposure was in two areas of the Company's Securities & Banking Unit. The first portion totaled $11.7 billion and included securities tied to subprime loans that were being held until they could be added to debt pools for investors. The second portion included $43 billion of super-senior securities, which are portions of CDOs backed in part by RMBS collateral.

By late 2007, it was apparent that Citigroup faced significant losses on its subprime-related assets, including the following as alleged by plaintiffs:

• *October 1, 2007:* Citigroup announced it would write-down approximately $1.4 billion on funded and unfunded highly leveraged finance commitments.

• *October 15, 2007:* Citigroup issued a press release reporting a net income of $2.38 billion, a 57% decline from the Company's prior year results.

• *November 4, 2007:* Citigroup announced significant declines on the fair value of the approximately $55 billion in the Company's U.S. subprime-related direct exposures, and estimated that further write downs would be between $8 and $11 billion.

• *November 6, 2007:* Citigroup disclosed that it provided $7.6 billion of emergency financing to the seven SIVs the Company operated after they were unable to repay maturing debt. The SIVs drew on the $10 billion of so-called committed liquidity provided by Citigroup. On December 13, 2007 Citigroup bailed out seven of its affiliated SIVs by bringing $49 billion in assets onto its balance sheet and taking full responsibility for the SIVs' $49 billion worth of assets.

• *January 15, 2008:* Citigroup announced it would take an additional $18.1 billion write-down for the fourth quarter 2007 and a quarterly loss of $9.83 billion. Citigroup also announced that the Company lowered its dividend to $0.32 per share, a 40% decline from the Company's previous dividend disbursement.

• By March 2008, Citigroup shares traded below book value and the Company announced that it would lay off an additional 2,000 employees, bringing

Citigroup's total layoff since the beginning of the subprime market crisis to more than 6,000.

• July 18, 2008: Citigroup announced it lost $2.5 billion in the second quarter, largely caused by $7.2 billion of write-downs of Citigroup's investments in mortgages and other loans and by weakness in the consumer market.

Plaintiffs also allege that Citigroup was exposed to the subprime mortgage market through its use of SIVs. Banks can create SIVs by borrowing cash (by selling commercial paper) and using the proceeds to purchase loans; in other words, the SIVs sell short term debt and buy longer-term, higher yielding assets. According to plaintiffs, Citigroup's SIVs invested in riskier assets, such as home equity loans, rather than the low-risk assets traditionally used by SIVs.

The problems in the subprime market left Citigroup's SIVs unable to pay their investors. The SIVs held subprime mortgages that had decreased in value, and the normally liquid commercial paper market became illiquid. Because the SIVs could no longer meet their cash needs by attracting new investors, they had to sell assets at allegedly "fire sale" prices. In November 2007, Citigroup disclosed that it provided $7.6 billion of emergency financing to the seven SIVs the Company operated after they were unable to repay maturing debt. Ultimately, Citigroup was forced to bail out seven of its affiliated SIVs by bringing $49 billion in assets onto its balance sheet, notwithstanding that Citigroup previously represented that it would manage the SIVs on an arms-length basis.

C. Plaintiffs' Claims

Plaintiffs allege that defendants are liable to the Company for breach of fiduciary duty for * * * failing to adequately oversee and manage Citigroup's exposure to the problems in the subprime mortgage market, even in the face of alleged "red flags"[.] * * * As will be more fully explained below, the "red flags" alleged in the eighty-six page Complaint are generally statements from public documents that reflect worsening conditions in the financial markets, including the subprime and credit markets, and the effects those worsening conditions had on market participants, including Citigroup's peers. By way of example only, plaintiffs' "red flags" include the following:

• *May 27, 2005:* Economist Paul Krugman of the *New York Times* said he saw "signs that America's housing market, like the stock market at the end of the last decade, is approaching the final, feverish stages of a speculative bubble."

• *May 2006:* Ameriquest Mortgage, one of the United States' leading wholesale subprime lenders, announced the closing of each of its 229 retail offices and reduction of 3,800 employees.

• *February 12, 2007:* ResMae Mortgage, a subprime lender, filed for bankruptcy. According to *Bloomberg,* in its Chapter 11 filing, ResMae stated that "[t]he subprime mortgage market has recently been crippled and a number of companies stopped originating loans and United States housing sales have slowed and defaults by borrowers have risen."

• *April 18, 2007:* Freddie Mac announced plans to refinance up to $20 billion of loans held by subprime borrowers who would be unable to afford their adjustable-rate mortgages at the reset rate.

• *July 10, 2007:* Standard and Poor's and Moody's downgraded bonds backed by subprime mortgages.

• *August 1, 2007:* Two hedge funds managed by Bear Stearns that invested heavily in subprime mortgages declared bankruptcy.

• *August 9, 2007:* American International Group, one of the largest United States mortgage lenders, warned that mortgage defaults were spreading beyond the subprime sector, with delinquencies becoming more common among borrowers in the category just above subprime.

• *October 18, 2007:* Standard & Poor's cut the credit ratings on $23.35 billion of securities backed by pools of home loans that were offered to borrowers during the first half of the year. The downgrades even hit securities rated AAA, which was the highest of the ten investment-grade ratings and the rating of government debt.

* * *

III. THE MOTION TO DISMISS UNDER RULE 23.1

A. The Legal Standard for Demand Excused

* * *

Under the familiar *Aronson* test, to show demand futility, plaintiffs must provide particularized factual allegations that raise a reasonable doubt that "(1) the directors are disinterested and independent [or] (2) the challenged transaction was otherwise the product of a valid exercise of business judgment." Where, however, plaintiffs complain of board inaction and do not challenge a specific decision of the board, there is no "challenged transaction," and the ordinary *Aronson* analysis does not apply. Instead, to show demand futility where the subject of the derivative suit is not a business decision of the board, a plaintiff must allege particularized facts that "create a reasonable doubt that, as of the time the complaint is filed, the board of directors could have properly exercised its independent and disinterested business judgment in responding to a demand."

* * *

B. Demand Futility Regarding Plaintiffs' Fiduciary Duty Claims

Plaintiffs' argument is based on a theory of director liability famously articulated by former-Chancellor Allen in *In re Caremark.* * * *

In *Stone v. Ritter,* the Delaware Supreme Court approved the *Caremark* standard for director oversight liability and made clear that liability was based on the concept of good faith, which the *Stone* Court held was embedded in the fiduciary duty of loyalty and did not constitute a freestanding fiduciary duty that could independently give rise to liability. As the *Stone* Court explained:

> *Caremark* articulates the necessary conditions predicate for director oversight liability: (a) the directors utterly failed to implement any reporting or information system or controls; *or* (b) having implemented such a system or controls, consciously failed to monitor or oversee its operations thus disabling themselves from being informed of risks or problems requiring their attention. In either case, imposition of liability requires a showing that the directors knew that they were not discharging their fiduciary obligations. Where directors fail to act in the face of a known duty to act, thereby demonstrating a conscious disregard for their responsibilities, they breach their duty of loyalty by failing to discharge that fiduciary obligation in good faith.

Thus, to establish oversight liability a plaintiff must show that the directors *knew* they were not discharging their fiduciary obligations or that the directors demonstrated a *conscious* disregard for their responsibilities such as by failing to act in the face of a known duty to act. The test is rooted in concepts of bad faith; indeed, a showing of bad faith is a *necessary condition* to director oversight liability.

1. *Plaintiffs' Caremark Allegations*

Plaintiffs' theory of how the director defendants will face personal liability is a bit of a twist on the traditional *Caremark* claim. In a typical *Caremark* case, plaintiffs argue that the defendants are liable for damages that arise from a failure to properly monitor or oversee employee misconduct or violations of law. * * * In contrast, plaintiffs' *Caremark* claims are based on defendants' alleged failure to properly monitor Citigroup's *business risk,* specifically its exposure to the subprime mortgage market. In their answering brief, plaintiffs allege that the director defendants are personally liable under *Caremark* for failing to "make a good faith attempt to follow the procedures put in place or fail[ing] to assure that adequate and proper corporate information and reporting systems existed that would enable them to be fully informed regarding Citigroup's risk to the subprime mortgage market." Plaintiffs point to so-called "red flags" that should have put defendants on notice of the problems in the subprime mortgage market and further allege that the board should have been especially conscious of these red flags because a majority of the directors (1) served on the Citigroup board during its previous Enron related conduct and (2) were members of the ARM Committee and considered financial experts.

Although these claims are framed by plaintiffs as *Caremark* claims, plaintiffs' theory essentially amounts to a claim that the director defendants should be personally liable to the Company because they failed to fully recognize the risk posed by subprime securities. When one looks past the lofty allegations of duties of oversight and red flags used to dress up these claims, what is left appears to be plaintiff shareholders attempting to hold the director defendants personally liable for making (or allowing to be made) business decisions that, in hindsight, turned out poorly for the Company. Delaware Courts have faced these types of claims many times and have developed doctrines to deal with them-the fiduciary duty of care and the business judgment rule. These doctrines properly focus on the decision-making process rather than on a substantive evaluation of the merits of the decision. This follows from the inadequacy of the Court, due in part to a concept known as hindsight bias, to properly evaluate whether corporate decision-makers made a "right" or "wrong" decision.

* * *

The Delaware Supreme Court has stated that bad faith conduct may be found where a director "intentionally acts with a purpose other than that of advancing the best interests of the corporation, ... acts with the intent to violate applicable positive law, or ... intentionally fails to act in the face of a known duty to act, demonstrating a conscious disregard for his duties." More recently, the Delaware Supreme Court held that when a plaintiff seeks to show that demand is excused because directors face a substantial likelihood of liability where "directors are exculpated from liability except for claims based on 'fraudulent,' 'illegal' or 'bad faith' conduct, a plaintiff must also plead particularized facts that demonstrate that the directors acted with scienter, *i.e.,* that they had 'actual or constructive knowledge' that their conduct was legally improper." A plaintiff can thus plead bad faith by alleging with particularity that a director *knowingly* violated a fiduciary duty or failed to act in violation of a *known* duty to act, demonstrating a *conscious* disregard for her duties.

* * * A plaintiff can show bad faith conduct by, for example, properly alleging particularized facts that show that a director *consciously* disregarded an obligation to be reasonably informed about the business and its risks or *consciously* disregarded the duty to monitor and oversee the business.

The Delaware Supreme Court made clear in *Stone* that directors of Delaware corporations have certain responsibilities to implement and monitor a system of oversight; however, this obligation does not eviscerate the core protections of the business judgment rule-protections designed to allow corporate managers and directors to pursue risky transactions without the specter of being held personally liable if those decisions turn out poorly. Accordingly, the burden required for a plaintiff to rebut the presumption of the business judgment rule by showing gross negligence is a difficult one, and the burden to show bad faith is even higher. * * *

To the extent the Court allows shareholder plaintiffs to succeed on a theory that a director is liable for a failure to monitor business risk, the Court risks undermining the well settled policy of Delaware law by inviting Courts to perform a hindsight evaluation of the reasonableness or prudence of directors' business decisions. Risk has been defined as the chance that a return on an investment will be different that expected. The essence of the business judgment of managers and directors is deciding how the company will evaluate the trade-off between risk and return. Businesses-and particularly financial institutions-make returns by taking on risk; a company or investor that is willing to take on more risk can earn a higher return. Thus, in almost any business transaction, the parties go into the deal with the knowledge that, even if they have evaluated the situation correctly, the return could be different than they expected.

It is almost impossible for a court, in hindsight, to determine whether the directors of a company properly evaluated risk and thus made the "right" business decision. In any investment there is a chance that returns will turn out lower than expected, and generally a smaller chance that they will be far lower than expected. When investments turn out poorly, it is possible that the decision-maker evaluated the deal correctly but got "unlucky" in that a huge loss-the probability of which was very small-actually happened. It is also possible that the decision-maker improperly evaluated the risk posed by an investment and that the company suffered large losses as a result.

Business decision-makers must operate in the real world, with imperfect information, limited resources, and an uncertain future. To impose liability on directors for making a "wrong" business decision would cripple their ability to earn returns for investors by taking business risks. Indeed, this kind of judicial second guessing is what the business judgment rule was designed to prevent, and even if a complaint is framed under a *Caremark* theory, this Court will not abandon such bedrock principles of Delaware fiduciary duty law. With these considerations and the difficult standard required to show director oversight liability in mind, I turn to an evaluation of the allegations in the Complaint.

a. The Complaint Does Not Properly Allege Demand Futility for Plaintiffs' Fiduciary Duty Claims

In this case, plaintiffs allege that the defendants are liable for failing to properly monitor the risk that Citigroup faced from subprime securities. * * *

The allegations in the Complaint amount essentially to a claim that Citigroup suffered large losses and that there were certain warning signs that could or should have put defendants on notice of the business risks related to Citigroup's investments in subprime assets. * * *

Plaintiffs do not contest that Citigroup had procedures and controls in place that were designed to monitor risk. Plaintiffs admit that Citigroup established the ARM Committee and in 2004 amended the ARM Committee charter to include the fact that one of the purposes of the ARM Committee was to assist the board in fulfilling its oversight responsibility relating to policy standards and guidelines for risk assessment and risk management. The ARM Committee was also charged with, among other things, (1) discussing with management and independent auditors the annual audited financial statements, (2) reviewing with management an evaluation of Citigroup's internal control structure, and (3) discussing with management Citigroup's major credit, market, liquidity, and operational risk exposures and the steps taken by management to monitor and control such exposures, including Citigroup's risk assessment and risk management policies. According to plaintiffs' own allegations, the ARM Committee met eleven times in 2006 and twelve times in 2007.

Plaintiffs nevertheless argue that the director defendants breached their duty of oversight either because the oversight mechanisms were not adequate or because the director defendants did not make a good faith effort to comply with the established oversight procedures. To support this claim, the Complaint alleges numerous facts that plaintiffs argue should have put the director defendants on notice of the impending problems in the subprime mortgage market and Citigroup's exposure thereto. Plaintiffs summarized some of these "red flags" in their answering brief as follows:

• the steady decline of the housing market and the impact the collapsing bubble would have on mortgages and subprime backed securities since as early as 2005;

• December 2005 guidance from the FASB staff-"The FASB staff is aware of loan products whose contractual features may increase the exposure of the originator, holder, investor, guarantor, or servicer to risk of nonpayment or realization.";

• the drastic rise in foreclosure rates starting in 2006;

• several large subprime lenders reporting substantial losses and filing for bankruptcy starting in 2006;

• billions of dollars in losses reported by Citigroup's peers, such as Bear Stearns and Merrill Lynch.

* * *

The warning signs alleged by plaintiffs are not evidence that the directors consciously disregarded their duties or otherwise acted in bad faith; at most they evidence that the directors made bad business decisions. The "red flags" in the Complaint amount to little more than portions of public documents that reflected the worsening conditions in the subprime mortgage market and in the economy generally. Plaintiffs fail to plead "particularized facts suggesting that the Board was presented with 'red flags' alerting it to potential misconduct" at the Company. * * *

* * *

To recognize such claims under a theory of director oversight liability would undermine the long established protections of the business judgment rule. It is well established that the mere fact that a company takes on business risk and suffers losses-even catastrophic losses-does not evidence misconduct, and without more, is not a basis for personal director liability. That there were signs in the market that reflected worsening conditions and suggested that conditions may deteriorate even further is not an invitation for this Court to disregard the presumptions of the business judgment rule and conclude that the directors are liable because they did not properly evaluate business risk. What plaintiffs are asking the Court to conclude from the presence of these "red flags" is that the directors failed to see the extent of Citigroup's business risk and therefore made a "wrong" business decision by allowing Citigroup to be exposed to the subprime mortgage market.

This Court's recent decision in *American International Group, Inc. Consolidated Derivative Litigation* [--- A.2d ----, 2009 WL 366613 (Del.Ch. Feb. 10, 2009)] demonstrates the stark contrast between the allegations here and allegations that are sufficient to survive a motion to dismiss. In *AIG,* the Court faced a motion to dismiss a complaint that included "well-pled allegations of pervasive, diverse, and substantial financial fraud involving managers at the highest levels of AIG." In concluding that the complaint stated a claim for relief * * * the Court held that the factual allegations in the complaint were sufficient to support an inference that AIG executives running those divisions knew of and approved much of the wrongdoing. The Court reasoned that huge fraudulent schemes were unlikely to be perpetrated without the knowledge of the executive in charge of that division of the company. Unlike the allegations in this case, the defendants in *AIG* allegedly failed to exercise reasonable oversight over pervasive *fraudulent* and *criminal* conduct. Indeed, the Court in *AIG* even stated that the complaint there supported the assertion that top AIG officials were leading a "criminal organization" and that "[t]he diversity, pervasiveness, and materiality of the alleged financial wrongdoing at AIG is extraordinary."

Contrast the *AIG* claims with the claims in this case. Here, plaintiffs argue that the Complaint supports the reasonable conclusion that the director defendants acted in bad faith by failing to see the warning signs of a deterioration in the subprime mortgage market and failing to cause Citigroup to change its investment policy to limit its exposure to the subprime market. Director oversight duties are designed to ensure reasonable reporting and information systems exist that would allow directors to know about and prevent wrongdoing that could cause losses for the Company. There are significant differences between failing to oversee employee fraudulent or criminal conduct and failing to recognize the extent of a Company's business risk. Directors should, indeed must under Delaware law, ensure that reasonable information and reporting systems exist that would put them on notice of fraudulent or criminal conduct within the company. Such oversight programs allow directors to intervene and prevent frauds or other wrongdoing that could expose the company to risk of loss as a result of such conduct. While it may be tempting to say that directors have the same duties to monitor and oversee business risk, imposing *Caremark*-type duties on directors to monitor business risk is fundamentally different. Citigroup was in the business of taking on and managing investment and other business risks. To impose oversight liability on directors for failure to monitor "excessive" risk would involve courts in conducting hindsight evaluations of decisions at the heart of the business judgment of directors. Oversight duties under Delaware law are not designed to subject directors, even expert directors, to *personal liability* for failure to predict the future and to properly evaluate business risk.

Instead of alleging facts that could demonstrate bad faith on the part of the directors, by presenting the Court with the so called "red flags," plaintiffs are inviting the Court to engage in the exact kind of judicial second guessing that is proscribed by the business judgment rule. * * *

Securities and Exchange Commission, Asset-Backed Securities, Release Nos. 33-9117; 34-61858

April 7, 2010

I. Executive Summary

A. Background

The recent financial crisis highlighted that investors and other participants in the securitization market did not have the necessary tools to be able to fully understand the risk underlying those securities and did not value those securities properly or accurately. The severity of this lack of understanding and the extent to which it pervaded the market and impacted the U.S. and worldwide economy calls into question the efficacy of several aspects of our regulation of asset-backed securities. In light of the problems exposed by the financial crisis, we are proposing significant revisions to our rules governing offers, sales and reporting with respect to asset-backed securities. These proposals are designed to improve investor protection and promote more efficient asset-backed markets.

Securitization generally is a financing technique in which financial assets, in many cases illiquid, are pooled and converted into instruments that are offered and sold in the capital markets as securities. This financing technique makes it easier for lenders to exchange payment streams coming from the loans for cash so that they can make additional loans or credit available to a wide range of borrowers and companies seeking financing. Some of the types of assets that are financed today through securitization include residential and commercial mortgages, agricultural equipment leases, automobile loans and leases, student loans and credit card receivables. Throughout this release, we refer to the securities sold through such vehicles as asset-backed securities, ABS, or structured finance products.

At its inception, securitization primarily served as a vehicle for mortgage financing. Since then, asset-backed securities have played a significant role in both the U.S. and global economy. At the end of 2007, there were more than $7 trillion of both agency and non-agency mortgage-backed securities and nearly $2.5 trillion of asset-backed securities outstanding. Securitization can provide liquidity to nearly all major sectors of the economy including the residential and commercial real estate industry, the automobile industry, the consumer credit industry, the leasing industry, and the commercial lending and credit markets.

Many of the problems giving rise to the financial crisis involved structured finance products, including mortgage-backed securities. Many of these mortgage-backed securities were used to collateralize other debt obligations such as collateralized debt obligations and collateralized loan obligations (CDOs or CLOs), types of asset-backed securities that are sold in private placements. As the default rate for subprime and other mortgages soared, such securities, including those with high credit ratings, lost their value. CDOs were noted, in particular, to have contributed to the collapse in liquidity during the financial crisis. As the crisis unfolded, investors increasingly became unwilling to purchase these securities, and today, this sentiment remains, as new issuances of asset-backed securities, except for government-sponsored issuances, have recently dramatically decreased. The absence of this financing option has negatively impacted the availability of credit.

The financial crisis highlighted a number of concerns with the operation of our rules in the securitization market. Certain regulations for asset-backed securities rely on the ratings for those securities provided by the ratings agencies, and much has been written about the failures of those ratings accurately to measure and describe the risks associated with certain of those products that were realized during the financial crisis.

In addition, investors have expressed concern regarding a lack of time to analyze securitization transactions and make investment decisions. While the Commission historically has not built minimum time periods into its registration process to deliberately slow down the market, and instead has believed investors can insist on adequate time to analyze securities (and refuse to invest if not provided sufficient time), we have been told that this is not generally possible in this market, particularly in an active market. In addition, market participants have expressed a desire for expanded disclosure relating to the assets underlying securitizations. Investors have complained that the mechanisms for enforcing the representations and warranties contained in securitization transaction documents are weak, and thus are not confident that even strong representations and warranties provide them with adequate protection. In the private market, we believe that, in many cases, investors did not have the information necessary to understand and properly analyze structured products, such as CDOs, that were sold in transactions in reliance on exemptions from registration. As a result of these and other factors, the financial crisis resulted in an absence of confidence in much of the securitization market.

We are proposing a number of changes to the offering process, disclosure, and reporting for asset-backed securities, which are designed to enhance investor protection in this market. The proposals are intended to provide investors with timely and sufficient information, including information in and about the private market for asset-backed securities, reduce the likelihood of undue reliance on credit ratings, and help restore investor confidence in the representations and warranties regarding the assets. Although these revisions are comprehensive and therefore would impose new burdens, if adopted, we believe they would protect investors and promote efficient capital formation. The proposals cover the following areas:

- revisions to the shelf offering process and criteria and prospectus delivery requirements;
- Securities Act and Exchange Act disclosure requirements, including new requirements to disclose standardized asset-level information or grouped asset data and a computer program that gives effect to the cash flow provisions of the transaction agreement (often referred to as the "waterfall"); and
- changes to the Securities Act safe harbors for exempt offerings and exempt resales for asset-backed securities.

In addition, we are proposing clarifying, technical and other changes to the current rules. The proposals are designed to address issues that contributed to or arose from the financial crisis. These proposals are also designed to be forward looking; some of these proposals are designed to improve areas that have the potential to raise issues similar to the ones highlighted in the financial crisis.

* * *

Our proposals are generally consistent with global initiatives that seek to improve practices in the securitization market. These initiatives include calls by international organizations to require greater disclosure by issuers of securitized products, including initial and ongoing information about underlying asset pool performance. Our focus on both the public and private markets for securitized products is supported by recommendations from international regulators about the type of disclosure that should be provided to investors in the private markets.

B. Securities Act Registration

Securities Act shelf registration provides important timing and flexibility benefits to issuers. An issuer with an effective shelf registration statement can conduct delayed offerings "off the shelf" under Securities Act Rule 415 without further staff clearance. Under our current rules, asset-backed securities may be registered on a Form S-3 registration statement and later offered "off the shelf" if, in addition to meeting other specified criteria, the securities are rated investment grade by a nationally recognized statistical rating organization (NRSRO). * * * [W]e are proposing to repeal that criterion and establish other criteria for shelf eligibility. We are also proposing changes to the Securities Act rules and forms for issuances of asset-backed securities.

We have undertaken a Commission-wide effort to consider whether references to NRSRO credit ratings in all the Commission's regulations are necessary or appropriate and whether they could cause investors to unduly rely on ratings. In this release, we are proposing to eliminate the current means of establishing shelf eligibility for an ABS transaction based on the credit ratings of the securities to be issued. Instead, we are proposing to require for shelf eligibility the following:

- A certification filed at the time of each offering off of a shelf registration statement, or takedown, by the chief executive officer of the depositor that the assets in the pool have characteristics that provide a reasonable basis to believe that they will produce, taking into account internal credit enhancements, cash flows to service any payments due and payable on the securities as described in the prospectus;
- Retention by the sponsor of a specified amount of each tranche of the securitization, net of the sponsor's hedging (also known as "risk retention" or "skin-in-the-game");
- A provision in the pooling and servicing agreement that requires the party obligated to repurchase the assets for breach of representations and warranties to periodically furnish an opinion of an independent third party regarding whether the obligated party acted consistently with the terms of the pooling and servicing agreement with respect to any loans

that the trustee put back to the obligated party for violation of representations and warranties and which were not repurchased; and

- An undertaking by the issuer to file Exchange Act reports so long as non-affiliates of the depositor hold any securities that were sold in registered transactions backed by the same pool of assets.

We also are proposing to replace Forms S-1 and S-3 with new forms for registered ABS offerings -- proposed Forms SF-1 and SF-3 -- and to revise the shelf offering structure for those securities. Form SF-3 would be the form used for ABS shelf offerings.

Given many ABS investors' stated desire for more time to consider the transaction and for more detailed information regarding the pool assets, we are proposing to revise the filing deadlines in shelf offerings to provide investors with additional time to analyze transaction-specific information prior to making an investment decision. These changes are designed to promote independent analysis of ABS by investors rather than reliance on credit ratings. Under the proposed ABS shelf procedures, an ABS issuer would be required to file a preliminary prospectus with the Commission for each takedown off of the proposed new shelf registration form for ABS (Form SF-3) at least five business days prior to the first sale in the offering. Under the proposal, issuers would use one prospectus for each transaction and the current practice of using core or base prospectuses plus supplements would be eliminated for ABS.

C. Disclosure

In 2004, we adopted a new set of rules prescribing the disclosure requirements for asset-backed issuers. Many disclosure requirements of Regulation AB are principles-based. Regulation AB currently requires that material, aggregate information about the composition and characteristics of the asset pool be filed with the Commission and provided to investors. * * * [W]e are proposing additional, and, in some cases, revised disclosure requirements for ABS offerings and ongoing reporting. For each loan or asset in the asset pool, we are proposing to require disclosure of specified data relating to the terms of the asset, obligor characteristics, and underwriting of the asset. Such data would be provided in a machine-readable, standardized format so that it is most useful to investors and the markets. Under our proposal, issuers would be required to provide the asset-level data or grouped account data at the time of securitization, when new assets are added to the pool underlying the securities, and on an ongoing basis.

We are proposing to require the filing of a computer program (the "waterfall computer program," as defined in the proposed rule) of the contractual cash flow provisions of the securities in the form of downloadable source code in Python, a commonly used computer programming language that is open source and interpretive. The computer program would be tagged in XML and required to be filed with the Commission as an exhibit. Under our proposal, the filed source code for the computer program, when downloaded and run (by loading it into an open "Python" session on the investor's computer), would be required to allow the user to programmatically input information from the asset data file that we are proposing to require as described above. We believe that, with the waterfall computer program and the asset data file, investors would be better able to conduct their own evaluations of ABS and may be less likely to be dependent on the opinions of credit rating agencies.

We also are proposing additional requirements to refine current disclosure requirements for asset-backed securities. Among other things, we are proposing to require:

- aggregated and loan-level data relating to the type and amount of assets that do not meet the underwriting criteria that is specified in the prospectus;
- for certain identified originators, information relating to the amount of the originator's publicly securitized assets that, in the last three years, has been the subject of a demand to repurchase or replace;
- for the sponsor, information relating to the amount of publicly securitized assets sold by the sponsor that, in the last three years, has been the subject of a demand to repurchase or replace;
- additional information regarding originators and sponsors;
- descriptions relating to static pool information, such as a description of the methodology used in determining or calculating the characteristics of the pool performance as well as any terms or abbreviations used;
- that static pool information for amortizing asset pools comply with the Item 1100(b) requirements for the presentation of historical delinquency and loss information; and
- the filing of Form 8-K for a one percent or more change in any material pool characteristic from what is described in the prospectus (rather than for a five percent or more change, as currently required).

We also are proposing to limit some of the existing exceptions to the discrete pool requirement in the definition of an asset-backed security. This is intended to not only address recent concerns arising out of the financial crisis but also serve to protect against future practices of participants along the chain of securitization that could result in the addition of assets into a securitization pool without a clear understanding of their quality.

D. Privately-Issued Structured Finance Products

A significant portion of securities transactions, including the offer and sale of all CDOs and ABCP, is conducted in the exempt private placement market, which includes both offerings eligible for Rule 144A resales and other private placements. CDOs are typically sold by the issuer in a private placement to one or more initial purchaser or purchasers in reliance upon the Section 4(2) private offering exemption in the Securities Act, which is available only to the issuer, followed by resales of the securities to "qualified institutional buyers" in reliance upon Rule 144A. Subsequent resales may also be made in reliance upon Rule 144A. Rule 144A provides a safe harbor for resellers from being deemed an underwriter within the meaning of Sections 2(a)(11) and 4(1) of the Securities Act for the sale of securities to qualified institutional buyers. If the conditions of the Rule 144A safe harbor are satisfied, sellers may rely on the exemption from Securities Act registration provided by Section 4(1) for transactions by persons other than issuers, underwriters or dealers.

Some have concluded that the events of the financial crisis have demonstrated that a lack of understanding of CDOs and other privately offered structured finance products by investors, rating agencies and other market participants may have significant consequences to the entire financial system. For example, the ratings of these products proved inaccurate, which significantly contributed to the financial crisis. This lack of understanding by credit rating agencies, investors, and other market participants indicates that the offering processes and disclosure available in the public and private market were inadequate to provide appropriate investor protection. Further, these securities are issued by special purpose vehicles whose only purpose is holding financial assets, with numerous parties involved in the securitization process. As a result, information about those assets and the structure of the vehicle is critical to an informed investment decision.

The safe harbors of Rule 144A and Regulation D that provide the ability to rely on an exemption from registration do not impose specific requirements on the disclosures provided to investors if those investors meet certain size requirements. However, the financial crisis has called into question the ability of our rules, as they relate to the private market for asset-backed securities, to ensure that investors had access to, and had sufficient time and incentives to adequately consider, appropriate information regarding these securities.

We are proposing to require enhanced disclosure by asset-backed issuers who wish to take advantage of the safe harbor provisions for these privately-issued securities. In addition, in order to provide additional transparency with respect to the private market for these securities, we are proposing amendments to Rule 144A to require a structured finance product issuer to file a public notice on EDGAR of the initial placement of structured finance products that are eligible for resale under Rule 144A. As we believe that the Commission may benefit from the availability of more information about private placements of structured finance products, we are proposing to require that in submitting such notice, the issuer undertakes to provide offering materials to the Commission upon written request.

All of our proposals, if adopted, would apply to new issuances of asset-backed securities. Therefore, the proposed rules, if adopted, would not impose new requirements on outstanding asset-backed securities.

Congressional Oversight Panel, Special Report on Regulatory Reform
Modernizing the American Financial Regulatory System: Recommendations for Improving Oversight, Protecting Consumers, and Ensuring Stability

January 2009.
pages 40-45.

6. Reform the Credit Rating System

***Problem with current system*: The credit rating system is ineffective and plagued with conflicts of interest.**

The major credit rating agencies played an important—and perhaps decisive—role in enabling (and validating) much of the behavior and decision making that now appears to have put the broader financial system at risk. In the subprime-related market specifically, high ratings for structured financial products—especially mortgage-backed securities (MBS), collateralized debt obligations (CDO), and CDOs that invested in other CDOs (frequently referred to as CDO-squared, or CDO^2)—were essential for ensuring broad demand for these products. High ratings not only instilled confidence in potentially risk-averse investors, but also helped satisfy investors' regulatory requirements, which were often explicitly linked to ratings from the major credit rating agencies. By 2006, Moody's business in rating structured financial products accounted for 44 percent of its revenues, as compared to 32 percent from its traditional corporate-bond rating business. It has also been reported that "roughly 60 percent of all global structured products were AAA-rated, in contrast to less than 1 percent of corporate issues." Financial firms, from Fannie Mae to AIG, also benefited greatly from having high credit ratings of their own—especially AAA—allowing them not only to borrow at low rates on the short-term markets to finance longer-term (and higher yielding) investments but also to sell guaranties of various sorts, effectively "renting out" their credit rating. Numerous explanations have been offered for credit rating agencies' apparent mistakes, including conflicts of interest, misuse of complex models, and their quasi-public status as nationally recognized statistical rating organizations (NRSROs).

Regarding conflicts of interests, worrisome is the rating agencies' practice of charging issuers for their ratings, a practice that began at Fitch and Moody's in 1970 and at Standard & Poor's a few years later. Although the practice of collecting payments from issuers has long provoked criticism, market observers often downplayed these concerns, suggesting that "the agencies have an overriding incentive to maintain a reputation for high-quality, accurate ratings." Others, however, claim that the "issuer pays" model biases ratings upward and also encourages "ratings shopping" by issuers, which in turn provokes a race to the bottom on the part of the rating agencies, each willing to lower quality standards to drum up more business.

Beyond the ratings themselves, credit rating agencies also charge issuers for advice, including pre-rating assessments (in which issuers learn what ratings will likely be under various hypothetical scenarios) and risk-management consulting. In some cases, credit rating agency analysts subsequently go to work for the companies they had been rating. This revolving-door practice creates not only the potential for conflicts of interest but also for gaming of the system, since former employees of the rating agencies presumably know how best to exploit weaknesses in the agencies' risk assessment models.

Many critics charge that it was the models themselves—and overreliance on them—that got the credit rating agencies into trouble in recent years, particularly in assigning ratings to structured financial products. "Instead of focusing on actual diligence of the risks involved, demanding additional issuer disclosures, or scrutinizing collateral appraisers' assessments," writes one skeptic, "rating agencies primarily relied on mathematical models that estimated the loss distribution and simulated the cash flows of RMBS [residential mortgage backed securities] and CDOs using historical data."

Many of the models involved excessively rosy assumptions about the quality of the underlying mortgages, ignoring the fact that these mortgages (especially subprime mortgages) were far riskier than ever before and were in fact becoming steadily riskier year by year. Credit rating agency modeling of mortgage-related securities may also have involved mistaken assumptions about the independence of the underlying mortgages—including the assumption that defaults would not be highly correlated across a broad bundle of mortgages or mortgage-related securities. By extension, many of the rating agencies' models may also have involved overly optimistic assumptions about the direction of housing prices (that is, that they would not fall by much, if at all). When asked on a conference call in March 2007 about how a 1 to 2 percent decline in home prices over an extended period of time would affect Fitch's modeling of certain subprime-related securities, a Fitch representative conceded, "The models would break down completely."

Yet another problem plaguing the rating agencies' models was the practice of embedded structuring by issuers, according to which CDOs would themselves become inputs into new CDOs (CDO^2). "With multiple rounds of structuring," three finance professors explain, "even minute errors at the level of the underlying securities, which would be insufficient to alter the security's rating, can dramatically alter the ratings of the structured finance securities." Of particular concern from a regulatory standpoint is the extent to which state and federal (and even global) financial regulations are linked to private credit ratings—and, in fact, to ratings issued by just a handful of specially designated credit rating agencies, the NRSROs). To the extent that leading credit rating agencies enjoy a protected status and virtually guaranteed demand as a result of their regulatory significance, they may face diminished incentives to maintain the quality of their ratings.

The SEC has recently undertaken a number of reforms aimed at the operations of the NRSROs pursuant to the passage of the Credit Rating Agency Reform Act of 2006 (the Rating Agency Act),[10] instituted examinations of NRSROs' practices;94 and proposed rules designed to enhance accountability, transparency, and competition. The Rating Agency Act and the SEC's recent regulatory activity are positive developments. However, since 2006 the financial

[10]Credit Rating Agency Reform Act of 2006, Pub. L. No. 109-291.

crisis has revealed the extent of the harmful consequences of the deep-seated conflicts of interest and distorted incentives associated with the credit ratings firms. With the knowledge that the contours of reform of credit rating agency regulation must take into account the SEC's actions, we propose the following recommendations.

Action item: **Adopt one or more regulatory options to address conflicts of interest and incentives.**

To address conflicts of interest, the SEC or a new regulatory body (see below) could impose limits on the proportion of revenues of rating agencies that are derived from issuers, though there is disagreement about whether alternative revenue sources would prove sufficient. Alternatively, for each rating, issuers could be required to pay into a pool, from which a rating agency would be chosen at random. Here, the challenge would be to maintain the quality of ratings after severing the link between pay and performance. One could also imagine the introduction of grace periods in which credit rating analysts could not take jobs with their clients. While this too would limit conflicts of interest, it might also interfere with the recruiting of high-quality credit analysts at the rating agencies.

To improve incentives, the SEC or some other regulatory body should further encourage additional competition by progressively expanding the ranks of the NRSROs. Other options would include additional disclosure requirements or prohibitions on rating agencies' use of nonpublic information. Since rating agencies currently face little if any legal liability for malfeasance in the production of ratings, a number of experts have proposed strategies for imposing liability on credit rating agencies to ensure appropriate accountability. Although such reforms might well prove helpful, they would be unlikely to solve the underlying problem by themselves.

Action item: **Reform the quasi-public role of NRSRO's and consider creating a Credit Rating Review Board.**

Perhaps the most pressing issue of all from a regulatory standpoint is the NRSRO designation itself. Particularly given all of the concerns that have been raised about the credit rating agencies and their poor performance leading up to the current crisis, state and federal policymakers will need to reassess whether they can continue to rely on these private ratings as a pillar of public financial regulation. In fact, it may be time to consider the possibility of eliminating, or at least dramatically scaling back, the NRSRO designation and replacing it with something else. One option would be to create a public entity—a Credit Rating Review Board—that would have to sign off on any rating before it took on regulatory significance. Even if an asset was rated as investment grade by a credit rating agency, it could still not be added to a bank or pension fund portfolio, for example, unless the rating was also approved by the review board. Ideally, the board would be given direction by lawmakers to favor simpler (plain vanilla) instruments with relatively long track records. New and untested instruments might not make the cut. Of course, such new instruments could still be actively bought and sold in the private marketplace. Only regulated transactions that currently require ratings would be effected. Two key advantages of this approach are that it would permit a dramatic opening of the market for private credit ratings and at the same time discontinue the unsuccessful outsourcing of vital regulatory monitoring.

Another, substantially different, option for the design of such a Credit Rating Review Board would be to model the board in part on the Public Company Accounting Oversight Board (PCAOB), a nont-for-profit corporation that was created by the Sarbanes-Oxley Act to oversee the auditors of public companies. Under this model, the Credit Rating Review Board would not rate instruments ex ante, but instead audit ratings after the fact, perhaps on an annual basis, to ensure that rating agencies are sufficiently disclosing their rating methodologies, the ratings agencies' methodologies are sound, and the rating agencies are adhering to their methodologies. Depending on the course of the SEC's rulemaking, the Credit Rating Review Board could coordinate with or assume some of the SEC's authority to regulate conflicts of interest and inspect, investigate, and discipline NRSROs.

The Senate version of the financial reform legislation, includes, as of this writing, a provision that will change the process for obtaining ratings on asset-backed securities (ABS). The provision would establish a credit ratings board to be overseen by the SEC. Every new ABS bond issue is to have a rating by one agency credit rating assigned by the board. Although the ABS underwriter could solicit additional ratings, it could not escape the verdict of the assigned agency. In theory, therefore, the underwriter could not shop around for the agency with the most favorable view. The SEC would determine the size of the board, a majority of be made up of investors; in addition, at least one member would be from a credit-rating company and at least one member would be from an investment bank.

SECTION D. HIGH LEVERAGE RESTRUCTURING

2. THE RISE, DECLINE, AND REAPPEARANCE OF LEVERAGED RESTRUCTURING

Insert after "Note: The Private Equity Restructurings of the 2000s," at Casebook page 320:

NOTE: HANGOVER

The second wave of leveraged restructuring ended when credit contracted during the summer of 2007. Most of the deals in the pipeline at the time closed nevertheless, albeit under painful circumstances.

The banks had committed to lend on the assumption that two-thirds of the leveraged loan paper received in exchange could be repackaged and resold in securitized packages, termed "Collateralized Loan Obligations" (CLOs). Through the "alchemy of securitization," the banks had been repackaging seventy percent of their portfolios of singe-B rated loans as AAA-rated paper. The banks, once having gotten their money back, promptly turned around and reloaned it in new private equity deals. As competition to make loans increased, interest rates fell and "covenant lite" and "PIK/toggle" terms became common.

The market for securitized loans collapsed abruptly in mid 2007, leaving the banks stuck with a mountain of $80 billion of low-rated LBO debt. The mountain's size has been reduced, but such paper as the banks have sold has been much discounted. The flow of new deals now amounts to a trickle, with private equity firms looking elsewhere for investment opportunities. Some took to investing in privately placed stock of financial companies with grim results. Others have bought LBO debt from the banks.

Attention now turns to the state of the junk bond and leveraged loan markets. By April 2009, 27 percent of speculative-grade issuers were rated by Moody's in the rock bottom range from Caa to C – ratings that render a borrower ineligible for credit. Projections of default rates on junk bonds and leveraged loans vary with the observer's projections for the economy, in a range from 13 to 19 percent for 2009. The peak annual default rates during the 1991 and 2001 recessions were 10 and 12 percent, respectively. Note that restructured firms with PIK loans may be able to stave off default until the PIK period expires or one or another covenant is violated. Unfortunately for many of these issuers, many of the their loans have intermediate terms. Leveraged companies will be looking to refinance $26 billion in 2009, $44 billion in 2010, and $120 billion in 2011.

At the same, it should be noted that junk bond and loan market values have turned upward a bit, at least as of the time of this writing. The S&P/LSTA U.S. Leveraged Loan 100, an index of loans rated below investment grade, rose 12 cents from Dec. 31, 2008 to 73.6 cents on the dollar on May 1, 2009. By early June 2009, the index had increased in value to 79 cents. CLOs also had recovered from their troughs by June 2009. AA-rated CLO paper went from 23 cents on the dollar in May 2009 to 42 cents in June; over the same period, A-rated CLO paper went from 10 cents to 23 cents.

SECTION E. DEBTOR DISTRESS

2. CREDIT DERIVATIVES

Insert after "Note: Credit Derivatives," at Casebook page 373:

VCG Special Opportunities Master Fund Ltd. v. Citibank, N.A.

United States District Court, Southern District of New York, 2008.
594 F. Supp. 2d 334.

BARBARA S. JONES, District Judge.

Defendant and Counterclaim-Plaintiff Citibank, N.A. ("Citibank") moves this Court for judgment on the pleadings * * * dismissing the complaint of Plaintiff and Counterclaim-Defendant VCG Special Opportunities Master Fund Limited ("VCG") and entering judgment in its favor on its counterclaim. For the reasons that follow, Citibank's motion is GRANTED * * *.

BACKGROUND

This action arises from a credit default swap (or "CDS") transaction between VCG and Citibank, by which VCG sold Citibank credit protection against the risk of a credit default by a collateralized debt obligation (or "CDO"). In a typical CDS transaction of this kind, the "protection buyer" makes regular payments to a "protection seller," with "reference" to a specific credit obligation. The credit obligation is generally referred to as the "reference obligation," and the issuer of that obligation is generally referred to as the "reference entity." In return for receiving the protection buyer's payments, the protection seller agrees to undertake the credit exposure of the underlying reference obligation.

The Parties' CDS Transaction

The primary contract documents governing the parties' rights and obligations under the CDS transaction are the 2002 version of the Master Agreement of the International Swap Dealers Association ("ISDA"), dated September 1, 2006 (the "ISDA Master Agreement"); the Schedule to the ISDA Master Agreement, dated September 1, 2006 (the "Schedule"); the 1994 ISDA Credit Support Annex, dated September 1, 2006 (the "Credit Support Annex"); and the Confirmation Letter by Citibank, dated July 5, 2007 (the "Confirmation Letter"). The Confirmation Letter incorporates the 2003 ISDA Credit Derivatives Definitions and the ISDA Standard Terms Supplement for use with Credit Transactions on Collateralized Debt Obligation with Pay-As-You-Go or Physical Settlement (the "Standard Terms Supplement"). In the event of any inconsistency between the Confirmation Letter and the ISDA Master Agreement, the terms of the Confirmation Letter control.

Pursuant to these documents (collectively, the "CDS Contract"), Citibank acted as the protection buyer in the parties' transaction. Citibank agreed to make, for the term of the CDS Contract, periodic "Fixed Payments" to VCG based on a fixed percentage of 5.50% per annum on an "Initial Face Amount" of the reference obligation, Class B Notes. The Class B Notes were issued by the reference entity, the Millstone III CDO Ltd. III-A (the "Millstone III CDO").[3]

VCG acted as the protection seller for the CDS transaction. As protection seller, VCG undertook the default risk of the reference obligation; that is, VCG agreed to pay Citibank a "Floating Payment" if certain credit events (or "Floating Amount Events") took place during the term of the CDS Contract. VCG also agreed to deposit collateral at the time of the execution of the CDS

3

Neither VCG nor Citibank own the Millstone III CDO. Rather, the parties simply trade in, or "hedge," the CDO's credit risk. *Aon Fin. Prods., Inc. v. Société Générale,* 476 F.3d 90, 96 (2d Cir.2007). The swap is not a contract of indemnity, but an instrumentality to shift default risk.

Contract to secure Citibank against the risk that VCG would not be in a position to make the Floating Payments. This collateral is called the "Independent Amount," the amount of which was specified in the Confirmation Letter.

Citibank Demands Additional Credit Support

Apart from the Independent Amount, some CDS transactions allow the protection buyer to demand additional collateral (or "variation margin") based upon a downward movement in the daily "mark-to-market value" of the underlying reference obligation. The parties disagree on whether the CDS Contract allowed Citibank to demand variation margin from VCG. [Citibank, which contends that the contract did so allow, demanded additional collateral from VCG four times in August 2007.] VCG alleges that while it delivered the sums requested, it nonetheless questioned Citibank's evaluation of the credit risk of the Class B Notes. Further, VCG maintains that it delivered the sums out of fear that Citibank might seize upon VCG's refusal to post variation margin as a reason to declare a technical default and seize VCG's collateral.

Declaration of a Floating Amount Event

Pursuant to the Standard Terms Supplement, the Floating Amount Events included a "Failure to Pay Principal," an "Interest Shortfall," or a "Writedown," each with respect to the reference obligation. On January 9, 2008, Citibank sent VCG a "Floating Amount Event Notice," stating in relevant part:

> This letter is notice to you that an Implied Writedown has occurred with respect to the Reference Obligation on or about January 4, 2008. The Implied Writedown Amount in respect of such Floating Amount Event is USD 10,000,000.00 (the "Floating Amount").

In other words, Citibank informed VCG that the Floating Payment Amount was due on the ground that an Implied Writedown had taken place.

According to the definition of "Implied Writedown Amount" provided in the Standard Terms Supplement,

> "Implied Writedown Amount" means, (i) if the Underlying Instruments do not provide for writedowns, applied losses, principal deficiencies or realized losses as described in (i) of the definition of "Writedown" to occur in respect of the Reference Obligation, on any Reference Obligation Payment Date, *an amount determined by the Calculation Agent [Citibank] equal to the excess, if any, of the Current Period Implied Writedown Amount over the Previous Period Implied Writedown Amount, in each case in respect of the Reference Obligation Calculation*

Period to which such Reference Obligation Payment Date relates, and (ii) in any other case, zero. (emphasis added).

"Writedown," in turn, is defined in relevant part as the occurrence at any time on or after the Effective Date of:

(i)(A) a writedown or applied loss (however, described in the Underlying Instruments) resulting in a reduction in the Outstanding Principal Amount (other than as a result of a scheduled or unscheduled payment of principal); or (B) the attribution of a principal deficiency or realized loss (however described in the Underlying Instruments) to the Reference Obligation resulting in a reduction or subordination of the current interest payable on the Reference Obligation; * * *

(iii) *if Implied Writedown is applicable and the Underlying Instruments do not provide for writedowns, applied losses, principal deficiencies, or realized losses as described in (i) above to occur in respect of the Reference Obligation, an Implied Writedown Amount being determined in respect of the Reference Obligation by the Calculation Agent.* (emphasis added)

As reflected in the Confirmation Letter, an "Implied Writedown" was "Applicable" to this CDS transaction. The parties disagree, however, on whether the Implied Writedown provision in the CDS Contract was exercised properly. This requires an initial determination of whether the Underlying Instruments to the Class B Notes provide for writedowns. If so, the Implied Writedown Amount is zero; if not, Citibank, as Calculation Agent, could determine an Implied Writedown Amount.

DISCUSSION

* * *

II. The Parties' Arguments

The gravamen of VCG's complaint is that Citibank improperly demanded from VCG additional collateral beyond the Independent Amount, and improperly declared a Floating Amount Event. The Court turns first to the issue of whether a Floating Amount Event occurred.

A. Floating Amount Event

There is no dispute that the Floating Amount Events that would trigger VCG's payment obligation to Citibank include: a "Failure to Pay Principal," an

"Interest Shortfall," or a "Writedown." There is also no dispute that the reference obligation has not experienced either a Failure to Pay Principal or an Interest Shortfall. Thus, the remaining question is whether a Writedown has taken place such that Citibank was entitled to demand VCG's Floating Payment obligation.

As reflected in the Confirmation Letter, the parties agree that "Implied Writedown" was "Applicable" to this CDS transaction and hence would constitute a "Writedown" as relevant to the CDS Contract. Pursuant to the terms of the Standard Terms Supplement incorporated by the Confirmation Letter, the amount of an Implied Writedown is zero in any case where the reference obligation's "Underlying Instruments" expressly provide for "writedowns, applied losses, principal deficiencies or realized losses" to occur. Where the reference obligation's Underlying Instruments do *not* provide for such events, the Calculation Agent is to determine whether an Implied Writedown has occurred.

VCG asserts that the Indenture between Millstone III CDO, Ltd., Millstone III CDO, LLC, and JP Morgan Chase Bank, N.A., dated July 5, 2006 (the "Millstone III Indenture"), actually provides for writedowns, applied losses, principal deficiencies and realized losses, which are passed on to the reference obligation, the Class B Notes. In response, Citibank argues that there can be no "serious dispute" that the Millstone III Indenture does *not* permit any express writedowns, or any of the other events listed, of the principal amounts of the Class B Notes. Thus, Citibank, as the designated Calculation Agent, properly calculated the Implied Writedown Amount resulting in the Floating Payment obligation.

The crux of the parties' disagreement centers on whether the portion of the Millstone III Indenture that accounts for a "Written Down Amount" concerns the reference obligation at issue, the Class B Notes, or instead refers to the possibility of the Millstone III CDO's securities being written down, which is not the type of Writedown contemplated in the CDS Contract. The Millstone III Indenture provides in relevant part:

> "Written Down Amount" means the sum, [sic] respect to each Written Down Security, of the amount to which the original Principal Balance of such Written Down Security is reduced as notified by or on behalf of the related issuer or trustee to the holders of such Written Down Security (including appraisal reductions on CMBS Securities).

"Written-Down Security" means any Collateral Asset (other than a Defaulted Obligation) as to which the aggregate par amount of such Collateral Asset and all other securities secured by the same pool of collateral that rank *pari passu* with or senior in priority of payment to such Collateral Asset exceeds the aggregate par amount (including reserved interest or other amounts available for overcollateralization) of all collateral securing such securities (excluding defaulted collateral)

Based upon this language, VCG contends that if a "Written Down Amount" is reported,[5] the outstanding principal amount of collateral in the pool available for distribution to noteholders, including Class B noteholders, is decreased. Assuming that the first class of notes affected were the Class B Notes, "writedowns, applied losses, principal deficiencies or realized losses" would, by definition, occur in respect of the reference obligation. In this regard, pursuant to the terms of the Standard Terms Supplement, VCG posits that the amount of the Implied Writedown is zero. (" 'Implied Writedown Amount' means, (i) if the Underlying do not provide for writedowns ... an amount determined by the Calculation Agent ..., and (ii) in any other case, zero.").

VCG's interpretation of the Millstone III Indenture is flawed in that the cited definition of "Written Down Amount" does not involve writedowns of the Class B Notes issued by the Millstone III CDO. Instead, the "Written Down Amount" refers to securities owned by the CDO. In other words, VCG confuses the CDO's assets (the securities it owns) with its liabilities (the securities it issues). The Class B Notes of the CDO are debt obligations *issued by* the Millstone III CDO; they are not a type of collateral asset *held by* the CDO.

Moreover, the Court is unpersuaded by VCG's claim that writedowns of the collateral assets owned by the Millstone III CDO is the equivalent of a writedown of the Class B Notes because a reduced collateral pool will be available for distribution to the noteholders in accordance with the priorities of payments of the CDO's obligations. Rather, under the Millstone III Indenture,

---

5

Before sums payable to the noteholders are allocated according to a priority of payments identified in Section 11.1 of the Millstone III Indenture (the "waterfall"), the issuer of the CDS is required to prepare a "Note Valuation Report," pursuant to Section 10.6(a) of the Indenture. Among other data taken into account in the Note Valuation Report is "a calculation showing the determination of the Net Outstanding Portfolio Collateral Balance," which in turn takes in to account the "Written Down Amount," quoted above.

deterioration in the CDO's collateral assets and any payment shortfalls do not result in any writedown of the principal amount of the *reference obligation,* which is the type of writedown contemplated under the CDS Contract. ("[I]f Implied Writedown is applicable and the Underlying Instruments to not provide for writedowns ...*in respect of the Reference Obligation,* an Implied Writedown Amount being determined *in respect of the Reference Obligation* by the Calculation Agent.") (emphasis added).) Thus, even if the collateral securities realize losses, the Class B Notes remain outstanding at their full principal amount, subject to the availability of funds. That is presumably why, in such a situation, the parties agreed that an Implied Writedown feature applies.

In sum, the Confirmation Letter makes clear that Implied Writedowns are applicable to this CDS transaction. Because the Millstone III Indenture does not expressly provide for writedowns of the Class B Notes, under the terms of the CDS Contract it is Citibank's responsibility, as the Calculation Agent, to determine whether an Implied Writedown has occurred. The CDS Contract sets forth a mathematical formula by which to calculate the Implied Writedown Amount. VCG does not challenge the use of this formula. Accordingly, the Court holds that Citibank properly determined that a Floating Amount Event in the form of an Implied Writedown occurred under the CDS Contract. Citibank's motion for judgment on the pleadings is therefore granted, and VCG's claim for a declaratory judgment based upon the non-occurrence of a Floating Amount Event is dismissed.

B. Additional Collateral

VCG argues that Citibank's requests for additional collateral were inconsistent with the terms set forth in the Confirmation Letter that the parties signed as part of the CDS Contract. The Court disagrees. The Credit Support Annex allowed for Citibank to request additional collateral from VCG depending upon Citibank's calculation of its "Exposure," or the amount of loss Citibank would incur (or gains it would realize) in replacing the CDS transaction with an economically equivalent transaction at the time of calculation. In turn, the Confirmation Letter states clearly that "[t]his Transaction shall be subject to the Credit Support Annex ... between Citibank and [VCG]." The Court finds nothing in the Confirmation Letter that modifies VCG's obligation to transfer additional collateral as set forth in the Credit Support Annex.

* * *

C. VCG's Alternative Claims

VCG alleges in the alternative claims of rescission, breach of the implied covenant of good faith and fair dealing, unjust enrichment, and conversion. For the following reasons, these claims are without merit.

1. Rescission

VCG claims that it believed it was agreeing "to sell credit protection on a credit default swap" and "not to take the risk of daily mark-to-market movement in the value of the reference obligation." * * *

VCG's claim of entitlement to rescission based upon unilateral mistake is not supportable here. First, the language of the Credit Support Annex makes clear that Citibank may request additional collateral from VCG depending on the current value of the CDS Contract at the time of Citibank's calculation of its Exposure. Second, VCG is a sophisticated hedge fund. No claim has been made by VCG that it was limited in its ability to review drafts of the agreement or to discuss the provisions of the CDS Contract before it was executed. Notwithstanding VCG's assertions to the contrary, it appears that the instant case presents a circumstance where VCG, a sophisticated hedge fund, simply failed to review carefully the terms of the parties' agreement. If VCG was negligent in this regard, this does not justify rescission.

2. Breach of the Implied Covenant of Good Faith and Fair Dealing

VCG next contends that Citibank breached the implied covenant of good faith and fair dealing by "making oppressive [variation] margin demands without justification", and by abusing the measure of discretion given to it as Calculation Agent. With regard to VCG's allegation of a breach of the implied covenant on the basis of variation margin, as discussed *supra,* this claim is waived in light of VCG's continued posting of the demanded collateral and acceptance of the benefits of the CDS Contract. With regard to VCG's allegation that Citibank abused its discretion as Calculation Agent, while it is true that under New York law a claim for arbitrary or irrational exercise of discretion under a contract can be separate and apart from a breach of contract claim, * * * VCG does not adduce specific facts of arbitrary or irrational conduct relating to Citibank's position as Calculation Agent. Indeed, in its opposition papers, VCG supports its claim by relying upon Citibank's supposedly unjustified demands of variation margin. Because that challenge is waived, however, the Court concludes that VCG has failed to state a claim for breach of the implied covenant of good faith and fair dealing.

* * *

NOTE: SETTLEMENT PROCESSES

The ISDA has successfully moved to regularize determinations respecting the occurrence of a credit event and the settlement of contracts in the event a credit event has occurred. The reform process involves amendment of standard CDS documentation, and has required the concurrence of dealers and CDS users.

Under the original practice, when a credit event occurs respecting a given issuer of debt, the risk seller, in order to perfect its right to payment, had to present the defaulted reference obligation to the risk buyer. Note that as a result, to the extent the defaulted security had a value, the risk buyer succeeded to it. The ISDA has moved the market toward cash settlement. Under the revised practice, when a credit event occurs respecting a reference entity, the ISDA issues a "protocol" under which an auction is scheduled for a stated future date. The auction determines the present value of the debt securities subject to CDSs. For example, assume that the auction prices an issue of defaulted bonds at $200 on a face value of $1,000. The $200 price facilitates cash settlement of outstanding CDSs, without requiring that risk seller present the reference obligation to the risk buyer. The risk buyer simply forwards $800 to the risk seller. Under the new practice, auction settlement will be provided for up front in the CDS contract. In addition, a "Determinations Committee" has been set up to determine whether a credit event in fact has occurred. The Committee is made up of dealer and buy-side representatives. Under its voting rules, at least one buy side representative will have to concur in binding determinations. One result of this will be a paucity of judicial opinions interpreting language in the ISDA's contracts.

The move to cash settlement reduces the market frictions that worried the Treasury and the Federal Reserve prior to the financial crisis. Ironically, it also makes it easier to use CDSs on a speculative basis. Actors wishing to profit by betting against a company now can buy risk through CDSs without having to worry about being long in the reference obligation in the wake of a credit event. It follows that the notional amount of reference obligations under CDSs more easily can exceed the actual principal amount of reference obligations outstanding. An analogy can be drawn to the "naked shorting" of equity securities.

Department of the Treasury, Financial Regulatory Reform, A New Foundation: Rebuilding Financial Supervision and Regulation

June, 2009
pp. 46-49

II. ESTABLISH COMPREHENSIVE REGULATION OF FINANCIAL MARKETS

B. Create Comprehensive Regulation of All OTC Derivatives, Including Credit Default Swaps (CDS)

OTC derivatives markets, including CDS markets, should be subject to comprehensive regulation that addresses relevant public policy objectives: (1) preventing activities in those markets from posing risk to the financial system; (2) promoting the efficiency and transparency of those markets; (3) preventing market manipulation, fraud, and other market abuses; and (4) ensuring that OTC derivatives are not marketed inappropriately to unsophisticated parties.

One of the most significant changes in the world of finance in recent decades has been the explosive growth and rapid innovation in the market for financial derivatives. Much of this development has occurred in the market for OTC derivatives, which are not executed on regulated exchanges. In 2000, the Commodity Futures Modernization Act (CFMA) explicitly exempted OTC derivatives, to a large extent, from regulation by the Commodity Futures Trading Commission. In addition, the law limited the SEC's authority to regulate certain types of OTC derivatives. As a result, the market for OTC derivatives has largely gone unregulated.

The downside of this lax regulatory regime for OTC derivatives – and, in particular, for credit default swaps (CDS) – became disastrously clear during the recent financial crisis. In the years prior to the crisis, many institutions and investors had substantial positions in CDS – particularly CDS that were tied to asset backed securities (ABS), complex instruments whose risk characteristics proved to be poorly understood even by the most sophisticated of market participants. At the same time, excessive risk taking by AIG and certain monoline insurance companies that provided protection against declines in the value of such ABS, as well as poor counterparty credit risk management by many banks, saddled our financial system with an enormous – and largely unrecognized – level of risk.

When the value of the ABS fell, the danger became clear. Individual institutions believed that these derivatives would protect their investments and provide return, even if the market went down. But, during the crisis, the sheer volume of these contracts overwhelmed some firms that had promised to provide payment on the CDS and left institutions with losses that they believed they had been protected against. Lacking authority to regulate the OTC derivatives market, regulators were unable to identify or mitigate the enormous systemic threat that had developed.

Government regulation of the OTC derivatives markets should be designed to achieve four broad objectives: (1) preventing activities in those markets from posing risk to the financial system; (2) promoting the efficiency and transparency of those markets; (3) preventing market manipulation, fraud, and other market abuses; and (4) ensuring that OTC derivatives are not marketed inappropriately to unsophisticated parties. To achieve these goals, it is critical that similar products and activities be subject to similar regulations and oversight.

To contain systemic risks, the Commodities Exchange Act (CEA) and the securities laws should be amended to require clearing of all standardized OTC derivatives through regulated central counterparties (CCPs). To make these measures effective, regulators will need to require that CCPs impose robust margin requirements as well as other necessary risk controls and that customized OTC derivatives are not used solely as a means to avoid using a CCP. For example, if an OTC derivative is accepted for clearing by one or more fully regulated CCPs, it should create a presumption that it is a standardized contract and thus required to be cleared.

All OTC derivatives dealers and all other firms whose activities in those markets create large exposures to counterparties should be subject to a robust and appropriate regime of prudential supervision and regulation. Key elements of that robust regulatory regime must include conservative capital requirements (more conservative than the existing bank regulatory capital requirements for OTC derivatives), business conduct standards, reporting requirements, and conservative requirements relating to initial margins on counterparty credit exposures. Counterparty risks associated with customized bilateral OTC derivatives transactions that should not be accepted by a CCP would be addressed by this robust regime covering derivative dealers. As noted above, regulatory capital requirements on OTC derivatives that are not centrally cleared also should be increased for all banks and BHCs.

The OTC derivatives markets should be made more transparent by amending the CEA and the securities laws to authorize the CFTC and the SEC, consistent with their respective missions, to impose recordkeeping and reporting requirements (including an audit trail) on all OTC derivatives. Certain of those requirements should be deemed to be satisfied by either clearing standardized transactions through a CCP or by reporting customized transactions to a regulated trade repository. CCPs and trade repositories should be required to, among other things, make aggregate data on open positions and trading volumes available to the public and make data on any individual counterparty's trades and positions available on a confidential basis to the CFTC, SEC, and the institution's primary regulators.

Market efficiency and price transparency should be improved in derivatives markets by requiring the clearing of standardized contracts through regulated CCPs as discussed earlier and by moving the standardized part of these markets onto regulated exchanges and regulated transparent electronic trade execution systems for OTC derivatives and by requiring development of a system for timely reporting of trades and prompt dissemination of prices and other trade information. Furthermore, regulated financial institutions should be encouraged to make greater use of regulated exchange-traded derivatives. Competition between appropriately regulated OTC derivatives markets and regulated exchanges would make both sets of markets more efficient and thereby better serve end-users of derivatives.

Market integrity concerns should be addressed by making whatever amendments to the CEA and the securities laws which are necessary to ensure that the CFTC and the SEC, consistent with their respective missions, have clear, unimpeded authority to police and prevent fraud, market manipulation, and other market abuses involving all OTC derivatives. The CFTC also should have authority to set position limits on OTC derivatives that perform or affect a significant price discovery function with respect to regulated markets. Requiring CCPs, trade repositories, and other market participants to provide the CFTC, SEC, and institutions' primary regulators with a complete picture of activity in the OTC derivatives markets will assist those regulators in detecting and deterring all such market abuses.

Current law seeks to protect unsophisticated parties from entering into inappropriate derivatives transactions by limiting the types of counterparties that could participate in those markets. But the limits are not sufficiently stringent. The CFTC and SEC are reviewing the participation limits in current law to recommend how the CEA and the securities laws should be amended to tighten the limits or to impose additional disclosure requirements or standards of care with respect to the marketing of derivatives to less sophisticated counterparties such as small municipalities.

SECTION F. INSOLVENCY REORGANIZATION

3. Reorganization under the Bankruptcy Code

Insert at Casebook page 455, after the third paragraph:

(C) ASSET SALES

In re Chrysler LLC

United States Court of Appeals, Second Circuit, 2009.
576 F.3d 108

Before: JACOBS, Chief Judge, KEARSE and SACK, Circuit Judges.

DENNIS JACOBS, Chief Judge:

The Indiana State Police Pension Trust, the Indiana State Teachers Retirement Fund, and the Indiana Major Moves Construction Fund (collectively, the "Indiana Pensioners" or "Pensioners"), along with various tort claimants and others, appeal from an order entered in the United States Bankruptcy Court for the Southern District of New York, Arthur J. Gonzalez, *Bankruptcy Judge,* dated June 1, 2009 (the "Sale Order"), authorizing the sale of substantially all of the debtor's assets to New CarCo Acquisition LLC ("New Chrysler"). On June 2, 2009 we granted the Indiana Pensioners' motion for a stay and for expedited appeal directly to this Court * * * .

In a nutshell, Chrysler LLC and its related companies (hereinafter "Chrysler" or "debtor" or "Old Chrysler") filed a pre-packaged bankruptcy petition under Chapter 11 on April 30, 2009. The filing followed months in which Chrysler experienced deepening losses, received billions in bailout funds from the Federal Government, searched for a merger partner, unsuccessfully sought additional government bailout funds for a stand-alone restructuring, and ultimately settled on an asset-sale transaction pursuant to 11 U.S.C. § 363 (the "Sale"), which was approved by the Sale Order. The key elements of the Sale were set forth in a Master Transaction Agreement dated as of April 30, 2009:

substantially all of Chrysler's operating assets (including manufacturing plants, brand names, certain dealer and supplier relationships, and much else) would be transferred to New Chrysler in exchange for New Chrysler's assumption of certain liabilities and $2 billion in cash. Fiat S.p.A agreed to provide New Chrysler with certain fuel-efficient vehicle platforms, access to its worldwide distribution system, and new management that is experienced in turning around a failing auto company. Financing for the sale transaction--$6 billion in senior secured financing, and debtor-in-possession financing for 60 days in the amount of $4.96 billion--would come from the United States Treasury and from Export Development Canada. The agreement describing the United States Treasury's commitment does not specify the source of the funds, but it is undisputed that prior funding came from the Troubled Asset Relief Program ("TARP"), 12 U.S.C. § 5211(a)(1), and that the parties expected the Sale to be financed through the use of TARP funds. Ownership of New Chrysler was to be distributed by membership interests, 55% of which go to an employee benefit entity created by the United Auto Workers union, 8% to the United States Treasury and 2% to Export Development Canada. Fiat, for its contributions, would immediately own 20% of the equity with rights to acquire more (up to 51%), contingent on payment in full of the debts owed to the United States Treasury and Export Development Canada.

At a hearing on May 5, 2009, the bankruptcy court approved the debtor's proposed bidding procedures. No other bids were forthcoming. From May 27 to May 29, the bankruptcy court held hearings on whether to approve the Sale. Upon extensive findings of fact and conclusions of law, the bankruptcy court approved the Sale by order dated June 1, 2009.

After briefing and oral argument, we affirmed the bankruptcy court's order on June 5, but we entered a short stay pending Supreme Court review. The Supreme Court, after an extension of the stay, declined a further extension. The Sale closed on June 10, 2009.

* * * The Sale Order is challenged essentially on four grounds. First, it is contended that the sale of Chrysler's auto-manufacturing assets, considered together with the associated intellectual property and (selected) dealership contractual rights, so closely approximates a final plan of reorganization that it constitutes an impermissible "*sub rosa* plan," and therefore cannot be accomplished under § 363(b). We consider this question first, because a determination adverse to Chrysler would have required reversal. Second, we consider the argument by the Indiana Pensioners that the Sale impermissibly subordinates their interests as secured lenders and allows assets on which they

have a lien to pass free of liens to other creditors and parties, in violation of § 363(f). We reject this argument on the ground that the secured lenders have consented to the Sale, as per § 363(f)(2). Third, the Indiana Pensioners challenge the constitutionality of the use of TARP funds to finance the Sale on a number of grounds, chiefly that the Secretary of the Treasury is using funds appropriated for relief of "financial institutions" to effect a bailout of an auto-manufacturer, and that this causes a constitutional injury to the Indiana Pensioners because the loss of their priorities in bankruptcy amounts to an economic injury that was caused or underwritten by TARP money. We conclude that the Indiana Pensioners lack standing to raise this challenge. Finally, we consider and reject the arguments advanced by present and future tort claimants.

DISCUSSION

* * *

I

The Indiana Pensioners characterize the Sale as an impermissible, *sub rosa* plan of reorganization. *See Pension Benefit Guar. Corp. v. Braniff Airways, Inc. (In re Braniff Airways, Inc.),* 700 F.2d 935, 940 (5th Cir.1983) (denying approval of an asset sale because the debtor "should not be able to short circuit the requirements of Chapter 11 for confirmation of a reorganization plan by establishing the terms of the plan *sub rosa* in connection with a sale of assets"). As the Indiana Pensioners characterize it, the Sale transaction "is a 'Sale' in name only; upon consummation, new Chrysler will be old Chrysler in essentially every respect. It will be called 'Chrysler.' ... Its employees, including most management, will be retained.... It will manufacture and sell Chrysler and Dodge cars and minivans, Jeeps and Dodge Trucks.... The real substance of the transaction is the underlying reorganization it implements."

Section 363(b) of the Bankruptcy Code authorizes a Chapter 11 debtor-in-possession to use, sell, or lease estate property outside the ordinary course of business, requiring in most circumstances only that a movant provide notice and a hearing. We have identified an "apparent conflict" between the expedient of a § 363(b) sale and the otherwise applicable features and safeguards of Chapter 11. *Comm. of Equity Sec. Holders v. Lionel Corp. (In re Lionel Corp.),* 722 F.2d 1063, 1071 (2d Cir.1983); *cf. Braniff,* 700 F.2d at 940.

In *Lionel,* we consulted the history and purpose of § 363(b) to situate § 363(b) transactions within the overall structure of Chapter 11. The origin of § 363(b) is the Bankruptcy Act of 1867, which permitted a sale of a debtor's assets when the estate or any part thereof was "of a perishable nature or liable to deteriorate in value." *Lionel,* 722 F.2d at 1066 (citing Section 25 of the Bankruptcy Act of 1867, Act of March 2, 1867, 14 Stat. 517). Typically, courts have approved § 363(b) sales to preserve " 'wasting asset[s].' " *Id.* at 1068. Most early transactions concerned perishable commodities; but the same practical necessity has been recognized in contexts other than fruits and vegetables. "[T]here are times when it is more advantageous for the debtor to begin to sell as many assets as quickly as possible in order to insure that the assets do not lose value." *Fla. Dep't of Revenue v. Piccadilly Cafeterias, Inc.,* --- U.S. ----, 128 S.Ct. 2326, 2342, 171 L.Ed.2d 203 (2008) (Breyer, J., dissenting); *see also In re Pedlow,* 209 F. 841, 842 (2d Cir.1913) (upholding sale of a bankrupt's stock of handkerchiefs because the sale price was above the appraised value and "Christmas sales had commenced and ... the sale of handkerchiefs depreciates greatly after the holidays"). Thus, an automobile manufacturing business can be within the ambit of the "melting ice cube" theory of § 363(b). As *Lionel* recognized, the text of § 363(b) requires no "emergency" to justify approval. *Lionel,* 722 F.2d at 1069. For example, if "a good business opportunity [is] presently available," *id.,* which might soon disappear, quick action may be justified in order to increase (or maintain) the value of an asset to the estate, by means of a lease or sale of the assets. Accordingly, *Lionel* "reject[ed] the requirement that only an emergency permits the use of § 363(b)." *Id.* "[I]f a bankruptcy judge is to administer a business reorganization successfully under the Code, then ... some play for the operation of both § 363(b) and Chapter 11 must be allowed for." *Id.* at 1071.

At the same time, *Lionel* "reject[ed] the view that § 363(b) grants the bankruptcy judge *carte blanche.*" *Id.* at 1069. The concern was that a quick, plenary sale of assets outside the ordinary course of business risked circumventing key features of the Chapter 11 process, which afford debt and equity holders the opportunity to vote on a proposed plan of reorganization after receiving meaningful information. Pushed by a bullying creditor, a § 363(b) sale might evade such requirements as disclosure, solicitation, acceptance, and confirmation of a plan. *See* 11 U.S.C. §§ 1122-29. "[T]he natural tendency of a debtor in distress," as a Senate Judiciary Committee Report observed, is "to pacify large creditors with whom the debtor would expect to do business, at the expense of small and scattered public investors." *Lionel,* 722 F.2d at 1070 (quoting S.Rep. No. 95-989, 2d Sess., at 10 (1978).

To balance the competing concerns of efficiency against the safeguards of the Chapter 11 process, *Lionel* required a "good business reason" for a § 363(b) transaction:

> [A bankruptcy judge] should consider all salient factors pertaining to the proceeding and, accordingly, act to further the diverse interests of the debtor, creditors and equity holders, alike. [A bankruptcy judge] might, for example, look to such relevant factors as the proportionate value of the asset to the estate as a whole, the amount of elapsed time since the filing, the likelihood that a plan of reorganization will be proposed and confirmed in the near future, the effect of the proposed disposition on future plans of reorganization, the proceeds to be obtained from the disposition vis-a-vis any appraisals of the property, which of the alternatives of use, sale or lease the proposal envisions and, most importantly perhaps, whether the asset is increasing or decreasing in value. This list is not intended to be exclusive, but merely to provide guidance to the bankruptcy judge.

722 F.2d at 1071.

After weighing these considerations, the Court in *Lionel* reversed a bankruptcy court's approval of the sale of Lionel Corporation's equity stake in another corporation, Dale Electronics, Inc. ("Dale"). The Court relied heavily on testimony from Lionel's Chief Executive Officer, who conceded that it was "only at the insistence of the Creditors' Committee that Dale stock was being sold and that Lionel 'would very much like to retain its interest in Dale,' " *id.* at 1072, as well as on a financial expert's acknowledgment that the value of the Dale stock was not decreasing. Since the Dale stock was not a wasting asset, and the proffered justification for selling the stock was the desire of creditors, no sufficient business reasons existed for approving the sale.

In the twenty-five years since *Lionel*, § 363(b) asset sales have become common practice in large-scale corporate bankruptcies. * * * A law review article recounts the phenomenon:

> Corporate reorganizations have all but disappeared.... TWA filed only to consummate the sale of its planes and landing gates to American Airlines. Enron's principal assets, including its trading operation and its most valuable pipelines, were sold within a few months of its bankruptcy petition. Within weeks of filing for Chapter 11, Budget sold most of its assets to the parent company of Avis. Similarly, Polaroid entered Chapter 11 and sold most of its assets to the private equity group at BankOne. Even when a large firm uses Chapter 11 as something other than a convenient auction block, its principal lenders are usually already in control and Chapter 11 merely puts in place a preexisting deal.

Douglas G. Baird & Robert K. Rasmussen, *The End of Bankruptcy,* 55 Stan. L.Rev. 751, 751-52 (2002). In the current economic crisis of 2008-09, § 363(b) sales have become even more useful and customary.[6] The "side door" of § 363(b) may well "replace the main route of Chapter 11 reorganization plans." Jason Brege, Note, *An Efficiency Model of Section 363(b) Sales,* 92 Va. L.Rev. 1639, 1640 (2006).

Resort to § 363(b) has been driven by efficiency, from the perspectives of sellers and buyers alike. The speed of the process can maximize asset value by sale of the debtor's business as a going concern. Moreover, the assets are typically burnished (or "cleansed") because (with certain limited exceptions) they are sold free and clear of liens, claims and liabilities. A § 363 sale can often yield the highest price for the assets because the buyer can select the liabilities it will assume and purchase a business with cash flow (or the near prospect of it). Often, a secured creditor can "credit bid," or take an ownership interest in the company by bidding a reduction in the debt the company owes. *See* 11 U.S.C. § 363(k) (allowing a secured creditor to credit bid at a § 363(b) sale).

This tendency has its critics. The objections are not to the quantity or percentage of assets being sold: it has long been understood (by the drafters of the Code, and the Supreme Court) that § 363(b) sales may encompass all or substantially all of a debtor's assets. Rather, the thrust of criticism remains what it was in *Lionel:* fear that one class of creditors may strong-arm the debtor-in-possession, and bypass the requirements of Chapter 11 to cash out quickly at the expense of other stakeholders, in a proceeding that amounts to a reorganization in all but name, achieved by stealth and momentum. *See, e.g., Motorola, Inc. v. Official Comm. of Unsecured Creditors and JPMorgan Chase Bank, N.A. (In re Iridium Operating LLC),* 478 F.3d 452, 466 (2d Cir.2007) ("The reason *sub rosa* plans are prohibited is based on a fear that a debtor-in-possession will enter into transactions that will, in effect, short circuit

---

6

For instance, Lehman Brothers sold substantially all its assets to Barclays Capital within five days of filing for bankruptcy. Lehman Brothers filed for bankruptcy in the early morning hours of September 15, 2008. On September 20, 2008, the bankruptcy court approved the sale to Barclays of Lehman's investment banking and capital markets operations, as well as supporting infrastructure including the Lehman headquarters in midtown Manhattan for $1.7 billion. *See Bay Harbour Mgmt., L.C. v. Lehman Bros. Holdings Inc. (In re Lehman Bros. Holdings Inc.),* No. 08-cv-8869(DLC), 2009 WL 667301, at *8 (2009) (affirming the § 363(b) sale order).

the requirements of Chapter 11 for confirmation of a reorganization plan."); Brege, *An Efficiency Model of Section 363(b) Sales,* 92 Va. L.Rev. at 1643 ("The cynical perspective is that [§ 363(b)] serves as a loophole to the otherwise tightly arranged and efficient Chapter 11, through which agents of the debtor-in-possession can shirk responsibility and improperly dispose of assets.")* * *.

As § 363(b) sales proliferate, the competing concerns identified in *Lionel* have become harder to manage. Debtors need flexibility and speed to preserve going concern value; yet one or more classes of creditors should not be able to nullify Chapter 11's requirements. A balance is not easy to achieve, and is not aided by rigid rules and prescriptions. *Lionel*'s multi-factor analysis remains the proper, most comprehensive framework for judging the validity of § 363(b) transactions.

Adopting the Fifth Circuit's wording in *Braniff,* 700 F.2d at 940, commentators and courts-including ours-have sometimes referred to improper § 363(b) transactions as "*sub rosa* plans of reorganization." *Braniff* rejected a proposed transfer agreement in large part because the terms of the agreement specifically attempted to "dictat[e] some of the terms of any future reorganization plan. The [subsequent] reorganization plan would have to allocate the [proceeds of the sale] according to the terms of the [transfer] agreement or forfeit a valuable asset." 700 F.2d at 940. As the Fifth Circuit concluded, "[t]he debtor and the Bankruptcy Court should not be able to short circuit the requirements of Chapter 11 for confirmation of a reorganization plan by establishing the terms of the plan *sub rosa* in connection with a sale of assets." *Id.*

The term "*sub rosa* " is something of a misnomer. It bespeaks a covert or secret activity, whereas secrecy has nothing to do with a § 363 transaction. Transactions blessed by the bankruptcy courts are openly presented, considered, approved, and implemented. *Braniff* seems to have used "*sub rosa* " to describe transactions that treat the requirements of the Bankruptcy Code as something to be evaded or subverted. But even in that sense, the term is unhelpful. The sale of assets is permissible under § 363(b); and it is elementary that the more assets sold that way, the less will be left for a plan of reorganization, or for liquidation. But the size of the transaction, and the residuum of corporate assets, is, under our precedent, just one consideration for the exercise of discretion by the bankruptcy judge(s), along with an open-ended list of other salient factors.\

Braniff's holding did not support the argument that a § 363(b) asset sale must be rejected simply because it is a sale of all or substantially all of a debtor's assets. Thus a § 363(b) sale may well be a reorganization in effect without being the kind of plan rejected in *Braniff. See, e.g., Fla. Dep't of Revenue v. Piccadilly Cafeterias, Inc.*, 128 S.Ct. at 2330 n. 2. Although *Lionel* did not involve a contention that the proposed sale was a *sub rosa* or *de facto* reorganization, a bankruptcy court confronted with that allegation may approve or disapprove a § 363(b) transfer that is a sale of all or substantially all of a debtor's assets, using the analysis set forth in *Lionel* in order to determine whether there was a good business reason for the sale.

The Indiana Pensioners argue that the Sale is a *sub rosa* plan chiefly because it gives value to unsecured creditors (*i.e.*, in the form of the ownership interest in New Chrysler provided to the union benefit funds) without paying off secured debt in full, and without complying with the procedural requirements of Chapter 11. However, Bankruptcy Judge Gonzalez demonstrated proper solicitude for the priority between creditors and deemed it essential that the Sale in no way upset that priority. The lien holders' security interests would attach to all proceeds of the Sale: "Not one penny of value of the Debtors' assets is going to anyone other than the First-Lien Lenders." Opinion Granting Debtor's Motion Seeking Authority to Sell, May 31, 2009, ("Sale Opinion") at 18. As Bankruptcy Judge Gonzalez found, all the equity stakes in New Chrysler were entirely attributable to *new* value-including governmental loans, new technology, and new management-which were not assets of the debtor's estate.

The Indiana Pensioners' arguments boil down to the complaint that the Sale does not pass the discretionary, multifarious *Lionel* test. The bankruptcy court's findings constitute an adequate rebuttal. Applying the *Lionel* factors, Bankruptcy Judge Gonzalez found good business reasons for the Sale. The linchpin of his analysis was that the only possible alternative to the Sale was an immediate liquidation that would yield far less for the estate-and for the objectors. The court found that, notwithstanding Chrysler's prolonged and well-publicized efforts to find a strategic partner or buyer, no other proposals were forthcoming. In the months leading up to Chrysler's bankruptcy filing, and during the bankruptcy process itself, Chrysler executives circled the globe in search of a deal. But the Fiat transaction was the *only* offer available.[10]

10

The bankruptcy court noted that Chrysler had discussed potential alliances with General Motors, Fiat, Nissan, Hyundai-Kia, Toyota, Volkswagen, Tata Motors, GAZ Group, Magna International, Mitsubishi Motors, Honda, Beijing

The Sale would yield $2 billion. According to expert testimony--not refuted by the objectors--an immediate liquidation of Chrysler as of May 20, 2009 would yield in the range of nothing to $800 million. Crucially, Fiat had conditioned its commitment on the Sale being completed by June 15, 2009. While this deadline was tight and seemingly arbitrary, there was little leverage to force an extension. To preserve resources, Chrysler factories had been shuttered, and the business was hemorrhaging cash. According to the bankruptcy court, Chrysler was losing going concern value of nearly $100 million each day.

On this record, and in light of the arguments made by the parties, the bankruptcy court's approval of the Sale was no abuse of discretion. With its revenues sinking, its factories dark, and its massive debts growing, Chrysler fit the paradigm of the melting ice cube. Going concern value was being reduced each passing day that it produced no cars, yet was obliged to pay rents, overhead, and salaries. Consistent with an underlying purpose of the Bankruptcy Code-maximizing the value of the bankrupt estate--it was no abuse of discretion to determine that the Sale prevented further, unnecessary losses.

The Indiana Pensioners exaggerate the extent to which New Chrysler will emerge from the Sale as the twin of Old Chrysler. New Chrysler may manufacture the same lines of cars but it will also make newer, smaller vehicles using Fiat technology that will become available as a result of the Sale--moreover, at the time of the proceedings, Old Chrysler was manufacturing no cars at all. New Chrysler will be run by a new Chief Executive Officer, who has experience in turning around failing auto companies. It may retain many of the same employees, but they will be working under new union contracts that contain a six-year no-strike provision. New Chrysler will still sell cars in some of its old dealerships in the United States, but it will also have new access to Fiat dealerships in the European market. Such transformative use of old and new assets is precisely what one would expect from the § 363(b) sale of a going concern.

II

The Indiana Pensioners next challenge the Sale Order's release of all liens on Chrysler's assets. In general, under § 363(f), assets sold pursuant to §

Automotive, Tempo International Group, Hawtai Automobiles, and Chery Automobile Co.

363(b) may be sold "free and clear of any interest" in the assets when, *inter alia,* the entity holding the interest consents to the sale. 11 U.S.C. § 363(f)(2). The bankruptcy court ruled that, although the Indiana Pensioners did not themselves consent to the release, consent was validly provided by the collateral trustee, who had authority to act on behalf of all first-lien credit holders.

We agree. Through a series of agreements, the Pensioners effectively ceded to an agent the power to consent to such a sale; the agent gave consent; and the Pensioners are bound. Accordingly, questions as to the status or preference of Chrysler's secured debt are simply not presented in this case.

The first-lien holders-among them, the Indiana Pensioners--arranged their investment in Chrysler by means of three related agreements: a First Lien Credit Agreement, a Collateral Trust Agreement, and a Form of Security Agreement. Together, these agreements create a framework for the control of collateral property. The collateral is held by a designated trustee for the benefit of the various lenders (including the Indiana Pensioners). In the event of a bankruptcy, the trustee is empowered to take any action deemed necessary to protect, preserve, or realize upon the collateral. The trustee may only exercise this power at the direction of the lenders' agent; but the lenders are required to authorize the agent to act on their behalf, and any action the agent takes at the request of lenders holding a majority of Chrysler's debt is binding on all lenders, those who agree and those who do not.

When Chrysler went into bankruptcy, the trustee had power to take any action necessary to realize upon the collateral--including giving consent to the sale of the collateral free and clear of all interests under § 363. The trustee could take such action only at the direction of the lenders' agent, and the agent could only direct the trustee at the request of lenders holding a majority of Chrysler's debt. But if those conditions were met--as they were here--then under the terms of the various agreements, the minority lenders could not object to the trustee's actions since they had given their authorization in the first place.

* * *

Anticipating the consequence of this contractual framework, the Indiana Pensioners argue as a last resort that the majority lenders were intimidated or bullied into approving the Sale in order to preserve or enhance relations with the government, or other players in the transaction. Absent this bullying, the Pensioners suggest, the majority lenders would not have requested the agent to direct the sale of the collateral, and the Sale would not have gone through. The Pensioners argue that this renders the lenders' consent ineffective or infirm.

The record before the bankruptcy court, and the record before this Court, does not support a finding that the majority lenders were coerced into agreeing to the Sale. On the whole, the record (and findings) support the view that they acted prudently to preserve substantial value rather than risk a liquidation that might have yielded nothing at all. Moreover, it is not at all clear what impact a finding of coerced consent would have on the validity of the consent given, or whether the bankruptcy court would have jurisdiction-or occasion-to adjudicate the Indiana Pensioners' allegation. Because the facts alleged by the Indiana Pensioners are not substantiated in this record, their arguments based on those allegations provide no ground for relief in this proceeding, and we decline to consider whether the allegations might give rise to some independent cause of action.

III

The Indiana Pensioners argue that the Secretary of the Treasury ("Secretary") exceeded his statutory authority and violated the Constitution by using TARP money to finance the sale of Chrysler's assets. Pensioners raise interesting and unresolved constitutional issues concerning the scope of the Secretary's authority under TARP and the use of TARP money to bail out an automobile manufacturer. However, federal courts are constrained by our own constitutional limitations, including the non-waivable Article III requirement that we have jurisdiction over the case or controversy before us. * * * We do not decide whether the Secretary's actions were constitutional or permitted by statute, because we conclude that the Indiana Pensioners lack standing to raise the TARP issue, and that we lack jurisdiction in this case to entertain that challenge.

Congress enacted the Emergency Economic Stabilization Act ("EESA") on October 3, 2008 in order "to immediately provide authority and facilities that the Secretary of the Treasury can use to restore liquidity and stability to the financial system of the Unites States...." 12 U.S.C. § 5201(1). Title I of EESA authorizes the Treasury Secretary "to establish the Troubled Asset Relief Program (or 'TARP') to purchase, and to make and fund commitments to purchase, troubled assets from any financial institution, on such terms and conditions as are determined by the Secretary." *Id.* § 5211(a)(1). Financial institutions include, but are not limited to, "any bank, savings association, credit union, security broker or dealer, or insurance company." *Id.* § 5202(5).

The statute details procedures for judicial review of the Secretary's decisions, limitations on available relief for TARP violations, and a host of legislative oversight mechanisms. *See, e.g., id.* §§ 5214-15, 5229(a), 5233. For example, courts review the Secretary's TARP decisions in accordance with standards set forth in the Administrative Procedure Act, 5 U.S.C. § 701 et. seq., and the Secretary's actions "shall be held unlawful and set aside if found to be arbitrary, capricious, an abuse of discretion, or not in accordance with law." 12 U.S.C. § 5229(a)(1). Injunctions are available only to remedy constitutional violations and must be "considered and granted or denied by the court on an expedited basis," *id.* § 5229(a)(2)(A), (C), (D); likewise, requests for temporary restraining orders must be considered and decided by the court "within 3 days of the date of the request," *id.* § 5229(a)(2)(B). As for legislative oversight, the statute calls for (among other things) the creation of the Financial Stability Oversight Board, which reviews the exercise of the Secretary's authority (§ 5214), the submission of periodic reports from the Secretary to Congress (§ 5215), the creation of a Congressional Oversight Panel to provide periodic updates to Congress (§ 5233), and the appointment of a special TARP Inspector General (§ 5214(a)(3)). In short, the statute provides swift, narrow, and deferential judicial review of the Secretary's TARP decisions, limits judicial relief, and relies instead on multi-faceted legislative oversight.

The Indiana Pensioners contend that the Secretary exceeded his statutory authority and violated the Constitution by using TARP money to fund the Sale because, *inter alia:* auto companies are not "financial institutions" under TARP; TARP does not authorize the Secretary to arrange and finance the reorganization of a private company; and the Sale effects an unconstitutional taking. In sum, they contend that the Secretary-and by extension, the Executive branch-violated the Constitution by dispensing federal money in excess of the statutory authority awarded by Congress under TARP.[13]

It is clear that TARP gives the Secretary broad discretion to apply financial aid when and where he decides it will best promote the stated goal of restoring stability to the financial markets. But, as detailed above, TARP also contains explicit limitations on the Secretary's authority, and provides for review and oversight, so that TARP is not all-purpose. At oral argument, the government suggested that any industry so "inter-related" with banks that its dealings could adversely impact the national banking system is, for TARP

13

See, e.g., Youngstown Sheet & Tube Co. v. Sawyer, 343 U.S. 579, 585, 72 S.Ct. 863, 96 L.Ed. 1153 (1952) (Executive power "must stem either from an act of Congress or from the Constitution itself.").

purposes, a financial institution. This is surely an expansive definition of "financial institution," albeit broadly protective of the nation's financial structures and arguably related to TARP's mandate of "restor[ing] liquidity and stability" to our markets. The scope of TARP is a consequential and vexed issue that may inevitably require resolution in some later case; but this Court lacks power to resolve it in the present dispute.

Article III of the Constitution limits the judicial power of the United States to the resolution of "cases" and "controversies." U.S. Const. art. III, § 2. This limitation is effectuated in part through the requirement of standing. * * *

At an "irreducible constitutional minimum," Article III standing requires that: (1) the plaintiff suffer an injury in fact; (2) the injury be fairly traceable to the challenged conduct; and (3) the injury will likely be redressed by a favorable decision from the court. * * * We conclude that the Indiana Pensioners lack standing because they cannot demonstrate they have suffered an injury in fact.

An injury in fact is "an invasion of a legally protected interest which is (a) concrete and particularized, and (b) 'actual or imminent, not conjectural or hypothetical.' " *Lujan*, 504 U.S. at 560, 112 S.Ct. 2130 (internal citations, quotation marks and footnote omitted). The Indiana Pensioners contend primarily that their injury in fact arises from the release of the collateral supporting their secured loans. But that collateral was released in exchange for a $2 billion cash payment and a residual deficiency claim. At oral argument, the Pensioners touted the value of the collateral at "around $25 billion" and complained that the value received pursuant to the Sale was a tithe of the actual asset value and an inadequate return on their investment. However, the Indiana Pensioners' argument ignores the bankruptcy court's *finding* that, in the absence of another buyer, the only viable alternative-liquidation-would yield an even *lower* return than the one achieved through the sale funded by TARP money. Judge Gonzalez found, as a fact, that the liquidation value of the collateral "was no greater than $2 billion, *i.e.*, the same amount the first lien secured lenders are receiving under the transaction." Opinion and Order Regarding Emergency Economic Stabilization Act of 2008 and Troubled Asset Relief Program, May 31, 2009, at 5. Since "the Indiana [Pensioners] will receive [their] pro-rata distribution of the value of the collateral," they simply "cannot allege injury in fact." *Id.* The release of collateral for fair (but less-than-hoped-for) value is not injury in fact sufficient to support standing.

* * *

IV

Finally, several objectors appeal from that portion of the Sale Order extinguishing all existing and future claims against New Chrysler, that "(a) arose prior to the Closing Date, (b) relate[ ] to the production of vehicles prior to the Closing Date or (c) otherwise [are] assertable against the Debtors or [are] related to the Purchased Assets prior to the closing date." The objectors can be divided into three groups: (1) plaintiffs with existing product liability claims against Chrysler; (2) plaintiffs with existing asbestos-related claims against Chrysler; and (3) lawyers undertaking to act on behalf of claimants who, although presently unknown and unidentified, might have claims in the future arising from Old Chrysler's production of vehicles. We consider each group's arguments in turn.

A. Existing Product Liability Claims

The Ad Hoc Committee of Consumer-Victims of Chrysler LLC and William Lovitz et al. challenge the foreclosing of New Chrysler's liability for product defects in vehicles produced by Old Chrysler. Section 363(f) provides, in relevant part, that a "trustee may sell property ... free and clear of *any interest in such property,*" under certain circumstances. 11 U.S.C. § 363(f) (emphasis added). The objectors argue that personal injury claims are not "interests in property," and that the district court's reliance on *In re Trans World Airlines, Inc.,* 322 F.3d 283 (3d Cir.2003) (" *TWA* "), which advances a broad reading of "interests in property," was misplaced.

* * *

Appellants argue that [decisions broadly] construing the phrase "any interest in such property" fail to account for the language of 11 U.S.C. § 1141(c), a provision involving confirmed plans of reorganization. Section 1141(c) provides that "except as otherwise provided in the [reorganization] plan or in the order confirming the plan, after confirmation of a plan, the property dealt with by the plan is free and clear of *all claims and interests* of creditors, equity security holders, and of general partners in the debtor." 11 U.S.C. § 1141(c). Appellants argue that Congress must have intentionally included the word "claims" in § 1141(c), and omitted the word from § 363(f), because it was willing to extinguish tort claims in the reorganization context, but unwilling to do so in the § 363 sale context. * * *

We do not place such weight on the absence of the word "claims" in § 363(f). The language and structure of § 1141(c) and § 363(f) differ in many respects. * * *

Given the expanded role of § 363 in bankruptcy proceedings, it makes sense to harmonize the application of § 1141(c) and § 363(f) to the extent permitted by the statutory language. * * * Courts have already done this in other contexts. * * *

We agree with *TWA* * * * that the term "any interest in property" encompasses those claims that "arise from the property being sold." * * *

"To allow the claimants to assert successor liability claims against [the purchaser] while limiting other creditors' recourse to the proceeds of the asset sale would be inconsistent with the Bankruptcy Code's priority scheme." *TWA,* 322 F.3d at 292. Appellants ignore this overarching principle and assume that tort claimants faced a choice between the Sale and an alternative arrangement that would have assured funding for their claims. But had appellants successfully blocked the Sale, they would have been unsecured creditors fighting for a share of extremely limited liquidation proceeds. Given the billions of dollars of outstanding secured claims against Old Chrysler, appellants would have fared no better had they prevailed.

The possibility of transferring assets free and clear of existing tort liability was a critical inducement to the Sale. As in *TWA,* "a sale of the assets of [Old Chrysler] at the expense of preserving successor liability claims was necessary in order to preserve some [55],000 jobs, ... and to provide funding for employee-related liabilities, including retirement benefits [for more than 106,000 retirees]." *TWA,* 322 F.3d at 293; *see also* Sale Opinion at 3.

It is the transfer of Old Chrysler's tangible and intellectual property to New Chrysler that could lead to successor liability (where applicable under state law) in the absence of the Sale Order's liability provisions. Because appellants' claims arose from Old Chrysler's property, § 363(f) permitted the bankruptcy court to authorize the Sale free and clear of appellants' interest in the property.

B. Asbestos Claims

On behalf of herself and others with outstanding or potential claims against Old Chrysler resulting from exposure to asbestos, Patricia Pascale argues that the Sale Order improperly grants New Chrysler immunity without assuring compliance with 11 U.S.C. § 524(g).

Section 524(g) * * * authorizes the court "to enjoin entities from taking legal action for the purpose of directly or indirectly collecting, recovering, or receiving payment or recovery with respect to any [asbestos-related] claim or demand." 11 U.S.C. § 524(g)(1)(B). * * *

By its terms, however, § 524(g) applies only to "a court that enters an order confirming a plan of reorganization under chapter 11." 11 U.S.C. § 524(g)(1)(A). Sections I and II of this opinion conclude that the Sale was proper under § 363. That determination forecloses the application of § 524(g) because there is no plan of reorganization as yet.

C. Future Claims

The Sale Order extinguished the right to pursue claims "on any theory of successor or transferee liability. whether known or unknown as of the Closing, now existing or hereafter arising, asserted or unasserted, fixed or contingent, liquidated or unliquidated." * * *

We affirm this aspect of the bankruptcy court's decision insofar as it constituted a valid exercise of authority under the Bankruptcy Code. However, we decline to delineate the scope of the bankruptcy court's authority to extinguish future claims, until such time as we are presented with an actual claim for an injury that is caused by Old Chrysler, that occurs after the Sale, and that is cognizable under state successor liability law.

(D) THE NEW VALUE EXCEPTION

Part III. FINANCING WITH HYBRID SECURITIES

SECTION A. PREFERRED STOCK FINANCING

1. RIGHTS AND PREFERENCES

(B) THE PREFERRED STOCK CONTRACT

Insert at Casebook page 493 before "(C) Issuer Motivations and Holder Expectations":

(c) Debt or Equity?

For balance sheet reporting purposes, preferred stock may or may not be classified below the debt-equity line on the right hand page. Since 2003, under Statement of Financial Accounting Standards No. 150, the Financial Accounting Standards Board ("FASB") has required that mandatorily redeemable stock be treated as long-term debt for financial statement purposes.

SFAS No. 150 extends this reclassification to three broad types of obligations:

(1) A financial instrument issued in the form of shares that is mandatorily redeemable—that embodies an unconditional obligation requiring the issuer to redeem it by transferring its assets at a specified or determinable date (or dates) or upon an event that is certain to occur.

(2) A financial instrument, other than an outstanding share, that, at inception, embodies an obligation to repurchase the issuer's equity shares, or is indexed to such an obligation, and that requires or may require the issuer to settle the obligation by transferring assets (for example, a forward purchase contract or written put option on the issuer's equity shares that is to be physically settled or net cash settled)

(3) A financial instrument that embodies an unconditional obligation, or a financial instrument other than an outstanding share that embodies a conditional obligation, that the issuer must or may settle by issuing a variable number of its equity shares, if, at inception, the monetary value of the obligation is based solely or predominantly on any of the following: (a) a fixed monetary amount known at inception, for example, a payable settleable with a variable number of the issuer's equity shares; (b) variations in something other than the fair value of the issuer's equity shares, for example, a financial instrument indexed to the S&P 500 and settleable with a variable number of the issuer's

equity shares; or (c) variations inversely related to changes in the fair value of the issuer's equity shares, for example, a written put option that could be net share settled.

The change in treatment does not cover conversion features, conditional redemption features, or other features embedded in financial instruments that are not derivatives in their entirety. It also does not affect the classification or measurement of convertible bonds, puttable stock, or other outstanding shares that are conditionally redeemable.

Does this change in the accounting treatment of mandatorily redeemable preferred hold out implications for the treatment of preferred under corporate law? **Harbinger Capital Partners Master Fund I Ltd. v. Granite Broadcasting Corp.**, 906 A.2d 218 (Del. Ch. 2006), considered a claim that it does. The plaintiff, a holder of mandatorily redeemable preferred stock, objected to the terms of a sale of assets on the ground that it constituted a fraudulent conveyance, claiming standing as a creditor and citing SFAS No. 150 as a primary justification. According to the plaintiff, even though FASB regulations do not control corporate law results, the factors that led to FASB's change of treatment at least raised a fact as to whether the preferred shares should be treated as debt or equity. The Delaware Chancery did consider the question of fact, treating it largely as a matter of contractual intent, and ruled that the plaintiff had not standing, 906 A.2d, 230-31:

"Examining the Granite preferred shares * * * leads clearly to the conclusion that these shares should be treated as equity for standing purposes. The defendants have conceded that these securities are classified as debt by Granite under FAS150. But, as this court noted above, that is not determinative. * * * Rather, the terms of the certificate of designation are clear and unambiguous and the question of whether the preferred shares are debt turns on an examination of those terms. What that analysis reveals is a hybrid security which falls decisively on the side of equity as a matter of law. Of course, the certificate of designation here calls the securities at issue 'shares.' But the fundamental reason that the preferred shares are equity is that they provide no guaranteed right of payment. As Harbinger has discovered, should Granite fail to perform, it has no financial rights other than a claim against the residual value of the corporation. In that sense, the fate of Harbinger's stock is tied directly to Granite's business fortunes, in a way that all the courts cited herein have held is peculiar to equity.

"Moreover, under the certificate of designation, the shares at issue provide Harbinger no right to redeem, no current dividend payments, and no right to have a dividend declared. * * * Further, as the certificate of designation makes clear, the preferred stockholders here do have a range of contractual rights against certain kinds of transactions. Although Harbinger is thus powerless in the sense that it has no vote in the corporation's management until a vote-triggering event, it is bound contractually to Granite in the very way that our courts have held characterizes preferred stock. And, * * * the liquidation preference in this case is tied directly to those assets of the corporation available for distribution to its stockholders. That fact demonstrates convincingly that, before the investment at issue here went poorly, the unambiguous intent of the parties was to create an equity instrument."

3. CLAIMS TO PRINCIPAL, INCLUDING ARREARAGES

(B) ALTERATION BY MERGER

Insert at the end of "Note: Preferred Class Voting In Respect of Mergers," at Casebook 538:

6. ***Distinguishing the Right to Vote from the Right to Consent.***

Matulich v. Aegis Communications Group, Inc., 942 A.2d 946 (Del. Supr. 2008), concerned a short form merger under Del. § 253. A small number of shares of Series B Preferred Stock not held by the majority shareholder remained outstanding. The charter provided explicitly that the preferred had "no voting rights." But the charter also reserved to the preferred the right of "consent to or approval of" charter amendments that impacted its rights and any merger or consolidation of the issuer. An earnest search for the remaining record holder of the preferred was conducted, but no holder was found. The issuer accordingly requested and obtained from the Court of Chancery an order deeming the holders of the preferred to have approved the merger.

A holder of common stock cashed out in the merger then appeared to claim that the § 253 merger was no statutorily authorized because a vote of the preferred was required and the majority shareholder owned less than 90 percent of the preferred. The Supreme Court rejected the claim:

> "The Series B shares possess no statutory voting rights, but do have a contractual right to consent and approve. We hold that Series B shareholders' contractual right to consent and approve does not

constitute a statutory right to vote on the merger. Therefore, the Court of Chancery properly concluded that the contractual rights of the Series B Preferred Shareholders were irrelevant in calculating whether [the majority shareholder] had the statutory voting power necessary to execute a short-form merger. Consequently, as a matter of law, [the] challenge to the Merger is without merit."

SECTION B. CONVERTIBLE SECURITIES AND WARRANTS

2. CONFLICTS OF INTEREST

(A) PROTECTIVE CONTRACT PROVISIONS

Insert at the bottom of Casebook 562, after "Note: Implied in Fact Anti-Diultion Protection":

NOTE: AUTHORIZED STOCK

For a convertible security to be converted or for a warrant to be exercised, there must be authorized common stock in a sufficient quantity available under the issuer's charter. It is customary for the issuer to make a representation respecting the availability of such stock at the closing at original issue. Such a representation, even if true, does not prevent the issuer and its shareholders from subsequently amending the charter to reduce the number of authorized shares. How then is a convertible or warrant contract to assure the availability of the stock? A covenant to this effect seems indicated. But suppose the issuer and its shareholders breach the covenant? Given an issue of convertible debt, a declaration of an event of default could follow. But the desirability of a default declaration can depend on the condition of the issuer at the time. If the convertibles are way in the money or our way out of the money, acceleration upon default might not get the convertible holders to the desired result. Common sense is called for when disputes occur.

Hildreth v. Castle Dental Centers, 939 A.2d 1281 (Del. Supr.. 2007), presents such a case. There a class of convertible preferred, if converted, would have taken the lion's share of the proceeds of a cash out merger. The problem was that issuer did not have sufficient available authorized common to permit conversion. The issuer had on two occasions attempted to amend its charter to increase the number of authorized shares, but in both instances had omitted to seek a ratifying vote of the common stock. The amendments, accordingly, were invalid. The merger agreement took this awkward state of affairs into account, providing that the merger proceeds be distributed as if the convertibles had been converted. The plaintiffs, holders of common stock, sought an appraisal. Their theory was that the merger proceeds should have been distributed to them on the assumption that the common stock had a right to 100 percent of the merger proceeds. The Delaware Supreme Court rejected the theory:

"It is true that in this case the merger agreement used the preferred stock's conversion feature to calculate the proportion of the total equity that would be paid to the preferred stockholders. But the parties to the agreement also could have used other metrics instead. For example, they could have "done the math" and assigned a dollar value to each share of preferred stock * * * and achieved the same result, irrespective of the applicable conversion formula.

"The issue in this appraisal is not what mechanism the parties to the merger agreement chose to allocate a price per share, but what proportion of the total equity, in fairness, should have been allocated to the common stock in this appraisal proceeding. The [plaintiffs] failed to present any evidence to the Court of Chancery concerning the proper allocation of value as between the preferred and common stock, separate and apart from the allocation method set forth in the merger agreement."

Insert at the end of "Note: Convertible Bond Contracts," at Casebook page 579:

5. Ratchet Averted.

Amazon.Com, Inc. v. Hoffman, 2009 WL 2031789 (Del.Ch.), concerns the operation of a "ratchet" type antidilution provision. Amazon held Series A convertible preferred stock of Basis Technology with a conversion price of $1.36 per share. The antidilution provisions provided for a downward adjustment if the Basis issued additional shares for less than $1.36. Basis issued new Series B convertible preferred stock for $1.39 per share. Amazon contended that the price was *above* the new stock's fair value and had been set to avoid triggering the antidilution clause, alleging breaches of fiduciary and good faith duties by the Basis board.

The fiduciary claim presented an obvious difficulty: How can a sale of *overpriced* stock by the board entail a breach of duty to the company? The Chancery Court dismissed the fiduciary claim as follows:

"The debate comes down to question of whether some fiduciary duty owed directly (and apart from any duty owed to the common shareholders) to the preferred shareholders is implicated. Putting aside the authority that preferred stockholders have no fiduciary duty claims against directors that are not also fiduciary duty claims of common stockholders, Series B Preferred stock (convertible into an equal number of common shares) was issued at a price greater than fair value. * * * This is not a case where shares were issued for less than fair value and thus, might have had a dilutive effect (but that would have been a claim shared with the common shareholders). In short, there was no breach of fiduciary duty and, to the extent that there might have been one in the nature of the duty of care, the exculpatory provision in the Charter precludes the pursuit of any such claim."

The Chancery court also dismissed the contractual claim:

"The covenant of good faith applies when the 'contract is truly silent with respect to the matter at hand, and only when the Court finds that the expectations of the parties were so fundamental that it is clear that they did not feel a need to negotiate about them.' The contractual requirements, set forth in the Designation, negotiated by Amazon, expressly and clearly define its rights with respect to this topic. If additional shares are issued at less than $1.36 per share, the anti-dilution provisions come into play. The Agreement, of course, does not expressly address what is to happen if shares are issued at a price equal to or greater than $1.36 per share, but the only plausible inference is that the parties considered the issue and reached agreement as to what price would trigger anti-dilution protection. * * *

"Another way of characterizing Amazon's complaint is that the defendant directors were motivated by a desire to circumvent the anti-dilution provisions of the Agreement. That is, the price was set not only without adequate process, but also with the specific purpose of avoiding the rights conferred on Amazon as the holder of Series A Preferred shares. Amazon attempts to blend its contractual rights with whatever fiduciary protections it may have. If one complies with the terms of the Agreement-as the director defendants did-there is no express breach of contract. Similarly, there was no breach of the duty of loyalty when the defendant directors authorized the issuance of shares for greater than fair value under these circumstances. In short, by combining independent contractual duties and fiduciary duties, Amazon cannot demonstrate a resulting and more powerful right. If nothing else, such a creative approach would run the risk of altering the carefully honed relationship among preferred shareholders and common shareholders."

(B) DUTIES IMPLIED IN LAW

Insert after "Note: Van Gemert's *Operative Theory," at the top of Casebook page 584*:

NOTE: THE DUTY TO NOTIFY IN DELAWARE

The Delaware Chancery Court got an opportunity to address a question respecting implied notice duties to holders of a warrant in **Corporate Property Associates 14 v. CHR Holding Corp.**, 2008 WL 963048 (Del.Ch.). The warrant issuer made substantial borrowings, the proceeds of which were funneled out to the stockholders as cash dividends. After effecting the dividends, the issuer sold itself in a cashout merger. The dividend amounts amounted to over thirty percent of the ultimate merger consideration. A warrant holder accordingly would have been better off exercising in advance of the dividends. But the warrants in question made no provision for notice in advance of a dividend paid on common stock and did not provide antidilution protection in the event of a cash dividend. The warrants did provide protections respecting mergers, termed "Liquidity Events." These included not only a requirement that the issuer provide notice but a further statement that, if necessary to consummate a liquidity event, the parties will work together in good faith to use means not provided for in the Warrants to balance the goals of "preserv[ing] for the [Warrantholder] the economic value of th[e] Warrant[s] while also ensuring that the Company has the maximum freedom to structure and consummate a Liquidity Event."

The Chancery brushed off the suggestion that a fiduciary duty to the warrantholders supported a right to notice. Nor did the good faith language applied to liquidity events support a good faith duty to provide notice:

"The problem with that argument is that a court cannot and should not use the implied covenant of good faith and fair dealing to fill a gap in a contract with an implied term unless it is clear from the contract that the parties would have agreed to that term had they thought to negotiate the matter. The protections that [plaintiff] cites in the contract convince me that the parties thought about and negotiated anti-dilution provisions. The parties agreed to protect the Warrants against dilution by stock dividend. They even created a broad gap-filling provision for liquidity events because they anticipated that the structure and exact details of such events are often difficult to predict in advance. Issuing cash dividends, however, is a simple and wellknown dilution technique. Sophisticated parties such as those involved in this transaction know that cash dividends are a dilution technique, that the only protection against dilution is contractual, and that there are methods for protecting themselves contractually. Because the Warrants evidence negotiation over anti-dilution provisions and because issuing a cash dividend is a dilution event well-known by sophisticated parties such as those involved in this transaction, the only reasonable inference to be drawn from the Warrants' silence on this point is that the parties did not agree to protect the Warrants against dilution by cash dividends. Using the implied covenant of good faith and fair dealing to imply contractual protection from dilution by cash dividends "would be to grant [plaintiff], by judicial fiat, contractual provisions that they failed to secure for themselves at the bargaining table."

Another count in the complaint grounded in fraud and negligent misrepresentation survived motion to dismiss. Prior to the second dividend, the plaintiffs inquired specifically of the issuer as to pending significant corporate developments, and received an answer that made no reference to the dividend.

Insert after "Note: Fair and Unfair Mergers," at Casebook page 596:

LC Capital Master Fund, Ltd.. v. James

Court of Chancery of Delaware, 2010.
990 A.2d 435.

STRINE, Vice Chancellor.

I. *Introduction*

Plaintiff LC Capital Master Fund, Ltd. ("LC Capital"), a preferred stockholder of QuadraMed Corporation ("QuadraMed"), seeks to enjoin the acquisition by defendant Francisco Partners II, L.P. ("Francisco Partners") of QuadraMed (the "Merger") because the consideration to be received by the preferred stockholders of QuadraMed does not exceed the "as if converted" value the preferred were contractually entitled to demand in the event of a merger. That "as if converted" value was based on a formula in the certificate of designation (the "Certificate") governing the preferred stock, and gave the preferred the bottom line right to convert into common at a specified ratio (the "Conversion Formula") and then receive the same consideration as the common in the Merger. The plaintiff purports to have the support of 95% of the preferred stockholders in seeking injunctive relief and I therefore refer to the plaintiff as the preferred stockholders.

* * *

* * * I find that the preferred stockholders have not proven a reasonable probability of success on the merits of their fiduciary duty claim. * * *

* * * [The preferred stockholders should] * * * seek relief through appraisal or through an equitable action for damages. * * *

II. *Factual Background*

* * *

Under the terms of the challenged merger agreement (the "Merger Agreement"), Francisco Partners will acquire QuadraMed at a price of $8.50 per share of common stock. The preferred stockholders will receive $13.7097 in cash in exchange for each share of preferred stock. The price for the preferred stock set forth in the Merger Agreement was pegged to the conversion right the Certificate granted to the preferred stockholders in the event of a merger. That conversion right allowed the preferred stockholders to convert their preferred shares into common shares and then to receive the same consideration as the common stock received in the merger. The conversion was determined by using the Conversion Formula of 1.6129 shares of preferred stock to one share of common stock. That is, in order to value the preferred stock, the merging parties agreed to simply cash out the preferred stock at the price the preferred

The preferred stockholders seek to enjoin the Merger on the grounds that the defendants breached their fiduciary duties of care and loyalty. But, the preferred stockholders do not allege that the defendants breached their *Revlon* duties as to *all* shareholders by approving a transaction that does not fully value QuadraMed as an entity. Instead, the preferred stockholders argue that the Merger consideration was unfairly allocated between the common and preferred stock. That is, the preferred stockholders do not challenge the overall adequacy of the Merger consideration. Rather, the preferred stockholders claim that they simply did not receive a big enough slice of the pie because the Board allocated the Merger consideration to the preferred stock on an "as-if converted" basis, which the preferred stockholders believe understates the value of their shares.

1. *The Rights Of The Preferred Stockholders*

Requesting a preliminary injunction is the only means the preferred stockholders have to block the transaction because, per the Certificate, the preferred stock does not have the right to vote on a merger. The circumstances in which the preferred stock has voting rights are limited to: (1) if the Certificate were to be amended in a way "that materially adversely affects the voting powers, rights or preferences" of the preferred stockholders; (2) if any class of shares with ranking before or in parity with the preferred stock were to be created; and (3) if the company were to incur "any long term, senior indebtedness of the Corporation in an aggregate principal amount exceeding $8,000,000." Relatedly, if four quarterly dividends are in arrears, the preferred stockholders can elect two substitute directors.

The Certificate includes a number of other rights for the preferred stock that are arguably relevant to the current dispute. As mentioned, the preferred stock has a dividend right. This provides for the payment of a dividend of $1.375 per year, but it is to be paid only "when, as and if authorized and declared" by the Board. The Certificate also provides a liquidation preference of $25 (plus accrued dividends) for each share of preferred stock. But, the Certificate does not afford the preferred stock a right to force a liquidation. Most relevantly, the Certificate expressly provides that a merger does not trigger the preferred stock's liquidation preference.

The preferred stockholders also point out that the Certificate includes a mandatory conversion right that allows QuadraMed to force the preferred stockholders to convert into common shares. The preferred stockholders stress that this provision of the Certificate may only be used by QuadraMed to force conversion when the company's common stock hits a price of $25 per share, far above the $8.50 per common share Merger value. But, like the liquidation preference, the mandatory conversion provision does not have bite in a merger. That is, the Certificate does not provide that, in the event of a merger, the preferred stockholders must be converted at a formula that affords the preferred stockholders an implied common stock value of $25 per share.

To the contrary, in a merger, the preferred stockholders will receive either: 1) the consideration determined by the Board in a merger agreement; or 2) if the preferred choose, the right to convert their shares using the Conversion Formula into common shares and redeem the same consideration as the common stockholders. The bottom line right of the preferred stockholders in a merger, therefore, is not tied to its healthy liquidation preference or the company's mandatory conversion strike price-it is simply the right to convert the shares into common stock at the Conversion Formula and then be treated pari passu with the common.

2. *The Board's Decision To Accept Francisco Partners' Bid For QuadraMed*

Over the years, QuadraMed received expressions of interest from a number of potential acquirors. From 2008 to date, QuadraMed has been seriously considering a sale. From early on in this strategic process, the preferred stockholders demanded a high price, even $25, for their stock, apparently under the mistaken view that they had a right to their liquidation preference in the event of a merger. Initially, some bidders indicated an interest in either meeting the preferred stockholders' asking price-which would mean paying much more for the preferred stock than the common-or at least allowing the preferred stock to remain outstanding after the consummation of a merger. For example, Francisco Partner's first bid for QuadraMed, made in October 2008, offered to acquire the company at $11 per share of common stock and to allow the preferred stock to remain outstanding. And, a later bid, received August 31, 2009 from a bidder referred to as "Bidder D" in the proxy materials, proposed acquiring QuadraMed for $10.00 per share of common stock, and $25.00 par value for each share of preferred stock. By "par value," Bidder D seems not to have meant to offer the preferred stockholders $25 per share in current value but a security with the future potential of reaching that value. But this was perhaps not as clearly expressed as it could have been.

As the negotiations continued, moreover, both Francisco Partners and Bidder D revised their offers downward. After several months of negotiating, Francisco Partners submitted a revised offer of $9.50 per share of common stock, with the requirement that the preferred stock be cashed-out. In March 2009, the Board rejected this offer, and negotiations with Francisco Partners were suspended. And, after its initial approach, Bidder D made very plain its earlier position and explained that it "never intended to offer face value" for the preferred stock and was instead interested in paying $10 per share of common stock and reaching agreement with the holders of preferred stock on the terms of a debt instrument with a $25 face value, but a present value equal to $10 per share on an as-if converted basis. Therefore, the treatment of the preferred stock and common stock under Bidder D's initial proposal and under the Merger is not as different as at first appears.

In light of the various bids being made for the company, QuadraMed's outside counsel, Crowell & Moring, LLP ("Crowell & Moring"), sent the QuadraMed Board a memorandum on September 1, 2009 addressing the legal issues relating to apportioning merger consideration between the common stock and preferred stock (the "September 2009 Memorandum"). In substance, the September 2009 Memorandum was Crowell & Moring's distillation of and update to a memorandum that Richards, Layton & Finger, P.A. ("Richards Layton"), QuadraMed's Delaware counsel, had prepared in June 2006. In 2006, while QuadraMed was in negotiations over a possible acquisition by a private equity firm, referred to as "Bidder B" in QuadraMed's proxy materials, Richards Layton authored a memorandum, dated June 22, 2006, that provided a general overview of the legal authority relevant to allocating merger consideration between common stock and preferred stock in a merger. The memorandum was addressed to counsel, Crowell & Moring, not the QuadraMed Board. Crowell & Moring's September 2009 Memorandum summarized Richards Layton's 2006 advice and discussed this court's April 2009 decision In re Appraisal of Metromedia Int'l Group, Inc., [971 A.2d 893 (Del.Ch.2009)] which addressed the allocation of merger consideration between common and preferred stock in the context of an appraisal action.

The QuadraMed Board formed a special committee of independent directors (the "Special Committee") to evaluate the various bids. QuadraMed's Board is comprised of six individuals: Duncan James, William Jurika, Lawrence English, James Peebles, Robert Miller, and Robert Pevenstein (collectively, the "Special Committee members"). The Special Committee was comprised of Jurika, English, Peebles, Miller, and Pevenstein-that is, all of the Special Committee members except James, who was also QuadraMed's Chief Executive Officer. With the exception of Jurika, who owns over 650,000 shares of QuadraMed common stock, the Special Committee members hold a nominal amount of QuadraMed shares and in the money stock options. The preferred stockholders have not presented any evidence that these members' holdings of QuadraMed shares and options constitute a material portion of their personal wealth.

In early autumn 2009, after Bidder D's approach in August, QuadraMed's investment bankers shopped the deal. At this time, Francisco Partners made a second bid, offering $8.50 per share of common stock and requiring the cash-out of the preferred stock on an as-if converted basis, which yielded a value of $13.7097 per preferred share. Francisco Partners insisted on cashing out the preferred stock because it did not want to bear the risk of a voluntary conversion of the preferred stock into common stock after the Merger. The evidence also indicates that Francisco Partners wanted to increase QuadraMed's borrowing after the Merger, and therefore wanted to eliminate the preferred stock because the Certificate gives the preferred stock a right to vote on any incurrence of debt in excess of $8,000,000.

Because the preferred stockholders were demanding more consideration than the common stock, one of the questions before the Special Committee was what fiduciary duties it owed to the common stock and preferred stock when allocating the proposed Merger's consideration. The evidence indicates that the Special Committee carefully considered the duties it owed to both the preferred and common stockholders, and was concerned about any perception that it was favoring one class over the other. In a series of meetings, the Special Committee reviewed the bids, and at those meetings, QuadraMed's counsel informed the Special Committee that the Board could adopt a merger agreement that cashed out the preferred stockholders, and that, if the Board respected the bottom line contractual rights of the preferred stockholders in a merger, it did not have to allocate additional value to the preferred stockholders. Indeed, Crowell & Moring said that the Board had to be careful about giving the preferred stockholders more unless there were special reasons to do so. Crowell & Moring also reported that Francisco Partner's counsel, Shearman & Sterling, LLP, had also reached the conclusion that a cash out of the preferred stock at closing was permissible under Delaware law, and that Francisco Partners would not insist on an "appraisal out" provision in the Merger Agreement so as to satisfy any concerns the Special Committee might have regarding the treatment of the preferred stock.

Meanwhile, Bidder D had been attempting to persuade the preferred stockholders to take a new debt security with a current value equal to what the common would receive but with a future upside. But, Bidder D found it "extremely difficult" to convince the holders of preferred stock to exchange their stock for a new debt security, and its bid foundered. Once Bidder D withdrew its offer on November 22, 2009, Francisco Partners became the only remaining bidder for QuadraMed. Although the Special Committee resisted cashing out the preferred stock for some time, the Committee eventually relented once it became clear that Francisco Partners would not do a deal that allowed QuadraMed's preferred stock to survive the Merger.

On December 7, 2009, a Special Committee meeting was held to consider approval of the Merger with Francisco Partners. At that meeting, Piper Jaffray, QuadraMed's financial advisor, presented an opinion that $8.50 per common share was fair to the common stockholders from a financial point of view. There was no separate opinion addressing the fairness of the Merger to the preferred stockholders. After deliberation, the Special Committee unanimously approved the Merger with Francisco Partners. From the meeting minutes, it appears that the Special Committee was wary of doing a deal that allocated more consideration to the preferred stock than to the common stock for two reasons: (1) shifting additional merger consideration to the preferred stock would cause the holders of common stock, who were the only stockholders who had a right to vote on the Merger, to vote against the transaction; and (2) there was no special reason to deviate from the Conversion Formula provided in the Certificate for allocating consideration to the preferred stock.

In the latter regard, it is fair to say that the Special Committee's equitable heartstrings were not moved to bestow upon the preferred stockholders anything better than receipt of the same treatment as the common stockholders on an as-if converted basis. Had a particular bidder insisted, after negotiations with the preferred, on doing a deal with differential consideration, the Special Committee would seem to have had an open and receptive mind if the proposal offered a more favorable valuation to all stockholders. But even then, the Special Committee, I infer, would have harbored a concern if the allocation system strayed too far (in either direction) from the Conversion Formula in the Certificate.

III. *Legal Analysis*

* * *

B. *The Preferred Stockholders Have Not Met Their Burden To Justify Enjoining The Merger*

1. *The Preferred Stockholders Have Not Shown That The QuadraMed Board Likely Breached Its Fiduciary Duties By Allocating To The Preferred Stock The Bottom Line Consideration Contractually Owed To Them*

* * * The preferred stockholders, pointing to the decisions of this court in *Jedwab v. MGM Grand Hotels, Inc.* [509 A.2d 584 (Del.Ch.1986),] and *In re FLS Holdings, Inc. Shareholders Litigation*, [1993 WL 104562 (Del.Ch. Apr. 2, 1993),] argue that the QuadraMed board had the duty to make a "fair" allocation of the Merger consideration between the common and preferred stockholders. To do this fairly, the preferred stockholders argue that the board had to set up some form of negotiating agent, with the duty and discretion to exert leverage on behalf of the preferred stockholders in the allocation process. This need, the preferred stockholders say, is heightened because of an unsurprising fact: the directors of QuadraMed own common stock and do not

own preferred stock. Indeed, the preferred stockholders say, every member of the Special Committee owned common stock and one member, Jurika, owned over five million dollars worth. How, they say, could such directors fairly balance the interests of the preferred against their own interest in having the common get as much as possible? At the very least, the preferred imply, the QuadraMed Board should have charged certain directors with representing the preferred, and enabled them to retain qualified legal and financial advisors to argue for the preferred and to value the preferred based on its unique contractual rights and their economic value.

* * *

* * * I perceive no basis to find that the directors sought to advantage the common stockholders at the unfair expense of the preferred stockholders. What the preferred stockholders complain about is that the directors did not perceive themselves as having a duty to allocate more Merger consideration to the preferred than the preferred could demand as an entitlement under the Certificate. Had the Board been advised properly and had the right mindset, the preferred stockholders say, they would have given weight to various contractual rights of the preferred, such as their liquidation preference rights, and determined that on the basis of those rights, they should get a higher share than the Certificate guaranteed they could demand. Ideally, in fact, the Board should have employed a bargaining agent on their behalf to vigorously contend for the proposition that the largest part of the roast should be put on the preferred stockholders' plate.

* * *

A close look at those cases, however, does not buttress the preferred stockholders' arguments. Notable in both cases was the absence of any contractual provision such as the one that exists in this case. That is, from what one can tell from *FLS Holdings* and *Jedwab,* there was no objective contractual basis-such as the conversion mechanism here-in either of those cases for the board to allocate the merger consideration between the preferred and the common. In the absence of such a basis, the only protection for the preferred is if the directors, as the backstop fiduciaries managing the corporation that sold them their shares, figure out a fair way to fill the gap left by incomplete contracting. Otherwise, the preferred would be subject to entirely arbitrary treatment in the context of a merger.

The broad language in *FLS Holdings* and *Jedwab* must, I think, be read against that factual backdrop. I say so for an important reason. Without this factual context, those opinions are otherwise in sharp tension with the great weight of our law's precedent in this area. In his recent decision in [*In re Trados Inc. Shareholder Litigation*, 2009 WL 2225958, at *7 (Del.Ch. July 24, 2009)], Chancellor Chandler summarized the weight of authority very well:

> Generally the rights and preferences of preferred stock are contractual in nature. This Court has held that directors owe fiduciary duties to preferred stockholders as well as common stockholders where the right claimed by the preferred "is not to a preference as against the common stock but rather a right shared equally with the common." Where this is not the case, however, "generally it will be the duty of the board, where discretionary judgment is to be exercised, to prefer the interests of the common stock-as the good faith judgment of the board sees them to be-to the interests created by the special rights, preferences, etc., of preferred stock, where there is a conflict." Thus, in circumstances where the interests of the common stockholders diverge from those of the preferred stockholders, it is *possible* that a director could breach her duty by improperly favoring the interests of the preferred stockholders over those of the common stockholders.

Notably, that summary relied heavily on decisions by Chancellor Allen, who authored both *Jedwab* and [*Equity-Linked Investors, L.P. v. Adams*, 705 A.2d 1040, 1042 (Del.Ch.1997)]. Does the summary of *Trados* expose some inconsistency in our law?

No, not when Chancellor Allen's decision in *HB Korenvaes Investments, L.P. v. Marriott Corp.* [1993 WL 205040 (Del.Ch. June 9, 1993),] is considered. In that case, a board took very aggressive action that was, objectively speaking, adverse to the interest of the preferred stockholders. The Marriott board agreed to a transaction that issued a large special dividend (of certain businesses!) to the common stock and indefinitely suspended dividends on the preferred stock. The preferred stockholders then sought to enjoin the payment of the special dividend, arguing that Marriott's directors breached their fiduciary duties to the preferred stockholders by agreeing to the transaction. Chancellor Allen rejected that argument, finding that even on the assumption that the board had acted to advantage the common in the transaction, no breach of duty of loyalty claim was stated.

* * * Chancellor Allen * * * found that the fact that the certificate of designation considered the possibility of an in-kind dividend and gave the

preferred certain rights in that context was dispositive of whether there was any fiduciary duty claim * * *.

The reasoning of *Korenvaes* reconciles the doctrine. When, by contract, the rights of the preferred in a particular transactional context are articulated, it is those rights that the board must honor. To the extent that the board does so, it need not go further and extend some unspecified fiduciary beneficence on the preferred at the expense of the common. When, however, as in *Jedwab* and *FLS Holdings,* there is no objective contractual basis for treatment of the preferred, then the board must act as a gap-filling agency and do its best to fairly reconcile the competing interests of the common and preferred.

This case is much closer to *Korenvaes* than it is to *Jedwab.* Although the preferred stockholders make much of the fact that the Certificate does not mandate that the Board accord the preferred stockholders the same treatment as the common in a merger, the only right that the preferred stockholders extracted for themselves was to receive the same consideration they would have received if they had converted their shares per the Conversion Formula set forth in the Certificate. In a situation where the preferred have no mandatory right to annual dividends, no voting rights on a merger, and where the Certificate plainly provides that a merger is not a liquidation event triggering a right to receipt of accrued dividends and the liquidation preferences before the common is paid, it is difficult to fathom any duty on the part of the QuadraMed Board to go further and allocate additional value to the preferred. * * *

This, of course, is not to say that the QuadraMed Board did not owe the preferred stockholders fiduciary duties in connection with the Merger. The Board certainly did. But those were the duties it also owed to the common. In the context of a sale of a company, those are the duties articulated in *Revlon* and its progeny; namely, to take reasonable efforts to secure the highest price reasonably available for the corporation. Notably, the preferred stockholders do not argue that the Board fell short of its obligations in this regard.[56] They simply

---

[56] Therefore, in this decision, I need not confront what might be considered a much harder case. Imagine an issuance of preferred stock that had an absolute right to annual dividend payments of a large amount. The corporation's discounted cash flow ("DCF") valuation indicates that the corporation could pay those dividends. The certificate of designation, like the one here, only gives the preferred the right to convert based on a formula, and does not give the preferred the right to vote on a merger, nor does it treat a merger as an event implicating the preferred's

right to a liquidation preference.

The corporation is valued fairly based on a DCF model in the merger. That is, the total consideration is fair. But, the conversion formula results in the preferred stockholders receiving a price for their shares that is lower than the discounted value of the dividends the preferred stockholders would be guaranteed to receive in the next five years. The board realizes this but chooses not to allocate more consideration to the preferred.

This hypothetical case is harder because the financial analysis undergirding the board's determination to proceed with the merger suggests that the corporation would have the financial capacity to pay the dividends to the preferred and that the certificate of designations would require that the board do so if the corporation remained as a going concern.

But remember that the preferred would not have bargained for, in the context of a merger, any contractual protection other than the bottom line right to be treated on as converted basis and the board would not have dishonored that protection. Under the reasoning of Chancellor Allen in *Korenvaes,* the board would not have owed any fiduciary duty of loyalty to somehow adjust upward the preferred stock's portion of the consideration. In that case, as mentioned, he sanctioned aggressive board action that clearly advantaged the common at the expense of the preferred. Because the preferred had bargained only for a limited right of protection in that context and the board has not deprived them of that protection, Chancellor Allen found that the board had no further duty and could take the action it did.

I need not answer the hard case here because the preferred stockholders have made no argument along these lines and have no right to demand that they actually receive annual dividends. The judicial sanctioning of the notion that the preferred get more merger consideration than they actually bargained for would, though, seem only to have appeal to those who believe that appraisal proceedings are now too predictable and non-burdensome. Indeed, the only thing rendering the future dividend stream in the hard case a non-speculative future source of income would be the judicial holding that preferred stockholders, who did not bargain for the right to block a merger that would result in the end of the corporation and therefore their future dividend stream, have to be compensated for the very stream that they did not procure a contractual right to force to continue. In that regard, the traditional appraisal use of the term "going concern" value cannot be rationally thought to have been intended to express the implicit notion that preferred stock, with no contractual right to block a merger or to receive any special economic treatment in a merger, can claim that the merger did not accord them fair value on the game theory-type speculation that: 1) if the want more of the proceeds than they are guaranteed by the Certificate. But I do not believe that the Board acted wrongly in viewing itself as under no obligation to satisfy that desire.

To indulge such a notion would create great uncertainty and inefficiency for corporations seeking to engage in mergers and acquisitions. Having had the chance to extract more and having only obtained the right to demand treatment under the Conversion Formula that operates to allocate any consideration in a merger between the preferred and the common on a basis the preferred assented to in the Certificate, why should the preferred have the right to ask the Board to give them more? The preferred stockholders' view of what the Board should do if this notion is embraced exemplifies the problem. The preferred stockholders would have the Board consider as relevant to value facts such as the preferred stock's dividend rights, rights in the event of liquidation, and limited voting rights. These, the preferred shareholders say, should be taken into account. But, of course, if that is so, it is also necessary to take into account the fact that the common get to vote on a merger and the preferred do not, and that the common

---

corporation did not engage in a merger, the preferred stockholders would have received a guaranteed share of the company's going concern cash flow; 2) that although the preferred stockholders received the bottom line consideration they were guaranteed by the certificate of designation and although the total price paid for the corporation was fair, the preferred stockholders' share of the merger consideration was less than fair in light of the *contractual* share of dividends they would have received even though they did not have the *contractual* right to block the merger that terminated that stream of future payments.

This example illustrates a tension that permeates the preferred stockholders' argument. Although they rely on the Board's supposed failure to comply with the equitable duties owed to them as preferred stockholders, the preferred stockholders continually refer back to their contractual rights as the basis for arguing for special fiduciary consideration. But in the context of a merger, they had no right to demand a special dividend, consideration equal to the liquidation preference formula, or any of the other sorts of things on which they base their argument for higher value. It is only to the extent that a judge implies that rights of this kind, which could have been but were not insulated by contractual protections from defeasement by merger, must be compensated for by equity that they have economic value in a merger. Our law has not, to date, embraced the notion that Chancery should create economic value for preferred stockholders that they failed to secure at the negotiating table.

stockholders get to elect a majority of the Board even if dividends are not paid to the preferred stockholders, and the preferred get to elect two substitute directors. That is, the Board would have to "weigh" these soft contractual possibilities against each other and somehow value them. Realizing that this is not so easy, the preferred stockholders say they have a simple answer: just form two special committees, have each retain their own advisors, and go at it. They can cut up the pie, and, while they do it, the acquiror will, in their hypothetical world, wait patiently for the results.

* * *

Another counterproductive consequence would result from accepting the preferred stockholders' arguments. For its entire history, our corporate law has tried to insulate the good faith decisions of disinterested corporate directors from judicial second-guessing for well-known policy reasons. The business judgment rule embodies that policy judgment. When mergers and acquisitions activity became a more salient and constant feature of corporate life, our law did not cast aside the values of the business judgment rule. * * *

To hold that independent directors are disabled from the protections of the business judgment rule when addressing a merger because they own common stock, and not the corporation's preferred stock, is not, therefore, something that should be done lightly. Corporate law must work in practice to serve the best interests of society and investors in creating wealth. Director compensation is already a difficult enough issue to address without adding on the need to ponder whether the independent directors need to buy or receive as compensation a share of any preferred stock issuance made by the corporation, for fear that, if they do not have an equally-weighted portfolio of some kind, they will not be able to impartially balance questions that potentially affect the common and preferred stockholders in different ways. Adhering to the rule of Equity-Linked Investors, *Trados,* and other similar cases, which hold that it is the duty of directors to pursue the best interests of the corporation and its common stockholders, if that can be done faithfully with the contractual promises owed to the preferred, avoids this policy dilemma. Admittedly, it does not solve for certain situations that directors might create themselves by authorizing multiple and sometimes exotic classes of common stock, situations that have led this court to, as a matter of necessity, consider the directors' portfolio balance, but it at least does not exacerbate the already complex challenge of compensating independent directors in a sensible way. And, given the unique nature of preferred stock and the often-fraught circumstances that lead to its issuance, our law should be chary to somehow suggest that otherwise independent directors should be receiving shares of this kind at the risk of facing being called "non-independent" or, worse, being deemed by loose reasoning to be "interested" and therefore somehow personally liable under the entire fairness standard for a merger allocation decision.

Here, the plaintiffs have also failed to impugn the Board's entitlement to the business judgment rule for a more mundane reason. Even if the court must, as I think it does not in this situation, consider whether the otherwise independent directors comprising the Special Committee could, because of their ownership of common stock and no preferred stock, impartially balance the interests at stake, the plaintiffs have not advanced facts that support a reasonable inference that any of the Special Committee members are materially self-interested. I say *any* forthrightly. As to director Jurika, who owns a large common stock stake, a shift in the merger consideration of 10% to the preferred would cost him approximately $500,000. That amount of money, of course, would be material to most Americans. But most Americans are not corporate directors, and do not have a $5.6 million stake of common stock in any company. And, the plaintiffs have not advanced any reason to believe that the hypothetical 10% shift would be important to Jurika. The man could be as rich as Croesus or Jimmy Buffett. The plaintiffs have a burden here and they have not even tried to meet it. As to the other directors on the Special Committee, they have failed even more obviously. Directors English, Miller, Peebles, and Pevenstein own only $61,284 worth of common stock and in the money options collectively. Even a fairly drastic shift of 20% of the merger consideration from the preferred to the common would only reduce those directors' collective take by approximately $28,000, and the plaintiffs do not make any attempt to show that this would be material to these directors' personal economic circumstances. Thus, even under the plaintiffs' theory, the business judgment rule, and not the entire fairness standard, applies to the Special Committee's decision.

* * *

NOTE: APPRAISAL RIGHTS

In re Appraisal of Metromedia International Group, Inc. --- A.2d ----, 2009 WL 1110663 (Del.Ch.), was an appraisal action brought by a group of convertible preferred stockholders in the wake of a reverse triangular merger in which the issuer was the survivor. The merger occurred after the acquiring corporation's acquisition subsidiary had already acquired in a friendly tender offer approximately 77 percent of the issuer's common shares. After the tender offer, the merger agreement granted the acquisition subsidiary the option (referred to as the "Top-Up Option") to obtain additional common shares from the issuer sufficient to raise the subsidiary's ownership stake in the issuer to 90 percent. The exercise of the option was followed by a short-form merger under Delaware § 253 in which the remaining common shares were cashed out for $1.80. The preferred was not cashed out in the merger, but its holders did have appraisal rights under Delaware § 262.

Each preferred share had a $50 liquidation preference; the issuer had an optional right to redeem each preferred share for $79.76. In addition, there were cumulative dividends in arrears of $29.40 per share.

The issuer claimed the fair value to be $18.07 per share. The preferred claimed a range from $67.50 per share to the redemption prince of $79.76. The Chancery Court awarded $38.92 per share.

The question was whether the charter provisions governing the preferred determined the payout formula:

"Thus, the most critical question in this action is whether the certificate of designation, which establishes the rights of [the issuer's] preferred shares, contractually establishes the metric for valuing the preferred shares in the event of a merger. I conclude that it does, which effectively renders irrelevant many of the underlying disputes among the testifying experts over the competing valuation models.

"Unlike common stock, the value of preferred stock is determined solely from the contract rights conferred upon it in the certificate of designation. The only reported post-*Weinberger* opinion involving an appraisal of preferred stock, *In re Appraisal of Ford Holdings, Inc. Preferred Stock,* demonstrates the primacy of contract as the measure of the preferred's value. There, former-Chancellor Allen analyzed the rights conferred upon preferred shareholders by the certificate of designation because, '[t]o the extent it possesses any special rights or powers and to the extent it is restricted or limited in any way, the relation between the holder of the preferred and the corporation is contractual.' When determining the fair value of preferred stock, therefore, I must first look to the contract upon which the preferred stock's value is based. In other words, the valuation of preferred stock must be viewed through the defining lens of its certificate of designation, unless the certificate is ambiguous or conflicts with positive law. As former-Chancellor Allen recognized in *Ford Holdings,* statutory appraisal rights can be modified or relinquished by contract, but in the case of unclear or indirect drafting, this Court will not 'cut stockholders off from a statutory right' to judicial appraisal of their preferred shares."

The Court looked to the carry over conversion rights section of the charter's antidilution provisions, which provided that the preferred would have the right to convert into the stock cash or other property that they would have received had they converted immediately prior to the merger. Under that provision, the value was the conversion value of 5.29 shares times the $1.80 merger price or $9.52 per share. The Court added the $29.40 dividends in arrears. Dividends were not mandatory under the charter. But the charter also provided that arrearages were to be paid in cash or stock (at the issuer's option) upon conversion.

Why treat the merger as a de facto conversion for purposes of valuing the preferred in an appraisal proceeding? Here the court relied on the language of the charter, section 8(g):

> In case of any capital reorganization or reclassification or other change of outstanding shares of Common Stock (other than a change in par value ...) or in case of any consolidation or merger of the Company with or into another Person ...each share of Preferred Stock then outstanding shall, without the consent of any holder of Preferred Stock, become convertible only into the kind and amount of shares of stock or other securities (of the Company or another issuer) or property or cash receivable upon such [merger] by a holder of the number of shares of Common Stock into which such share of Preferred Stock could have been converted immediately prior to such [merger] after giving effect to any adjustment event. The provisions of this Section 8(g) and any equivalent thereof in any such certificate similarly shall apply to successive [mergers]. *The provisions of this Section 8(g) shall be the sole right of holders of Preferred Stock in connection with any [merger] and such holders shall have no separate vote thereon.*

The phrase "sole right of the holder" in the last sentence was deemed to cover an appraisal proceeding.

The plaintiffs, in contrast, valued the stock based on its liquidation and redemption prices, projecting future scenarios under which the issuer might have liquidated or redeemed.

SECTION C. VENTURE CAPITAL FINANCE

Insert in "Note: Cases for Comparison," at Casebook 617:

3. *ThoughtWorks v. SV Investment.*

ThoughtWorks, Inc. v. SV Investment Partners, LLC, 902 A.2d 745 (Del. Ch. 2006), concerned a venture capitalist in a position similar to that of *Equity-Linked Investors*, but outfitted with more effective charter provisions.

ThoughtWorks, an information technology firm, in 2000 raised $26.6 million from SV Investment Partners, LLC ("SVIP"), a venture capital firm, in exchange for 3,137,954 shares of ThoughtWorks's Series A convertible preferred stock. Both parties believed that ThoughtWorks would in the next few years undertake an initial public offering that would allow SVIP to cash out its investment.

Article IV, Section 4(a) of the governing charter provisions provided that SVIP would have a right to put, or have the company redeem, all of its preferred shares for approximately $43 million on the fifth anniversary of the closing:

> On the date that is the fifth anniversary of the Closing Date, if prior to such date, the Company has not issued shares of Common Stock to the public in a Qualified Public Offering ... each holder of Preferred Stock shall be entitled to require the Corporation to redeem for cash out of any funds legally available therefor and which have not been designated by the Board of Directors as necessary to fund the working capital requirements of the Corporation for the fiscal year of the Redemption Date, not less than 100% of the Preferred Stock held by each holder on that date.

The "Redemption Date" was defined as "the date that is the fifth anniversary of the Closing Date (as such date may be postponed pursuant to Section 4(c) hereof)." Section 4(d) went on to state that the redemption requirement shall be continuous such that "funds available pursuant to Section 4(a) shall be applied therefor until such requirements are fully satisfied."

The charter also provided that ThoughtWorks would have to obtain consent from the holders of the majority of the preferred stock to conduct certain business transactions. Article IV, Section 5 of the corporate charter set out those situations. Specifically, Section 5(j) provided that the consent of the holders of the preferred stock would be needed before the company could:

> [E]nter, or allow any subsidiary to enter into, any contractual arrangement providing for the payment of $500,000 or more per year by either party thereto and that is outside the ordinary course of business or that was not contemplated by the Corporation's annual budget.

ThoughtWorks got into difficulty when the tech bubble burst and was unable to redeem the preferred on the fifth anniversary. It attempted, but failed to find debt financing to fund the redemption. In consequence, it made a formal offer to the preferred stockholders to redeem their stock for $12.8 million in cash. Some of the preferred stockholders accepted the company's proposal; however, SVIP did not respond to the offer.

As the redemption date approached, the ThoughtWorks board determined that "the funds required to fund the working capital requirements of the Company [were] an amount in excess of available cash," and that the preferred shares accordingly would not be redeemed.

Thereafter, ThoughtWorks sought an increase in its line of bank credit from $3 million to $10 million to manage its cash flow so that it could timely pay its employees and other expenses. SVIP objected, citing its rights under the charter.

ThoughtWorks followed up with a declaratory judgment action, asserting, for the first time, that the charter allowed it to postpone the payment of its redemption obligation beyond 2005, on the theory that Article IV, Section 4 of the charter allowed it, in years after the fiscal year of the redemption date, to set aside an amount designated by the board of directors as necessary to fund the working capital requirements of the company when determining the funds available to satisfy its redemption obligation. In addition, it asked the court to declare that it could enter into a $10 million line of credit with the LaSalle bank without obtaining the consent of SVIP.

The Chancery Court ruled for SVIP:

"ThoughtWorks argues that Section 4(d) allows it to set aside funds needed for working capital in fulfilling its redemption obligation. ThoughtWorks contends that, since it had insufficient funds to redeem SVIP's stock in 2005, Section 4(d) provides that funds available pursuant to Section 4(a) shall be continuously applied until the obligation is fully discharged. Thus, it argues that in determining what funds the company has available to satisfy the redemption obligation, ThoughtWorks must apply the same methodology provided for in Section 4(a), *i.e.,* all legally available funds except those determined by the board as necessary to meet the company's working capital requirements. Simply put, ThoughtWorks argues that it has the right, ongoing from year to year, to exclude necessary working capital from the funds available to pay the redemption obligation.

* * *

"ThoughtWorks's contention that Section 4(d) gave it the right to continually set aside working capital in fulfilling the redemption obligation is unavailing. Section 4(d) states that, if at any time after the redemption date, the redemption obligation 'shall not be fully discharged,' 'funds available pursuant to Section 4(a) shall be applied therefor until such requirements are fully discharged.' Under Section 4(a), it is clear that the working capital set-aside is only available during the fiscal year of the redemption date. The reason Section 4(d) does not simply refer to funds 'legally available' but instead refers back to Section 4(a) appears to stem from the fact that the continuing nature of ThoughtWorks redemption obligation included the remainder of fiscal 2005 beyond the redemption date. Thus, for example, if ThoughtWorks had experienced such positive developments in the second half of fiscal 2005 that the legally available funds exceeded its working capital requirements, it would have had an obligation to apply such excess funds to its continuing redemption obligation under Section 4(d). Once fiscal 2005 ended, however, ThoughtWorks was obliged to apply all legally available funds to its redemption obligation without regard to the working capital set-aside found in Section 4(a).

"This reading of the document is entirely consistent with the evidence at trial relating to the negotiation and drafting of the document that clearly established the parties' intention that the working capital exclusion be limited to the fiscal year of the redemption date. * * *

"ThoughtWorks also seeks a declaration that Article IV, Section 5 of its certificate of incorporation does not provide the preferred stockholders with consent rights over the board's decision to enter into an operating line of credit, even one that substantially limits by contract its ability to apply any cash in satisfaction of its redemption obligation. It argues that the consent rights provided to the preferred stockholders in the charter do not extend to debt transactions of this type. According to ThoughtWorks, neither SVIP nor its lawyers, all of whom are sophisticated businesspeople with experience in transactions of this kind, negotiated for the right to consent to ThoughtWorks's incurrence of debt. In addition, ThoughtWorks argues that SVIP violated the implied duty of good faith and fair dealing by interfering with its right to obtain an increase in its line of credit. Because this last claim was not asserted in ThoughtWorks's complaint or in any submissions prior to trial, but rather was made for the first time in its post-trial brief, the court will not address it.

"SVIP responds that Section 5(j) of the charter requires that ThoughtWorks obtain the consent of a majority of the preferred stockholders if it enters into any contractual arrangement providing for the payment of $500,000 or more per year by either party if the transaction is either (1) outside the ordinary course of business or (2) not contemplated by the corporation's annual budget. SVIP contends that the decision to obtain a major line of credit falls within the parameters of Section 5(j) because it is a contractual arrangement that provides for the payment of $500,000 or more per year. SVIP argues that ThoughtWorks's decision to enter into a $10 million line of credit * * * without first obtaining SVIP's consent violates both prongs of Section 5(f). Furthermore, SVIP argues that the previous dealings of the parties support its interpretation of the charter. Particularly, in the past, ThoughtWorks sought the consent of SVIP prior to entering into or increasing a line of credit.

"Recognizing that the certificate of incorporation does not contain a prototypical material indebtedness provision, the court, nevertheless, concludes that ThoughtWorks's proposed $10 million line of credit falls within the scope of Section 5(j) as a 'contractual arrangement providing for the payment of $500,000 or more per year by either party.' ThoughtWorks's contention that Section 5(j) is only a material contracts provision and cannot be read to relate to the incurrence of material indebtedness is not persuasive. The plain language of the section clearly states that it broadly applies to 'any contractual arrangement providing for the payment of $500,000 or more.' Such contractual arrangements can be easily read to include debt transactions. Therefore, if the line of credit is either outside of ThoughtWorks's ordinary course of business or not contemplated by ThoughtWorks's annual budget, ThoughtWorks must obtain prior consent from a majority of the preferred stockholders, or, in this case, SVIP.

"Although only one of these conditions need be satisfied for the consent requirement of Section 5(j) to apply, the court finds that both conditions were met. First, no $10 million line of credit was contemplated in ThoughtWorks's budget. By ThoughtWorks's own admissions at trial, annual budgets had not been generated or presented to the holders of the preferred stock for approval pursuant to Section 5(f) of the charter since 2002. Loughmiller [the CEO] testified at trial that, after ThoughtWorks had a disagreement with SVIP in 2002 over the budget, he decided not to present a budget to SVIP for its approval, even though he believed SVIP had a right under the charter to approve the budget. Instead, he explained that ThoughtWorks prepared what he called 'operating plans,' financial projections which were not approved by the majority of the preferred stockholders. Because those 'operating plans' included

ThoughtWorks's operating lines of credit, ThoughtWorks argues it did not need to obtain the consent of the preferred stockholders pursuant to Section 5(j) of the charter prior to obtaining them.

"The court disagrees. The purpose of Section 5(j) is to ensure that major contractual agreements are approved by a majority of the preferred stockholders. That approval may take place either in the process of approving the budget, pursuant to Section 5(f), or later through the consent of a majority of the preferred stockholders. ThoughtWorks's position that it complied with Section 5(j) because it prepared 'operating plans' that included lines of credit eviscerates the protections of Section 5 because it allows ThoughtWorks to enter into a significant transaction without obtaining either of the two approvals prescribed in the charter. In effect, ThoughtWorks's argument allows it to avoid seeking approval of its budget under Section 5(f) and also allows it to avoid seeking consent under Section 5(j) for a major transaction. This is clearly inconsistent with the plain meaning of the charter.

"Second, the evidence showed that a large line of credit, such as $10 million, is outside of ThoughtWorks's ordinary course of business. When SVIP invested in ThoughtWorks, the parties agreed that ThoughtWorks would use part of the proceeds for the repayment of all of the company's outstanding debt. In fact, ThoughtWorks's credit facility was extinguished as a condition of closing the transaction. Thus, at the time of SVIP's investment, it was assumed by both parties that ThoughtWorks would not need to take on debt.

"When ThoughtWorks later needed to borrow for working capital purposes, it sought and obtained formal written consent from SVIP for a $3 million line of credit. "These facts clearly support a finding that any line of credit fell outside the ordinary course of business, and thus required consent from a majority of the preferred stockholders."

In re Trados Incorporated Shareholder Litigation

Delaware Court of Chancery, 2009.
2009 WL 2225958.

CHANDLER, Chancellor.

This is a purported class action brought by a former stockholder of Trados Incorporated ("Trados," or the "Company") for breach of fiduciary duty arising out of a transaction whereby Trados became a wholly owned subsidiary of SDL, plc ("SDL"). Of the $60 million contributed by SDL, Trados' preferred stockholders received approximately $52 million. The remainder was distributed to the Company's executive officers pursuant to a previously approved bonus plan. Trados' common stockholders received nothing for their common shares.

Plaintiff contends that this transaction was undertaken at the behest of certain preferred stockholders that desired a transaction that would trigger their large liquidation preference and allow them to exit their investment in Trados. * * *

As explained below, plaintiff has alleged facts sufficient, at this preliminary stage, to demonstrate that at least a majority of the members of Trados' seven member board were unable to exercise independent and disinterested business judgment in deciding whether to approve the merger. Accordingly, I decline to dismiss the breach of fiduciary duty claims arising out of the board's approval of the merger. * * *

I. BACKGROUND

A. The Parties

Before the merger, Trados developed software and services used by businesses to make the translation of text and material into other languages more efficient. Founded in 1984 as a German entity, Trados moved to the United States in the mid-1990s with the hope of going public, and became a Delaware corporation in March 2000. To better position itself for the possibility of going public, Trados accepted investments from venture capital firms and other entities. As a result, preferred stockholders had a total of four designees on Trados' seven member board. Each of the seven members of Trados' board at the time of the board's approval of the merger is named as a defendant in this action.

David Scanlan was the board designee of, and a partner in, Wachovia Capital Partners, LLC ("Wachovia"). At the time of the merger, Wachovia owned 3,640,000 shares of Trados' Series A preferred stock (100% of that series) and 1,007,151 shares of Trados' Series BB preferred stock (approximately 24% of that series).

Lisa Stone was the board designee of Rowan Entities Limited and Rowan Nominees Limited RR (together, the "Rowan Entities"), transferees of Trados' preferred stock held by Hg Investment Managers Limited (collectively,

"Hg"). Stone was a director and employee of both Hg Investment Managers Limited and the Rowan Entities. At the time of the merger, Hg owned 1,379,039 shares of Trados' common stock (approximately 4.3%), 2,014,302 shares of Trados' Series BB preferred stock (approximately 48.3% of that series), 5,333,330 shares of Trados' Series C preferred shares (all of that series), and 862,976 shares of Trados' Series D preferred stock (approximately 28.6% of that series).

Sameer Gandhi was a board designee of, and a partner in, several entities known as Sequoia. Sequoia owned 5,255,913 shares of Trados' Series E preferred stock (approximately 32% of that series).

Joseph Prang was also a board designee of Sequoia. Prang owned Mentor Capital Group LLC ("Mentor Capital"), which owned 263,810 shares of Trados' Series E preferred stock (approximately 1% of that series).

Wachovia, Hg, Sequoia, and Mentor combined owned approximately 51% of Trados' outstanding preferred stock. Plaintiff alleges that these preferred stockholders desired to exit their investment in Trados.

Two of the three remaining director defendants were employees of Trados. Jochen Hummel was acting President of Trados from April 2004 until September or October 2004, and was also the Company's chief technology officer. Joseph Campbell was Trados' CEO from August 23, 2004 until the merger. The remaining Trados director was Klaus-Dieter Laidig.

B. The Negotiations

In April 2004, the Trados board began to discuss a potential sale of the Company, and later formed a mergers and acquisitions committee, consisting of Stone, Gandhi, and Scanlan, to explore a sale or merger of Trados. Around the same time, the Company's President and CEO was terminated due to, among other issues, a perception by the rest of the board that Trados was underperforming. The board appointed Hummel as an interim President, but instructed him to consult with Gandhi and Scanlan before taking material action on behalf of the Company. In July 2004, Campbell was hired as the Company's CEO, effective August 23, 2004. Gandhi described Campbell as "a hard-nosed CEO whose task is to grow the company profitably or sell it." At the time Campbell joined Trados, however, the Company was losing money and had little cash to fund continuing operations. At a July 7, 2004 meeting, Trados' board determined that the fair market value of Trados' common stock was $0 .10 per share.

In June 2004, Trados engaged JMP Securities, LLC, an investment bank, to assist in identifying potential alternatives for a merger or sale of the Company. By July 2004, JMP Securities had identified twenty seven potential buyers of Trados, and contacted seven of them, including SDL. By August 2004, JMP Securities had conducted discussions with SDL CEO Mark Lancaster, who made an acquisition proposal in the $40 million range. Trados informed Lancaster that it was not interested in a deal at that price, and Campbell formally terminated JMP Securities in September 2004.

In July 2004, Scanlan expressed concern that the executive officers of the Company might not have sufficient incentives to remain with the Company or pursue a potential acquisition of the Company, due to the high liquidation preference of the Company's preferred stock. The board instructed Scanlan to develop a bonus plan to address these concerns. This led to the December 2004 board approval of the Management Incentive Plan (the "MIP"), which set a graduated compensation scale for the Company's management based on the price obtained for the Company in an acquisition.

Trados' financial condition improved markedly during the fourth quarter of 2004, in part due to Campbell's efforts to reduce spending and bring in additional cash through debt financing. By the time of the December 2004 board meeting, Trados had arranged to borrow $2.5 million from Western Technology Investment, with the right to borrow an additional $1.5 million.

Despite the Company's improved performance, the board continued to work toward a sale of the Company. In December 2004, Gandhi reported to Sequoia Capital that the Company's performance was improving, but that Campbell's "mission is to architect an M & A event as soon as practicable." At a February 2, 2005 board meeting, Campbell presented positive financial results from the fourth quarter of 2004, including record revenue and profit from operations. As a result of its improved performance and the lack of an immediate need for cash, the board extended by six months the period during which it could obtain additional cash from Western Technology Investment.

In January 2005, SDL initiated renewed merger discussions with Campbell. Upon learning of SDL's interest, the Trados board expressed that it was not interested in any transaction involving less than a "60-plus" million dollar purchase price. Lancaster first discussed a transaction at $50 million, but later offered $60 million. At the February 2, 2005 meeting, the board instructed Campbell to continue negotiating with Lancaster under the general terms SDL proposed, including the $60 million price. In mid-February 2005, Campbell made inquiries with two other potential acquirers of Trados, but neither expressed any substantive interest.

In a theme that runs throughout his allegations, plaintiff alleges that there was no need to sell Trados at the time because the Company was well financed and experiencing improved performance under Campbell's leadership. For example, plaintiff contends that by February 2005 Trados was beating its revenue budget for the year, a trend that continued as Trados beat its revenue projections for the first quarter of 2005 and through the end of May 2005.

By February 2005, Campbell and Lancaster agreed to the basic terms of a merger at $60 million. Trados then re-engaged JMP securities, which plaintiff alleges acted as little more than a "go-between." In April 2005, SDL and Trados signed the letter of intent for the merger at the $60 million price.

* * *

D. The Merger

The director defendants unanimously approved the merger, and on June 19, 2005 Trados and SDL entered into an Agreement and Plan of Merger. Of the $60 million merger price, approximately $7.8 million would go to management pursuant to the MIP, and the remainder would go to the preferred stockholders in partial satisfaction of their $57.9 million liquidation preference. Plaintiff alleges that the directors know both of these facts, and thus knew that the common shareholders would receive nothing in the merger. The merger was consummated on July 7, 2005.

Plaintiff alleges that Campbell and Hummel received benefits as a result of the merger. Campbell became a director of SDL and received $775,000 through the MIP, $1,315,000 in exchange for a non-compete agreement, and a $250,000 bonus. Campbell took $702,000 of his MIP compensation in SDL stock, and $73,000 in cash. Hummel became "SDL's general manager of Europe, the Middle East, and Asia (technology division)," and received $1,092,000 under the MIP, of which he took $436,800 in SDL stock and $655,200 in cash.

II. ANALYSIS

* * *

C. Fiduciary Duty Claims

Count I of the Complaint asserts a claim that the director defendants breached their fiduciary duty of loyalty to Trados' common stockholders by approving the merger. Plaintiff alleges that there was no need to sell Trados at the time because the Company was well-financed, profitable, and beating revenue projections. Further, plaintiff contends, "in approving the Merger, the Director Defendants never considered the interest of the common stockholders in continuing Trados as a going concern, even though they were obliged to give priority to that interest over the preferred stockholders' interest in exiting their investment."

* * *

* * * A plaintiff can survive a motion to dismiss under Rule 12(b)(6) by pleading facts from which a reasonable inference can be drawn that a majority of the board was interested or lacked independence with respect to the relevant decision.

A director is interested in a transaction if "he or she will receive a personal financial benefit from a transaction that is not equally shared by the stockholders" or if "a corporate decision will have a materially detrimental impact on a director, but not on the corporation and the stockholders." The receipt of any benefit is not sufficient to cause a director to be interested in a transaction. Rather, the benefit received by the director and not shared with stockholders must be "of a sufficiently material importance, in the context of the director's economic circumstances, as to have made it improbable that the director could perform her fiduciary duties ... without being influenced by her overriding personal interest....

"Independence means that a director's decision is based on the corporate merits of the subject before the board rather than extraneous considerations or influences. At this stage, a lack of independence can be shown by pleading facts that support a reasonable inference that the director is beholden to a controlling person or "so under their influence that their discretion would be sterilized."

Plaintiff's theory of the case is based on the proposition that, for purposes of the merger, the preferred stockholders' interests diverged from the interests of the common stockholders. Plaintiff contends that the merger took place at the behest of certain preferred stockholders, who wanted to exit their investment. Defendants contend that plaintiff ignores the "obvious alignment" of the interest of the preferred and common stockholders in obtaining the highest price available for the company. Defendants assert that because the preferred stockholders would not receive their entire liquidation preference in the merger, they would benefit if a higher price were obtained for the Company. Even accepting this proposition as true, however, it is not the case that the interests of the preferred and common stockholders were aligned with respect to the decision of whether to pursue a sale of the company or continue to operate the Company without pursuing a transaction at the time.

The merger triggered the $57.9 million liquidation preference of the preferred stockholders, and the preferred stockholders received approximately $52 million dollars as a result of the merger. In contrast, the common stockholders received nothing as a result of the merger, and lost the ability to ever receive anything of value in the future for their ownership interest in Trados. It would not stretch reason to say that this is the worst possible outcome for the common stockholders. The common stockholders would certainly be no worse off had the merger not occurred.

Taking, as I must, the well-pleaded facts in the Complaint in the light most favorable to plaintiff, it is reasonable to infer that the common stockholders would have been able to receive some consideration for their Trados shares at some point in the future had the merger not occurred. This inference is supported by plaintiff's allegations that the Company's performance had significantly improved and that the Company had secured additional capital through debt financing. Thus, it is reasonable to infer from the factual allegations in the Complaint that the interests of the preferred and common stockholders were not aligned with respect to the decision to pursue a transaction that would trigger the liquidation preference of the preferred and result in no consideration for the common stockholders.

Generally, the rights and preferences of preferred stock are contractual in nature. This Court has held that directors owe fiduciary duties to preferred stockholders as well as common stockholders where the right claimed by the preferred "is not to a preference as against the common stock but rather a right shared equally with the common." Where this is not the case, however, "generally it will be the duty of the board, where discretionary judgment is to be exercised, to prefer the interests of common stock-as the good faith judgment of the board sees them to be-to the interests created by the special rights, preferences, *etc.,* of preferred stock, where there is a conflict." Thus, in circumstances where the interests of the common stockholders diverge from those of the preferred stockholders, it is *possible* that a director could breach her duty by improperly favoring the interests of the preferred stockholders over those of the common stockholders. [*Blackmore Partners, L.P. v. Link Energy LLC,* 864 A.2d 80, 85-86 (Del.Ch.2004).] As explained above, the factual allegations in the Complaint support a reasonable inference that the interests of the preferred and common stockholders diverged with respect to the decision of whether to pursue the merger. Given this reasonable inference, plaintiff can avoid dismissal if the Complaint contains well-pleaded facts that demonstrate that the director defendants were interested or lacked independence with respect to this decision.

1. *The Director Defendants' Approval of the Merger*

Plaintiff has alleged facts that support a reasonable inference that Scanlan, Stone, Gandhi, and Prang, the four board designees of preferred stockholders, were interested in the decision to pursue the merger with SDL, which had the effect of triggering the large liquidation preference of the preferred stockholders and resulted in no consideration to the common stockholders for their common shares. Each of these four directors was designated to the Trados board by a holder of a significant number of preferred shares. While this, alone, may not be enough to rebut the presumption of the business judgment rule, plaintiff has alleged more. Plaintiff has alleged that Scanlan, Stone, Gandhi, and Prang each had an ownership or employment relationship with an entity that owned Trados preferred stock. Scanlan was a partner in Wachovia; Stone was a director, employee and part owner of Hg; Gandhi was a partner in several entities referred to as Sequoia; and Prang owned Mentor Capital. Plaintiff further alleges that each of these directors was dependent on the preferred stockholders for their livelihood. As detailed above, each of these entities owned a significant number of Trados' preferred shares, and together these entities owned approximately 51 % of Trados' outstanding preferred stock. The allegations of the ownership and other relationships of each of Scanlan, Stone, Gandhi, and Prang to preferred stockholders, combined with the fact that each was a board designee of one of these entities, is sufficient, under the plaintiff-friendly pleading standard on a motion to dismiss, to rebut the business judgment presumption with respect to the decision to approve the merger with SDL.

* * *

Defendants * * * rely on *Orban v. Field,* [1997 WL 153831 (Del.Ch. Apr.1, 1997),] but that decision does not counsel in favor of dismissal at this stage of the litigation. In *Orban,* the Court was evaluating whether a board breached its duties where it "deploy [ed] corporate power against its own shareholders" by "eliminating the leverage of the common stockholders by diluting their ownership interest below 10%" in order to prevent the common stockholder from using his ability to block a transaction to extract value for his shares. The Court, in deciding to grant summary judgment in favor of defendants, asked whether defendants had met their burden "to show that their conduct was taken in good faith pursuit of valid ends and was reasonable in the circumstances." Although this inquiry was "inevitably one that must be applied in the rich particularity of context," the Court was still able to conclude, based on the evidence in the record, that the plaintiff's "threat to impede the realization of th[e] transaction by the corporation was thwarted by legally permissible action that was measured and appropriate in the circumstances." In making this determination, the Court assumed that the business judgment rule did not apply to the challenged actions.

Here, in contrast, the issue on the motion to dismiss is whether plaintiff has rebutted the presumption of the business judgment rule. Unlike on a motion for summary judgment, I must accept the well-pleaded factual allegations in the Complaint as true. As explained above, those allegations, with the benefit of reasonable inferences, are sufficient, at this stage, to rebut the presumption of the business judgment rule. Unlike in *Orban,* I am unable, at this stage, to make determinations based on the record, such as that the board acted "both in good faith and reasonably." Those determinations must wait for another day.

Plaintiff has alleged facts that support a reasonable inference that a majority of the board was interested or lacked independence with respect to the decision to approve the merger. Accordingly, plaintiff has alleged sufficient facts to survive defendants' motion to dismiss the fiduciary duty claims based on the board's decision to approve the merger.

Part IV. EQUITY CAPITAL STRUCTURE – PAYOUT POLICY AND OWNERSHIP STAKES

SECTION A. PAYOUT POLICY–DIVIDENDS, REPURCHASES, AND RETAINED EARNINGS

5. REPURCHASES OF OUTSTANDING SHARES

(B) REPURCHASES–FIDUCIARY AND DISCLOSURE OBLIGATIONS

(4) Federal Securities Laws–Open Market Repurchases

(b) safe-harbor for potentially manipulative repurchases

Insert at Casebook page 693, before "Note: OMRs and Market Efficiency:"

The SEC proposes to amend Rule 10b-18. Securities Exchange Act Release No. 34-61414, January 25, 2010, describes this initiative at pages 5-7 and 11:

> Since Rule 10b-18's adoption in 1982, there have been significant market changes with respect to trading strategies and developments in automated trading systems and technology that have increased the speed of trading and changed the profile of how issuer repurchases are effected. We understand that the increased speed of today's market activity, as evidenced by flickering quotes, has made it increasingly difficult for issuers to ensure that every purchase of its common stock during the day will meet the Rule's current price condition. As discussed below, currently, failure to meet any one of the four conditions under the Rule with respect to any of the issuer's repurchases during the day will disqualify all of the issuer's other Rule 10b-18 purchases from the safe harbor for that day. Moreover, the opportunity for issuers to effect repurchases using alternative trading strategies or pricing mechanisms, such as repurchases effected on a volume-weighted average price ("VWAP") basis (i.e., where a security's price is generally derived from adding up the dollar amounts traded for each transaction in the security (price multiplied by shares traded) and then dividing by the total number of shares traded for the day), has increased significantly. However, because such transactions may be priced without reference to the quoted price of the stock at the time of

execution and, thus, possibly above Rule 10b-18's current price limitation, many issuers that repurchase their shares using such trading strategies must forego the protections of the safe harbor for such purchases.

In connection with the 2003 amendments to Rule 10b-18, the Commission sought comment as to whether Rule 10b-18's price condition should apply where the issuer has no control, directly or indirectly, over the price at which a Rule 10b-18 purchase will be effected, for example, "passive" or independently-derived pricing, such as the VWAP. While the Commission did not adopt an exception for VWAP transactions at that time, it stated that it would take into account commenters' recommendations, as well as current market practices involving VWAP transactions, in considering whether any future changes to Rule 10b-18 were appropriate. Since that time, we understand from the industry that VWAP has become one of the most widely recognized and accepted pricing mechanisms and trading benchmarks.

Based on our experience with the operation of Rule 10b-18 and to respond to these market developments, we propose to revise Rule 10b-18 as described below. The proposed amendments are intended to clarify and modernize the safe harbor provisions. In particular, our proposal to modify the price condition would provide issuers with greater flexibility to conduct their issuer repurchase programs within the safe harbor under conditions designed to reduce the potential for abuse. Our proposal to limit the general disqualification provision would also provide issuers with additional flexibility to conduct their share repurchase programs in fast moving markets. At the same time, our proposals to modify the timing condition and the "merger exclusion" provision under the Rule are intended to maintain reasonable limits on the safe harbor consistent with the objectives of the Rule to minimize the market impact of the issuer's repurchases, thereby allowing the market to establish a security's price based on independent market forces without undue influence by the issuer, and to promote safe harbor availability only during normal market conditions for an issuer.

* * *

In this release, we are proposing revisions to the safe harbor rule. In particular, we propose to:

- modify the timing condition to preclude Rule 10b-18 purchases as the opening purchase in the principal market for the security and in the market where the purchase is effected (in addition to the current prohibition against effecting Rule 10b-18 purchases as the opening purchase reported in the consolidated system);
- relax the price condition for certain VWAP transactions;
- limit the disqualification provision in fast moving markets under certain specific conditions;
- modify the "merger exclusion" provision to extend the time in which the safe harbor is unavailable in connection with an acquisition by a special purpose acquisition company ("SPAC"); and
- update certain definitional provisions consistent with the current Rule.

SECTION B. EQUITY OWNERSHIP AND THE VALUE OF THE FIRM

1. Executive Stock Options

(A) STOCK OPTIONS AND SHAREHOLDER VALUE

Insert after "Note: After Exercise," at Casebook page 706:

AT&T Corp. v. Lillis

Delaware Supreme Court, 2008
953 A.2d 241

Before STEELE, Chief Justice, HOLLAND, BERGER, JACOBS and RIDGELY, Justices, constituting the court en banc.

STEELE, Chief Justice.

Plaintiffs-appellees, who are former directors and officers of MediaOne Corp., seek compensation for stock options that were cashed out in a 2004 merger between AT & T Wireless and Cingular. MediaOne originally granted its directors and officers options under a 1994 stock option plan. An anti-destruction, anti-dilution clause in that 1994 stock option plan preserved the option holders' "economic position" upon the happening of certain specified events, including a merger. [More particularly, Section XVIII.A of the 1994 plan reads as follows:

> In the event there is any change in the Common Stock by reason of any consolidation, combination, liquidation, reorganization, recapitalization, stock dividend, split-up, split-off, spin-off, combination of shares, exchange of shares or other like change in capital structure of the [MediaOne], the number or kind of shares or interests subject to an Award and the per share price or value thereof shall be appropriately adjusted by the Committee at the time of such event, provided that each Participant's *economic position* with respect to the Award shall not, as a result of such adjustment, *be worse than it had been immediately prior to such event.* (emphasis added)]

AT & T acquired MediaOne in a stock for stock merger in 1999. In that merger, plaintiffs-appellees' MediaOne options were converted into AT & T options and continued to be governed by the terms of the 1994 MediaOne plan.

In 2001, AT & T spun off Wireless. In that transaction, *all* AT & T options holders, including plaintiffs-appellees, received new options in Wireless. An Employee Benefits Agreement and Wireless Adjustment Agreement governed the new Wireless options created through the spin off. In addition to those two agreements, the 1994 MediaOne stock option plan also continued to govern *plaintiffs-appellees'* new options in Wireless.

In 2004, Cingular agreed to a cash out merger with Wireless. In that transaction, which gave rise to this dispute, Wireless options holders were cashed out at $15 per share minus the exercise price of the option.

The plaintiffs-appellees who originally received options in MediaOne that were converted into Wireless options as a result of the foregoing transaction filed a complaint in the Court of Chancery against defendant-appellant AT & T and defendant-cross appellee Cingular. The plaintiffs claimed that Wireless (now Cingular) violated the terms of the 1994 plan when it cashed out plaintiffs-appellees' Wireless options without any compensation for the lost "time value" of their options. Plaintiffs-appellees argued, in the alternative, that AT & T is liable for any breach of the 1994 plan by Wireless because AT & T had a duty to obligate Wireless legally to observe those terms.

In a letter to plaintiffs' counsel and in its answer to the complaint, AT & T initially took the position that Wireless could not cash out *any* Wireless options based on AT & T's understanding of the Employee Benefits Plan and the Wireless Adjustment Plan, which governed *all* Wireless options created in the 2005 spin off. In order to bind Wireless to its contractual duties as AT & T saw them, AT & T arbitrated its dispute with Wireless. After a hearing, the arbitration panel found that Wireless did not breach either of those plans. AT & T then changed litigation strategy in the Court of Chancery, by asserting that the 1994 plan did not proscribe Wireless from cashing out the options. Although AT & T acknowledged that the 1994 plan required AT & T to preserve plaintiffs-appellees' "economic position" "immediately prior" to a merger, it argued that in the context of a cash out merger, plaintiffs-appellees' "economic position" was limited to the intrinsic value of the options.

A Vice Chancellor denied cross motions for summary judgment, holding that Section XVIII.A of the 1994 plan controlled the plaintiffs-appellees' options, but that the term "economic position" in that section was ambiguous. The Vice Chancellor then held a trial to consider extrinsic evidence that could aid him in interpreting that term.

Interpreting Section XVIII.A., the Vice Chancellor noted AT & T's initial position that Wireless could not cancel the stock options and accorded "great weight" to AT & T's initial stance. The Vice Chancellor also found that the parties' earlier transactions, where stock options were replaced with new stock options, demonstrated that the parties intended to preserve the time value of the options in each transaction. Because Wireless did not preserve the time value of the options in the 2004 merger, he found AT & T liable for a breach of the 1994 plan. The Vice Chancellor further found that AT & T had not transferred the 1994 MediaOne plan's obligation to Wireless and, thus, did not hold Cingular liable.

* * *

The Vice Chancellor calculated damages and entered judgment against AT & T for $11,306,986, plus prejudgment interest.

DISCUSSION

I. *INTERPRETATION OF SECTION XVIII.A*

* * *

Our task on *de novo* review * * * is to determine "what a reasonable person in the position of the parties would have thought" the term "economic position" meant. Plaintiffs-appellees assert that "economic position" means "full economic value." Plaintiffs-appellees maintain that, in this context, "full economic value" means that the options' time value must be preserved. On the other hand, AT & T contends that "economic position" simply refers to the "intrinsic value" of the options "immediately prior to" a cash out merger.

The language of Section XVIII.A protects the "economic position" of plaintiffs-appellees' options "immediately prior" to a merger. The important question, here, is: what exactly was plaintiffs-appellees' "economic position" in the face of an impending cash out merger?

On the one hand, a stock option's worth can increase substantially over time. It therefore is logical that the "economic position" of the stock option *might* include time value. On the other hand, at the point of time "immediately prior" to a cash out merger, the "economic position" of the stock options retains no time value because the options will be immediately exchanged for the right to receive a cash sum. In light of the impending cash out merger, there is no prospect that the option will ever be worth anything more than that exact cash sum. Thus, the "economic position" of the stock option might relate only to the cash sum for which the option will be exchanged.

We find both interpretations of Section XVIII.A to be reasonable. Therefore, the Vice Chancellor appropriately found the term "economic position" to be ambiguous and properly considered extrinsic evidence.

II. *EXTRINSIC EVIDENCE*

Plaintiffs-appellees urge us to find that the 1994 plan required AT & T and Wireless to preserve the time value of their options based upon AT & T's course of conduct and AT & T's alleged admissions. The Vice Chancellor considered three items of extrinsic evidence to find that the term "economic position" included the time value of plaintiffs-appellees' stock options. First, he considered the parties' course of conduct in earlier transactions. Second, he looked to the fact that MediaOne's officers and directors received a significant proportion of their compensation through options. Finally, he gave "great weight" to AT & T's supposed admissions.

A. *The Parties' Course of Conduct*

Plaintiffs-appellees suggest, and the Vice Chancellor accepted, that AT & T's course of conduct established AT & T's belief that the options' time value was required to be preserved--a course of conduct arguably supporting the parties' intended meaning of the term "economic position." But, plaintiffs-appellees and the Vice Chancellor spent no time discussing the fact that, in each of the previous transactions, the transactions were stock for stock transactions-not cash outs. When reviewing the MediaOne-AT & T merger, the Vice Chancellor noted "[t]his discussion here focuses on the adjustment calculated for those persons who elected to receive adjusted AT & T options." The Vice Chancellor never explained why he disregarded the cash election in that merger, nor did he address why the stock for stock election better evidenced the parties' intent in the context of the dispute in this case-a cash out merger.

In the transactions the Vice Chancellor considered, AT & T replaced plaintiffs-appellees' options to buy stock in the pre-merger company with options to buy post-merger stock. AT & T argues that "these prior events demonstrate that options were adjusted consistently to mirror adjustments to the underlying security." But these transactions were also distinguishable from the Cingular-Wireless merger precisely because they were stock for stock transactions. Therefore, they did not necessarily evidence what the parties intended to occur in a cash out merger. In the case of a stock for stock merger, option holders expect to have their old options replaced with new options because the old (underlying) stock is being replaced with new (underlying) stock. In such a transaction, by its very nature, the "economic position" of the options will invariably incorporate the expected time value of the new options.

But where the stock and the options are to be cashed out in a merger, the option holders can have no expectation of receiving replacement options in new stock. Instead, option holders will, and expect to, receive only cash representing intrinsic value for their options. The question presented in this case is whether, in order to protect option holders' "economic position," the option holders must receive additional compensation where they receive cash and not stock. The cash election in the MediaOne-AT & T merger is the only earlier transaction that included a cash component. It, therefore, is the only transaction similar to the one at issue here.

In the MediaOne-AT & T merger, shareholders and option holders could elect to receive (1) cash, (2) new stock or (in the case of option holders) new options, or (3) a combination of both cash and stock (or options). Stockholders electing cash would receive \$85 per share, and the option holder would receive \$85 per share minus the exercise price of the options. Under plaintiffs-appellees' interpretation of Section XVIII.A, option holders in the MediaOne-AT & T merger should have received additional compensation above the cash out for $85 per share in order to compensate option holders for the lost time value. Yet, in that merger, option holders who might have chosen the cash out would have received intrinsic value *only*. They would not have received additional compensation for the time value of the options. Logically, option holders in that merger electing cash would have received the intrinsic value, $85, cash only, because those who wished to preserve time value would have elected the offered options designed to preserve time value in the surviving entity.

Because the Vice Chancellor did not address the distinction between a cash out merger and a stock for stock merger and the significance of that distinction in evaluating the extrinsic evidence of contractual intent, we remand this case for him to reconsider the evidentiary importance of the parties' course of conduct in the MediaOne-AT & T transaction.

B. *AT & T's Admissions*

We also are constrained to comment on the "great weight" that the Vice Chancellor afforded to AT & T's supposed admissions. The Vice Chancellor found (1) AT & T's admissions in its answer and (2) the letter sent from AT & T's counsel to plaintiffs-appellees' counsel to be persuasive evidence that AT & T, in fact, believed that it needed to preserve the time value of plaintiffs-appellees' options under the 1994 plan. We find, however, that AT & T's letter to plaintiffs-appellees admitted nothing relating to the parties' intended meaning of the phrase "economic position" in Section XVIII.A. Moreover, **AT & T** consistently denied plaintiffs-appellees' interpretation of Section XVIII.A.

Having reviewed AT & T's alleged admission in its letter, we conclude that that letter does not refer to the 1994 plan at all. Rather, the letter refers to the Employee Benefit Agreement and the Adjustment Plan--separate documents that were created when AT & T spun off Wireless. AT & T's spin off of Wireless preserved *all* AT & T's options holders' rights by issuing options to acquire the new Wireless stock. To protect *all* of *these* options in the future, AT & T obligated Wireless under the Employee Benefits Agreement and the Wireless Adjustment Plan. When it wrote plaintiffs-appellees' counsel, AT & T explained that it, too, was concerned that Wireless had cashed out *all* options holders at $15 per share minus the exercise price. AT & T asserted that the Employee Benefits Agreement and the Wireless Adjustment Plan prevented Wireless from cashing out *any* options. AT & T spoke in order to protect the interests of *all* Wireless options created by the spin off, which of course included--but was not limited to--options held by plaintiffs-appellees. Because AT & T was attempting to protect *all* former AT & T (and now Wireless) options holders, AT & T did not refer to the 1994 plan or to Section XVIII.A, because that plan and provision governed only *plaintiffs-appellees'* options. Thus, in its letter, AT & T never admitted that *Section XVIII.A* proscribed Wireless from cashing out plaintiffs-appellees' options or that *Section XVIII.A* required Wireless to compensate plaintiffs-appellees for the lost time value of their options following a cash out merger.

Nor did AT & T ever admit in its answer that Section XVIII.A preserved the time value of plaintiffs-appellees' options. In paragraph 17 of their complaint, plaintiffs-appellees specifically alleged an interpretation of Section XVIII.A that an equivalent option must be granted in any merger. AT & T denied that allegation. AT & T initially made certain admissions that the options maintained value. However, these 'admissions are consistent with AT & T's theory that all options holders were protected under the Employee Benefits Agreement and the Wireless Adjustment Plan. Thus, any admissions that AT & T made about the value of the options did not relate to an interpretation of Section XVIII.A, but, rather, related to the Employee Benefits Agreement and the Wireless Adjustment Plan.

Further, the Vice Chancellor correctly ruled that AT & T made no judicial admissions in its answer. * * *

CONCLUSION

NOW, THEREFORE, IT IS ORDERED that the judgment of the Court of Chancery is REMANDED for proceedings consistent with this opinion.

NOTE: SUBSEQUENT PROCEEDINGS

On remand, in **Lillis v. AT & T Corp.**, 2008 WL 2811153 (Del.Ch.), the Court of Chancery reversed itself: "This court's conclusion in the Trial Opinion concerning the interpretation of Section XVIII.A hinged primarily on AT & T's admissions. Without that evidence, the plaintiffs have failed to demonstrate that, in the case of the all cash Cingular/Wireless merger, Section XVIII.A required an adjustment to preserve both the intrinsic value and the time value of their options." Id. at 8.

The plaintiffs appealed. In **AT&T Corp. v. Lillis**, --- A.2d ----, 2009 WL 604917 (Del.Supr.), the Delaware Supreme Court in turn reversed itself, splitting three to two:

"In our first opinion, this Court instructed the Court of Chancery to disregard AT & T's admissions because we concluded that those admissions did not relate to the 1994 Plan. We were mistaken. The relevant allegations and admissions do relate to the 1994 Plan, as AT & T acknowledges. Nonetheless, AT & T argues that the remand instruction was appropriate because the admissions are irrelevant to determining the meaning of 'economic position.' We disagree. Several of AT & T's answers, and statements in its brief in opposition to the Option Holders' motion for judgment on the pleadings, support a conclusion that AT & T agreed with the Option Holders' interpretation of Section XVIII.A.

* * *

"If AT & T did not agree with the Option Holders' interpretation of 'economic position,' it would not have admitted that the cancellation of the options would leave them 'worse off.' The only options being cancelled were the out-of-the-money options. If those options had no time value, then they were worthless at the time of the merger, and the Option Holders could not have been made 'worse off' by their cancellation. Therefore, AT & T must have believed that 'economic position' included value in addition to intrinsic value.

* * *

"In their separate opinion, the dissenting Justices acknowledge that AT & T's original answer contained admissions that relate to the 1994 Plan. Their position, however, is that those admissions in AT & T's original answer were legal, rather than factual. Based upon that distinction, the dissent concludes that the admissions are not binding and, regardless, that a party's legal theory does not reveal a party's intention when the agreement was drafted. We disagree with this analysis for several reasons.

"First, the analysis in the dissenting opinion is limited to the admissions in AT & T's original answer. It does not confront the fact that similar admissions also were made in AT & T's Answering Brief in Opposition to Plaintiffs' Motion for Judgment on the Pleadings. Second, although the admissions, once withdrawn, were no longer legally binding *as admissions,* their withdrawal did not eliminate or alter their probative value *as evidence* of a disputed material fact-the parties' intended meaning of the ambiguous term 'economic position.' It is hornbook law that the contracting parties' course of conduct may be considered as evidence of their intended meaning of an ambiguous contractual term. In this case, that course of conduct included the undisputed fact that AT & T made certain admissions in its original answer, which it later withdrew."

(B) FIDUCIARY DUTIES

Insert at the end of "Note: Spring-Loading," at Casebook page 728:

Weiss v. Swanson, 948 A.2d 433 (Del. Ch. 2008), extends *Tyson* to the converse practice -- "bullet-dodging," where the board waits until after the bad news has been made public before awarding the options. Said the Chancery Court:

"* * * In considering the materiality of the Director Defendants' alleged practice of timing options, it is important to note that this court has yet to consider the precise allegations presented here. *Tyson* considered only whether a practice of spring-loading is material information, and this court has had no occasion to consider whether a practice of bullet-dodging is material information directors have a duty to disclose. Taking Weiss's allegations in this case as true, it is reasonable to infer that stockholders would consider the practice of timing options described in the complaint to be important in deciding whether to approve the option plans or to reelect board members. In other words, the well-pleaded allegations in the complaint support an inference that the Director Defendants' alleged practice of granting spring-loaded and bullet-dodged options in conjunction with earnings releases was material information. Under *Tyson,* because the allegations of the complaint support an inference that the Director Defendants never disclosed this practice in the plans themselves, subsequent proxy statements, or SEC filings describing the option grants, the allegations in the complaint also give rise to an inference that the Director Defendants, in violation of their fiduciary duties, intended to circumvent the restrictions found in the plans."

(C) NEW FEDERAL REGULATION

Congressional Oversight Panel, Special Report on Regulatory Reform.

Modernizing the American Financial Regulatory System: Recommendations for Improving Oversight, Protecting Consumers, and Ensuring Stability

January 2009

pages 37-40

5. Create Executive Pay Structures that Discourage Excessive Risk Taking

***Problem with current system:* Executive pay packages incentivize excessive risk.**

Executive pay is a key issue in modernizing the financial regulatory system. However, the common focus on the themes of inequality and "pay for performance" misses the unnecessary risk that many compensation schemes introduce into the financial sector. Altering the incentives that encourage this risk through the tax code, regulation, and corporate governance reform will help mitigate systemic risk in future crises.

Executive compensation has been one of the most controversial issues in American business since the late 1980s. In response to criticism that executives' and shareholders' interests did not sufficiently align, executive compensation packages began to contain more and more stock options, to the point where options now represent the lion's share of a high-ranking executive's pay.

Much criticism of executive pay has had its origins in the increase in the ratio of the pay of public company executives to average worker pay, from 42:1 in 1982 to over 400:1 in the early years of this decade. Recent executive pay scandals, such as those associated with the backdating of stock options, have centered on efforts by executives to disconnect pay from performance without informing investors. Numerous accounts of executive pay in the context of the financial crisis of 2007–08 have focused on large severance packages, often described as once again disconnecting pay from performance.[1]

---

[1] The most prominent example is that of Angelo Mozilo, the former Chief Executive Officer of Countrywide Financial Corporation. Countrywide was rescued from bankruptcy by being acquired by Bank of America, which is now itself seeking additional financial assistance from the TARP. Mozilo realized more than $400 million in compensation from 2001 to 2007, most of it in the form of stock related compensation that he received and cashed out during the period. *Executive Incentives*, Wall Street Journal (Nov. 20, 2008). Similarly, three of Merrill Lynch's

However, even before the current crises, many criticized such incentive plans for encouraging excessive focus on the short term at the expense of consideration of the risks involved. This short-term focus led to unsustainable stock buyback programs, accounting manipulations, risky trading and investment strategies, or other unsustainable business practices that merely yield short-term positive financial reports. Executive pay should be designed, regulated, and taxed to incentivize financial executives to prioritize long-term objectives, and to avoid both undertaking excessive, unnecessary risk and socializing losses with the help of the federal taxpayer.

***Action item*: Create tax incentives to encourage long-term–oriented pay packages.**

Financial firm packages typically have a number of features that introduce short-term biases in business decision making. Most equity-linked compensation is either in the form of performance bonuses, typically awarded on an annual basis, and options on restricted stock, typically awarded in the form of grants with three-year vesting periods, and no restrictions on sale after vesting. These structures, together with the typical five-years-or-less tenure of public company CEOs, often lead to a focus on investment horizons of less than three years. Altering the tax treatment of executive compensation packages in the interests of encouraging stability, lessening risks, and orienting finance executives toward long-term goals represents a relatively simple step toward solving the incentive problem. Such a change could result from revising applicable tax rates, changing the treatment of compensation as income versus capital gains, or other relatively simple measures.

***Action item*: Encourage financial regulators to guard against asymmetric pay packages in financial institutions, such as options combined with large severance packages.**

Asymmetric links between compensation and risk create incentives for executives to pursue potentially systemically threatening high-risk–high-reward strategies without sufficient regard for the downside potential. Encouraging regulators to spot and discourage compensation packages that excessively

---

top executives realized a combined $200 million in bonuses shortly before Bank of America absorbed that firm. Andrew Clark, *Banking Crisis: Merrill Lynch Top Brass Set to Share $200m*, The Guardian (Sept. 17, 2008) (online at www.guardian.co.uk/business/2008/sep/17/merrilllynch.executivesalaries).

insulate executives from losses will help resolve this asymmetry and promote stability.

Stock options create incentives that are tied to stock price, but the overall compensation package's asymmetric link to stock price actually helps encourage more dramatic risk taking. As the price of the underlying stock declines, the option holder become less sensitive to further declines in value of the underlying stock, and more interested in the possibility of achieving dramatic gains, regardless of the risk of further losses. A number of common features of executive pay practice that further protect executives against downside risk exacerbate this asymmetry problem. Among these features are the prevalence of option repricing when the underlying company stock falls below the option strike price for sustained periods of time and large severance packages paid to failed executives. While asymmetries in executive compensation are potentially harmful in the context of any company, they create particular difficulties in the context of regulated financial institutions. Most regulated financial institutions are the beneficiaries of explicit or implicit guarantees. The FDIC insurance system is an explicit guarantee to some depositors, which in the current crisis has been extended to all bank debt. The current Treasury and Federal Reserve rescues of Fannie Mae, Freddie Mac, and AIG, and the recent TARP actions in relation to Citigroup and Bank of America—and perhaps all nine major TARP recipient banks—all raise issues of implicit guarantees. These guarantees provide regulators with an opportunity to ensure that problematically asymmetrical compensation plans do not reappear in these institutions.

***Action item*: Regulators should consider requiring executive pay contracts to provide for clawbacks of bonus compensation for executives of failing institutions.**

Financial system regulators should consider revoking bonus compensation for executives of failing institutions that require federal intervention. Whether the federal government promises to support the institution before a crisis develops, as with Fannie Mae and Freddie Mac, or after, as with TARP recipients, the prospect of losing bonus compensation could deter risky practices that make the federal rescue more probable.

The cases of the Fannie Mae and Freddie Mac seem particularly relevant. In both companies, executive pay in the course of the 1990s moved from a model focused on corporate stability to a model focused on stock price maximization through asymmetric, short-term incentives. It appears that this change fed pressures to increase margins in ways that were only possible by engaging in riskier investment practices. This approach to executive pay is inconsistent with federal guarantees of solvency; inevitably, if it is not abandoned, taxpayers will end up paying for imprudent risk taking by improperly incentivized executives.

As the financial crisis has developed, there has been a fair amount of discussion of clawbacks of executive pay. The Sarbanes-Oxley Act of 2002 required clawbacks of executive pay awarded as a result of fraudulent financial statements. Similar clawback provisions could help restore symmetry and a longer-term perspective to executive compensation systems. As such, regulators should consider adding them to the tools at their disposal.

***Action item*: Encourage corporate governance structures with stronger board and long-term investor oversight of pay packages.**

The Associated Press recently reported that "even where banks cut back on pay, some executives were left with seven- or eight-figure compensation that most people can only dream about. Richard D. Fairbank, the chairman of Capital One Financial Corp., took a $1 million hit in compensation after his company had a disappointing year, but still got $17 million in stock options. The McLean, Va.-based company received $3.56 billion in bailout money on Nov. 14." Corporate governance regulations should strengthen the role of boards and long-term shareholders in the executive pay process with the goal of encouraging executive pay practices that align executives' interests with the long-term performance of the businesses they manage.

The problems of asymmetric and short-term-focused executive pay have been the subject of a number of reform efforts by business groups. Such reform recommendations have come from the Conference Board, in its report on the origins of the financial crisis, and from the Aspen Institute's Principles for Long Term Value Creation, endorsed by the U.S. Chamber of Commerce and the Business Roundtable, as well as by the Council of Institutional Investors and the AFL-CIO.

Financial regulators should encourage these efforts wherever possible and provide assistance wherever practicable. Financial regulators should ncourage these efforts wherever possible and provide assistance wherever practicable. Congressional Oversight Panel, Special Report on Regulatory Reform.

Section 111 of the Emergency Economic Stabilization Act of 2008, as amended by section 7001 of American Recovery and Reinvestment Act of 2009 set out restrictions on executive pay at companies receiving federal financial assistance. The Regulations described below effectuated this legislation.

U. S. Treasury Press Release – New Restrictions On Executive Compensation
February 4, 2009
Updated: March 2, 2009

Today, the Treasury Department is issuing a new set of guidelines on executive pay for financial institutions that are receiving government assistance to address our current financial crisis. These measures are designed to ensure that public funds are directed only toward the public interest in strengthening our economy by stabilizing our financial system and not toward inappropriate private gain. The measures announced today are designed to ensure that the compensation of top executives in the financial community is closely aligned not only with the interests of shareholders and financial institutions, but with the taxpayers providing assistance to those companies.

The Treasury guidelines on executive pay seek to strike the correct balance between the need for strict monitoring and accountability on executive pay and the need for financial institutions to fully function and attract the talent pool that will maximize the chances of financial recovery and taxpayers being paid back on their investments. The proposals below, such as emphasizing restricted stock that vests as the government is repaid with interest, seek to strike exactly that balance.

The guidelines distinguish between banks participating in any new generally available capital access program and banks needing " exceptional assistance." Generally available programs have the same terms for all recipients, with limits on the amount each institution may receive and specified returns for taxpayers. The goal of these programs is to help ensure the financial system as a whole can provide the credit necessary for recovery, including providing capital to smaller community banks that play a critical role in lending to small businesses, families and others. The previously announced Capital Purchase Program is an example of a generally available capital access program.

If a firm needs more assistance than is allowed under a widely available standard program, then that is exceptional assistance. Banks falling under the "exceptional assistance" standard have bank-specific negotiated agreements with

Treasury. Examples include AIG, and the Bank of America and Citi transactions under the Targeted Investment Program.

As part of President Obama's efforts to promote systemic regulatory reform, the standards today mark the beginning of a long-term effort to examine both the degree that executive compensation structures at financial institutions contributed to our current financial crisis and how corporate governance and compensation rules can be reformed to better promote long-term value and growth for shareholders, companies, workers and the economy at large and to prevent such financial crises from occurring again.

I. COMPLIANCE AND CERTIFICATION:

All Companies Receiving Government Assistance Must Ensure Compliance with Executive Compensation Provisions: The chief executive officers of all companies that have to this point received or do receive any form of government assistance must provide certification that the companies have strictly complied with statutory, Treasury, and contractual executive compensation restrictions. Chief executive officers must re-certify compliance with these restrictions on an annual basis. In addition, the compensation committees of all companies receiving government assistance must provide an explanation of how their senior executive compensation arrangements do not encourage excessive and unnecessary risk-taking.

II. ENHANCED CONDITIONS ON EXECUTIVE COMPENSATION GOING FORWARD:

1. Companies Receiving Exceptional Financial Recovery Assistance:

Limit Senior Executives to $500,000 in Total Annual Compensation – Other than Restricted Stock: Current programs providing exceptional assistance to financial institutions forbid recipients of government funds from taking a tax deduction for senior executive compensation above $500,000. Today's guidance takes this restriction further by limiting the total amount of compensation to no more than $500,000 for these senior executives except for restricted stock awards.

Any Additional Pay for Senior Executives Must Be in Restricted Stock that Vests When the Government Has Been Repaid with Interest: Any pay to a senior executive of a company receiving exceptional assistance beyond $500,000 <u>must be made in restricted stock</u> or other similar long-term incentive arrangements. The senior executive receiving such restricted stock will only be able to cash in either after the government has been repaid – including the contractual dividend payments that ensure taxpayers are compensated for the time value of their money – or after a specified period according to conditions that consider among other factors the degree a company has satisfied repayment obligations, protected taxpayer interests or met lending and stability standards. Such a restricted stock strategy will help assure that senior executives of companies receiving exceptional assistance have incentives aligned with both the long-term interests of shareholders as well as minimizing the costs to taxpayers.

Executive Compensation Structure and Strategy Must be Fully Disclosed and Subject to a "Say on Pay" Shareholder Resolution: The senior executive compensation structure and the rationale for how compensation is tied to sound risk management must be submitted to a non-binding shareholder resolution. There are no "Say on Pay" provisions in the existing programs.

Require Provisions to Clawback Bonuses for Top Executives Engaging in Deceptive Practices: Under the existing programs providing exceptional assistance, only the top five senior executives were subject to a clawback provision. Going forward, a company receiving exceptional assistance must have in place provisions to claw back bonuses and incentive compensation from any of the next twenty senior executives if they are found to have knowingly engaged in providing inaccurate information relating to financial statements or performance metrics used to calculate their own incentive pay.

Increase Ban on Golden Parachutes for Senior Executives: The existing programs providing exceptional assistance to financial institutions prohibited the top five senior executives from receiving any golden parachute payment upon severance from employment, a ban that will be expanded to include the top ten senior executives. In addition, and at a minimum, the next twenty-five executives will be prohibited from receiving any golden parachute payment greater than one year's compensation upon severance from employment.

Require Board of Directors' Adoption of Company Policy Relating to Approval of Luxury Expenditures: The boards of directors of companies receiving exceptional assistance from the government must adopt a company-wide policy on any expenditures related to aviation services, office and facility renovations, entertainment and holiday parties, and conferences and events. This policy is not intended to cover reasonable expenditures for sales conferences, staff development, reasonable performance incentives and other measures tied to a company's normal business operations. These new rules go beyond current guidelines, and would require certification by chief executive officers for expenditures that could be viewed as excessive or luxury items. Companies should also now post the text of the expenditures policy on their web sites.

2. Financial Institutions Participating in Generally Available Capital Access Programs:

The Treasury intends to issue proposed guidance subject to public comment on the following executive compensation requirements relating to future *generally available* capital access programs.

Limit Senior Executives to $500,000 in Total Annual Compensation Plus Restricted Stock – Unless Waived with Full Public Disclosure and Shareholder Vote: Companies that participate in generally available capital access programs may waive the $500,000 plus restricted stock rule only by disclosure of their compensation and, if requested, a non-binding "say on pay" shareholder resolution. All firms participating in a future capital access program must review and disclose the reasons that compensation arrangements of both the senior executives and other employees do not encourage excessive and unnecessary risk taking. Under the current Capital Purchase Program, the companies were only required to review and certify that the top five executives' compensation arrangements did not encourage excessive and unnecessary risk-taking.

Require Provisions to Clawback Bonuses for Top Executives Engaging in Deceptive Practices: The same clawback provision that applies to companies receiving exceptional assistance will apply to those in generally available capital access programs. Thus, in addition to the clawback provision applicable to the top five executives as under the Capital Purchase Program, a company receiving assistance must have in place provisions to claw back bonuses and incentive compensation from any of the next twenty senior executives if they are found to have knowingly engaged in providing inaccurate information relating to financial statements or performance metrics used to calculate their own incentive pay.

Increase Ban on Golden Parachutes for Senior Executives: Even under generally available capital access programs, the golden parachute ban will be strengthened: Upon a severance from employment, the top five senior executives will not be allowed a golden parachute payment greater than one year's compensation, as opposed to three years under the current Capital Purchase Program.

Require Board of Directors' Adoption of Company Policy Relating to Approval of Luxury Expenditures: This policy will be the same for companies accessing generally available capital programs as it is for those receiving exceptional assistance. There are no guidelines on luxury expenditures under the current Capital Purchase Program.

[*These new standards will not apply retroactively to existing investments or to programs already announced such as the Capital Purchase Program and the Term Asset-Backed Securities Loan Facility.*]

III. LONG-TERM REGULATORY REFORM: COMPENSATION STRATEGIES ALIGNED WITH PROPER RISK MANAGEMENT AND LONG-TERM VALUE AND GROWTH:

Even as we work to recover from current market events, it is not too early to begin a serious effort to both examine how company-wide compensation strategies at financial institutions – not just those related to top executives – may have encouraged excessive risk-taking that contributed to current market events and to begin developing model compensation policies for the future. Such steps should include:

Requiring all Compensation Committees of Public Financial Institutions to Review and Disclose Strategies for Aligning Compensation with Sound Risk-Management: The Secretary of the Treasury and the Chairman of the Securities and Exchange Commission should work together to require compensation committees of all public financial institutions – not just those receiving government assistance – to review and disclose executive and certain employee compensation arrangements and explain how these compensation arrangements are consistent with promoting sound risk management and long-term value creation for their companies and their shareholders.

Compensation of Top Executives Should Include Incentives That Encourage a Long-Term Perspective: Over the last decade there has been an emerging consensus that top executives should receive compensation that encourages more of a long-term perspective on creating economic value for their shareholders and the economy at large. One idea worthy of serious consideration is requiring top executives at financial institutions to hold stock for several years after it is awarded before it can be cashed-out as this would encourage a more long-term focus on the economic interests of the firm.

Pass Say on Pay Shareholder Resolutions on Executive Compensation: Even beyond companies receiving financial recovery assistance, owners of financial institutions – the shareholders – should have a non-binding resolution on both the levels of executive compensation as well as how the structure of compensation incentives help promote risk management and long-term value creation for the firm and the economy as a whole.

White House -Treasury Conference on Long-Term Executive Pay Reform: The Secretary of the Treasury will host a conference with shareholder advocates, major public pension and institutional investor leaders, policy-makers, executives, academics, and others on executive pay reform at financial institutions. Treasury will seek testimony, comment, and white papers on model executive pay initiatives in the cause of establishing best practices and guidelines on executive compensation arrangements for financial institutions.

Part V. MERGERS AND ACQUISITIONS

SECTION C. THE MERGER AGREEMENT

Insert after IPB, Inc. v. Tyson Foods, Inc., *at the bottom of Casebook page 805:*

Hexion Specialty Chemicals, Inc. v. Huntsman Corp.

Court of Chancery of Delaware, 2008.
965 A.2d 715.

LAMB, Vice Chancellor.

In July 2007, just before the onset of the ongoing crisis affecting the national and international credit markets, two large chemical companies entered into a merger agreement contemplating a leveraged cash acquisition of one by the other. The buyer is a privately held corporation, 92% owned by a large private equity group.

Because the buyer and its parent were eager to be the winning bidder in a competitive bidding situation, they agreed to pay a substantially higher price than the competition and to commit to stringent deal terms, including no "financing out." In other words, if the financing the buyer arranged (or equivalent alternative financing) is not available at the closing, the buyer is not excused from performing under the contract. In that event, and in the absence of a material adverse effect relating to Huntsman's business as a whole, the issue becomes whether the buyer's liability to the seller for failing to close the transaction is limited to $325 million by contract or, instead, is uncapped.

The answer to that question turns on whether the buyer committed a knowing and intentional breach of any of its covenants found in the merger agreement that caused damages in excess of the contractual limit. Among other things, the buyer covenanted that it would use its reasonable best efforts to take all actions and do all things "necessary, proper or advisable" to consummate the financing on the terms it had negotiated with its banks and further covenanted that it would not take any action "that could be reasonably be expected to materially impair, delay or prevent consummation" of such financing.

While the parties were engaged in obtaining the necessary regulatory approvals, the seller reported several disappointing quarterly results, missing the numbers it projected at the time the deal was signed. After receiving the seller's first quarter 2008 results, the buyer and its parent, through their counsel, began exploring options for extricating the seller from the transaction. At first, this process focused on whether the seller had suffered a material adverse effect. By early May, however, attention shifted to an exploration of the prospective solvency of the combined entity, leading them to retain the services of a well-known valuation firm to explore the possibility of obtaining an opinion that the combined entity would be insolvent. After making a number of changes to the inputs into the deal model that materially and adversely effected the viability of the transaction, and without consulting with the seller about those changes or about other business initiatives that might improve the prospective financial condition of the resulting entity, the buyer succeeded in obtaining an "insolvency" opinion.

The insolvency opinion was presented to the buyer's board of directors on June 18, 2008, and later published in a press release claiming that the merger could not be consummated because the financing would not be available due to the prospective insolvency of the combined entity and because the seller had suffered a material adverse effect, as defined in the merger agreement. The buyer and a host of its affiliated entities immediately filed the complaint in this action, alleging a belief that the merger cannot be consummated since the financing will not be available.

The complaint alleges financing will be unavailable because, (1) the amounts available under that financing are no longer sufficient to close the transaction and (2) the combined entity would be insolvent. The complaint seeks a declaration that the buyer is not obligated to consummate the merger if the combined company would be insolvent and a further declaration that its liability (and that of its affiliates) to the seller for nonconsummation of the transaction cannot exceed the $325 million termination fee. The complaint also seeks a declaration that the seller suffered a material adverse effect, thus excusing the buyer's obligation to close. The seller answered and filed counterclaims seeking, among other things, an order directing the buyer to specifically perform its obligations under the merger agreement.

The court conducted six days of trial on certain of the claims for declaratory and injunctive relief raised by the pleadings. In this post-trial opinion, the court finds that the seller has not suffered a material adverse effect, as defined in the merger agreement, and further concludes that the buyer has knowingly and intentionally breached numerous of its covenants under that contract. Thus, the court will grant the seller's request for an order specifically enforcing the buyer's contractual obligations to the extent permitted by the merger agreement itself.

The court also determines that it should not now rule on whether the combined entity, however it may ultimately be capitalized, would be solvent or insolvent at closing. In this connection, the court rejects the buyer's argument that it can be excused from performing its freely undertaken contractual obligations simply because its board of directors concluded that the performance of those contractual obligations risked insolvency. Instead, it was the duty of the buyer's board of directors to explore the many available options for mitigating the risk of insolvency while causing the buyer to perform its contractual obligations in good faith. If, at closing, and despite the buyer's best efforts, financing had not been available, the buyer could then have stood on its contract rights and faced no more than the contractually stipulated damages. The buyer and its parent, however, chose a different course.

The court recognizes that there remain substantial obstacles to closing the transaction. Some of those result from the current unsettled credit environment, others result from the difficult macroeconomic conditions facing both the seller and the buyer in running their businesses. Some other of those obstacles appear to result from the course of action the buyer and its parent have pursued in place of the continued good faith performance of the buyer's contractual obligations. Despite these obstacles, the seller has asked for an order of specific performance and, given the realistic possibility that the buyer and its parent may now regard closing the deal to be a superior outcome to not closing, the court concludes that such an order should issue requiring Hexion to perform all of its covenants and obligations (other than the ultimate obligation to close).

I.

* * *

The plaintiffs and counterclaim defendants in this action are Hexion Specialty Chemicals, Inc., Apollo Global Management, LLC, and various entities through which Apollo Global Management conducts its business (Apollo Global Management and its related entities are collectively referred to as "Apollo"). Hexion, a New Jersey corporation, is the world's largest producer of binder, adhesive, and ink resins for industrial applications. Apollo Global Management, a Delaware limited liability company, is an asset manager focusing on private equity transactions. Through its ownership in Hexion's holding company, Apollo owns approximately 92% of Hexion.

The defendant and counterclaim plaintiff in this action is Huntsman Corporation, a Delaware corporation. Huntsman, a global manufacturer and marketer chemical products, operates five primary lines of business: Polyurethanes, Advanced Materials, Textile Effects, Performance Products and Pigments.

* * *

In late 2005 and early 2006, Apollo and Hexion entered negotiations with Huntsman concerning a proposed transaction whereby Hexion would merge with Huntsman's specialty chemical business and Huntsman's commodity business would be spun out and acquired by Apollo. Hexion and Apollo performed substantial due diligence on Huntsman, but the deal died when Huntsman missed earnings targets and Apollo advised Huntsman that it could no longer justify the $25 per share price then being discussed.

* * *

In May 2007, Huntsman, through its financial advisor Merrill Lynch & Co., Inc., began to solicit bids for the company. Apollo (through Hexion) and Basell, the world's largest polypropylene maker, emerged among the potential buyers. Huntsman signed confidentiality agreements and began to negotiate merger agreements with both Hexion and Basell. On June 25, 2007, Huntsman rejected Hexion's offer of $26 per share and executed a merger agreement with Basell for $25.25 per share. The same day, but after the agreement was signed, Hexion raised its bid to $27 per share. Basell refused to raise its bid, stating that its deal remained superior because it was more certain to close. On June 29, 2007, Huntsman re-entered negotiations with Hexion after Hexion further increased its bid to $27.25 per share. On July 12, 2007, Huntsman terminated its deal with Basell and signed an all cash deal at $28 per share with Hexion.

* * *

One day before the signing of the merger agreement, Hexion signed a commitment letter with affiliates of Credit Suisse and Deutsche Bank (the "lending banks") to secure financing for the deal. In section 3.2(e) of the merger agreement, Hexion represented that the "aggregate proceeds contemplated to be provided by the Commitment Letter will be sufficient ... to pay the aggregate Merger Consideration." The commitment letter required a "customary and reasonably satisfactory" solvency certificate from the Chief Financial Officer of

Hexion, the Chief Financial Officer of Huntsman, or a reputable valuation firm as a condition precedent to the lending banks obligation to provide financing.

* * *

Due to the existence of a signed agreement with Basell and Apollo's admittedly intense desire for the deal, Huntsman had significant negotiating leverage. As a result, the merger agreement is more than usually favorable to Huntsman. For example, it contains no financing contingency and requires Hexion to use its "reasonable best efforts" to consummate the financing. In addition, the agreement expressly provides for uncapped damages in the case of a "knowing and intentional breach of any covenant" by Hexion and for liquidated damages of $325 million in cases of other enumerated breaches. The narrowly tailored MAE clause is one of the few ways the merger agreement allows Hexion to walk away from the deal without paying Huntsman at least $325 million in liquidated damages.

* * *

II.

Hexion argues that its obligation to close is excused as a result of a Company Material Adverse Effect in the business of Huntsman. For the reasons detailed below, Hexion's argument fails.

A. *The "Chemical Industry" Carve-Outs are Inapplicable*

Section 6.2(e) of the merger agreement states that Hexion's obligation to close is conditioned on the absence of "any event, change, effect or development that has had or is reasonably expected to have, individually or in the aggregate," an MAE. MAE is defined in section 3.1(a)(ii) as:

> any occurrence, condition, change, event or effect that is materially adverse to the financial condition, business, or results of operations of the Company and its Subsidiaries, taken as a whole; *provided, however,* that in no event shall any of the following constitute a Company Material Adverse Effect: (A) any occurrence, condition, change, event or effect resulting from or relating to changes in general economic or financial market conditions, except in the event, and only to the extent, that such occurrence, condition, change, event or effect has had a disproportionate effect on the Company and its Subsidiaries, taken as a whole, as compared to other Persons engaged in the chemical industry;

> (B) any occurrence, condition, change, event or effect that affects the chemical industry generally (including changes in commodity prices, general market prices and regulatory changes affecting the chemical industry generally) except in the event, and only to the extent, that such occurrence, condition, change, event or effect has had a disproportionate effect on the Company and its Subsidiaries, taken as a whole, as compared to other Persons engaged in the chemical industry....

The parties disagree as to the proper reading of this definition. Hexion argues that the relevant standard to apply in judging whether an MAE has occurred is to compare Huntsman's performance since the signing of the merger agreement and its expected future performance to the rest of the chemical industry. Huntsman, for its part, argues that in determining whether an MAE has occurred the court need reach the issue of comparing Huntsman to its peers if and only if it has first determined that there has been an "occurrence, condition, change, event or effect that is materially adverse to the financial condition, business, or results of operations of the Company and its Subsidiaries, taken as a whole...." Huntsman here has the better argument. The plain meaning of the carve-outs found in the proviso is to prevent certain occurrences which would *otherwise* be MAE's being found to be so. If a catastrophe were to befall the chemical industry and cause a material adverse effect in Huntsman's business, the carve-outs would prevent this from qualifying as an MAE under the Agreement. But the converse is not true-Huntsman's performance being disproportionately worse than the chemical industry in general does not, in itself, constitute an MAE. Thus, unless the court concludes that the company has suffered an MAE as defined in the language coming before the proviso, the court need not consider the application of the chemical industry carve-outs.

Hexion bases its argument that Huntsman has suffered an MAE principally on a comparison between Huntsman and other chemical industry firms. Hexion's expert witness, Telly Zachariades of The Valence Group, largely focused on this at trial. Zachariades testified regarding a comparison of the performance of Huntsman during the second half of 2007 and first half of 2008, relative to two sets of benchmark companies which he chose as representative of the industry-the Bloomberg World Chemical Index and the Chemical Week 75 Index. Zachariades compared Huntsman to these two benchmarks in a variety of different areas, both backward and forward-looking, and, in each, found Huntsman significantly worse than the mean, and, in most, in the bottom decile. This potentially would be compelling evidence if it was necessary to reach the carve-outs, although Huntsman's expert, Mark Zmijewski, managed to cast doubt on Zachariades's analysis. However, because, as discussed below,

Huntsman has not suffered an MAE, the court need not reach the question of whether Huntsman's performance has been disproportionately worse than the chemical industry taken as a whole.

B. *Huntsman Has Not Suffered An MAE*

For the purpose of determining whether an MAE has occurred, changes in corporate fortune must be examined in the context in which the parties were transacting. In the absence of evidence to the contrary, a corporate acquirer may be assumed to be purchasing the target as part of a long-term strategy. The important consideration therefore is whether there has been an adverse change in the target's business that is consequential to the company's long-term earnings power over a commercially reasonable period, which one would expect to be measured in years rather than months. A buyer faces a heavy burden when it attempts to invoke a material adverse effect clause in order to avoid its obligation to close. Many commentators have noted that Delaware courts have never found a material adverse effect to have occurred in the context of a merger agreement. This is not a coincidence. The ubiquitous material adverse effect clause should be seen as providing a "backstop protecting the acquirer from the occurrence of unknown events that substantially threaten the overall earnings potential of the target in a durationally-significant manner. A short-term hiccup in earnings should not suffice; rather [an adverse change] should be material when viewed from the longer-term perspective of a reasonable acquirer." This, of course, is not to say that evidence of a significant decline in earnings by the target corporation during the period after signing but prior to the time appointed for closing is irrelevant. Rather, it means that for such a decline to constitute a material adverse effect, poor earnings results must be expected to persist significantly into the future.

Hexion protests being shouldered with the burden of proof here, urging the court that Huntsman bears the burden of showing the absence of an MAE, because that is a condition precedent to closing. In support of this proposition Hexion cites no cases directly related to material adverse effect clauses. Instead, Hexion cites two cases for the general proposition that "a party who seeks to recover upon a contract must prove such facts as are necessary to establish a compliance with conditions precedent thereto cannot be denied." This is undoubtedly true, so far as it goes. Hexion argues that *IBP,* in placing the burden to prove a material adverse effect on the buyer, is distinguishable because in *IBP* the material adverse effect clause was drafted in the form of a representation and warranty that no material adverse effect had occurred. But material adverse effect clauses are strange animals, *sui generis* among their contract clause brethren. It is by no means clear to this court that the form in which a material adverse effect clause is drafted (i.e., as a representation, or warranty, or a condition to closing), absent more specific evidence regarding the intention of the parties, should be dispositive on the allocation of the burden of proof. Typically, conditions precedent are easily ascertainable objective facts, generally that a party performed some particular act or that some independent event has occurred. A material adverse effect clause does not easily fit into such a mold, and it is not at all clear that it ought to be treated the same for this purpose. Rather, for the same practical reasons that the court in *IBP* cites, it seems the preferable view, and the one the court adopts, that absent clear language to the contrary, the burden of proof with respect to a material adverse effect rests on the party seeking to excuse its performance under the contract. This outcome is also in accord with this court's holding that in determining the allocation of the burden of proof in suits for declaratory judgment, "the better view is that a plaintiff in a declaratory judgment action should always have the burden of going forward." This rule would also place the burden of proof that an MAE has occurred on Hexion, as the initial seeker of a declaratory judgment that an MAE has occurred. Furthermore, as the parties jointly stipulate, the question is "[w]hether Hexion has established that a 'Company Material Adverse Effect,' as defined in the Merger Agreement, has occurred." This again places the burden to show the existence of an MAE squarely on Hexion.

The issue then becomes what benchmark to use in examining changes in the results of business operations post-signing of the merger agreement-EBITDA or earnings per share. In the context of a cash acquisition, the use of earnings per share is problematic. Earnings per share is very much a function of the capital structure of a company, reflecting the effects of leverage. An acquirer for cash is replacing the capital structure of the target company with one of its own choosing. While possible capital structures will be constrained by the nature of the acquired business, where, as here, both the debt and equity of the target company must be acquired, the capital structure of the target prior to the merger is largely irrelevant. What matters is the results of operation of the business. Because EBITDA is independent of capital structure, it is a better measure of the operational results of the business. Changes in Huntsman's fortunes will thus be examined through the lens of changes in EBITDA. This is, in any event, the metric the parties relied on most heavily in negotiating and modeling the transaction.

Hexion focuses its argument that Huntsman has suffered an MAE along several lines: (1) disappointing results in Huntsman's earnings performance over the period from July 2007 through the present; (2) Huntsman's increase in net debt since signing, contrary to the expectations of the parties; and (3) underperformance in Huntsman's Textile Effects and Pigments lines of business.

1. *Huntsman Has A Difficult Year After The Signing Of The Merger Agreement*

There is no question that Huntsman's results from the time of signing in July 2007 until the end of the first half of 2008 have been disappointing. Huntsman's first-half 2008 EBITDA was down 19.9% year-over-year from its first-half 2007 EBITDA. And its second-half 2007 EBITDA was 22% below the projections Huntsman presented to bidders in June 2007 for the rest of the year.

Realizing, however, that these results, while disappointing, were not compelling as a basis to claim an MAE, Hexion focused its arguments on Huntsman's repeated misses from its forecasts. In its "Project Nimbus" forecasts, Huntsman management projected 2008 consolidated EBITDA of $1.289 billion. As of August 1, 2008, Huntsman management projected EBITDA for 2008 was $879 million, a 32% decrease from the forecast the year before. Hexion points to these shortfalls from the 2007 projections and claims that Huntsman's failure to live up to its projections are key to the MAE analysis.

But this cannot be so. Section 5.11(b) of the merger agreement explicitly disclaims any representation or warranty by Huntsman with respect to "any projections, forecasts or other estimates, plans or budgets of future revenues, expenses or expenditures, future results of operations ..., future cash flows ... or future financial condition ... of [Huntsman] or any of its Subsidiaries ... heretofore or hereafter delivered to or made available to [Hexion or its affiliates] ...." The parties specifically allocated the risk to Hexion that Huntsman's performance would not live up to management's expectations at the time. If Hexion wanted the short-term forecasts of Huntsman warranted by Huntsman, it could have negotiated for that. It could have tried to negotiate a lower base price and something akin to an earn-out, based not on Huntsman's post-closing performance but on its performance between signing and closing. Creative investment bankers and deal lawyers could have structured, at the agreement of the parties, any number of potential terms to shift to Huntsman some or all of the risk that Huntsman would fail to hit its forecast targets. But none of those things happened. Instead, Hexion agreed that the contract contained no representation or warranty with respect to Huntsman's forecasts. To now allow the MAE analysis to hinge on Huntsman's failure to hit its forecast targets during the period leading up to closing would eviscerate, if not render altogether void, the meaning of section 5.11(b). It is a maxim of contract law that, given ambiguity between potentially conflicting terms, a contract should be read so as not to render any term meaningless. Thus, the correct interpretation cannot be that section 6.2(e) voids section 5.11(b), making it a condition precedent to Hexion's obligation to consummate the merger that Huntsman substantially meet its forecast targets. Rather, the correct analysis is that Huntsman's failure to hit its forecasts cannot be a predicate to the determination of an MAE in Huntsman's business. Moreover, at trial Jordan Zaken, one of the Apollo partners involved in negotiating the Huntsman deal on behalf of Hexion, admitted on cross-examination that Hexion and Apollo never fully believed Huntsman's forecasts. Those forecasts, therefore, cannot be the basis of a claim of an MAE, since they never formed part of the expectations of the parties (in a strict contractual sense) to begin with.

Rather, as Huntsman's expert Zmijewski testified at trial, the terms "financial condition, business, or results of operations" are terms of art, to be understood with reference to their meaning in Regulation S-K and Item 7, the "Management's Discussion and Analysis of Financial Condition and Results of Operations" section of the financial statements public companies are required to file with the SEC. In this section, a company is required to disclose its financial result for the period being reported, along with its pro forma financial results for the same time period for each of the previous two years. Zmijewski testified at trial that these results are analyzed by comparing the results in each period with the results in the same period for the prior year (i.e., year-end 2007 results to year-end 2006 results, first-quarter 2005 results to first-quarter 2004 results, and so forth). The proper benchmark then for analyzing these changes with respect to an MAE, according to Zmijewski (and the analysis the court adopts here), is to examine each year and quarter and compare it to the prior year's equivalent period. Through this lens, it becomes clear that no MAE has occurred. Huntsman's 2007 EBITDA was only 3% below its 2006 EBITDA, and, according to Huntsman management forecasts, 2008 EBITDA will only be 7% below 2007 EBITDA. Even using Hexion's much lower estimate of Huntsman's 2008 EBITDA, Huntsman's 2008 EBITDA would still be only 11% below its 2007 EBITDA. And although Huntsman's fourth quarter 2007 EBITDA was 19% below its third quarter 2007 results, which were in turn 3% below its second quarter 2007 results, Huntsman has historically been down on a quarter-over-quarter basis in each of the third and fourth quarters of the year. Moreover, comparing the trailing-twelve-months EBITDA for second quarter 2007 to second quarter 2008, the 2008 result is only down 6% from 2007.

Of course, the expected future performance of the target company is also relevant to a material adverse effect analysis. Hexion, on the basis of its estimates of Huntsman's future profitability, urges that Huntsman has or is expected to suffer an MAE. Hexion estimates that Huntsman will earn only $817 million in 2008, and that its earnings will contract further in 2009, to $809 million.

Huntsman responds with its own projections, that it will generate $878 million of EBITDA in 2008, and $1.12 billion of EBITDA in 2009. To support its projections, Huntsman offered testimony at trial by Peter Huntsman, its CEO, Kimo Esplin, its CFO, Tony Hankins, the President of its Polyurethanes division, Paul Hulme, President of its Materials and Effects Division, and Simon Turner, Senior Vice President of its Pigments division. Each of the division managers described in detail how he expected to reach his target earnings for the following year, and described both how macroeconomic effects such as sharp increases in the prices of crude oil and natural gas, and the weakening of the dollar relative to the euro, contributed to a reduction in Huntsman's 2008 earnings and how the recent reversal of the trend in several of those macroeconomic effects could be expected to positively change future EBITDA results. While the court recognizes that management's expectations for a company's business often skew towards the overly optimistic, especially in the presence of litigation, the court ultimately concludes that Hexion's projections reflect an overly pessimistic view of Huntsman's future earnings.

The fact that Hexion offered little detail as to how it arrived at its projections for Huntsman's business also diminishes the weight its projections deserve. Ultimately, the likely outcome for Huntsman's 2009 EBITDA is somewhere in the middle. This proposition is confirmed by current analyst estimates for Huntsman 2009 EBITDA, which average around $924 million. This would represent a mere 3.6% decrease in EBITDA from 2006 to 2009, and a result essentially flat from 2007 to 2009. The court also notes that in two of the four original deal models Apollo produced in June of 2007 to justify its $28 per share offer, Huntsman's projected 2009 EBITDA was significantly below this estimate, at $833 million in the "Hexion Management Flat Case," and at a mere $364 million in its recession case. The other two models ("Hexion Management Case" and "Hexion Management Case with Interest Rates Run at Caps") are essentially the same as each other except with respect to the expected interest rates on the debt facilities. Thus in only one of Hexion's three views of future operating performance of Huntsman at the time of signing did Huntsman perform better in 2009 than it is presently expected to by analysts.

These results do not add up to an MAE, particularly in the face of the macroeconomic challenges Huntsman has faced since the middle of 2007 as a result of rapidly increased crude oil and natural gas prices and unfavorable foreign exchange rate changes. Ultimately, the burden is on Hexion to demonstrate the existence of an MAE in order to negate its obligation to close, and that is a burden it cannot meet here.

2. *Huntsman's Net Debt Expands During The Same Period*

Hexion urges that Huntsman's results of operations cannot be viewed in isolation, but should be examined in conjunction with Huntsman's increase in net debt. As of the end of June 2007, Huntsman forecast that its net debt at the end of 2008 would be $2.953 billion. At the time, its net debt stood at $4.116 billion. It expected that this reduction in debt would be financed by the divestiture of three of its divisions (which was accomplished by the end of 2007) and by its operating cash flows. Things did not go according to plan. Driven largely by dramatic increases in the prices of inputs and growth in accounts receivables, working capital expanded during this time by $265 million, while foreign exchange effects on the outstanding debt balances resulted in a dollar-denominated increase in the notional value of Huntsman's debt of an additional $178 million. All told, rather than shrinking by a billion dollars, Huntsman's net debt since signing has expanded by over a quarter of a billion dollars.

Hexion points to this debt expansion as further evidence (when combined with the results of operations discussed above) of an MAE based on changes in the financial condition of Huntsman. Huntsman, of course, points out that this increase in net debt from signing until the present is only on the order of 5% or 6% (depending upon which date one chooses to measure Huntsman's debt, since weekly changes in the total debt as a result of working capital fluctuations can be as much as plus or minus $100 million), a far cry from an MAE based on financial condition. Hexion responds that this view ignores the fact that "post-signing Huntsman received $794 million in cash proceeds from divestitures that were to have been used to repay debt. The assets were sold along with their revenue generating capacity. An apples-to-apples comparison (adjusting to eliminate the divestiture proceeds) would show an increase in net debt of 32%." This argument initially appears attractive, but examination of Apollo's initial deal-model negates any persuasive power it might have initially held. In all four of the cases which Apollo modeled, Huntsman's net debt at closing is assumed to be $4.1 billion. All of Hexion's assumptions about the value of the deal were predicated on Huntsman net debt levels on that order-the projected decrease in Huntsman's net debt of a billion dollars was simply an added attraction. Hexion cannot now claim that a 5% increase in net debt from its expectations in valuing the deal, even combined with the reduced earnings, should excuse it from its obligation to perform on the merger agreement.

3. *Challenging Times At Textile Effects And Pigments*

Both in its pretrial brief and at trial, Hexion focused most of its attention on two Huntsman divisions which have been particularly troubled since the signing of the merger agreement-Pigments and Textile Effects. These two divisions were expected to compose only 25% of Huntsman's adjusted EBITDA in 2008-14% coming from Pigments, and 11% coming from Textile Effects. Little space need be spent on this argument as it falls under its own weight.

First, as already discussed, under the terms of the merger agreement, an MAE is to be determined based on an examination of Huntsman taken as a whole. A close examination of two divisions anticipated to generate at most a fourth of Huntsman's EBITDA is therefore only tangentially related to the issue. Although the results in each of these two divisions, if standing alone, might be materially impaired, as already illustrated above, Huntsman as a whole is not materially impaired by their results. If it is unconvincing to say Huntsman's business as a whole has been materially changed for the worse, it is even more unconvincing to claim that 75% of Huntsman's business is fine, but that troubles in the other 25% materially changes the business as a whole.

Additionally, there is reason to believe that much of Huntsman's troubles in each of these divisions are short-term in nature. Paul Hulme, the President of Huntsman's Advanced Materials and Textile Effects business, testified at trial regarding the headwinds Textile Effects has faced over the last year. Huntsman first acquired the Textile Effects business from CIBA in June 2006, just over two years ago, for $158 million. At that time, Textile Effects was burdened with an inflated cost structure, which Hulme set about to change as part of Huntsman's Project Columbus (which is still ongoing). Included in this restructuring is the closing of certain plants in Europe and the construction and expansion of Huntsman's Textile Effects presence in Asia, allowing Huntsman to follow the shift in the textile manufacturing market there and minimize its manufacturing costs and foreign exchange rate change exposures. Moreover, the Textile Effects business faced a so-called "perfect storm" of macroeconomic challenges in the first-half of 2008: its costs for inputs were inflated by the dramatic weakening of the dollar against the euro, and the strengthening of the Swiss franc, Indian rupee, and Chinese ren minh bi. Additionally, petroleum derivatives form a large portion of the inputs to the Textile Effects manufacturing processes, and the dramatic increase in the price of crude oil over the same period caused input costs to balloon further. Notably, most of these macroeconomic changes have been reversing over the period since the end of the second quarter of 2008. In addition, Huntsman has been able to develop some traction in passing price increases into the market since July 2008.

As for Pigments, titanium dioxide is a notoriously cyclical business, which Apollo well knew at the time of bidding. During an initial presentation meeting with the management of Huntsman, Josh Harris of Apollo expressed to Peter Huntsman that Apollo knew as much about the titanium dioxide business as Huntsman did. Apollo had over the year prior to negotiating the Huntsman deal been in negotiations with Kerr McGee, one of Huntsman's competitors in the titanium dioxide business, to acquire Kerr McGee's pigments business. Apollo was therefore well familiar with the cyclicality that business is known to face. Hexion focuses its argument on Huntsman's use predominantly of the sulfate process, while the majority of its competitors use the chlorine process for manufacturing titanium dioxide. As a result of a recent run-up in the price of sulfuric acid, a key input to the sulfate process, Huntsman has thus faced increased input costs that its competitors have not shared. Nevertheless, Tronox, one of Huntsman's major competitors in the pigments business and a user of the chlorine process, is itself facing financial distress, partly as a result of its own cost increases, illustrating that the present pain in the pigments business is not restricted to those manufacturers using the sulfate process.

III.

Both parties seek declaratory judgment on the subject of knowing and intentional breach. Hexion seeks a declaratory judgment that no "knowing and intentional breach" of the merger agreement has occurred, and therefore its liability for any breach of the merger agreement is capped at $325 million. Huntsman seeks the obverse-a declaratory judgment that Hexion has engaged in a "knowing and intentional breach" of the merger agreement, and therefore it is entitled to full contract damages, not capped or liquidated by the $325 million figure in section 7.3(d) of the merger agreement. For the reasons detailed below, the court concludes that Hexion has engaged in a knowing and intentional breach, and that the liquidated damages clause of section 7.3(d) is therefore inapplicable.

The court first turns to the meaning of "knowing and intentional breach" as it is used in the merger agreement. "Knowing and intentional," a phrase which echoes with notes of criminal and tort law, is not normally associated with contract law. In fact, the term does not appear at all in either WILLISTON

ON CONTRACTS or the RESTATEMENT OF THE LAW OF CONTRACTS. Hexion argues in its pretrial brief that a "knowing" breach "requires that Hexion not merely know of its actions, but have *actual knowledge* that such actions *breach* the covenant," and that negligence or a mistake of law or fact will not suffice to establish a knowing breach. Moreover, it argues, for such breach to also be "intentional," Hexion must have "acted 'purposely' with the 'conscious object' of breaching."

Hexion commits the same fundamental error in its analysis of both terms. Hexion interprets the terms "knowing" and "intentional" as modifying the violation of the legal duty supposed, rather than modifying the act which gives rise to the violation. This is simply wrong. * * * [Hexion] would make "knowing and intentional breach" synonymous with willful and malicious breach, a concept ultimately having no place in an action sounding in contract rather than tort. It is a fundamental proposition of contract law that damages in contract are solely to give the non-breaching party the "benefit of the bargain," and not to punish the breaching party. It is for this very reason that penalty clauses are unenforceable. Instead, the best definition of "knowing and intentional breach" is the one suggested by Hexion's citation to the entry for "knowing" in Black's Law Dictionary. Black's lists "deliberate" as one of its definitions for knowing. Thus a "knowing and intentional" breach is a deliberate one-a breach that is a direct consequence of a deliberate act undertaken by the breaching party, rather than one which results indirectly, or as a result of the breaching party's negligence or unforeseeable misadventure. In other words, a "knowing and intentional" breach, as used in the merger agreement, is the taking of a deliberate act, which act constitutes in and of itself a breach of the merger agreement, even if breaching was not the conscious object of the act. It is with this definition in mind that Hexion's actions will be judged.

A. *Hexion's Failure to Use Reasonable Best Efforts to Consummate the Financing and Failure to Give Huntsman Notice of its Concerns*

Hexion claims that it will be unable to consummate the merger because, if it were to do so, the resulting company would, according to Hexion, be insolvent. The commitment letter requires as a condition precedent to the banks' obligation to fund that the banks receive a solvency certificate or opinion indicating that the combined entity would be solvent. Hexion argues that no qualified party will be able to deliver such an opinion in good faith, and as such the banks will be neither willing nor obligated to fund. Furthermore, Hexion claims, even if it were able to convince the banks to fund under the commitment letter, there would still be insufficient funds available to close the deal. Notably however, such was Apollo and Hexion's ardor for Huntsman in July 2007 that there is no "financing out" in this deal-the conditions precedent to Hexion's obligation to close do not contain any requirement regarding the availability of the financing under the commitment letter. Nor is there a "solvency out," which would make Hexion's obligation to close contingent on the solvency of the combined entity. Nevertheless, as Apollo's desire for Huntsman cooled through the spring of 2008, Apollo and Hexion attempted to use the purported insolvency of the combined entity as an escape hatch to Hexion's obligations under the merger agreement.

Section 5.12(a) of the merger agreement contains Hexion's covenant to use its reasonable best efforts to consummate the financing:

> (a) [Hexion] shall use its reasonable best efforts to take, or cause to be taken, all actions and to do, or cause to be done, all things necessary, proper or advisable to arrange and consummate the Financing on the terms and conditions described in the Commitment Letter, including (i) using reasonable best efforts to (x) satisfy on a timely basis all terms, covenants and conditions set forth in the Commitment Letter; (y) enter into definitive agreements with respect thereto on the terms and conditions contemplated by the Commitment Letter; and (z) consummate the Financing at or prior to Closing; and (ii) seeking to enforce its rights under the Commitment Letter. Parent will furnish correct and complete copies of all such definitive agreements to the Company promptly upon their execution.

Put more simply, to the extent that an act was both commercially reasonable and advisable to enhance the likelihood of consummation of the financing, the onus was on Hexion to take that act. To the extent that Hexion deliberately chose not to act, but instead pursued another path designed to *avoid* the consummation of the financing, Hexion knowingly and intentionally breached this covenant.

Likewise, section 5.12(b) of the merger agreement provides in pertinent part:

> (b) [Hexion] shall keep the Company informed with respect to all material activity concerning the status of the Financing contemplated by the Commitment Letter and shall give [Huntsman] prompt notice of any material adverse change with respect to such Financing. Without limiting the foregoing, [Hexion] agrees to notify [Huntsman] promptly, and in any event within two Business Days, if at any time ... (iii) for any reason [Hexion] no longer believes in good faith that it will be able to obtain all or any portion of the Financing contemplated by the Commitment Letter on the terms described therein.

This provision is equally simple. Hexion covenants that it will let Huntsman know within two business days if it no longer believes in good faith it will be able to draw upon the commitment letter financing.

Sometime in May 2008, Hexion apparently became concerned that the combined entity, after giving effect to the merger agreement and the commitment letter, would be insolvent. At that time a reasonable response to such concerns might have been to approach Huntsman's management to discuss the issue and potential resolutions of it. This would be particularly productive to the extent that such potential insolvency problems rested on the insufficiency of operating liquidity, which could be addressed by a number of different "levers" available to management. This is not what Hexion did. Instead Hexion, through Wachtell Lipton, engaged Duff & Phelps ostensibly to provide them guidance as to whether the combined entity would be in danger of being considered insolvent. At that point, Hexion's actions could not definitively be said to have been in breach of its obligations under section 5.12(a).

By early June, Duff & Phelps reported back to Wachtell Lipton and Hexion that, based on the information they had been provided, the combined company appeared to fail all three of the customary insolvency tests (the failure of any one of which is sufficient to render a company, for the purposes of delivering a solvency opinion, insolvent). By this point Hexion, assuming *arguendo* it believed in the projections it provided to Duff & Phelps in order to conduct the analysis, would have had a justifiable good faith concern that it would not be able to provide the required solvency certificate, and that the bank financing pursuant to the commitment letter might be imperiled. Hexion was then clearly obligated to approach Huntsman management to discuss the appropriate course to take to mitigate these concerns. Moreover, Hexion's obligations under the notification covenant in section 5.12(b) of the merger agreement was now in play. Because Hexion now had (again giving Hexion the benefit of the doubt) a good faith belief that the combined entity would be insolvent, Hexion had an absolute obligation to notify Huntsman of this concern within two days of coming to this conclusion, *i.e.* within two days of receiving Duff & Phelps's initial report.

But Hexion did nothing to approach Huntsman management, either to discuss ways the solvency problems might be addressed, or even to put Huntsman on notice of its concerns. This choice alone would be sufficient to find that Hexion had knowingly and intentionally breached its covenants under the merger agreement. Hexion in the days that followed would compound its breach further.

B. *Hexion Affirmatively Acts To Scuttle The Financing*

Section 5.12(b) of the merger agreement contains more than an affirmative requirement that Hexion provide prompt notice to Huntsman if the financing is imperiled. It also contains a negative covenant:

> *[Hexion] shall not, and shall not* permit any of its Affiliates to, *without the prior written consent of [Huntsman], take or fail to take any action* or enter into any transaction, including any merger, acquisition, joint venture, disposition, lease, contract or debt or equity financing, *that could reasonably be expected to materially impair, delay or prevent consummation of the Financing contemplated by the Commitment Letter* or any Alternate Financing contemplated by any Alternate Financing. (emphasis added).

Hexion's obligation under the covenant here is again quite simple: do nothing without Huntsman's written consent which might reasonably be expected to scuttle or otherwise harm the likelihood or timing of the financing under the commitment letter.

Apparently considering Duff & Phelps's initial determination that the combined entity would likely be insolvent insufficient for its purposes, on June 2, 2008, Hexion engaged a second Duff & Phelps team headed by Wisler, to provide a formal solvency opinion, or, more to the point, a formal insolvency opinion.

The Duff & Phelps formal opinion team eventually delivered a formal insolvency opinion to Hexion on June 18, 2008, which opinion was presented to the Hexion board the same day. Concluding that the board could rely on the opinion, Hexion's did not contact Huntsman to discuss the issue. If Hexion had contacted Huntsman at this point and requested a meeting between Hexion and Huntsman management to discuss strategies to address the apparent insolvency problem, Hexion would once again have been in compliance with its obligations under the covenants in sections 5.12(a) and (b), and any knowing and intentional breach resulting from its earlier failure to notify Huntsman would have been cured, as no prejudice to Huntsman would have occurred by Hexion's delay. But Hexion chose an alternative tack. Upon adopting the findings of the Duff & Phelps insolvency opinion on June 18, the Hexion board approved the filing of this lawsuit, and the initial complaint was filed that day. In that complaint, Hexion publicly raised its claim that the combined entity would be insolvent, thus placing the commitment letter financing in serious peril. The next day, June 19, 2008, Credit Suisse, the lead bank under the commitment letter, received a copy of the Duff & Phelps insolvency opinion from Hexion, all but killing any possibility that the banks would be willing to fund under the commitment letter. Morrison testified on cross-examination that he was well aware that this was virtually certain to be the consequence of delivering the insolvency opinion to the banks:

Q Okay. And it's correct that you sent the banks both a copy of this lawsuit complaint and a copy of the Duff & Phelps insolvency opinion. Correct?

A I believe so, yes.

Q And you carefully considered the consequences of your doing that, did you not?

A Yes.

Q Okay. You knew that providing this to the banks would make it virtually impossible for them to go forward with the financing?

A Yes.

* * *

Q Let's look back at the contract. You mentioned the contract. Again, JX 1. Let's look at 5.12(b). And let's go down toward the-yes. Here we go. Right there. This is out of 5.12(b). Hexion, without the written consent of Huntsman, cannot take any action that would be reasonably expected to materially impair, delay or prevent the financing contemplated by the commitment letter. Correct?

A Yes.

Q And you are aware of this obligation. Correct?

A Yes.

Q All right. And you didn't seek Huntsman's consent to deliver the Duff & Phelps insolvency opinion to the banks?

A No.

Q Right. And even though you knew that delivering that insolvency opinion would prevent consummation of the financing, you went ahead and did it, anyway?

A Yes.

Given the court's conclusion that a "knowing and intentional" breach must be the deliberate commission of an act that constitutes a breach of a covenant in the merger agreement, Morrison's testimony makes clear that a knowing and intentional breach by Hexion had occurred by June 19, 2008.

Hexion * * * to justify its taking such dramatic and irrevocable action [argues] that it wanted to secure its status as first filer in any lawsuit arising out of the contract in order to ensure for itself a Delaware forum for litigation. Although the merger agreement explicitly lays exclusive jurisdiction over such suits in the Delaware Court of Chancery, Zaken testified at trial that Apollo and Hexion were concerned that Huntsman might choose to bring suit in Texas instead. But this is clearly no defense to a claim that Hexion knowingly and intentionally breached its covenant not to act in any way which could be reasonably expected to harm the likelihood of the consummation of the financing without Huntsman's express written consent. This proposed defense amounts to nothing more than "we were afraid they might breach, so we breached first." Even if Huntsman had filed suit in Texas prior to Hexion's breach of section 5.12(b), to the extent that Huntsman's filing of a suit in Texas might not constitute a material breach of the merger agreement, Hexion's performance under the contract *still* would not be excused and it would have remained obligated to comply with the terms of the covenants under the merger agreement. *A fortiori,* Hexion's obligation under the section 5.12(b) covenant cannot have been excused by Hexion's mere fear that Huntsman would breach the merger agreement by bringing suit in Texas.

* * *

* * * Hexion [also] focuses on the conception that, once in possession of the insolvency opinion, and the board of directors having determined the opinion was reliable, Hexion was obligated to deliver the opinion to the banks. However, Hexion had been feeding the banks Huntsman's updated forecasts as it received them. Its obligations to update the banks ended there. It was under no obligation, even once it obtained the insolvency opinion, to deliver the opinion to the banks, as the opinion did not constitute information of the type delivered to the banks up to that point. Solvency is not an issue to be measured prior to closing-rather, all that is required is that a suitable solvency letter can be delivered in good faith in connection with closing.

* * *

C. *Hexion's Counterargument*

Hexion offers as a counterargument to the contention that it failed to use its best efforts to consummate the financing and the merger the argument that "[a] 'reasonable best efforts' covenant does not prevent a company or its board from seeking expert advice to rely upon in assessing its own future solvency, or, once it has made an assessment that insolvency would ensue, from taking actions to avoid insolvency." The first contention (that it is permissible to seek expert advice) is undoubtedly true, and the second (that it may take actions to avoid insolvency) is on its face reasonable as well. But that Hexion's board was permitted to take steps to avoid insolvency upon closing the merger if it believed in good faith that would ensue if it stayed on its present course is not the same thing as saying that Hexion could therefore attempt to abandon the merger entirely before satisfying itself that there were not commercially reasonable steps it could take to meet its obligations under the merger agreement while still avoiding bankruptcy. Indeed, the case that Hexion cites in support for its proposition, *Bloor v. Falstaff Brewing Corp.*, [601 F.2d 609 (2d Cir.1979) (Friendly, J)] ultimately undercuts it. Hexion cites the case as stating that "a promise to use best efforts does not strip the party of the 'right to give reasonable consideration to its own interests' and does not require the party to 'spend itself into bankruptcy.' " This is no doubt true, but it is also not all that *Bloor* says on the subject. The sentence that Hexion quotes from *Bloor* in its entirety reads:

> Although we agree that even this [the best efforts clause under consideration] did not require [the defendant] to spend itself into bankruptcy to promote the sales of [plaintiff's products], *it did prevent the application to them of [defendant's controlling shareholder's] philosophy of emphasizing profit uber alles without fair consideration of the effect on [plaintiff's] volume.* [*Bloor*, 601 F.2d at 614 (emphasis added).]

Bloor continues:

> Plaintiff was not obliged to show just what steps [defendant] could reasonably have taken to maintain a high volume for [plaintiff's] products. It was sufficient to show that [defendant] simply didn't care about [plaintiff's] volume and was content to allow this to plummet so long as that course was best for [plaintiff's] overall profit picture, an inference which the judge permissibly drew. The burden then shifted to [defendant] to prove there was nothing significant it could have done to promote [plaintiff's] sales that would not have been financially disastrous. [Id. at 614-15.]

The situation in the instant case is analogous. Huntsman was not obligated to show that Hexion had viable options to avoid insolvency while performing its obligation to close, it merely needed to show (which it succeeded in doing) that Hexion simply did not care whether its course of action was in Huntsman's best interests so long as that course of action was best for Hexion. At that point the burden shifted to Hexion to show that there were no viable options it could exercise to allow it to perform without disastrous financial consequences. Hexion has not met this burden, nor has it attempted to. Rather, its contention from the outset of this lawsuit has been that once it determined that the combined entity would be insolvent, its obligations to Huntsman were at an end. The fact that a conference with Huntsman management to discuss these concerns would have been virtually costless only underscores the fact that Hexion made no attempts to seek out its available options. Far from making "every conceivable effort," Hexion appears to have made no effort at all. Similarly, Hexion cites *Triple-A Baseball Club Association v. Northeastern Baseball, Inc.* [, 832 F.2d 214, 222 (1st Cir.1987),] for the proposition that although the "reasonable best efforts" standard is separate and distinct from good faith, the court in *Triple-A Baseball Club* was "unable to find any case in which a court found ... that a party acted in good faith but did not use its best efforts." This court will not change that score. Rather, Hexion's utter failure to make any attempt to confer with Huntsman when Hexion first became concerned with the potential issue of insolvency, both constitutes a failure to use reasonable best efforts to consummate the merger and shows a lack of good faith.

D. *Hexion Drags Its Feet On Receiving Antitrust Clearance*

Section 5.4 of the merger agreement requires Hexion to "take any and all action necessary" to obtain antitrust approval for the transaction, and prohibits Hexion from taking "any action with the intent to or that could reasonably be expected to hinder or delay the obtaining of" such approval. Unlike the reasonable best efforts Hexion is obligated to make under other covenants in the merger agreement, both parties have characterized this obligation as "come hell or high water."

In spite of this obligation, as of the time of trial (a mere three weeks before the Termination Date) Hexion still had not received consent from the FTC to consummate the merger. * * * Yet * * * Hexion had come to an agreement in principal with the FTC staff as to a divestiture plan to satisfy the FTC's concerns in April, and by August had a buyer for the assets to be divested. * * *

* * *

In the face of this overwhelming evidence, it is the court's firm conclusion that by June 19, 2008 Hexion had knowingly and intentionally breached its covenants and obligations under the merger agreement. To the extent that it is at some later time necessary for this court to determine damages in this action, any damages which were proximately caused by that knowing and intentional breach will be uncapped and determined on the basis of standard contract damages or any special provision in the merger agreement. Because of the difficulty in separating out causation of damages in such an action, the burden will be on Hexion to demonstrate that any particular damage was not proximately caused by its knowing and intentional breach. To the extent Hexion can make such a showing, those damages which were not proximately caused by Hexion's knowing and intentional breach will be limited to the liquidated damages amount of $325 million, pursuant to section 7.3(d) of the merger agreement.

IV.

Hexion strenuously argues, and urges the court to declare, that on a pro forma basis (assuming the merger closes on the financing terms contemplated in the commitment letter), the combined entity will be insolvent. In support of its contention, Hexion offers the opinion it obtained from Duff & Phelps, based on Hexion's gloomy projections of Huntsman's future performance. It also points to a rudimentary solvency analysis done by a Merrill Lynch analyst in May 2008.

Huntsman argues, in opposition, that solvency is not even an issue under the merger agreement and, thus, is not a proper subject for declaratory relief at this time. Huntsman also contends that the combined entity (1) will be solvent; (2) to the extent that it is not solvent, that would come as a result of Hexion's knowing and intentional breach of contract, and (3) Hexion is, in any event, obligated to put in whatever equity is necessary to close the transaction and make the combined entity solvent. To support its argument regarding solvency, Huntsman relies on Resnick's expert valuation opinion, based on Huntsman's revised July 2008 projections. In addition, at trial Huntsman introduced evidence suggesting that American Appraisal Associates, Inc. has determined that, if engaged for that purpose, it expected to be able to deliver a favorable solvency opinion. Even more recently, Huntsman filed a Form 8-K stating that it has engaged American Appraisal for this purpose, and asks the court to take judicial notice of that fact.

The court thus finds itself asked to referee a battle of the experts in which there is no clear answer and no possibility of splitting the difference. For the reasons briefly discussed below, the court determines not to reach the issue of solvency at this time because that issue will not arise unless and until a solvency letter or opinion is delivered to the lending banks and those banks then either fund or refuse to fund the transaction.

To begin with, Huntsman is correct that the solvency of the combined entity is not a condition precedent to Hexion's obligations under the merger agreement. In fact, looking only at terms of the merger agreement, Hexion's avowed inability to deliver a suitable solvency opinion does not negate its obligation to close: rather, the receipt of such an opinion is merely a condition precedent to Huntsman's duty to close, protects Huntsman (and its shareholders), and is, therefore, waivable by Huntsman. To put it differently, Hexion's fear that it has agreed to pay too high a price for Huntsman does not provide a basis for it to get out of the transaction.

The issue of solvency is only relevant to the obligation of the lending banks to fund when the time comes for them to do so. Paragraph 6 of exhibit D to the commitment letter makes it a condition precedent to funding that the lending banks receive a reasonably satisfactory solvency letter in such form and substance as has been customary in prior Apollo transaction. But Huntsman, in order to avoid or ameliorate the very situation it now finds itself in, specifically bargained for and obtained the right to have its CFO provide such a letter. Esplin, Huntsman's CFO, testified that he was prepared to provide the required letter. Moreover, it now appears that Huntsman has retained American Appraisal to furnish a back up opinion to support such a letter.

Thus, there is only one point in time at which it is necessary to make a determination of solvency-at (or as of) closing. For the reasons discussed elsewhere in this opinion, the court is issuing a judgment and order that will require Hexion to specifically perform its covenants and obligations under the merger agreement (other than its obligation to close). Thus, if the other conditions to closing are met, Hexion will be obligated to call upon the lending banks to perform on their funding obligations. In that circumstance, the banks will then have to choose whether to fund on the basis of the solvency letter delivered by Huntsman or, instead, reject that letter as unsatisfactory and refuse to fund. If the lending banks refuse to fund, they will, of course, be opening themselves to the potential for litigation, including a claim for damages for breach of contract. In such litigation, the prospective insolvency of the combined entity would likely be a important issue.

If the banks agree to fund, Hexion will then have to determine whether it considers it in its best interests to close the transaction, or instead refuse to close, subjecting itself to the possibility of an additional finding of knowing and intentional breach of contract and uncapped contract damages. If Hexion chooses to close, the issue will be moot. If it does not, the posture of the matter, and the decision presented to the court, will be far more concrete and capable of judicial resolution than the issue now framed by the parties.

For the foregoing reasons, the court will not now resolve the question of whether the combined entity would be solvent or not. * * *

V.

Huntsman asks the court to enter a judgment ordering Hexion and its merger subsidiary, Nimbus, to specifically perform their covenants and obligations under the merger agreement. For the reasons explained below, the court finds that, under the agreement, Huntsman cannot force Hexion to consummate the merger, but that Huntsman is entitled to a judgment ordering Hexion to specifically perform its other covenants and obligations.

The court first examines whether the merger agreement, somewhat unusually, contains a provision prohibiting the issuance of an order specifically directing Hexion to comply with its duty to close the transaction. Section 8.11 provides that generally a non-breaching party may seek and obtain specific performance of any covenant or obligation set forth in the agreement. However, that section goes on to state, in virtually impenetrable language, as follows: "In circumstances where [Hexion is] obligated to consummate the Merger and the Merger has not been consummated on or prior to the earlier of the last day of the Marketing Period or the Termination Date (other than as a result of [Huntsman's] refusal to close in violation of this Agreement) the parties acknowledge that [Huntsman] shall *not* be entitled to enforce specifically the obligations of [Hexion] to consummate the Merger."

Hexion argues that section 8.11 entirely precludes specific performance as a remedy for breach of its obligation to close. Andrew Nussbaum, a Wachtell Lipton partner advising Hexion during the negotiation and drafting of the merger agreement, testified that "[i]t was [Hexion's] position that we would agree to specific performance of our covenants under the agreement, with the exception of the obligation to close the merger." Nussbaum further testified that Huntsman accepted Hexion's position in the executed version of the agreement.

Huntsman did not question Nussbaum at trial regarding the parties' understanding of the specific performance section and did not offer contrary testimony by any of its lawyers. Instead, Huntsman attempts to undercut Nussbaum's testimony by arguing in its post-trial brief that the phrase "[i]n circumstances where ... [Huntsman] shall not be entitled to enforce specifically the obligation[ ] of [Hexion] to consummate the Merger" implies that some other circumstances must exist where specific performance of the obligation to close is available; otherwise, Huntsman argues, the drafters simply would have written "[u]nder no circumstances ... shall [Huntsman] be entitled to enforce specifically the obligations of [Hexion] to consummate the merger." Huntsman then explains that the reason for the exception to its general right to demand specific performance was to protect the Marketing Period during which the lending banks were to syndicate the debt. Furthermore, Huntsman argues, the parties agreed that if the Marketing Period had passed or the Termination Date had arrived Huntsman *could* force Hexion to consummate the merger, as the lending banks would have had a chance to syndicate the debt. While Huntsman's argument makes commercial sense, the inartfully drafted provision does not say what Huntsman says it does.

The problem clause is the second condition to the carve-out from specific performance: if "the Merger has not been consummated on or prior to the earlier of the last day of the Marketing Period or the Termination Date," Huntsman cannot force Hexion to close. Literally the clause does not allow specific performance in any case where Huntsman could employ the remedy.

While generally Delaware courts attempt to interpret contracts in a manner that gives meaning to each provision, the meaning of the phrase at issue is unclear. When a provision is "fairly susceptible of different interpretations," as is the case here, "the court may consider extrinsic evidence." Here, Huntsman merely offers an unsupported argument about what the parties intended to mean, based on logic, but provides no evidence. In addition, Huntsman's argument contradicts how it explained the merger in the proxy statement it filed with the Security and Exchange Commission. * * *

Nussbaum's uncontradicted testimony at trial coupled with the extrinsic evidence provided in Huntsman's own publicly filed proxy statement leads the court to find that the agreement does not allow Huntsman to specifically enforce Hexion's duty to consummate the merger. Instead, if all other conditions precedent to closing are met, Hexion will remain free to choose to refuse to close. Of course, if Hexion's refusal to close results in a breach of contract, it will remain liable to Huntsman in damages.

Turning to the remaining questions, there is no dispute that section 8.11 of the merger agreement reflects the parties' express agreement that irreparable injury would occur "in the event that any of the provisions of this Agreement were not performed in accordance with its specific terms or were otherwise breached." That same section also contains the parties' general agreement that, in the event of any breach, the non-breaching party shall be entitled to obtain an order of specific performance "to enforce the observance and performance of such covenant or obligation." Finally, section 8.11 provides that no party seeking an order of specific performance "shall be required to obtain, furnish or post any bond or similar instrument."

In view of these provisions, and considering all the circumstances, the court concludes that it is appropriate to require Hexion to specifically perform its obligations under the merger agreement, other than the obligation to close. Hexion does not argue otherwise. When it is known whether the financing contemplated by the commitment letter is available or not, Hexion and its shareholders will thus be placed in the position to make an informed judgment about whether to close the transaction (in light of, among other things, the findings and conclusions in this opinion) and, if so, how to finance the combined operations. As the parties recognize, both Hexion and Huntsman are solvent, profitable businesses. The issues in this case relate principally to the cost of the merger and whether the financing structure Apollo and Hexion arranged in July 2007 is adequate to close the deal and fund the operations of the combined enterprise. The order the court is today issuing will afford the parties the opportunity to resolve those issues in an orderly and sensible fashion.

SECTION E. FAIRNESS AND DISCLOSURE

1. FREEZEOUTS AND BUYOUTS: FAIR DEALING, FAIR PRICE, AND THE APPRAISAL REMEDY

(A) FREEZE-OUTS

(1) Fiduciary Duties

(b) Fair Dealing and Fair Price

Insert after Glassman v. Unocal Exploration Corp., at Casebook page 884:

NOTE: QUASI APPRAISAL

Berger v. Pubco Corporation, 2008 WL 2224107 (Del.Ch.), concerned a $20 cashout merger of the minority interest under section 253. Robert Kanner, the majority shareholder owned more than 90 percent of the stock. Although the corporation's stock was sporadically traded over the counter, the corporation was not subject to the federal mandatory disclosure regime. The minority shareholders received the required statutory notice of their right to pursue an appraisal. The notice, however, was summarily drafted, even as it included the corporation's most recent financial statements.

The plaintiffs alleged that the notice should have specified the means by which Kanner had determined the $20 per share price. The defendants countered that this failure to disclose was immaterial because Kanner could have used whatever valuation methodology he desired, including even "rolling the dice." The Chancery court disagreed with Kanner:

"Defendants' argument entirely misses the mark, however, because the issue is not about necessity--it is about materiality. In the context of Pubco, an unregistered company that made no public filings and whose Notice was relatively terse and short on details, the method by which Kanner set the merger consideration is a fact that is substantially likely to alter the total mix of information available to the minority stockholders. Where, as here, a minority shareholder needs to decide only whether to accept the merger consideration or to seek appraisal, the question is partially one of trust: can the minority shareholder trust that the price offered is good enough, or does it likely undervalue the Company so significantly that appraisal is a worthwhile endeavor? When faced with such a question, it would be material to know that the price offered was set by arbitrarily rolling dice. In a situation like Pubco's, where so little information is available about the Company, such a disclosure would significantly change the landscape with respect to the decision of whether or not to trust the price offered by the parent. This does not mean that Kanner should have provided picayune details about the process he used to set the price; it simply means he should have disclosed in a broad sense what the process was, assuming he followed a process at all and did not simply choose a number randomly."

As regards a remedy, recissory damages being inappropriate and the time for an actual appraisal proceeding having long past, the Chancery court accorded a "quasi appraisal." As to this, the plaintiffs argued for a class-action proceeding with an "opt out right." The defendants, citing *Gilliland v. Motorola, Inc.*, 873 A.2d 305 (Del.Ch.2005), argued for an "opt in" proceeding in which participating shareholders would be required to escrow a portion of the merger consideration they received. The Chancery Court went with the defendant's process proposal. The Delaware Supreme Court reversed, **Berger v. Pubco Corporation**, 976 A.2d 132 (Del. 20009). Justice Jacobs reasoned as follows, 976 A.2d at 142-144:

"[W]hich remedy is the more appropriate--the one that imposes the opt in and partial escrow requirements or the one that does not? Considerations of utility and fairness impel us to conclude that the latter is the more appropriate remedy for the disclosure violation that occurred here. Because neither the opt-in nor the escrow requirement is mandated as a matter of law and because those requirements involve different equities, we analyze each requirement separately.

"We start with the 'opt in' issue. The approach adopted by the Court of Chancery requires the minority shareholders to opt in to become members of the plaintiff class. The other choice would treat those shareholders automatically as members of the class--that is, as having already opted in. Those shareholders would continue as members of the class, unless and until individual members opt out after receiving the remedial supplemental disclosure and the Rule 23 notice of class action informing them of their opt out right. From the minority's standpoint, the first alternative is potentially more burdensome than the second, because shareholders that fail either to opt in or to opt in within a prescribed time, forfeit the opportunity to seek an appraisal recovery. On the other hand, structuring the remedy as an 'opt out' class action avoids that risk of forfeiture, and thus benefits the minority shareholders. To the corporation, however, neither alternative is more burdensome than the other. Under either alternative the company will know at a relatively early stage which shareholders are (and are not) members of the class.

"Given these choices, it is self evident which alternative is optimal. As between an opt in requirement that would potentially burden shareholders desiring to seek an appraisal recovery but would impose no burden on the corporation, and an opt out requirement that would impose a lesser burden on the shareholders but again no burden on the corporation, the latter alternative is superior and is the remedy that the trial court should have ordered.

"That leaves the requirement that the minority shareholders electing to participate in the quasi-appraisal must escrow a portion of the merger proceeds that they received. The rationale for this requirement, as stated in *Gilliland,* is 'to mimic, at least in small part, the risks of a statutory appraisal ... to promote well-reasoned judgments by potential class members and to avoid awarding a "windfall" to those shareholders who made an informed decision [after receiving the original notice of merger] to take the cash rather than pursue their statutory appraisal remedy.'

"The defendants-appellees argue that it is fair and equitable to require the minority shareholders to escrow some portion of the merger proceeds. Otherwise (defendants say), the shareholders would have it both ways: they could retain the merger proceeds they received and at the same time litigate to recover a higher amount-a dual benefit they would not have in an actual appraisal. It is true that the minority shareholders would enjoy that 'dual benefit.' But, does that make it inequitable from the fiduciary's standpoint? We think not. No positive rule of law cited to us requires replicating the burdens imposed in an actual statutory appraisal. Indeed, our law allows the minority to enjoy that dual benefit in the related setting of a class action challenging a long form merger on fiduciary duty grounds. In that setting the shareholder class members may retain the merger proceeds and simultaneously pursue the class action remedy. The defendants cite no case authority, nor are we aware of any, holding that that in the long form merger context that benefit is inequitable to the majority shareholder accused of breaching its fiduciary duty.

"Lastly, fairness requires that the corporation be held to the same strict standard of compliance with the appraisal statute as the minority shareholders. Our case law is replete with examples where dissenting minority shareholders that failed to comply strictly with certain technical requirements of the appraisal statute, were held to have lost their entitlement to an appraisal, and, consequently, lost the opportunity to recover the difference between the fair value of their shares and the merger price. These technical statutory violations were not curable, so that irrespective of the equities the unsuccessful appraisal claimant could not proceed anew. That result effectively allowed the corporation to retain the entire difference between fair value and the merger price attributable to the shares for which appraisal rights were lost. The appraisal statute should be construed even-handedly, not as a one-way street. Minority shareholders who fail to observe the appraisal statute's technical requirements risk forfeiting their statutory entitlement to recover the fair value of their shares. In fairness, majority stockholders that deprive their minority shareholders of material information should forfeit their statutory right to retain the merger proceeds payable to shareholders who, if fully informed, would have elected appraisal.

"In cases where the corporation does not comply with the disclosure requirement mandated by *Glassman,* the quasi-appraisal remedy that operates in the fairest and most balanced way and that best effectuates the legislative intent underlying Section 253, is the one that does not require the minority shareholders seeking a recovery of fair value to escrow a portion of the merger proceeds they received. We hold, for these reasons, that the quasi-appraisal remedy ordered by the Court of Chancery was legally erroneous in the circumstances presented here."

2. The Duty of Care

Insert after "Note: The Duty of Care and Merger Negotiations," at Casebook page 933:

NOTE: THE DUTY OF CARE AND ASSET SALES

McFadden v. Sidhu, 964 A.2d 1262 (Del. Ch. 2008), concerned i2 Technology Inc.'s sale of its wholly owned subsidiary, Trade Services Corp.(TSC). The buyer was an internal management buyout team led by a TSC vice president, Anthony Dubreville. The sale price was $3 million. Six months after the sale, Dubreville rejected an offer of $18.5 million for TSC as too low. Two years after the sale Dubreville sold TSC for $25 million.

The plaintiff brought a derivative action against both the i2 board and Dubreville. The action against the i2 board rested on a breach of the duty of care. The Chancery Court excused the demand requirement, finding that the complaint pleaded with particularity sufficient to create a reasonable doubt that the transaction followed from a valid exercise of business judgment. Indeed, the Court found the board to have been grossly negligent. The court faulted the board for delegating responsibility for the sale process to Dubreville, known to be an interested buyer, and then engaging in little or no oversight of Dubreville's half hearted efforts in soliciting bids. Dubreville had not contacted the class of buyers with the greatest potential interest – TSC's competitors. But plaintiff's action failed nonetheless. The directors had the benefit of a section 102(b)(7) exculpatory provision and the plaintiff had not adequately alleged action in bad faith.

The Court, 964 A.2d at 1274-75, relied on *In re Walt Disney Co. Derivative Litigation*:

" * * * Recently * * * the Supreme Court has modified Delaware's understanding of the definition of gross negligence in the context of fiduciary duty. In analyzing 'three different categories of fiduciary behavior [that] are candidates for the "bad faith" pejorative label,' the Court made quite clear that gross negligence cannot be such an example of bad faith conduct: '[t]here is no basis in policy, precedent or common sense that would justify dismantling the distinction between gross negligence and bad faith.' Instead, the Court concluded that conduct motivated by subjective bad intent and that resulting from gross negligence are at opposite ends of the spectrum. The Court then considered a third category of conduct: the intentional dereliction of duty or the conscious disregard for one's responsibilities. The Court determined that such misconduct must be treated as a non-exculpable, non-indemnifiable violation of the fiduciary duty to act in good faith, a duty that the Court later confirmed was squarely within the duty of loyalty. Thus, from the sphere of actions that was once classified as grossly negligent conduct that gives rise to a violation of the duty of care, the Court has carved out one specific type of conduct-the intentional dereliction of duty or the conscious disregard for one's responsibilities-and redefined it as bad faith conduct, which results in a breach of the duty of loyalty. Therefore, Delaware's current understanding of gross negligence is conduct that constitutes reckless indifference or actions that are without the bounds of reason.

"The conduct of the Director Defendants here fits precisely within this revised understanding of gross negligence. In finding that demand is excused as futile, I have already concluded that plaintiff has pleaded with particularity so as to raise a reasonable doubt that the actions of the board were a product of the valid exercise of their business judgment. Thus, for the reasons explained above, the Director Defendants' actions, beginning with placing Dubreville in charge of the sale process of TSC and continuing through their failure to act in any way so as to ensure that the sale process employed was thorough and complete, are properly characterized as either recklessly indifferent or unreasonable. Plaintiff has not, however, sufficiently alleged that the Director Defendants acted in bad faith through a conscious disregard for their duties. Instead, plaintiff has ably pleaded that the Director Defendants quite clearly were not careful enough in the discharge of their duties-that is, they acted with gross negligence or else reckless indifference. Because such conduct breaches the Director Defendants' duty of care, this violation is exculpated by the Section 102(b)(7) provision in the Company's charter and therefore the Director Defendants' motion to dismiss for failure to state a claim must be granted."

The complaint against Dubreville for breach of fiduciary duty and unjust enrichment did go forward. Dubreville, as an officer, did not have the benefit of section 102(b)(7) even as his position as an officer did entail fiduciary duties identical to those owed by the directors.

SECTION F. THE TENDER OFFER

3. MANAGEMENT DEFENSES AND FIDUCIARY DUTIES

(B) DEFENSIVE TACTICS AND THE DUTY OF LOYALTY

(2) The Operation of the Unocal Standard

Insert after "Note: No Hand Pills," at Casebook page 1052:

NOTE: A 5 PERCENT TRIGGER

Selectica, Inc. v. Versata Enterprises, Inc. , 2010 WL 703062 (Del.Ch.), concerned an unusual poison pill. Selectica went public in 2000 and earned no money thereafter, accumulating $160 million in net operating loss tax carry forwards (NOLs). Selectica was looking for an acquisition partner. Its NOLs were a primary asset, at least to the extent that it could find a partner with taxable earnings that the NOLs might protect.

Trilogy Inc. acquired just under 5 percent of Selectica's stock. Selectica's board became concerned about the impact of Trilogy's stockholding on the status of the NOLs. The threat, said the board, was the permanent diminution of the value of the NOLs to zero under the tax code if a new or existing 5 percent shareholder acquired 10 percent or more of Selectica's stock. The Board accordingly amended Selectica's poison pill to lower the triggering threshhold (and bestow the status of "Acquiring Person" on the stockholder) from 15 percent of the stock to 4.99 percent.

Trilogy thereafter increased its ownership percentage to 6.7 percent and became an "Acquiring Person" under the pill. Selectica, acting through an independent director committee, thereupon, effected an exchange of the rights under the pill and reloaded the pill to effect a new distribution of rights. The triggering of the pill doubled the number of Selectica shares held by each shareholder other than Trilogy, diluting Trilogy's holding.

Both Selectica and Trilogy took the matter to the Delaware courts. Trilogy argued that to sanction a low-threshold poison pill employed for the purpose of protecting NOLs would be to acquiesce to an unreasonable expansion of the universe of takeover defenses in order to protect assets of questionable, even dubious, value.

The Chancery court ruled for Selectica:

"The first part of the *Unocal* test requires a board to show that it had reasonable grounds for concluding that a threat to a corporate objective existed. This case presents unique grounds for establishing this first part of the *Unocal* test as employing a poison pill for the ostensible purpose of protecting NOLs is a distinct departure from the poison pill's originally intended use: the prevention of hostile takeovers. Delaware courts have only considered the poison pill in the context of an anti-takeover device, and the *Unocal* test is one that analyzes the board's response to such an outside threat. In contrast, an NOL pill's principal function is to prevent the inadvertent forfeiture of potentially valuable assets, not to protect against hostile takeover attempts.

"As a result of its unique objective, a pill designed to protect NOLs necessitates precluding a lesser accumulation of shares than might be appropriate for a pill designed to prevent a hostile acquirer from establishing a control position in the company. Consequently, the 5% trigger necessary for an NOL pill to serve its function imposes a far greater cost on shareholders than the pill thresholds traditionally employed and held as acceptable by our courts in the anti-takeover context. Not surprisingly, pills with a 5% trigger remain fairly uncommon, though they have been employed with greater frequency in recent years.

* * *

"Trilogy is correct in pointing out that it is not sufficient to conclude that an asset with potential value is worth protecting without considering the probability of that value being realized, and that Selectica's failure to generate taxable income in prior years colors this probability. However, the absence of a formal study calculating such a value does not mean that the directors were unreasonable in concluding that a sufficiently material probability existed to merit the asset's preservation, or that such a determination was not implicit in their calculus. In connection with the expert advice it received, the Court is satisfied that the Board was reasonable in concluding that Selectica's NOLs were worth preserving and that Trilogy's actions presented a serious threat to their impairment.

* * *

"The second prong of *Unocal* requires an evaluation of whether a board's defensive response to the threat was preclusive or coercive and, if not, whether it was 'reasonable in relation to the threat' identified. * * *

* * *

"Trilogy asserts that the NOL Pill and the Reloaded NOL Pill are distinctly more preclusive than those poison pills previously evaluated by Delaware courts and that, consequently, they should be declared invalid.

Specifically, Trilogy claims that a 4.99% pill renders the possibility of an effective proxy contest realistically unattainable. Trilogy argues that, because a proxy contest can only be successful where the challenger has sufficient credibility, the 4 .99% pill prevents a potential dissident from signaling its financial commitment to the company sufficient to establish such credibility. * * *

"Though Trilogy's expert testimony suggests that a poison pill with a less than 5% trigger 'has a substantial preclusive effect,' the Court cannot conclude that the NOL Pill, Exchange, and Reloaded NOL Pill were preclusive, and thereby draconian. Such a high standard operates to exclude only the most egregious defensive responses. * * * To find a measure preclusive (and avoid the reasonableness inquiry altogether), the measure must render a successful proxy contest a near impossibility or else utterly moot, given the specific facts at hand. The NOL Pill and Reloaded NOL Pill do not meet this standard.

* * *

[The] Court [also] finds that the combination of the NOL Pill, the Exchange, and the Reloaded NOL Pill was a proportionate response to the threatened loss of Selectica's NOLs.

There is, of course, the risk that accumulated net operating losses could provide a convenient pretext for perpetuating a board-preferred shareholder structure. For this reason, shareholder rights plans, such as the ones adopted by Selectica, must be subject to careful review. In this instance, however, the Board reasonably believed, based on the guidance of appropriate experts, that the NOLs had value, a value worth protecting. In its view of the actual value of the NOLs, the Board may have been incorrect. It is not for the Court, however, to substitute its judgment for the reasonable conclusions of the Board * * * . Moreover, the threat posed by Trilogy was reasonably viewed as qualitatively different from the normal corporate control dispute that leads to the adoption of a shareholder rights plan. In this instance, Trilogy, a competitor with a contentious history, recognized that harm would befall its rival if it purchased sufficient shares of Selectica stock, and Trilogy proceeded to act accordingly. It was reasonable for the Board to respond, and the timing of Trilogy's campaign required the Board to act promptly. Moreover, the 4.99% threshold for the NOL Pill was driven by our tax laws and regulations; the threshold, low as it is, was measured by reference to an external standard, one created neither by the Board nor by the Court."

(3) The Revlon Auction Duty

Insert after Omnicare, Inc. v.NCS Healthcare, Inc., *at Casebook page 1120:*

Lyondell Chemical Company v. Ryan

Supreme Court of Delaware, 2009.
– A.2d. – ; 2009 WL 1024764

Before STEELE, Chief Justice, HOLLAND, BERGER, JACOBS and RIDGELY, Justices, constituting the Court en Banc.

BERGER, Justice.

We accepted this interlocutory appeal to consider a claim that directors failed to act in good faith in conducting the sale of their company. The Court of Chancery decided that "unexplained inaction" permits a reasonable inference that the directors may have consciously disregarded their fiduciary duties. The trial court expressed concern about the speed with which the transaction was consummated; the directors' failure to negotiate better terms; and their failure to seek potentially superior deals. But the record establishes that the directors were disinterested and independent; that they were generally aware of the company's value and its prospects; and that they considered the offer, under the time constraints imposed by the buyer, with the assistance of financial and legal advisors. At most, this record creates a triable issue of fact on the question of whether the directors exercised due care. There is no evidence, however, from which to infer that the directors knowingly ignored their responsibilities, thereby breaching their duty of loyalty. Accordingly, the directors are entitled to the entry of summary judgment.

FACTUAL AND PROCEDURAL BACKGROUND

Before the merger at issue, Lyondell Chemical Company ("Lyondell") was the third largest independent, publicly traded chemical company in North America. Dan Smith ("Smith") was Lyondell's Chairman and CEO. Lyondell's other ten directors were independent and many were, or had been, CEOs of other large, publicly traded companies. Basell AF ("Basell") is a privately held Luxembourg company owned by Leonard Blavatnik ("Blavatnik") through his ownership of Access Industries. Basell is in the business of polyolefin technology, production and marketing.

In April 2006, Blavatnik told Smith that Basell was interested in acquiring Lyondell. A few months later, Basell sent a letter to Lyondell's board offering $26.50-$28.50 per share. Lyondell determined that the price was inadequate and that it was not interested in selling. During the next year, Lyondell prospered and no potential acquirors expressed interest in the company. In May 2007, an Access affiliate filed a Schedule 13D with the Securities and Exchange Commission disclosing its right to acquire an 8.3% block of Lyondell stock owned by Occidental Petroleum Corporation. The Schedule 13D also disclosed Blavatnik's interest in possible transactions with Lyondell.

In response to the Schedule 13D, the Lyondell board immediately convened a special meeting. The board recognized that the 13D signaled to the market that the company was "in play," but the directors decided to take a "wait and see" approach. A few days later, Apollo Management, L.P. contacted Smith to suggest a management-led LBO, but Smith rejected that proposal. In late June 2007, Basell announced that it had entered into a $9.6 billion merger agreement with Huntsman Corporation ("Huntsman"), a specialty chemical company. Basell apparently reconsidered, however, after Hexion Specialty Chemicals, Inc. made a topping bid for Huntsman. Faced with competition for Huntsman, Blavatnik returned his attention to Lyondell.

On July 9, 2007, Blavatnik met with Smith to discuss an all-cash deal at $40 per share. Smith responded that $40 was too low, and Blavatnik raised his offer to $44-$45 per share. Smith told Blavatnik that he would present the proposal to the board, but that he thought the board would reject it. Smith advised Blavatnik to give Lyondell his best offer, since Lyondell really was not on the market. The meeting ended at that point, but Blavatnik asked Smith to call him later in the day. When Smith called, Blavatnik offered to pay $48 per share. Under Blavatnik's proposal, Basell would require no financing contingency, but Lyondell would have to agree to a $400 million break-up fee and sign a merger agreement by July 16, 2007.

Smith called a special meeting of the Lyondell board on July 10, 2007 to review and consider Basell's offer. The meeting lasted slightly less than one hour, during which time the board reviewed valuation material that had been prepared by Lyondell management for presentation at the regular board meeting, which was scheduled for the following day. The board also discussed the Basell offer, the status of the Huntsman merger, and the likelihood that another party might be interested in Lyondell. The board instructed Smith to obtain a written offer from Basell and more details about Basell's financing.

Blavatnik agreed to the board's request, but also made an additional demand. Basell had until July 11 to make a higher bid for Huntsman, so Blavatnik asked Smith to find out whether the Lyondell board would provide a firm indication of interest in his proposal by the end of that day. The Lyondell board met on July 11, again for less than one hour, to consider the Basell proposal and how it compared to the benefits of remaining independent. The board decided that it was interested, authorized the retention of Deutsche Bank Securities, Inc. ("Deutsche Bank") as its financial advisor, and instructed Smith to negotiate with Blavatnik.

Basell then announced that it would not raise its offer for Huntsman, and Huntsman terminated the Basell merger agreement. From July 12-July 15 the parties negotiated the terms of a Lyondell merger agreement; Basell conducted due diligence; Deutsche Bank prepared a "fairness" opinion; and Lyondell conducted its regularly scheduled board meeting. The Lyondell board discussed the Basell proposal again on July 12, and later instructed Smith to try to negotiate better terms. Specifically, the board wanted a higher price, a go-shop provision, and a reduced break-up fee. As the trial court noted, Blavatnik was "incredulous." He had offered his best price, which was a substantial premium, and the deal had to be concluded on his schedule. As a sign of good faith, however, Blavatnik agreed to reduce the break-up fee from $400 million to $385 million.

On July 16, 2007, the board met to consider the Basell merger agreement. Lyondell's management, as well as its financial and legal advisers, presented reports analyzing the merits of the deal. The advisors explained that, notwithstanding the no-shop provision in the merger agreement, Lyondell would be able to consider any superior proposals that might be made because of the "fiduciary out" provision. In addition, Deutsche Bank reviewed valuation models derived from "bullish" and more conservative financial projections. Several of those valuations yielded a range that did not even reach $48 per share, and Deutsche Bank opined that the proposed merger price was fair. Indeed, the bank's managing director described the merger price as "an absolute home run." Deutsche Bank also identified other possible acquirors and explained why it believed no other entity would top Basell's offer. After considering the presentations, the Lyondell board voted to approve the merger and recommend it to the stockholders. At a special stockholders' meeting held on November 20, 2007, the merger was approved by more than 99% of the voted shares.

* * * The Court of Chancery issued its opinion on July 29, 2008, denying summary judgment as to the "*Revlon*" and the "deal protection" claims.

This Court accepted the Lyondell directors' application for certification of an interlocutory appeal on September 15, 2008.

DISCUSSION

The class action complaint challenging this $13 billion cash merger alleges that the Lyondell directors breached their "fiduciary duties of care, loyalty and candor ... and ... put their personal interests ahead of the interests of the Lyondell shareholders." Specifically, the complaint alleges that: 1) the merger price was grossly insufficient; 2) the directors were motivated to approve the merger for their own self-interest; 3) the process by which the merger was negotiated was flawed; 4) the directors agreed to unreasonable deal protection provisions; and 5) the preliminary proxy statement omitted numerous material facts. The trial court rejected all claims except those directed at the process by which the directors sold the company and the deal protection provisions in the merger agreement.

The remaining claims are but two aspects of a single claim, under *Revlon v. MacAndrews & Forbes Holdings, Inc.*, [506 A.2d 173, 182 (Del.1986),] that the directors failed to obtain the best available price in selling the company. As the trial court correctly noted, *Revlon* did not create any new fiduciary duties. It simply held that the "board must perform its fiduciary duties in the service of a specific objective: maximizing the sale price of the enterprise." The trial court reviewed the record, and found that Ryan might be able to prevail at trial on a claim that the Lyondell directors breached their duty of care. But Lyondell's charter includes an exculpatory provision, pursuant to 8 *Del. C.* § 102(b)(7), protecting the directors from personal liability for breaches of the duty of care. Thus, this case turns on whether any arguable shortcomings on the part of the Lyondell directors also implicate their duty of loyalty, a breach of which is not exculpated. Because the trial court determined that the board was independent and was not motivated by self-interest or ill will, the sole issue is whether the directors are entitled to summary judgment on the claim that they breached their duty of loyalty by failing to act in good faith.

This Court examined "good faith" in two recent decisions. In *In re Walt Disney Co. Deriv. Litig.*, [906 A.2d 27 (Del.2006),] the Court discussed the range of conduct that might be characterized as bad faith, and concluded that bad faith encompasses not only an intent to harm but also intentional dereliction of duty:

> [A]t least three different categories of fiduciary behavior are candidates for the "bad faith" pejorative label. The first category involves so-called

> "subjective bad faith," that is, fiduciary conduct motivated by an actual intent to do harm.... [S]uch conduct constitutes classic, quintessential bad faith....
>
> The second category of conduct, which is at the opposite end of the spectrum, involves lack of due care-that is, fiduciary action taken solely by reason of gross negligence and without any malevolent intent.... [W]e address the issue of whether gross negligence (including failure to inform one's self of available material facts), without more, can also constitute bad faith. The answer is clearly no.
>
> * * *
>
> That leaves the third category of fiduciary conduct, which falls in between the first two categories.... This third category is what the Chancellor's definition of bad faith-intentional dereliction of duty, a conscious disregard for one's responsibilities-is intended to capture. The question is whether such misconduct is properly treated as a non-exculpable, nonindemnifiable violation of the fiduciary duty to act in good faith. In our view, it must be.... [*Id.* at 64-66.]

The *Disney* decision expressly disavowed any attempt to provide a comprehensive or exclusive definition of "bad faith."

A few months later, in *Stone v. Ritter,*[911 A.2d 362 (Del.2006),] this Court addressed the concept of bad faith in the context of an "oversight" claim. We adopted the standard articulated ten years earlier, in *In re Caremark Int'l Deriv. Litig.* [698 A.2d 959, 971 (Del.Ch.1996)]:

> [W]here a claim of directorial liability for corporate loss is predicated upon ignorance of liability creating activities within the corporation ... only a sustained or systematic failure of the board to exercise oversight-such as an utter failure to attempt to assure a reasonable information and reporting system exists-will establish the lack of good faith that is a necessary condition to liability.

The *Stone* Court explained that the *Caremark* standard is fully consistent with the *Disney* definition of bad faith. *Stone* also clarified any possible ambiguity about the directors' mental state, holding that "imposition of liability requires a showing that the directors knew that they were not discharging their fiduciary obligations."

The Court of Chancery recognized these legal principles, but it denied summary judgment in order to obtain a more complete record before deciding whether the directors had acted in bad faith. Under other circumstances, deferring a decision to expand the record would be appropriate. Here, however, the trial court reviewed the existing record under a mistaken view of the applicable law. Three factors contributed to that mistake. First, the trial court imposed *Revlon* duties on the Lyondell directors before they either had decided to sell, or before the sale had become inevitable. Second, the court read *Revlon* and its progeny as creating a set of requirements that must be satisfied during the sale process. Third, the trial court equated an arguably imperfect attempt to carry out Revlon duties with a knowing disregard of one's duties that constitutes bad faith.

Summary judgment may be granted if there are no material issues of fact in dispute and the moving party is entitled to judgment as a matter of law. The facts, and all reasonable inferences, must be considered in the light most favorable to the non-moving party. The Court of Chancery identified several undisputed facts that would support the entry of judgment in favor of the Lyondell directors: the directors were "active, sophisticated, and generally aware of the value of the Company and the conditions of the markets in which the Company operated." They had reason to believe that no other bidders would emerge, given the price Basell had offered and the limited universe of companies that might be interested in acquiring Lyondell's unique assets. Smith negotiated the price up from $40 to $48 per share-a price that Deutsche Bank opined was fair. Finally, no other acquiror expressed interest during the four months between the merger announcement and the stockholder vote.

Other facts, however, led the trial court to "question the adequacy of the Board's knowledge and efforts...." After the Schedule 13D was filed in May, the directors apparently took no action to prepare for a possible acquisition proposal. The merger was negotiated and finalized in less than one week, during which time the directors met for a total of only seven hours to consider the matter. The directors did not seriously press Blavatnik for a better price, nor did they conduct even a limited market check. Moreover, although the deal protections were not unusual or preclusive, the trial court was troubled by "the Board's decision to grant considerable protection to a deal that may not have been adequately vetted under *Revlon.*"

The trial court found the directors' failure to act during the two months after the filing of the Basell Schedule 13D critical to its analysis of their good faith. The court pointedly referred to the directors' "two months of slothful indifference despite *knowing* that the Company was in play," and the fact that they "languidly awaited overtures from potential suitors...." In the end, the trial court found that it was this "failing" that warranted denial of their motion for summary judgment:

> [T]he Opinion clearly questions whether the Defendants "engaged" in the sale process.... This is where the 13D filing in May 2007 and the subsequent two months of (apparent) Board inactivity become critical.... [T]he Directors made *no apparent effort* to arm themselves with *specific knowledge* about the present value of the Company in the May through July 2007 time period, despite *admittedly knowing* that the 13D filing ... effectively put the Company "in play," and, therefore, presumably, also knowing that an offer for the sale of the Company could occur at any time. It is these facts that raise the specter of "bad faith" in the present summary judgment record....

The problem with the trial court's analysis is that *Revlon* duties do not arise simply because a company is "in play." The duty to seek the best available price applies only when a company embarks on a transaction-on its own initiative or in response to an unsolicited offer-that will result in a change of control. Basell's Schedule 13D did put the Lyondell directors, and the market in general, on notice that Basell was interested in acquiring Lyondell. The directors responded by promptly holding a special meeting to consider whether Lyondell should take any action. The directors decided that they would neither put the company up for sale nor institute defensive measures to fend off a possible hostile offer. Instead, they decided to take a "wait and see" approach. That decision was an entirely appropriate exercise of the directors' business judgment. The time for action under *Revlon* did not begin until July 10, 2007, when the directors began negotiating the sale of Lyondell.

The Court of Chancery focused on the directors' two months of inaction, when it should have focused on the one week during which they considered Basell's offer. During that one week, the directors met several times; their CEO tried to negotiate better terms; they evaluated Lyondell's value, the price offered and the likelihood of obtaining a better price; and then the directors approved the merger. The trial court acknowledged that the directors' conduct during those seven days might not demonstrate anything more than lack of due care. But the court remained skeptical about the directors' good faith-at least on the present record. That lingering concern was based on the trial court's synthesis of the *Revlon* line of cases, which led it to the erroneous conclusion that directors must follow one of several courses of action to satisfy their *Revlon* duties.

There is only one *Revlon* duty-to "[get] the best price for the stockholders at a sale of the company." No court can tell directors exactly how to accomplish that goal, because they will be facing a unique combination of circumstances, many of which will be outside their control. As we noted in

Barkan v. Amsted Industries, Inc.,"there is no single blueprint that a board must follow to fulfill its duties." [567 A.2d 1279, 1286 (Del.1989).] That said, our courts have highlighted both the positive and negative aspects of various boards' conduct under *Revlon.* The trial court drew several principles from those cases: directors must "engage actively in the sale process,"and they must confirm that they have obtained the best available price either by conducting an auction, by conducting a market check, or by demonstrating "an impeccable knowledge of the market."

The Lyondell directors did not conduct an auction or a market check, and they did not satisfy the trial court that they had the "impeccable" market knowledge that the court believed was necessary to excuse their failure to pursue one of the first two alternatives. As a result, the Court of Chancery was unable to conclude that the directors had met their burden under *Revlon.* In evaluating the totality of the circumstances, even on this limited record, we would be inclined to hold otherwise. But we would not question the trial court's decision to seek additional evidence if the issue were whether the directors had exercised due care. Where, as here, the issue is whether the directors failed to act in good faith, the analysis is very different, and the existing record mandates the entry of judgment in favor of the directors.

As discussed above, bad faith will be found if a "fiduciary intentionally fails to act in the face of a known duty to act, demonstrating a conscious disregard for his duties." The trial court decided that the *Revlon* sale process must follow one of three courses, and that the Lyondell directors did not discharge that "known set of [*Revlon*] 'duties'." But, as noted, there are no legally prescribed steps that directors must follow to satisfy their *Revlon* duties. Thus, the directors' failure to take any specific steps during the sale process could not have demonstrated a conscious disregard of their duties. More importantly, there is a vast difference between an inadequate or flawed effort to carry out fiduciary duties and a conscious disregard for those duties.

Directors' decisions must be reasonable, not perfect. "In the transactional context, [an] extreme set of facts [is] required to sustain a disloyalty claim premised on the notion that disinterested directors were intentionally disregarding their duties." [*In re Lear Corp. S'holder Litig.,* 2008 WL 4053221 at *11 (Del.Ch.).]]The trial court denied summary judgment because the Lyondell directors' "unexplained inaction" prevented the court from determining that they had acted in good faith. But, if the directors failed to do all that they should have under the circumstances, they breached their duty of care. Only if they knowingly and completely failed to undertake their responsibilities would they breach their duty of loyalty. The trial court approached the record from the wrong perspective. Instead of questioning whether disinterested, independent directors did everything that they (arguably) should have done to obtain the best sale price, the inquiry should have been whether those directors utterly failed to attempt to obtain the best sale price.

Viewing the record in this manner leads to only one possible conclusion. The Lyondell directors met several times to consider Basell's premium offer. They were generally aware of the value of their company and they knew the chemical company market. The directors solicited and followed the advice of their financial and legal advisors. They attempted to negotiate a higher offer even though all the evidence indicates that Basell had offered a "blowout" price. Finally, they approved the merger agreement, because "it was simply too good not to pass along [to the stockholders] for their consideration." We assume, as we must on summary judgment, that the Lyondell directors did absolutely nothing to prepare for Basell's offer, and that they did not even consider conducting a market check before agreeing to the merger. Even so, this record clearly establishes that the Lyondell directors did not breach their duty of loyalty by failing to act in good faith. In concluding otherwise, the Court of Chancery reversibly erred.

NOTE: LEAR CORPORATION

In re Lear Corp. Shareholder Litigation, 967 A.2d 640 (Del. Ch. 2008), also concerned the good faith of a board of directors negotiating the sale of the company. Vice-Chancellor Strine summarized as follows:

"In this case, stockholder plaintiffs seek to hold the board of Lear Corporation * * * responsible in damages for agreeing to pay a bidder a termination fee payable upon a no vote on a merger in exchange for that bidder increasing its bid from the original merger agreement by $1.25 per share * * * . The bidder did not face competition from a rival bidder; in fact, Lear had been fully shopped, and no topping bid had emerged. Rather, in a frothy M & A market, stockholders perceived that the original merger price of $36 per share was inadequate and that the original bidder could do better. Facing likely defeat on the $36 merger at the polls, the Lear board bargained to get another $1.25 per share. In exchange, the bidder demanded $25 million in compensation contingent solely upon a no vote, in contrast to the original termination fee, the bulk of which was payable only if Lear consummated an alternative transaction within twelve months. The $25 million represented only 0.9% of the total deal value. According to the amended complaint, the Lear board approved the

'Revised Merger Agreement' knowing that it was improbable that its stockholders would agree to the enhanced deal. And, in fact, the shareholders did not approve, and the Merger was defeated.

"The defendants have moved to dismiss the complaint against them, primarily arguing that the complaint fails to state with particularity a non-exculpated claim for breach of fiduciary duty. In this opinion, I grant that motion. At bottom, the plaintiffs' theory is that directors who believe in good faith that a merger is good for the stockholders cannot adopt it if stockholder approval is unlikely. That notion is at odds with our law.

"Directors are entitled to make good faith business decisions even if the stockholders might disagree with them. Where, as here, the complaint itself indicates that an independent board majority used an adequate process, employed reputable financial, legal, and proxy solicitation experts, and had a substantial basis to conclude a merger was financially fair, the directors cannot be faulted for being disloyal simply because the stockholders ultimately did not agree with their recommendation. In particular, where, as here, the directors are protected by an exculpatory charter provision, it is critical that the complaint plead facts suggesting a fair inference that the directors breached their duty of loyalty by making a bad faith decision to approve the merger for reasons inimical to the interests of the corporation and its stockholders. Where a complaint, as here, does not even create an inference of mere negligence or gross negligence, it certainly does not satisfy the far more difficult task of stating a non-exculpated duty of loyalty claim."

Insert after "Note: Comments on the Delaware Antitakeover Cases," at Casebook page 1124:

(4) Lock Ups and Bail Outs

In re the Bear Stearns Companies, Inc. Shareholder Litigation

Court of Chancery of Delaware, 2008.
2008 WL 959992 (Del.Ch.)

PARSONS, Vice Chancellor.

* * *

I. FACTS

A. The Parties

Plaintiff Police and Fire Retirement System of the City of Detroit owns, and at all relevant times owned, more than 13,000 shares of Bear Stearns common stock. Plaintiff Wayne County Employees' Retirement System ("Wayne County") owns, and at all relevant times owned, approximately 5,500 shares of Bear Stearns common stock. Defendant The Bear Stearns Companies Inc. ("Bear Stearns") is a Delaware corporation. Bear Stearns is a holding company and, through its broker-dealer and international bank subsidiaries, is a leading investment, securities, and derivatives trading, clearance, and brokerage firm serving corporations, governments, and institutional and individual investors worldwide. The individual Defendants comprise the board of directors of Bear Stearns. Defendant JPMorgan Chase & Co. ("JPMorgan"), a Delaware corporation, is a leading global financial services firm with assets of $1.5 trillion and operations in more than fifty countries. The firm is a leader in investment banking, financial services for consumers, small business, and commercial banking, financial transaction processing, asset management, and private equity.

B. Bear Stearns' Liquidity Crisis

Because of rumors circulating throughout the financial community regarding Bear Stearns' financial condition, customers began withdrawing their funds from Bear Stearns and, toward the latter part of the week of March 10, 2008, Bear Stearns was faced with a liquidity crisis. In accordance with customary industry practice, Bear Stearns held a substantial portfolio of investment grade assets and financed its operations through short term (largely day-to-day) borrowings secured by those assets. By March 13 and 14, counterparties to Bear Stearns declined to provide it short-term funding on customary terms. This unwillingness to fund on a secured basis placed enormous stress on the liquidity of Bear Stearns. On Thursday, March 13, Bear Stearns' liquidity pool fell sharply; it continued to fall on Friday, March 14, and the market rumors became self-fulfilling.

Amid these conditions, Bear Stearns found itself facing bankruptcy and the imminent threat of a disorderly wind-down. According to Treasury Secretary Paulson, it is the job of regulators to address times of turmoil in the capital markets, such as the recent reduced access to short-term funding and liquidity issues. To preserve the stability and orderliness of the financial markets, the Federal Reserve acted promptly to resolve the Bear Stearns situation.

On Friday, March 14, 2008, the Federal Reserve and JPMorgan, with the support of the Department of the Treasury, agreed to provide emergency funding to Bear Stearns. Under the terms of the agreement, the Federal Reserve Bank of New York and JPMorgan agreed to provide an unspecified amount of secured funding to Bear Stearns for up to 28 days. Further, through its Discount Window, the Federal Reserve Bank of New York would provide a form of non-recourse financing to JPMorgan. Also, on March 14, the per share price of Bear Stearns common stock decreased from a close of $57.00 on March 13, to a close of $30.00, the largest one-day decrease in nearly two decades. Credit-ratings firms downgraded Bear Stearns to two or three levels above junk status. Banks and other counterparties stopped taking collateral on short-term lines of credit, even those secured by the highest quality mortgage bonds backed by Fannie Mae and Freddie Mac.

C. The Merger Agreements

On March 16, 2008, Bear Stearns and JPMorgan announced a merger (the "Merger Agreement"). Under the terms of the Merger Agreement, JPMorgan agreed to acquire Bear Stearns in a stock merger transaction, in which Bear Stearns stockholders would receive 0.05473 JPMorgan shares per Bear Stearns share, or approximately $2 (at announcement). In a related move, the Federal Reserve agreed to lend JPMorgan up to $30 billion on a non-recourse basis secured by a pool of Bear Stearns' less liquid assets. Additionally, JPMorgan agreed to provide an immediate, broad guaranty of Bear Stearns' trading obligations.

The Merger Agreement and related agreements also contained deal protection measures including, among other things: a Section 203 waiver; an option for JPMorgan to purchase Bear Stearns' corporate headquarters building for $1.1 billion (the "Asset Option"); and an option for JPMorgan to purchase approximately 19.9% of Bear Stearns stock for $2 per share.

After the announcement of the Merger Agreement, Bear Stearns' prime brokerage customers continued moving their assets to other brokerages. This customer flight reportedly resulted from widespread concern and uncertainty over whether JPMorgan's proposed merger with Bear Stearns would be consummated, heightened by speculation that Bear Stearns stockholders would vote down the deal and take their chances if Bear Stearns were liquidated. Notwithstanding JPMorgan's guaranty-which was to stay in place for a substantial period even if the merger was voted down-customers feared that Bear

Stearns would not survive and that, as a result, its business operations would be jeopardized and its customers would not have ready access to their securities.

On March 24, 2008, Bear Stearns and JPMorgan announced an amended merger agreement (the "Amended Merger Agreement") and related Share Exchange Agreement ("SEA"). Among other things, the Amended Merger Agreement increased the merger consideration to 0.21753 JPMorgan shares per Bear Stearns share, or approximately $10. The Amended Merger Agreement also limited the guarantee by JPMorgan and the Federal Reserve. It carried forward some of the deal protection devices, such as the Section 203 waiver and the Asset Option. Moreover, under the terms of the SEA, JPMorgan will exchange, for the same per-share consideration, 95 million newly issued, non-transferable shares of Bear Stearns common stock, or 39.5% of the outstanding common after giving effect to the issuance (the "JPMorgan Shares"). [JPMorgan can now exercise the Asset Option even if Bear Stearns shareholders vote down the Amended Merger Agreement and 120 days elapse after the vote.] The share exchange was expected to be completed on April 8, 2008, before the record date for the Bear Stearns shareholder vote on the Amended Merger Agreement.

The merger remains subject to stockholder approval, which will require the preparation and dissemination of a proxy statement, followed by a vote of Bear Stearns' stockholders. Due to the need for SEC clearance of the proxy/registration statement to be issued in connection with the meeting, and applicable notice requirements, the parties do not anticipate a stockholder vote on the merger before May 14, 2008.

II. PROCEDURAL HISTORY

[In March 2008, five purported class actions were filed in New York Supreme Court alleging that the proposed merger is at an inadequate price and was approved by the Bear Stearns directors in breach of their fiduciary duties. The New York actions, now consolidated, are before Justice Herman Cahn. A hearing is pending on a motion for a preliminary injunction to prevent the voting of the JPMorgan Shares at the mid-May stockholders meeting to approve the proposed merger.]

On March 20 and 24, 2008, three days and seven days after the filing of the first New York cases, the pension fund plaintiffs in Delaware filed their respective complaints in this Court. Both actions purport to be class actions on behalf of all Bear Stearns shareholders. * * *

The Delaware Action closely parallels the New York Action. The Delaware Plaintiffs challenged the Amended Merger Agreement and related transactions, and requested, among other relief, an order temporarily restraining the "Lock Up Stock Sale" of the JPMorgan Shares or, alternatively, the voting of those Shares. On March 25, the Delaware Plaintiffs filed a joint application for a temporary restraining order against the anticipated April 8 "Lock Up Stock Sale," but later abandoned that application in favor of pursuing a preliminary injunction preventing JPMorgan from voting any of the shares acquired through that sale.

On March 27, 2008, Defendants moved to dismiss or in the alternative stay the Delaware Action. * * * This is the Court's ruling on Defendants' motion.

III. THE PARTIES' CONTENTIONS

The claims asserted in the New York and Delaware Actions are essentially the same. In each forum, the plaintiffs assert the merger consideration is too low and the merger process was unfair, such that the defendant directors breached their fiduciary duties by virtue of their involvement with the merger. Because Defendants in this action have moved to stay or dismiss it, they have not yet addressed the merits of Plaintiffs' claims.

Bear Stearns and JPMorgan seek to stay the Delaware Action, arguing that otherwise Defendants and the broader public interest uniquely implicated here will be subject to the risks, burdens, and uncertainties of two parallel, expedited proceedings brought on behalf of the same class asserting the same claims in different jurisdictions. Specifically, Bear Stearns and JPMorgan seek to stay the contemporaneously filed Delaware Action based on a balancing of the factors considered in a *forum non conveniens* analysis. They assert that under such a balancing approach, the following factors are paramount: New York is a more convenient forum; the New York court intends to proceed with a preliminary injunction hearing; the challenged merger and related transactions involve unique facts and circumstances, not likely to be repeated; and the hardship and irrationality posed by dual preliminary injunction proceedings outweighs Delaware's interest in this dispute. Among the unusual factual circumstances of the challenged transaction, Defendants emphasize the perceived need for the merger in order to avert disorder in the financial markets and the material involvement of third parties based in New York, such as the Federal Reserve Bank of New York.

Plaintiffs respond that Delaware is the proper forum because this dispute involves numerous novel and substantial issues of Delaware law. Specifically, Plaintiffs contend the proposed transactions include perhaps the most extreme combination of deal protections approved by a board of directors of a public Delaware corporation ever considered by this Court. Additionally, Plaintiffs argue that this litigation should proceed here because Delaware has the authority to regulate the internal affairs of its corporations, and this Court is uniquely positioned as the regular arbiter of corporate law disputes to resolve the contested issues.

IV. ANALYSIS

* * * In assessing which of multiple actions challenging the same conduct should proceed, the Court of Chancery often applies the *McWane* doctrine [*McWane Cast Iron Pipe Corp. v. McDowell-Wellman Eng'g Co.,* 263 A.2d 281 (Del.1970)], also known as the first-filed rule. Under the first-filed rule, this Court freely exercises its broad discretion to grant a stay "when there is a prior action pending elsewhere, in a court capable of doing prompt and complete justice, involving the same parties and the same issues."

Where the multiple actions are contemporaneously filed, however, this Court evaluates a motion to stay " 'under the traditional *forum non conveniens* framework without regard to a *McWane*-type preference of one action over the other.' " The *forum non conveniens* factors are:

> (1) the applicability of Delaware law, (2) the relative ease of access to proof, (3) the availability of compulsory process for witnesses, (4) the pendency or non-pendency of a similar action or actions in another jurisdiction, (5) the possibility of a need to view the premises, and (6) all other practical considerations that would make the trial easy, expeditious, and inexpensive.

Motions to stay litigation on grounds of *forum non conveniens* are granted only in the rare case.

Here, because the first New York action and the first Delaware action were filed in the same general time frame, only three days apart, I consider them contemporaneous filings. * * *

Turning to the unusual circumstances of this case, the fourth and sixth *forum non conveniens* factors predominate in terms of importance-*i.e.,* the pendency or non-pendency of a similar action or actions in another jurisdiction and all other practical considerations relevant to the orderly and efficient administration of justice. Before addressing those factors, however, I briefly discuss Plaintiffs' argument regarding the applicability of Delaware law.

Plaintiffs note that Bears Stearns was formed under the laws of Delaware and both the Amended Merger Agreement and the SEA provide that they shall be governed in accordance with the laws of Delaware and that any action arising out of or in connection with the agreements or transactions contemplated by them shall be brought in Delaware. Further, Plaintiffs contend this litigation implicates both novel and important issues of Delaware corporate law.

Defendants acknowledge the applicability of Delaware law, but dispute Plaintiffs' characterization of the issues presented here. They contend the applicable law cited by Plaintiffs involves settled principles articulated in cases decided a number of years ago. Defendants also emphasize that the facts of this case are unique.

Despite Plaintiffs' protestations to the contrary, the claims asserted in the Complaint only require the application of well-settled principles of Delaware law to evaluate the deal protections in the merger and the alleged breaches of fiduciary duty. There is no dispute that these principles will be applied by some court. Although the facts of the case are unusual, the uniqueness of facts does not transform settled law into new or novel legal issues. Moreover, several facts make it unlikely this extraordinary situation will recur or have wide application. Indeed, Christopher Cox, Chairman of the Securities and Exchange Commission, in reported testimony before a Congressional Committee characterized Bear Stearns' failure to obtain financing even though it had "high quality collateral" as "an unprecedented occurrence." Thus, Delaware's interest in having this case heard in its courts is not quite as strong as in [other cases] in which this Court declined to stay Delaware actions involving novel issues having widespread application in favor of similar litigation in another state.

That is not to say, however, that the issues of Delaware law presented by this dispute are not important; in fact, such issues ordinarily would be heard in this Court. Rather, I find the circumstances of this case to be *sui generis*. What is paramount is that this Court not contribute to a situation that might cause harm to a number of affected constituencies, including U.S. taxpayers and citizens, by creating the risk of greater uncertainty. In that sense, the key factors in determining whether to stay this litigation are the pendency of an identical action in another jurisdiction that is more procedurally advanced than Delaware (factor 4) and the other unique practical considerations (factor 6) of this case. I therefore turn to those factors.

In terms of the fourth *forum non conveniens* factor, the pendency of a similar action in another jurisdiction, there is a virtually identical action pending in New York, and it is proceeding on an expedited basis. * * *

Defendants contend that if the Delaware Action is not stayed, there is a real risk that both the New York and Delaware Actions will go forward on parallel, expedited tracks, creating unseemly and inefficient duplicative proceedings. Duplicative proceedings are disfavored because they waste judicial and financial resources, and because the competing proceedings create the appearance of an unseemly race to decide with a potential for inconsistent rulings. Defendants further argue that in this extraordinary factual setting, the threat of harm is even greater. The hardship is allegedly magnified because duplicative and parallel preliminary injunction proceedings alone could undermine the market's perception of the Bear Stearns rescue plan and because the parties and third parties involved already are functioning in a pressure cooker, continuously monitoring the attempted rescue and the overall stability of the financial markets.

Plaintiffs downplay the significance of the related case pending in New York in comparison to the important issues of Delaware law presented by this dispute. First, they argue that whatever potential harm defendants face from the prospect of litigation in two forums is of their own making. In that regard, Plaintiffs imply Defendants colluded with the New York plaintiffs to position the New York Action ahead of this one by stipulating to a schedule immediately after being notified, on or about March 24, that the Delaware Plaintiffs were about to request a temporary injunction against the anticipated April 8 issuance of the JPMorgan Shares. Defendants deny any such collusion. Rather, they contend they were caught in a dispute among competing plaintiff stockholders and reacted in a forum neutral manner. * * *

* * * An important factor * * * in deciding whether to permit the Delaware Action to proceed in parallel with the New York Action is the risk of harm such competing litigations would create.

Regarding the sixth factor, all other practical considerations that would make the trial easy, expeditious, and inexpensive, this case raises practical considerations far beyond the typical concerns The practical considerations here include: two sets of plaintiffs in two fora; the risk that inconsistent rulings would negatively impact not only the parties involved, but also the U.S. financial markets and the national economy; and the involvement of unusual third party players, including, *inter alia,* the Federal Reserve Bank and the Department of the Treasury. Given these important and atypical practical considerations, this is the rare case where a stay may be appropriate.

Under a balancing of the relevant considerations in a *forum non conveniens* framework, the relatively unique circumstances of the Bear Stearns and JPMorgan merger and the dangers posed by multiple competing actions relating to that merger support a stay of the Delaware Action. * * * In this case, considering that the New York court has scheduled an expedited preliminary injunction hearing, the issues presented involve application of established precedents of Delaware corporate law to an unusual set of facts, which is unlikely to recur, and the persuasive practical reasons against embarking unnecessarily on a collision course with our sister court in New York in these extraordinary circumstances, I find Defendants have shown that failing to stay this action would result in overwhelming hardship. Accordingly, I will stay the Delaware Action.

APPENDIX A

FINANCIAL CONTRACT FORMS

Insert at Casebook Page A-186:

FORM 6 – TARP PREFERRED STOCK

CERTIFICATE OF DESIGNATIONS

OF

FIXED RATE CUMULATIVE PERPETUAL PREFERRED STOCK,

SERIES [●]

OF

[●]

[***Insert name of Corporation***], a [corporation] organized and existing under the laws of the [***Insert jurisdiction of organization***] (the Corporation"), in accordance with the provisions of Section[s] [●] of the [***Insert applicable statute***] thereof, does hereby certify:

The board of directors of the Corporation (the "Board of Directors") or an applicable committee of the Board of Directors, in accordance with the [certificate of incorporation and bylaws] of the Corporation and applicable law, adopted the following resolution on [●] creating a series of [●] shares of Preferred Stock of the Corporation designated as "Fixed Rate Cumulative Perpetual Preferred Stock, Series [●]".

RESOLVED, that pursuant to the provisions of the [certificate of incorporation and the bylaws] of the Corporation and applicable law, a series of Preferred Stock, par value $[●] per share, of the Corporation be and hereby is created, and that the designation and number of shares of such series, and the voting and other powers, preferences and relative, participating, optional or other rights, and the qualifications, limitations and restrictions thereof, of the shares of such series, are as follows:

Part 1. Designation and Number of Shares. There is hereby created out of the authorized and unissued shares of preferred stock of the Corporation a series of preferred stock designated as the "Fixed Rate Cumulative Perpetual Preferred Stock, Series [●]" (the "Designated Preferred Stock"). The authorized number of shares of Designated Preferred Stock shall be [●].

Part 2. Standard Provisions. The Standard Provisions contained in Annex A attached hereto are incorporated herein by reference in their entirety and shall be deemed to be a part of this Certificate of Designations to the same extent as if such provisions had been set forth in full herein.

Part. 3. Definitions. The following terms are used in this Certificate of Designations (including the Standard Provisions in Annex A hereto) as defined below:

(a) "Common Stock" means the common stock, par value $[●] per share, of the Corporation.

(b) "Dividend Payment Date" means [February 15, May 15, August 15 and November 15] of each year.

(c) "Junior Stock" means the Common Stock, [***Insert titles of any existing Junior Stock***] and any other class or series of stock of the Corporation the terms of which expressly provide that it ranks junior to Designated Preferred Stock as to dividend rights and/or as to rights on liquidation, dissolution or winding up of the Corporation.

(d) "Liquidation Amount" means $[1,000][1] per share of Designated Preferred Stock.

(e) "Minimum Amount" means $[***Insert $ amount equal to 25% of the aggregate value of the Designated Preferred Stock issued on the Original Issue Date***].

(f) "Parity Stock" means any class or series of stock of the Corporation (other than Designated Preferred Stock) the terms of which do not expressly provide that such class or series will rank senior or junior to Designated Preferred Stock as to dividend rights and/or as to rights on liquidation, dissolution or winding up of the Corporation (in each case without regard to whether dividends accrue cumulatively or non-cumulatively). Without limiting the foregoing, Parity Stock shall include the Corporation's [***Insert title(s) of existing classes or series of Parity Stock***].

(g) "Signing Date" means [***Insert date of applicable securities purchase agreement***].

1 If issuer desires to issue shares with a higher dollar amount liquidation preference, liquidation preference references will be modified accordingly. In such case (in accordance with Section 4.7 of the Securities Purchase Agreement), the issuer will be required to enter into a deposit agreement.

Part. 4. Certain Voting Matters. [***To be inserted if the Charter provides for voting in proportion to liquidation preferences*:** Whether the vote or consent of the holders of a plurality, majority or other portion of the shares of Designated Preferred Stock and any Voting Parity Stock has been cast or given on any matter on which the holders of shares of Designated Preferred Stock are entitled to vote shall be determined by the Corporation by reference to the specified liquidation amount of the shares voted or covered by the consent as if the Corporation were liquidated on the record date for such vote or consent, if any, or, in the absence of a record date, on the date for such vote or consent. For purposes of determining the voting rights of the holders of Designated Preferred Stock under Section 7 of the Standard Provisions forming part of this Certificate of Designations, each holder will be entitled to one vote for each $1,000 of liquidation preference to which such holder's shares are entitled.] [***To be inserted if the Charter does not provide for voting in proportion to liquidation preferences:*** Holders of shares of Designated Preferred Stock will be entitled to one vote for each such share on any matter on which holders of Designated Preferred Stock are entitled to vote, including any action by written consent.]

[*Remainder of Page Intentionally Left Blank*]

IN WITNESS WHEREOF, [***Insert name of Corporation***] has caused this Certificate of Designations to be signed by [●], its [●], this [●] day of [●].

[***Insert name of Corporation***]

By: ______________________

Name:
Title:

ANNEX A

STANDARD PROVISIONS

Section 1. General Matters. Each share of Designated Preferred Stock shall be identical in all respects to every other share of Designated Preferred Stock. The Designated Preferred Stock shall be perpetual, subject to the provisions of Section 5 of these Standard Provisions that form a part of the Certificate of Designations. The Designated Preferred Stock shall rank equally with Parity Stock and shall rank senior to Junior Stock with respect to the payment of dividends and the distribution of assets in the event of any dissolution, liquidation or winding up of the Corporation.

Section 2. Standard Definitions. As used herein with respect to Designated Preferred Stock:

(a) "Applicable Dividend Rate" means (i) during the period from the Original Issue Date to, but excluding, the first day of the first Dividend Period commencing on or after the fifth anniversary of the Original Issue Date, 5% per annum and (ii) from and after the first day of the first Dividend Period commencing on or after the fifth anniversary of the Original Issue Date, 9% per annum.

(b) "Appropriate Federal Banking Agency" means the "appropriate Federal banking agency" with respect to the Corporation as defined in Section 3(q) of the Federal Deposit Insurance Act (12 U.S.C. Section 1813(q)), or any successor provision.

(c) "Business Combination" means a merger, consolidation, statutory share exchangeor similar transaction that requires the approval of the Corporation's stockholders.

(d) "Business Day" means any day except Saturday, Sunday and any day on which banking institutions in the State of New York generally are authorized or required by law or other governmental actions to close.

(e) "Bylaws" means the bylaws of the Corporation, as they may be amended from time to time.

(f) "Certificate of Designations" means the Certificate of Designations or comparable instrument relating to the Designated Preferred Stock, of which these Standard Provisions form a part, as it may be amended from time to time.

(g) "Charter" means the Corporation's certificate or articles of incorporation, articles of association, or similar organizational document.

(h) "Dividend Period" has the meaning set forth in Section 3(a).

(i) "Dividend Record Date" has the meaning set forth in Section 3(a).

(j) "Liquidation Preference" has the meaning set forth in Section 4(a).

(k) "Original Issue Date" means the date on which shares of Designated Preferred Stock are first issued.

(l) "Preferred Director" has the meaning set forth in Section 7(b).

(m) "Preferred Stock" means any and all series of preferred stock of the Corporation, including the Designated Preferred Stock.

(n) "Qualified Equity Offering" means the sale and issuance for cash by the Corporation to persons other than the Corporation or any of its subsidiaries after the Original Issue Date of shares of perpetual Preferred Stock, Common Stock or any combination of such stock, that, in each case, qualify as and may be included in Tier 1 capital of the Corporation at the time of issuance under the applicable risk-based capital guidelines of the Corporation's Appropriate Federal Banking Agency (other than any such sales and issuances made pursuant to agreements or arrangements entered into, or pursuant to financing plans which were publicly announced, on or prior to October 13, 2008).

(o) "Share Dilution Amount" has the meaning set forth in Section 3(b).

(p) "Standard Provisions" mean these Standard Provisions that form a part of the Certificate of Designations relating to the Designated Preferred Stock.

(q) "Successor Preferred Stock" has the meaning set forth in Section 5(a).

(r) "Voting Parity Stock" means, with regard to any matter as to which the holders of Designated Preferred Stock are entitled to vote as specified in Sections 7(a) and 7(b) of these Standard Provisions that form a part of the Certificate of Designations, any and all series of Parity Stock upon which like voting rights have been conferred and are exercisable with respect to such matter.

Section 3. Dividends.

(a) Rate. Holders of Designated Preferred Stock shall be entitled to receive, on each share of Designated Preferred Stock if, as and when declared by the Board of Directors or any duly authorized committee of the Board of Directors, but only out of assets legally available therefor, cumulative cash dividends with respect to each Dividend Period (as defined below) at a rate per annum equal to the Applicable Dividend Rate on (i) the Liquidation Amount per share of Designated Preferred Stock and (ii) the amount of accrued and unpaid dividends for any prior Dividend Period on such share of Designated Preferred Stock, if any. Such dividends shall begin to accrue and be cumulative from the Original Issue Date, shall compound on each subsequent Dividend Payment Date (*i.e.*, no dividends shall accrue on other dividends unless and until the first Dividend Payment Date for such other dividends has passed without such other dividends having been paid on such date) and shall be payable quarterly in arrears on each Dividend Payment Date, commencing with the first such Dividend Payment Date to occur at least 20 calendar days after the Original Issue Date. In the event that any Dividend Payment Date would otherwise fall on a day that is not a Business Day, the dividend payment due on that date will be postponed to the next day that is a Business Day and no additional dividends will accrue as a result of that postponement. The period from and including any Dividend Payment Date to, but excluding, the next Dividend Payment Date is a "Dividend Period", provided that the initial Dividend Period shall be the period from and including the Original Issue Date to, but excluding, the next Dividend Payment Date.

Dividends that are payable on Designated Preferred Stock in respect of any Dividend Period shall be computed on the basis of a 360-day year consisting of twelve 30-day months. The amount of dividends payable on Designated Preferred Stock on any date prior to the end of a Dividend Period, and for the initial Dividend Period, shall be computed on the basis of a 360-day year consisting of twelve 30-day months, and actual days elapsed over a 30-day month.

Dividends that are payable on Designated Preferred Stock on any Dividend Payment Date will be payable to holders of record of Designated Preferred Stock as they appear on the stock register of the Corporation on the applicable record date, which shall be the 15th calendar day immediately preceding such Dividend Payment Date or such other record date fixed by the Board of Directors or any duly authorized committee of the Board of Directors that is not more than 60 nor less than 10 days prior to such Dividend Payment Date (each, a "Dividend Record Date"). Any such day that is a Dividend Record Date shall be a Dividend Record Date whether or not such day is a Business Day.

Holders of Designated Preferred Stock shall not be entitled to any dividends, whether payable in cash, securities or other property, other than dividends (if any) declared and payable on Designated Preferred Stock as specified in this Section 3 (subject to the other provisions of the Certificate of Designations).

(b) <u>Priority of Dividends</u>. So long as any share of Designated Preferred Stock remains outstanding, no dividend or distribution shall be declared or paid on the Common Stock or any other shares of Junior Stock (other than dividends payable solely in shares of Common Stock) or Parity Stock, subject to the immediately following paragraph in the case of Parity Stock, and no Common Stock, Junior Stock or Parity Stock shall be, directly or indirectly, purchased, redeemed or otherwise acquired for consideration by the Corporation or any of its subsidiaries unless all accrued and unpaid dividends for all past Dividend Periods, including the latest completed Dividend Period (including, if applicable as provided in Section 3(a) above, dividends on such amount), on all outstanding shares of Designated Preferred Stock have been or are contemporaneously declared and paid in full (or have been declared and a sum sufficient for the payment thereof has been set aside for the benefit of the holders of shares of Designated Preferred Stock on the applicable record date). The foregoing limitation shall not apply to (i) redemptions, purchases or other acquisitions of shares of Common Stock or other Junior Stock in connection with the administration of any employee benefit plan in the ordinary course of business (including purchases to offset the Share Dilution Amount (as defined below) pursuant to a publicly announced repurchase plan) and consistent with past practice, *provided* that any purchases to offset the Share Dilution Amount shall in no event exceed the Share Dilution Amount; (ii) purchases or other acquisitions by a broker-dealer subsidiary of the Corporation solely for the purpose of market-making, stabilization or customer facilitation transactions in

Junior Stock or Parity Stock in the ordinary course of its business; (iii) purchases by a brokerdealer subsidiary of the Corporation of capital stock of the Corporation for resale pursuant to an offering by the Corporation of such capital stock underwritten by such broker-dealer subsidiary; (v) any dividends or distributions of rights or Junior Stock in connection with a stockholders' rights plan or any redemption or repurchase of rights pursuant to any stockholders' rights plan; (v) the acquisition by the Corporation or any of its subsidiaries of record ownership in Junior Stock or Parity Stock for the beneficial ownership of any other persons (other than the Corporation or any of its subsidiaries), including as trustees or custodians; and (vi) the exchange or conversion of Junior Stock for or into other Junior Stock or of Parity Stock for or into other Parity Stock (with the same or lesser aggregate liquidation amount) or Junior Stock, in each case, solely to the extent required pursuant to binding contractual agreements entered into prior to the Signing Date or any subsequent agreement for the accelerated exercise, settlement or exchange thereof for Common Stock. "Share Dilution Amount" means the increase in the number of diluted shares outstanding (determined in accordance with generally accepted accounting principles in the United States, and as measured from the date of the Corporation's consolidated financial statements most recently filed with the Securities and Exchange Commission prior to the Original Issue Date) resulting from the grant, vesting or exercise of equity-based compensation to employees and equitably adjusted for any stock split, stock dividend, reverse stock split, reclassification or similar transaction.

When dividends are not paid (or declared and a sum sufficient for payment thereof set aside for the benefit of the holders thereof on the applicable record date) on any Dividend Payment Date (or, in the case of Parity Stock having dividend payment dates different from the Dividend Payment Dates, on a dividend payment date falling within a Dividend Period related to such Dividend Payment Date) in full upon Designated Preferred Stock and any shares of Parity Stock, all dividends declared on Designated Preferred Stock and all such Parity Stock and payable on such Dividend Payment Date (or, in the case of Parity Stock having dividend payment dates different from the Dividend Payment Dates, on a dividend payment date falling within the Dividend Period related to such Dividend Payment Date) shall be declared *pro rata* so that the respective amounts of such dividends declared shall bear the same ratio to each other as all accrued and unpaid dividends per share on the shares of Designated Preferred Stock (including, if applicable as provided in Section 3(a) above, dividends on such amount) and all Parity Stock payable on such Dividend Payment Date (or, in the case of Parity Stock having dividend payment dates different from the Dividend Payment Dates, on a dividend payment date falling within the Dividend Period related to such Dividend Payment Date) (subject to their having been declared by the Board of Directors or a duly authorized committee of the Board of Directors out of legally available funds and including, in the case of Parity Stock that bears cumulative dividends, all accrued but unpaid dividends) bear to each other. If the Board of Directors or a duly authorized committee of the Board of Directors determines not to pay any dividend or a full dividend on a Dividend Payment Date, the Corporation will provide written notice to the holders of Designated Preferred Stock prior to such Dividend Payment Date.

Subject to the foregoing, and not otherwise, such dividends (payable in cash, securities or other property) as may be determined by the Board of Directors or any duly authorized committee of the Board of Directors may be declared and paid on any securities, including Common Stock and other Junior Stock, from time to time out of any funds legally available for such payment, and holders of Designated Preferred Stock shall not be entitled to participate in any such dividends.

Section 4. Liquidation Rights.

(a) Voluntary or Involuntary Liquidation. In the event of any liquidation, dissolution or winding up of the affairs of the Corporation, whether voluntary or involuntary, holders of Designated Preferred Stock shall be entitled to receive for each share of Designated Preferred Stock, out of the assets of the Corporation or proceeds thereof (whether capital or surplus) available for distribution to stockholders of the Corporation, subject to the rights of any creditors of the Corporation, before any distribution of such assets or proceeds is made to or set aside for the holders of Common Stock and any other stock of the Corporation ranking junior to Designated Preferred Stock as to such distribution, payment in full in an amount equal to the sum of (i) the Liquidation Amount per share and (ii) the amount of any accrued and unpaid dividends (including, if applicable as provided in Section 3(a) above, dividends on such amount), whether or not declared, to the date of payment (such amounts collectively, the "Liquidation Preference").

(b) Partial Payment. If in any distribution described in Section 4(a) above the assets of the Corporation or proceeds thereof are not sufficient to pay in full the amounts payable with respect to all outstanding shares of Designated Preferred Stock and the corresponding amounts payable with respect of any other stock of the Corporation ranking equally with Designated Preferred Stock as to such distribution, holders of Designated Preferred Stock and the holders of such other stock shall share ratably in any such distribution in proportion to the full respective distributions to which they are entitled.

(c) Residual Distributions. If the Liquidation Preference has been paid in full to all holders of Designated Preferred Stock and the corresponding amounts payable with respect of any other stock of the Corporation ranking equally with Designated Preferred Stock as to such distribution has been paid in full, the holders of other stock of the Corporation shall be entitled to receive all remaining assets of the Corporation (or proceeds thereof) according to their respective rights and preferences.

(d) Merger, Consolidation and Sale of Assets Not Liquidation. For purposes of this Section 4, the merger or consolidation of the Corporation with any other corporation or other entity, including a merger or consolidation in which the holders of Designated Preferred Stock receive cash, securities or other property for their shares, or the sale, lease or exchange (for cash, securities or other property) of all or substantially all of the assets of the Corporation, shall not constitute a liquidation, dissolution or winding up of the Corporation.

Section 5. Redemption.

(a) Optional Redemption. Except as provided below, the Designated Preferred Stock may not be redeemed prior to the first Dividend Payment Date falling on or after the third anniversary of the Original Issue Date. On or after the first Dividend Payment Date falling on or after the third anniversary of the Original Issue Date, the Corporation, at its option, subject to the approval of the Appropriate Federal Banking Agency, may redeem, in whole or in part, at any time and from time to time, out of funds legally available therefor, the shares of Designated Preferred Stock at the time outstanding, upon notice given as provided in Section 5(c) below, at a redemption price equal to the sum of (i) the Liquidation Amount per share and (ii) except as otherwise provided below, any accrued and unpaid dividends (including, if applicable as provided in Section 3(a) above, dividends on such amount) (regardless of whether any dividends are actually declared) to, but excluding, the date fixed for redemption.

Notwithstanding the foregoing, prior to the first Dividend Payment Date falling on or after the third anniversary of the Original Issue Date, the Corporation, at its option, subject to the approval of the Appropriate Federal Banking Agency, may redeem, in whole or in part, at any time and from time to time, the shares of Designated Preferred Stock at the time outstanding, upon notice given as provided in Section 5(c) below, at a redemption price equal to the sum of (i) the Liquidation Amount per share and (ii) except as otherwise provided below, any accrued and unpaid dividends (including, if applicable as provided in Section 3(a) above, dividends on such amount) (regardless of whether any dividends are actually declared) to, but excluding, the date fixed for redemption; *provided* that (x) the Corporation (or any successor by Business Combination) has received aggregate gross proceeds of not less than the Minimum Amount (plus the "Minimum Amount" as defined in the relevant certificate of designations for each other outstanding series of preferred stock of such successor that was originally issued to the United States Department of the Treasury (the "Successor Preferred Stock") in connection with the Troubled Asset Relief Program Capital Purchase Program) from one or more Qualified Equity Offerings (including Qualified Equity Offerings of such successor), and (y) the aggregate redemption price of the Designated Preferred Stock (and any Successor Preferred Stock) redeemed pursuant to this paragraph may not exceed the aggregate net cash proceeds received by the Corporation (or any successor by Business Combination) from such Qualified Equity Offerings (including Qualified Equity Offerings of such successor).

The redemption price for any shares of Designated Preferred Stock shall be payable on the redemption date to the holder of such shares against surrender of the certificate(s) evidencing such shares to the Corporation or its agent. Any declared but unpaid dividends payable on a redemption date that occurs subsequent to the Dividend Record Date for a Dividend Period shall not be paid to the holder entitled to receive the redemption price on the redemption date, but rather shall be paid to the holder of record of the redeemed shares on such Dividend Record Date relating to the Dividend Payment Date as provided in Section 3 above.

(b) No Sinking Fund. The Designated Preferred Stock will not be subject to any mandatory redemption, sinking fund or other similar provisions. Holders of Designated Preferred Stock will have no right to require redemption or repurchase of any shares of Designated Preferred Stock.

(c) Notice of Redemption. Notice of every redemption of shares of Designated Preferred Stock shall be given by first class mail, postage prepaid, addressed to the holders of record of the shares to be redeemed at their respective last addresses appearing on the books of the Corporation. Such mailing shall be at least 30 days and not more than 60 days before the date fixed for redemption. Any notice mailed as provided in this Subsection shall be conclusively presumed to have been duly given, whether or not the holder receives such notice, but failure duly to give such notice by mail, or any defect in such notice or in the mailing thereof, to any holder of shares of Designated Preferred Stock designated for redemption shall not affect the validity of the proceedings for the redemption of any other shares of Designated Preferred Stock. Notwithstanding the foregoing, if shares of Designated Preferred Stock are issued in book-entry form through The Depository Trust Corporation or any other similar facility, notice of redemption may be given to the holders of Designated Preferred Stock at such time and in any manner permitted by such facility. Each notice of redemption given to a holder shall state: (1) the redemption date; (2) the number of shares of Designated Preferred Stock to be redeemed and, if less than all the shares held by such holder are to be redeemed, the number of such shares to be redeemed from such holder; (3) the redemption price; and (4) the place or places where certificates for such shares are to be surrendered for payment of the redemption price.

(d) Partial Redemption. In case of any redemption of part of the shares of Designated Preferred Stock at the time outstanding, the shares to be redeemed shall be selected either *pro rata* or in such other manner as the Board of Directors or a duly authorized committee thereof may determine to be fair and equitable. Subject to the provisions hereof, the Board of Directors or a duly authorized committee thereof shall have full power and authority to prescribe the terms and conditions upon which shares of Designated Preferred Stock shall be redeemed from time to time. If fewer than all the shares represented by any certificate are redeemed, a new certificate shall be issued representing the unredeemed shares without charge to the holder thereof.

(e) Effectiveness of Redemption. If notice of redemption has been duly given and if on or before the redemption date specified in the notice all funds necessary for the redemption have been deposited by the Corporation, in trust for the *pro rata* benefit of the holders of the shares called for redemption, with a bank or trust company doing business in the Borough of Manhattan, The City of New York, and having a capital and surplus of at least $500 million and selected by the Board of Directors, so as to be and continue to be available solely therefor, then, notwithstanding that any certificate for any share so called for redemption has not been surrendered for cancellation, on and after the redemption date dividends shall cease to accrue on all shares so called for redemption, all shares so called for redemption shall no longer be deemed outstanding and all rights with respect to such shares shall forthwith on such redemption date cease and terminate, except only the right of the holders thereof to receive the amount payable on such redemption from such bank or trust company, without interest. Any funds unclaimed at the end of three years from the redemption date shall, to the extent permitted by law, be released to the

Corporation, after which time the holders of the shares so called for redemption shall look only to the Corporation for payment of the redemption price of such shares.

(f) Status of Redeemed Shares. Shares of Designated Preferred Stock that are redeemed, repurchased or otherwise acquired by the Corporation shall revert to authorized but unissued shares of Preferred Stock (*provided* that any such cancelled shares of Designated Preferred Stock may be reissued only as shares of any series of Preferred Stock other than Designated Preferred Stock).

Section 6. Conversion.

Holders of Designated Preferred Stock shares shall have no right to exchange or convert such shares into any other securities.

Section 7. Voting Rights.

(a) General. The holders of Designated Preferred Stock shall not have any votingrights except as set forth below or as otherwise from time to time required by law.

(b) Preferred Stock Directors. Whenever, at any time or times, dividends payable on the shares of Designated Preferred Stock have not been paid for an aggregate of six quarterly Dividend Periods or more, whether or not consecutive, the authorized number of directors of the Corporation shall automatically be increased by two and the holders of the Designated Preferred Stock shall have the right, with holders of shares of any one or more other classes or series of Voting Parity Stock outstanding at the time, voting together as a class, to elect two directors (hereinafter the "Preferred Directors" and each a "Preferred Director") to fill such newly created directorships at the Corporation's next annual meeting of stockholders (or at a special meeting called for that purpose prior to such next annual meeting) and at each subsequent annual meeting of stockholders until all accrued and unpaid dividends for all past Dividend Periods, including the latest completed Dividend Period (including, if applicable as provided in Section 3(a) above, dividends on such amount), on all outstanding shares of Designated Preferred Stock have been declared and paid in full at which time such right shall terminate with respect to the Designated Preferred Stock, except as herein or by law expressly provided, subject to revesting in the event of each and every subsequent default of the character above mentioned; *provided* that it shall be a qualification for election for any Preferred Director that the election of such Preferred Director shall not cause the

Corporation to violate any corporate governance requirements of any securities exchange or other trading facility on which securities of the Corporation may then be listed or traded that listed or traded companies must have a majority of independent directors. Upon any termination of the right of the holders of shares of Designated Preferred Stock and Voting Parity Stock as a class to vote for directors as provided above, the Preferred Directors shall cease to be qualified as directors, the term of office of all Preferred Directors then in office shall terminate immediately and the authorized number of directors shall be reduced by the number of Preferred Directors elected pursuant hereto. Any Preferred Director may be removed at any time, with or without cause, and any vacancy created thereby may be filled, only by the affirmative vote of the holders a majority of the shares of Designated Preferred Stock at the time outstanding voting separately as a class together with the holders of shares of Voting Parity Stock, to the extent the voting rights of such holders described above are then exercisable. If the office of any Preferred Director becomes vacant for any reason other than removal from office as aforesaid, the remaining Preferred Director may choose a successor who shall hold office for the unexpired term in respect of which such vacancy occurred.

(c) Class Voting Rights as to Particular Matters. So long as any shares of Designated Preferred Stock are outstanding, in addition to any other vote or consent of stockholders required by law or by the Charter, the vote or consent of the holders of at least 66 2/3% of the shares of Designated Preferred Stock at the time outstanding, voting as a separate class, given in person or by proxy, either in writing without a meeting or by vote at any meeting called for the purpose, shall be necessary for effecting or validating:

(i) Authorization of Senior Stock. Any amendment or alteration of the Certificate of Designations for the Designated Preferred Stock or the Charter to authorize or create or increase the authorized amount of, or any issuance of, any shares of, or any securities convertible into or exchangeable or exercisable for shares of, any class or series of capital stock of the Corporation ranking senior to Designated Preferred Stock with respect to either or both the payment of dividends and/or the distribution of assets on any liquidation, dissolution or winding up of the Corporation;

(ii) Amendment of Designated Preferred Stock. Any amendment, alteration or repeal of any provision of the Certificate of Designations for the Designated Preferred Stock or the Charter (including, unless no vote on such merger or consolidation is required by Section 7(c)(iii) below, any amendment, alteration or repeal by means of a merger, consolidation or otherwise) so as to adversely affect the rights, preferences, privileges or voting powers of the Designated Preferred Stock; or (iii) Share Exchanges, Reclassifications, Mergers and Consolidations. Any consummation of a binding share exchange or reclassification involving the Designated Preferred Stock, or of a merger or consolidation of the Corporation with another corporation or other entity, unless in each case (x) the shares of Designated Preferred Stock remain outstanding or, in the case of any such merger or consolidation with respect to which the Corporation is not the surviving or resulting entity, are converted into or exchanged for preference securities of the surviving or resulting entity or its ultimate parent, and (y) such shares remaining outstanding or such preference securities, as the case may be, have such rights, preferences, privileges and voting powers, and limitations and restrictions thereof, taken as a whole, as are not materially less favorable to the holders thereof than the rights, preferences, privileges and voting powers, and limitations and restrictions thereof, of Designated Preferred Stock immediately prior to such consummation, taken as a whole; *provided*, *however*, that for all purposes of this Section 7(c), any increase in the amount of the authorized Preferred Stock, including any increase in the authorized amount of Designated Preferred Stock necessary to satisfy preemptive or similar rights granted by the Corporation to other persons prior to the Signing Date, or the creation and issuance, or an increase in the authorized or issued amount, whether pursuant to preemptive or similar rights or otherwise, of any other series of Preferred Stock, or any securities convertible into or exchangeable or exercisable for any other series of Preferred Stock, ranking equally with and/or junior to Designated Preferred Stock with respect to the payment of dividends (whether such dividends are cumulative or non-cumulative) and the distribution of assets upon liquidation, dissolution or winding up of the Corporation will not be deemed to adversely affect the rights, preferences, privileges or voting powers, and shall not require the affirmative vote or consent of, the holders of outstanding shares of the Designated Preferred Stock.

(d) Changes after Provision for Redemption. No vote or consent of the holders of Designated Preferred Stock shall be required pursuant to Section 7(c) above if, at or prior to the time when any such vote or consent would otherwise be required pursuant to such Section, all outstanding shares of the Designated Preferred Stock shall have been redeemed, or shall have been called for redemption upon proper notice and sufficient funds shall have been deposited in trust for such redemption, in each case pursuant to Section 5 above.

(e) Procedures for Voting and Consents. The rules and procedures for calling and conducting any meeting of the holders of Designated Preferred Stock (including, without limitation, the fixing of a record date in connection therewith), the solicitation and use of proxies at such a meeting, the obtaining of written consents and any other aspect or matter with regard to such a meeting or such consents shall be governed by any rules of the Board of Directors or any duly authorized committee of the Board of Directors, in its discretion, may adopt from time to time, which rules and procedures shall conform to the requirements of the Charter, the Bylaws, and applicable law and the rules of any national securities exchange or other trading facility on which Designated Preferred Stock is listed or traded at the time.

Section 8. Record Holders.

To the fullest extent permitted by applicable law, the Corporation and the transfer agent for Designated Preferred Stock may deem and treat the record holder of any share of Designated Preferred Stock as the true and lawful owner thereof for all purposes, and neither the Corporation nor such transfer agent shall be affected by any notice to the contrary.

Section 9. Notices.

All notices or communications in respect of Designated Preferred Stock shall be sufficiently given if given in writing and delivered in person or by first class mail, postage prepaid, or if given in such other manner as may be permitted in this Certificate of Designations, in the Charter or Bylaws or by applicable law. Notwithstanding the foregoing, if shares of Designated Preferred Stock are issued in book-entry form through The Depository Trust Corporation or any similar facility, such notices may be given to the holders of Designated Preferred Stock in any manner permitted by such facility.

Section 10. No Preemptive Rights.

No share of Designated Preferred Stock shall have any rights of preemption whatsoever as to any securities of the Corporation, or any warrants, rights or options issued or granted with respect thereto, regardless of how such securities, or such warrants, rights or options, may be designated, issued or granted.

Section 11. Replacement Certificates.

The Corporation shall replace any mutilated certificate at the holder's expense upon surrender of that certificate to the Corporation. The Corporation shall replace certificates that become destroyed, stolen or lost at the holder's expense upon delivery to the Corporation of reasonably satisfactory evidence that the certificate has been destroyed, stolen or lost, together with any indemnity that may be reasonably required by the Corporation.

Section 12. Other Rights.

The shares of Designated Preferred Stock shall not have any rights, preferences, privileges or voting powers or relative, participating, optional or other special rights, or qualifications, limitations or restrictions thereof, other than as set forth herein or in the Charter or as provided by applicable law.

FORM 7 – TARP WARRANT

FORM OF WARRANT TO PURCHASE COMMON STOCK

THE SECURITIES REPRESENTED BY THIS INSTRUMENT HAVE NOT BEEN REGISTERED UNDER THE SECURITIES ACT OF 1933, AS AMENDED, OR THE SECURITIES LAWS OF ANY STATE AND MAY NOT BE TRANSFERRED, SOLD OR OTHERWISE DISPOSED OF EXCEPT WHILE A REGISTRATION STATEMENT RELATING THERETO IS IN EFFECT UNDER SUCH ACT AND APPLICABLE STATE SECURITIES LAWS OR PURSUANT TO AN EXEMPTION FROM REGISTRATION UNDER SUCH ACT OR SUCH LAWS. THIS INSTRUMENT IS ISSUED SUBJECT TO THE RESTRICTIONS ON TRANSFER AND OTHER PROVISIONS OF A SECURITIES PURCHASE AGREEMENT BETWEEN THE ISSUER OF THESE SECURITIES AND THE INVESTOR REFERRED TO THEREIN, A COPY OF WHICH IS ON FILE WITH THE ISSUER. THE SECURITIES REPRESENTED BY THIS INSTRUMENT MAY NOT BE SOLD OR OTHERWISE TRANSFERRED EXCEPT IN COMPLIANCE WITH SAID AGREEMENT. ANY SALE OR OTHER TRANSFER NOT IN COMPLIANCE WITH SAID
AGREEMENT WILL BE VOID.

WARRANT
to purchase

____
Shares of Common Stock of

____

Issue Date: _______________________

1. Definitions. Unless the context otherwise requires, when used herein the following terms shall have the meanings indicated.

"*Affiliate*" has the meaning ascribed to it in the Purchase Agreement.

"*Appraisal Procedure*" means a procedure whereby two independent appraisers, one chosen by the Company and one by the Original Warrantholder, shall mutually agree upon the determinations then the subject of appraisal. Each party shall deliver a notice to the other appointing its appraiser within 15 days after the Appraisal Procedure is invoked. If within 30 days after appointment of the two appraisers they are unable to agree upon the amount in question, a third independent appraiser shall be chosen within 10 days thereafter by the mutual consent of such first two appraisers. The decision of the third appraiser so appointed and chosen shall be given within 30 days after the selection of such third appraiser. If three appraisers shall be appointed and the determination of one appraiser is disparate from the middle determination by more than twice the amount by which the other determination is disparate from the middle determination, then the determination of such appraiser shall be excluded, the remaining two determinations shall be averaged and such average shall be binding and conclusive upon the Company and the Original Warrantholder; otherwise, the average of all three determinations shall be binding upon the Company and the Original Warrantholder. The costs of conducting any Appraisal Procedure shall be borne by the Company.

"*Board of Directors*" means the board of directors of the Company, including any duly authorized committee thereof.

"*Business Combination*" means a merger, consolidation, statutory share exchange or similar transaction that requires the approval of the Company's stockholders.

"*business day*" means any day except Saturday, Sunday and any day on which banking institutions in the State of New York generally are authorized or required by law or other governmental actions to close.

"*Capital Stock*" means (A) with respect to any Person that is a corporation or company, any and all shares, interests, participations or other equivalents (however designated) of capital or capital stock of such Person and (B) with respect to any Person that is not a corporation or company, any and all partnership or other equity interests of such Person.

"*Charter*" means, with respect to any Person, its certificate or articles of incorporation, articles of association, or similar organizational document.

"*Common Stock*" has the meaning ascribed to it in the Purchase Agreement.

"*Company*" means the Person whose name, corporate or other organizational form and jurisdiction of organization is set forth in Item 1 of Schedule A hereto.

"*conversion*" has the meaning set forth in Section 13(B).

"*convertible securities*" has the meaning set forth in Section 13(B).

"*CPP*" has the meaning ascribed to it in the Purchase Agreement.

"*Exchange Act*" means the Securities Exchange Act of 1934, as amended, or any successor statute, and the rules and regulations promulgated thereunder.

"*Exercise Price*" means the amount set forth in Item 2 of Schedule A hereto.

"*Expiration Time*" has the meaning set forth in Section 3.

"*Fair Market Value*" means, with respect to any security or other property, the fair market value of such security or other property as determined by the Board of Directors, acting in good faith or, with respect to Section 14, as determined by the Original Warrantholder acting in good faith. For so long as the Original Warrantholder holds this Warrant or any portion thereof, it may object in writing to the Board of Director's calculation of fair market value within 10 days of receipt of written notice thereof. If the Original Warrantholder and the Company are unable to agree on fair market value during the 10-day period following the delivery of the Original Warrantholder's objection, the Appraisal Procedure may be invoked by either party to determine Fair Market Value by delivering written notification thereof not later than the 30th day after delivery of the Original Warrantholder's objection.

"*Governmental Entities*" has the meaning ascribed to it in the Purchase Agreement.

"*Initial Number*" has the meaning set forth in Section 13(B).

"*Issue Date*" means the date set forth in Item 3 of Schedule A hereto.

"*Market Price*" means, with respect to a particular security, on any given day, the last reported sale price regular way or, in case no such reported sale takes place on such day, the average of the last closing bid and ask prices regular way, in either case on the principal national securities exchange on which the applicable securities are listed or admitted to trading, or if not listed or admitted to trading on any national securities exchange, the average of the closing bid and ask prices as furnished by two members of the Financial Industry Regulatory Authority, Inc. selected from time to time by the Company for that purpose.

"Market Price" shall be determined without reference to after hours or extended hours trading. If such security is not listed and traded in a manner that the quotations referred to above are available for the period required hereunder, the Market Price per share of Common Stock shall be deemed to be (i) in the event that any portion of the Warrant is held by the Original Warrantholder, the fair market value per share of such security as determined in good faith by the Original Warrantholder or (ii) in all other circumstances, the fair market value per share of such security as determined in good faith by the Board of Directors in reliance on an opinion of a nationally recognized independent investment banking corporation retained by the Company for this purpose and certified in a resolution to the Warrantholder. For the purposes of determining the Market Price of the Common Stock on the "trading day" preceding, on or following the occurrence of an event, (i) that trading day shall be deemed to commence immediately after the regular scheduled closing time of trading on the New York Stock Exchange or, if trading is closed at an earlier time, such earlier time and (ii) that trading day shall end at the next regular scheduled closing time, or if trading is closed at an earlier time, such earlier time (for the avoidance of doubt, and as an example, if the Market Price is to be determined as of the last trading day preceding a specified event and the closing time of trading on a particular day is 4:00 p.m. and the specified event occurs at 5:00 p.m. on that day, the Market Price would be determined by reference to such 4:00 p.m. closing price).

"*Ordinary Cash Dividends*" means a regular quarterly cash dividend on shares of Common Stock out of surplus or net profits legally available therefor (determined in accordance with generally accepted accounting principles in effect from time to time), *provided* that Ordinary Cash Dividends shall not include any cash dividends paid subsequent to the Issue Date to the extent the aggregate per share dividends paid on the outstanding Common Stock in any quarter exceed the amount set forth in Item 4 of Schedule A hereto, as adjusted for any stock split, stock dividend, reverse stock split, reclassification or similar transaction.

"*Original Warrantholder*" means the United States Department of the Treasury. Any actions specified to be taken by the Original Warrantholder hereunder may only be taken by such Person and not by any other Warrantholder.

"*Permitted Transactions*" has the meaning set forth in Section 13(B).
"*Person*" has the meaning given to it in Section 3(a)(9) of the Exchange Act and as used in Sections 13(d)(3) and 14(d)(2) of the Exchange Act.

"*Per Share Fair Market Value*" has the meaning set forth in Section 13(C).

"*Preferred Shares*" means the perpetual preferred stock issued to the Original Warrantholder on the Issue Date pursuant to the Purchase Agreement.

"*Pro Rata Repurchases*" means any purchase of shares of Common Stock by the Company or any Affiliate thereof pursuant to (A) any tender offer or exchange offer subject to Section 13(e) or 14(e) of the Exchange Act or Regulation 14E promulgated thereunder or (B) any other offer available to substantially all holders of Common Stock, in the case of both (A) or (B), whether for cash, shares of Capital Stock of the Company, other securities of the Company, evidences of indebtedness of the Company or any other Person or any other property (including, without limitation, shares of Capital Stock, other securities or evidences of indebtedness of a subsidiary), or any combination thereof, effected while this Warrant is outstanding. The "*Effective Date*" of a Pro Rata Repurchase shall mean the date of acceptance of shares for purchase or exchange by the Company under any tender or exchange offer which is a Pro Rata Repurchase or the date of purchase with respect to any Pro Rata Repurchase that is not a tender or exchange offer.

"*Purchase Agreement*" means the Securities Purchase Agreement – Standard Terms incorporated into the Letter Agreement, dated as of the date set forth in Item 5 of Schedule A hereto, as amended from time to time, between the Company and the United States Department of the Treasury (the "*Letter Agreement*"), including all annexes and schedules thereto.

"*Qualified Equity Offering*" has the meaning ascribed to it in the Purchase Agreement.

"*Regulatory Approvals*" with respect to the Warrantholder, means, to the extent applicable and required to permit the Warrantholder to exercise this Warrant for shares of Common Stock and to own such Common Stock without the Warrantholder being in violation of applicable law, rule or regulation, the receipt of any necessary approvals and authorizations of, filings and registrations with, notifications to, or expiration or termination of any applicable waiting period under, the Hart-Scott-Rodino Antitrust Improvements Act of 1976, as amended, and the rules and regulations thereunder.

"*SEC*" means the U.S. Securities and Exchange Commission.

"*Securities Act*" means the Securities Act of 1933, as amended, or any successor statute, and the rules and regulations promulgated thereunder.

"*Shares*" has the meaning set forth in Section 2.

"*trading day*" means (A) if the shares of Common Stock are not traded on any national or regional securities exchange or association or over-the-counter market, a business day or (B) if the shares of Common Stock are traded on any national or regional securities exchange or association or over-the-counter market, a business day on which such relevant exchange or quotation system is scheduled to be open for business and on which the shares of Common Stock (i) are not suspended from trading on any national or regional securities exchange or association or over-the-counter market for any period or periods aggregating one half hour or longer; and (ii) have traded at least once on the national or regional securities exchange or association or over-the-counter market that is the primary market for the trading of the shares of Common Stock.

"*U.S. GAAP*" means United States generally accepted accounting principles.

"*Warrantholder*" has the meaning set forth in Section 2.

"*Warrant*" means this Warrant, issued pursuant to the Purchase Agreement.

2. <u>Number of Shares; Exercise Price</u>. This certifies that, for value received, the United States Department of the Treasury or its permitted assigns (the "*Warrantholder*") is entitled, upon the terms and subject to the conditions hereinafter set forth, to acquire from the Company, in whole or in part, after the receipt of all applicable Regulatory Approvals, if any, up to an aggregate of the number of fully paid and nonassessable shares of Common Stock set forth in Item 6 of Schedule A hereto, at a purchase price per share of Common Stock equal to the Exercise Price. The number of shares of Common Stock (the "*Shares*") and the Exercise Price are subject to adjustment as provided herein, and all references to "Common Stock," "Shares" and "Exercise Price" herein shall be deemed to include any such adjustment or series of adjustments.

3. <u>Exercise of Warrant; Term</u>. Subject to Section 2, to the extent permitted by applicable laws and regulations, the right to purchase the Shares represented by this Warrant is exercisable, in whole or in part by the

Warrantholder, at any time or from time to time after the execution and delivery of this Warrant by the Company on the date hereof, but in no event later than 5:00 p.m., New York City time on the tenth anniversary of the Issue Date (the "*Expiration Time*"), by (A) the surrender of this Warrant and Notice of Exercise annexed hereto, duly completed and executed on behalf of the Warrantholder, at the principal executive office of the Company located at the address set forth in Item 7 of Schedule A hereto (or such other office or agency of the Company in the United States as it may designate by notice in writing to the Warrantholder at the address of the Warrantholder appearing on the books of the Company), and (B) payment of the Exercise Price for the Shares thereby purchased:

(i) by having the Company withhold, from the shares of Common Stock that would otherwise be delivered to the Warrantholder upon such exercise, shares of Common stock issuable upon exercise of the Warrant equal in value to the aggregate Exercise Price as to which this Warrant is so exercised based on the Market Price of the Common Stock on the trading day on which this Warrant is exercised and the Notice of Exercise is delivered to the Company pursuant to this Section 3, or

(ii) with the consent of both the Company and the Warrantholder, by tendering in cash, by certified or cashier's check payable to the order of the Company, or by wire transfer of immediately available funds to an account designated by the Company.

If the Warrantholder does not exercise this Warrant in its entirety, the Warrantholder will be entitled to receive from the Company within a reasonable time, and in any event not exceeding three business days, a new warrant in substantially identical form for the purchase of that number of Shares equal to the difference between the number of Shares subject to this Warrant and the number of Shares as to which this Warrant is so exercised. Notwithstanding anything in this Warrant to the contrary, the Warrantholder hereby acknowledges and agrees that its exercise of this Warrant for Shares is subject to the condition that the Warrantholder will have first received any applicable Regulatory Approvals.

4. Issuance of Shares; Authorization; Listing. Certificates for Shares issued upon exercise of this Warrant will be issued in such name or names as the Warrantholder may designate and will be delivered to such named Person or Persons within a reasonable time, not to exceed three business days after the date on which this Warrant has been duly exercised in accordance with the terms of this Warrant. The Company hereby represents and warrants that any Shares

issued upon the exercise of this Warrant in accordance with the provisions of Section 3 will be duly and validly authorized and issued, fully paid and nonassessable and free from all taxes, liens and charges (other than liens or charges created by the Warrantholder, income and franchise taxes incurred in connection with the exercise of the Warrant or taxes in respect of any transfer occurring contemporaneously therewith). The Company agrees that the Shares so issued will be deemed to have been issued to the Warrantholder as of the close of business on the date on which this Warrant and payment of the Exercise Price are delivered to the Company in accordance with the terms of this Warrant, notwithstanding that the stock transfer books of the Company may then be closed or certificates representing such Shares may not be actually delivered on such date. The Company will at all times reserve and keep available, out of its authorized but unissued Common Stock, solely for the purpose of providing for the exercise of this Warrant, the aggregate number of shares of Common Stock then issuable upon exercise of this Warrant at any time. The Company will (A) procure, at its sole expense, the listing of the Shares issuable upon exercise of this Warrant at any time, subject to issuance or notice of issuance, on all principal stock exchanges on which the Common Stock is then listed or traded and (B) maintain such listings of such Shares at all times after issuance. The Company will use reasonable best efforts to ensure that the Shares may be issued without violation of any applicable law or regulation or of any requirement of any securities exchange on which the Shares are listed or traded.

5. No Fractional Shares or Scrip. No fractional Shares or scrip representing fractional Shares shall be issued upon any exercise of this Warrant. In lieu of any fractional Share to which the Warrantholder would otherwise be entitled, the Warrantholder shall be entitled to receive a cash payment equal to the Market Price of the Common Stock on the last trading day preceding the date of exercise less the pro-rated Exercise Price for such fractional share.

6. No Rights as Stockholders; Transfer Books. This Warrant does not entitle the Warrantholder to any voting rights or other rights as a stockholder of the Company prior to the date of exercise hereof. The Company will at no time close its transfer books against transfer of this Warrant in any manner which interferes with the timely exercise of this Warrant.

7. Charges, Taxes and Expenses. Issuance of certificates for Shares to the Warrantholder upon the exercise of this Warrant shall be made without charge to the Warrantholder for any issue or transfer tax or other incidental expense in respect of the issuance of such certificates, all of which taxes and expenses shall be paid by the Company.

8. Transfer/Assignment.

(A) Subject to compliance with clause (B) of this Section 8, this Warrant and all rights hereunder are transferable, in whole or in part, upon the books of the Company by the registered holder hereof in person or by duly authorized attorney, and a new warrant shall be made and delivered by the Company, of the same tenor and date as this Warrant but registered in the name of one or more transferees, upon surrender of this Warrant, duly endorsed, to the office or agency of the Company described in Section 3. All expenses (other than stock transfer taxes) and other charges payable in connection with the preparation, execution and delivery of the new warrants pursuant to this Section 8 shall be paid by the Company.

(B) The transfer of the Warrant and the Shares issued upon exercise of the Warrant are subject to the restrictions set forth in Section 4.4 of the Purchase Agreement. If and for so long as required by the Purchase Agreement, this Warrant shall contain the legends as set forth in Sections 4.2(a) and 4.2(b) of the Purchase Agreement.

9. Exchange and Registry of Warrant. This Warrant is exchangeable, upon the surrender hereof by the Warrantholder to the Company, for a new warrant or warrants of like tenor and representing the right to purchase the same aggregate number of Shares. The Company shall maintain a registry showing the name and address of the Warrantholder as the registered holder of this Warrant. This Warrant may be surrendered for exchange or exercise in accordance with its terms, at the office of the Company, and the Company shall be entitled to rely in all respects, prior to written notice to the contrary, upon such registry.

10. Loss, Theft, Destruction or Mutilation of Warrant. Upon receipt by the Company of evidence reasonably satisfactory to it of the loss, theft, destruction or mutilation of this Warrant, and in the case of any such loss, theft or destruction, upon receipt of a bond, indemnity or security reasonably satisfactory to the Company, or, in the case of any such mutilation, upon surrender and cancellation of this Warrant, the Company shall make and deliver, in lieu of such lost, stolen, destroyed or mutilated Warrant, a new Warrant of like tenor and representing the right to purchase the same aggregate number of Shares as provided for in such lost, stolen, destroyed or mutilated Warrant.

11. Saturdays, Sundays, Holidays, etc. If the last or appointed day for the taking of any action or the expiration of any right required or granted herein

shall not be a business day, then such action may be taken or such right may be exercised on the next succeeding day that is a business day.

12. Rule 144 Information. The Company covenants that it will use its reasonable best efforts to timely file all reports and other documents required to be filed by it under the Securities Act and the Exchange Act and the rules and regulations promulgated by the SEC thereunder (or, if the Company is not required to file such reports, it will, upon the request of any Warrantholder, make publicly available such information as necessary to permit sales pursuant to Rule 144 under the Securities Act), and it will use reasonable best efforts to take such further action as any Warrantholder may reasonably request, in each case to the extent required from time to time to enable such holder to, if permitted by the terms of this Warrant and the Purchase Agreement, sell this Warrant without registration under the Securities Act within the limitation of the exemptions provided by (A) Rule 144 under the Securities Act, as such rule may be amended from time to time, or (B) any successor rule or regulation hereafter adopted by the SEC. Upon the written request of any Warrantholder, the Company will deliver to such Warrantholder a written statement that it has complied with such requirements.

13. Adjustments and Other Rights. The Exercise Price and the number of Shares issuable upon exercise of this Warrant shall be subject to adjustment from time to time as follows; *provided*, that if more than one subsection of this Section 13 is applicable to a single event, the subsection shall be applied that produces the largest adjustment and no single event shall cause an adjustment under more than one subsection of this Section 13 so as to result in duplication:

(A) Stock Splits, Subdivisions, Reclassifications or Combinations If the Company shall (i) declare and pay a dividend or make a distribution on its Common Stock in shares of Common Stock, (ii) subdivide or reclassify the outstanding shares of Common Stock into a greater number of shares, or (iii) combine or reclassify the outstanding shares of Common Stock into a smaller number of shares, the number of Shares issuable upon exercise of this Warrant at the time of the record date for such dividend or distribution or the effective date of such subdivision, combination or reclassification shall be proportionately adjusted so that the Warrantholder after such date shall be entitled to purchase the number of shares of Common Stock which such holder would have owned or been entitled to receive in respect of the shares of Common Stock subject to this Warrant after such date had this Warrant been exercised immediately prior to such date. In such event, the Exercise Price in effect at the time of the record date for such dividend or distribution or the effective date of such subdivision, combination or reclassification shall be adjusted to the number obtained by dividing (x) the product of (1) the number of Shares issuable upon the exercise of this Warrant before such adjustment and (2) the Exercise Price in effect immediately prior to the record or effective date, as the case may be, for the dividend, distribution, subdivision, combination or reclassification giving rise to this adjustment by (y) the new number of Shares issuable upon exercise of the Warrant determined pursuant to the immediately preceding sentence.

(B) Certain Issuances of Common Shares or Convertible Securities. Until the earlier of (i) the date on which the Original Warrantholder no longer holds this Warrant or any portion thereof and (ii) the third anniversary of the Issue Date, if the Company shall issue shares of Common Stock (or rights or warrants or other securities exercisable or convertible into or exchangeable (collectively, a "*conversion*") for shares of Common Stock) (collectively, "*convertible securities*") (other than in Permitted Transactions (as defined below) or a transaction to which subsection (A) of this Section 13 is applicable) without consideration or at a consideration per share (or having a conversion price per share) that is less than 90% of the Market Price on the last trading day preceding the date of the agreement on pricing such shares (or such convertible securities) then, in such event:

(A) the number of Shares issuable upon the exercise of this Warrant immediately prior to the date of the agreement on pricing of such shares (or of such convertible securities) (the "*Initial Number*") shall be increased to the number obtained by multiplying the Initial Number by a fraction (A) the numerator of which shall be the sum of (x) the number of shares of Common Stock of the Company outstanding on such date and (y) the number of additional shares of Common Stock issued (or into which convertible securities may be exercised or convert) and

(B) the denominator of which shall be the sum of (I) the number of shares of Common Stock outstanding on such date and (II) the number of shares of Common Stock which the aggregate consideration receivable by the Company for the total number of shares of Common Stock so issued (or into which convertible securities may be exercised or convert) would purchase at the Market Price on the last trading day preceding the date of the agreement on pricing such shares (or such convertible securities); and (B) the Exercise Price payable upon exercise of the Warrant shall be adjusted by multiplying such Exercise Price in effect immediately prior to the date of the agreement on pricing of such shares (or of such convertible securities) by a fraction, the numerator of which shall be the number of shares of Common Stock issuable upon exercise of this Warrant prior to such date and the denominator of which shall be the number of shares of Common Stock issuable upon exercise of this Warrant immediately after the adjustment described in clause (A) above.

For purposes of the foregoing, the aggregate consideration receivable by the Company in connection with the issuance of such shares of Common Stock or convertible securities shall be deemed to be equal to the sum of the net offering price (including the Fair Market Value of any non-cash consideration and after deduction of any related expenses payable to third parties) of all such securities plus the minimum aggregate amount, if any, payable upon exercise or conversion of any such convertible securities into shares of Common Stock; and "*Permitted Transactions*" shall mean issuances (i) as consideration for or to fund the acquisition of businesses and/or related assets, (ii) in connection with employee benefit plans and compensation related arrangements in the ordinary course and consistent with past practice approved by the Board of Directors, (iii) in connection with a public or broadly marketed offering and sale of Common Stock or convertible securities for cash conducted by the Company or its affiliates pursuant to registration under the Securities Act or Rule 144A thereunder on a basis consistent with capital raising transactions by comparable financial institutions and (iv) in connection with the exercise of preemptive rights on terms existing as of the Issue Date. Any adjustment made pursuant to this Section 13(B) shall become effective immediately upon the date of such issuance.

(C) Other Distributions. In case the Company shall fix a record date for the making of a distribution to all holders of shares of its Common Stock of securities, evidences of indebtedness, assets, cash, rights or warrants (excluding Ordinary Cash Dividends, dividends of its Common Stock and other dividends or distributions referred to in Section 13(A)), in each such case, the Exercise Price in effect prior to such record date shall be reduced immediately thereafter to the price determined by multiplying the Exercise Price in effect immediately prior to the reduction by the quotient of (x) the Market Price of the Common Stock on the last trading day preceding the first date on which the Common Stock trades regular way on the principal national securities exchange on which the Common Stock is listed or admitted to trading without the right to receive such distribution, minus the amount of cash and/or the Fair Market Value of the securities, evidences of indebtedness, assets, rights or warrants to be so distributed in respect of one share of Common Stock (such amount and/or Fair

Market Value, the "*Per Share Fair Market Value*") divided by (y) such Market Price on such date specified in clause (x); such adjustment shall be made successively whenever such a record date is fixed. In such event, the number of Shares issuable upon the exercise of this Warrant shall be increased to the number obtained by dividing (x) the product of (1) the number of Shares issuable upon the exercise of this Warrant before such adjustment, and (2) the Exercise Price in effect immediately prior to the distribution giving rise to this adjustment by (y) the new Exercise Price determined in accordance with the immediately preceding sentence. In the case of adjustment for a cash dividend that is, or is coincident with, a regular quarterly cash dividend, the Per Share Fair Market Value would be reduced by the per share amount of the portion of the cash dividend that would constitute an Ordinary Cash Dividend. In the event that such distribution is not so made, the Exercise Price and the number of Shares issuable upon exercise of this Warrant then in effect shall be readjusted, effective as of the date when the Board of Directors determines not to distribute such shares, evidences of indebtedness, assets, rights, cash or warrants, as the case may be, to the Exercise Price that would then be in effect and the number of Shares that would then be issuable upon exercise of this Warrant if such record date had not been fixed.

(D) Certain Repurchases of Common StockIn case the Company effects a Pro Rata Repurchase of Common Stock, then the Exercise Price shall be reduced to the price determined by multiplying the Exercise Price in effect immediately prior to the Effective Date of such Pro Rata Repurchase by a fraction of which the numerator shall be (i) the product of (x) the number of shares of Common Stock outstanding immediately before such Pro Rata Repurchase and (y) the Market Price of a share of Common Stock on the trading day immediately preceding the first public announcement by the Company or any of its Affiliates of the intent to effect such Pro Rata Repurchase, minus (ii) the aggregate purchase price of the Pro Rata Repurchase, and of which the denominator shall be the product of (i) the number of shares of Common Stock outstanding immediately prior to such Pro Rata Repurchase minus the number of shares of Common Stock so repurchased and (ii) the Market Price per share of Common Stock on the trading day immediately preceding the first public announcement by the Company or any of its Affiliates of the intent to effect such Pro Rata Repurchase. In such event, the number of shares of Common Stock issuable upon the exercise of this Warrant shall be increased to the number obtained by dividing (x) the product of (1) the number of Shares issuable upon the exercise of this Warrant before such adjustment, and (2) the Exercise Price in effect immediately prior to the Pro Rata Repurchase giving rise to this adjustment by (y) the new Exercise Price determined in accordance with the immediately preceding sentence. For the avoidance of doubt, no increase to the Exercise Price or decrease in the number of Shares issuable upon exercise of this Warrant shall be made pursuant to this Section 13(D).

(E) Business Combinations. In case of any Business Combination or reclassification of Common Stock (other than a reclassification of Common Stock referred to in Section 13(A)), the Warrantholder's right to receive Shares upon exercise of this Warrant shall be converted into the right to exercise this Warrant to acquire the number of shares of stock or other securities or property (including cash) which the Common Stock issuable (at the time of such Business Combination or reclassification) upon exercise of this Warrant immediately prior to such Business Combination or reclassification would have been entitled to receive upon consummation of such Business Combination or reclassification; and in any such case, if necessary, the provisions set forth herein with respect to the rights and interests thereafter of the Warrantholder shall be appropriately adjusted so as to be applicable, as nearly as may reasonably be, to the Warrantholder's right to exercise this Warrant in exchange for any shares of stock or other securities or property pursuant to this paragraph. In determining the kind and amount of stock, securities or the property receivable upon exercise of this Warrant following the consummation of such Business Combination, if the holders of Common Stock have the right to elect the kind or amount of consideration receivable upon consummation of such Business Combination, then the consideration that the Warrantholder shall be entitled to receive upon exercise shall be deemed to be the types and amounts of consideration received by the majority of all holders of the shares of common stock that affirmatively make an election (or of all such holders if none make an election).

(F) Rounding of Calculations; Minimum Adjustments. All calculations under this Section 13 shall be made to the nearest one-tenth (1/10th) of a cent or to the nearest onehundredth (1/100th) of a share, as the case may be. Any provision of this Section 13 to the contrary notwithstanding, no adjustment in the Exercise Price or the number of Shares into which this Warrant is exercisable shall be made if the amount of such adjustment would be less than $0.01 or one-tenth (1/10th) of a share of Common Stock, but any such amount shall be carried forward and an adjustment with respect thereto shall be made at the time of and together with any subsequent adjustment which, together with such amount and any other amount or amounts so carried forward, shall aggregate $0.01 or 1/10th of a share of Common Stock, or more.

(G) Timing of Issuance of Additional Common Stock Upon Certain Adjustments. In any case in which the provisions of this Section 13 shall require that an adjustment shall become effective immediately after a record date for an event, the Company may defer until the occurrence of such event (i) issuing to the Warrantholder of this Warrant exercised after such record date and before the occurrence of such event the additional shares of Common Stock issuable upon such exercise by reason of the adjustment required by such event over and above the shares of Common Stock issuable upon such exercise before giving effect to such adjustment and (ii) paying to such Warrantholder any amount of cash in lieu of a fractional share of Common Stock; *provided*, *however*, that the Company upon request shall deliver to such Warrantholder a due bill or other appropriate instrument evidencing such Warrantholder's right to receive such additional shares, and such cash, upon the occurrence of the event requiring such adjustment.

(H) Completion of Qualified Equity Offering. In the event the Company (or any successor by Business Combination) completes one or more Qualified Equity Offerings on or prior to December 31, 2009 that result in the Company (or any such successor) receiving aggregate gross proceeds of not less than 100% of the aggregate liquidation preference of the Preferred Shares (and any preferred stock issued by any such successor to the Original Warrantholder under the CPP), the number of shares of Common Stock underlying the portion of this Warrant then held by the Original Warrantholder shall be thereafter reduced by a number of shares of Common Stock equal to the product of (i) 0.5 and (ii) the number of shares underlying the Warrant on the Issue Date (adjusted to take into account all other theretofore made adjustments pursuant to this Section 13).

(I) Other Events. For so long as the Original Warrantholder holds this Warrant or any portion thereof, if any event occurs as to which the provisions of this Section 13 are not strictly applicable or, if strictly applicable, would not, in the good faith judgment of the Board of Directors of the Company, fairly and adequately protect the purchase rights of the Warrants in accordance with the essential intent and principles of such provisions, then the Board of Directors shall make such adjustments in the application of such provisions, in accordance with such essential intent and principles, as shall be reasonably necessary, in the good faith opinion of the Board of Directors, to protect such purchase rights as aforesaid. The Exercise Price or the number of Shares into which this Warrant is exercisable shall not be adjusted in the event of a change in the par value of the Common Stock or a change in the jurisdiction of incorporation of the Company.

(J) Statement Regarding Adjustments. Whenever the Exercise Price or the number of Shares into which this Warrant is exercisable shall be adjusted as provided in Section 13, the Company shall forthwith file at the principal office of the Company a statement showing in reasonable detail the facts requiring such adjustment and the Exercise Price that shall be in effect and the number of Shares into which this Warrant shall be exercisable after such adjustment, and the Company shall also cause a copy of such statement to be sent by mail, first class postage prepaid, to each Warrantholder at the address appearing in the Company's records.

(K) Notice of Adjustment Event. In the event that the Company shall propose to take any action of the type described in this Section 13 (but only if the action of the type described in this Section 13 would result in an adjustment in the Exercise Price or the number of Shares into which this Warrant is exercisable or a change in the type of securities or property to be delivered upon exercise of this Warrant), the Company shall give notice to the Warrantholder, in the manner set forth in Section 13(J), which notice shall specify the record date, if any, with respect to any such action and the approximate date on which such action is to take place. Such notice shall also set forth the facts with respect thereto as shall be reasonably necessary to indicate the effect on the Exercise Price and the number, kind or class of shares or other securities or property which shall be deliverable upon exercise of this Warrant. In the case of any action which would require the fixing of a record date, such notice shall be given at least 10 days prior to the date so fixed, and in case of all other action, such notice shall be given at least 15 days prior to the taking of such proposed action. Failure to give such notice, or any defect therein, shall not affect the legality or validity of any such action.

(L) Proceedings Prior to Any Action Requiring Adjustment. As a condition precedent to the taking of any action which would require an adjustment pursuant to this Section 13, the Company shall take any action which may be necessary, including obtaining regulatory, New York Stock Exchange, NASDAQ Stock Market or other applicable national securities exchange or stockholder approvals or exemptions, in order that the Company may thereafter validly and legally issue as fully paid and nonassessable all shares of Common Stock that the Warrantholder is entitled to receive upon exercise of this Warrant pursuant to this Section 13.

(M) Adjustment Rules. Any adjustments pursuant to this Section 13 shall be made successively whenever an event referred to herein shall occur. If an adjustment in Exercise Price made hereunder would reduce the Exercise Price to an amount below par value of the Common Stock, then such adjustment in Exercise Price made hereunder shall reduce the Exercise Price to the par value of the Common Stock.

14. Exchange. At any time following the date on which the shares of Common Stock of the Company are no longer listed or admitted to trading on a national securities exchange (other than in connection with any Business Combination), the Original Warrantholder may cause the Company to exchange all or a portion of this Warrant for an economic interest (to be determined by the Original Warrantholder after consultation with the Company) of the Company classified as permanent equity under U.S. GAAP having a value equal to the Fair Market Value of the portion of the Warrant so exchanged. The Original Warrantholder shall calculate any Fair Market Value required to be calculated pursuant to this Section 14, which shall not be subject to the Appraisal Procedure.

15. No Impairment. The Company will not, by amendment of its Charter or through any reorganization, transfer of assets, consolidation, merger, dissolution, issue or sale of securities or any other voluntary action, avoid or seek to avoid the observance or performance of any of the terms to be observed or performed hereunder by the Company, but will at all times in good faith assist in the carrying out of all the provisions of this Warrant and in taking of all such action as may be necessary or appropriate in order to protect the rights of the Warrantholder.

16. Governing Law. **This Warrant will be governed by and construed in accordance with the federal law of the United States if and to the extent such law is applicable, and otherwise in accordance with the laws of the State of New York applicable to contracts made and to be performed entirely within such State. Each of the Company and the Warrantholder agrees (a) to submit to the exclusive jurisdiction and venue of the United States District Court for the District of Columbia for any civil action, suit or proceeding arising out of or relating to this Warrant or the transactions contemplated hereby, and (b) that notice may be served upon the Company at the address in Section 20 below and upon the Warrantholder at the address for the Warrantholder set forth in the registry maintained by the Company pursuant to Section 9 hereof. To the extent permitted by applicable law, each of the Company and the Warrantholder hereby unconditionally waives trial by jury in any civil legal action or proceeding relating to the Warrant or the transactions contemplated hereby or thereby.**

17. Binding Effect. This Warrant shall be binding upon any successors or assigns of the Company.

18. Amendments. This Warrant may be amended and the observance of any term of this Warrant may be waived only with the written consent of the Company and the Warrantholder.

19 . Prohibited Actions. The Company agrees that it will not take any action which would entitle the Warrantholder to an adjustment of the Exercise Price if the total number of shares of Common Stock issuable after such action upon exercise of this Warrant, together with all shares of Common Stock then outstanding and all shares of Common Stock then issuable upon the exercise of all outstanding options, warrants, conversion and other rights, would exceed the total number of shares of Common Stock then authorized by its Charter.

20. Notices. Any notice, request, instruction or other document to be given hereunder by any party to the other will be in writing and will be deemed to have been duly given (a) on the date of delivery if delivered personally, or by facsimile, upon confirmation of receipt, or (b) on the second business day following the date of dispatch if delivered by a recognized next day courier service. All notices hereunder shall be delivered as set forth in Item 8 of Schedule A hereto, or pursuant to such other instructions as may be designated in writing by the party to receive such notice.

21. Entire Agreement. This Warrant, the forms attached hereto and Schedule A hereto (the terms of which are incorporated by reference herein), and the Letter Agreement (including all documents incorporated therein), contain the entire agreement between the parties with respect to the subject matter hereof and supersede all prior and contemporaneous arrangements or undertakings with respect thereto.

[Remainder of page intentionally left blank]

[Form of Notice of Exercise]

Date: ________

TO: **[Company]**

RE: Election to Purchase Common Stock

The undersigned, pursuant to the provisions set forth in the attached Warrant, hereby agrees to subscribe for and purchase the number of shares of the Common Stock set forth below covered by such Warrant. The undersigned, in accordance with Section 3 of the Warrant, hereby agrees to pay the aggregate Exercise Price for such shares of Common Stock in the manner set forth below. A new warrant evidencing the remaining shares of Common Stock covered by such Warrant, but not yet subscribed for and purchased, if any, should be issued in the name set forth below.

Number of Shares of Common Stock ____________________________

Method of Payment of Exercise Price (note if cashless exercise pursuant to Section 3(i) of the Warrant or cash exercise pursuant to Section 3(ii) of the Warrant, with consent of the Company and the Warrantholder) ____________________________

Aggregate Exercise Price: ____________________________

Holder: ____________________________
By: ____________________________
Name: ____________________________
Title: ____________________________

IN WITNESS WHEREOF, the Company has caused this Warrant to be duly executed by a duly authorized officer.

Dated: _______________

COMPANY:____________________
By:____________________________
Name:
Title:
Attest:____________________________

By:______________________________
Name:
Title:

[Signature Page to Warrant]

SCHEDULE A

Item 1
Name:
Corporate or other organizational form:
Jurisdiction of organization:
Item 2
Exercise Price: [1]
Item 3
Issue Date:
Item 4
Amount of last dividend declared prior to the Issue Date:
Item 5
Date of Letter Agreement between the Company and the United States Department of the
Treasury:
Item 6
Number of shares of Common Stock:
Item 7
Company's address:
Item 8
Notice information:

[1] Initial exercise price to be calculated based on the average of closing prices of the Common Stock on the 20trading days ending on the last trading day prior to the date the Company's application for participation in the Capital Purchase Program was approved by the United States Department of the Treasury.